Advances in APPLIED BIOLOGY

Advances in
APPLIED BIOLOGY

Vol. X

Edited by

T. H. Coaker

Department of Applied Biology, University of Cambridge,
Cambridge, England

1984

ACADEMIC PRESS, INC.
Harcourt Brace Jovanovich, Publishers
London San Diego New York Berkeley
Boston Sydney Tokyo Toronto

ACADEMIC PRESS LTD.
24–28 Oval Road
LONDON NW1 7DX

United States Edition, published by
ACADEMIC PRESS, INC.
San Diego, CA 92101

Second Printing 1987

ISBN 0-12-040910-0

ISSN 0309-1791

Printed in Great Britain by
St Edmundsbury Press Ltd, Bury St Edmunds, Suffolk

Contents

Contributors

K. ANAND KUMAR, *Pearl Millet Improvement Program, ICRISAT Sahelian Centre, B. P. 12404, Niamey, Niger.*

D. J. ANDREWS, *Pearl Millet Improvement Program, ICRISAT Centre, Patancheru P.O., Andhra Pradesh 502 324, India.*

P. K. EVANS, *Department of Biology, University of Southampton, Southampton 309 5NH, England.*

N. W. GALWEY, *Department of Applied Biology, University of Cambridge, Cambridge CB2 3DX, England.*

S. MATTHEWS, *Department of Agriculture, University of Aberdeen, Aberdeen AB9 1UD, Scotland.*

M. DE A. OLIVEIRA, *Department of Agriculture, University of Aberdeen, Aberdeen AB9 1UD, Scotland.*

ALISON A. POWELL, *Department of Agriculture, University of Aberdeen, Aberdeen AB9 1UD, Scotland.*

J. RISI C., *Department of Applied Biology, University of Cambridge, Cambridge CB2 3DX, England.*

D. C. SASTRI, *ICRISAT Centre, Patancheru P.O., Andhra Pradesh 502 324, India.*

V. M. WILSON, *Department of Biology, University of Southampton, Southampton 309 5NH, England.*

Preface

The main purpose of the series is to draw together subject matter from currently important fields of Applied Biology to produce a synthesis for students, teachers, and specialists from other fields. The widely diversified and multidisciplinary nature of Applied Biology emphasizes the importance of the series since interdependence of the various subjects it embraces cannot be ignored, especially if the fruits of research are ultimately to be applied for the benefit of man.

Contributions to the series are written by specialists in the field, some with a biological background, others with chemical or physical qualifications, each presenting their subject matter in their style. Each article seeks to fulfill four aims. They review the state of the subject generally and select where possible one or more aspect for particular critical discussion; they summarize what is known to be of practical importance and indicate where each author sees the greatest need for future work.

The papers in this volume cover the genetical and physiological improvement of seed stocks by the application of traditional methods to new crops as well as by the development of new methods.

December 1984 T. H. COAKER

Advances in
APPLIED BIOLOGY

Plant Somatic Hybridization

P. K. EVANS AND V. M. WILSON

Department of Biology, University of Southampton, Southampton, England

I. Introduction

Somatic hybridization, as its name implies, is the process whereby somatic cells from different plants, as opposed to specialized haploid gametes, are induced to fuse. A hybrid cell is formed from which, through the process of repeated cell division, an entire plant is finally recovered. Each cell of such plants contains genetic material from both parents. The method exploits several fundamental principles of plant cell biology. The first principle is that the wall can be removed from the plant cell without irreparable damage to its viability. The removal of this wall is clearly a necessity since the plasma membranes cannot be brought into the close contact required for fusion with it *in situ.* These naked cells, or isolated protoplasts, must, however, be stabilized by maintaining them in a medium in which the osmotic potential is such as to prevent excessive uptake of water that would lead to protoplast expansion and eventual rupture of the plasma membrane. The second principle is that the plasma membrane can be reversibly destabilized, allowing the plasma membranes of two protoplasts to combine, resulting in protoplast fusion. Third, the technique seeks to exploit the totipotency of the plant cell. This is the concept that living nucleated cells in the tissue of the plant, although they may be highly specialized and never destined to divide again, retain all their genetic

ISBN 0-12-040910-0

information, their differentiation merely being the repression of the appropriate parts of the genome. If suitable nutrient and environmental conditions can be provided, this repressed information can once again be expressed, resulting, in the first instance, in a resumption of cell division and then by repeated cycles of division in the formation of organized structures such as shoots and roots. In other words, somatic cells of the plant retain a capacity to revert to an embryonic condition.

Somatic hybridization involves a series of individual steps. For success, methods need to be perfected for protoplast isolation, fusion, the selection and culture of the hybrid cells, and the recovery of entire plants from the selected colonies. Finally, the properties of the hybrid plants in terms of their genetic composition have to be characterized. Each of these various steps will be considered, with particular emphasis being placed on the selection, characterization, and properties of somatic hybrids.

The desire to go to these lengths to produce a hybrid was prompted largely by the realization that the technique might provide a means of overcoming incompatibility barriers, which offers the possibility of producing hitherto unobtainable gene combinations. Plants have evolved complex mechanisms to screen out unacceptable pollen and prevent promiscuous crossings, thereby maintaining the integrity of the species. Some of these screening mechanisms prevent the growth of the pollen tube, thus denying contact between male and female gametes. When the pollen tube does penetrate the egg sac, there may be a failure of the gametes to fuse. Clearly, this prezygotic incompatibility is circumvented by the use of isolated protoplasts for somatic hybridization. When the gametes are able to fuse, there may be a failure of the zygote to develop, namely, zygotic incompatibility. This developmental breakdown may arise as a result of a failure of the genomes to become fully integrated, possibly caused by disparities in the replication times of the two genomes. Alternatively, the zygote may progress some way toward becoming an embryo and then abort. This postzygotic incompatibility may be due to a failure of the endosperm to develop, possibly as a result of an imbalance between the hormone levels in the embryo and maternal tissue. This postzygotic incompatibility would not be expected to operate in somatic hybridization, whereas the zygotic incompatibility is still likely to be encountered. It seems reasonable to expect, therefore, that at least some of the incompatibility barriers are likely to be breached as a result of somatic hybridization.

II. Protoplast Isolation and Culture

Before somatic hybridization can even be considered it is necessary to obtain large quantities of viable protoplasts. The parameters for successful protoplast isolation have now been defined, and the isolation of viable protoplasts is a routine procedure in many laboratories. In fact, protoplast preparations are used not only for the production of somatic hybrids but also in basic studies on plant cell biology (see Galun, 1981). The various techniques required for protoplast isolation have been reviewed (I. K. Vasil and Vasil, 1980) and consequently only the basic principles will be outlined here.

There are two major prerequisites for any successful protoplast isolation. First, the cell wall must be removed without affecting the viability of the enclosed protoplast. Second, since the living protoplast is an osmotic system, it will take up water, expand, and burst once it is removed from the confines of the cell wall unless the osmotic potential of the external environment is suitably regulated. The correct osmotic potential is one in which the cells are just plasmolyzed, as too high an osmotic potential in the external medium will lead to irreversible damage to the protoplast.

In early attempts at protoplast isolation, inorganic salts were used as osmotic stabilizers (Klercker, 1892), and although satisfactory protoplast isolation has been obtained using salts such as KCl, $CaCl_2$, and $MgSO_4$ as osmotic stabilizers (Kameya and Uchimiya, 1972), there is some evidence that cell wall regeneration and cell division may be adversely affected (Meyer and Abel, 1975).

The sugar alcohols, mannitol and sorbitol, are now commonly used as osmotic stabilizers. Used separately or in combination at total concentrations of 0.3–0.8 *M* they have proved particularly useful. Mannitol has the advantage that it penetrates only slowly into plant cells; in addition, it is relatively metabolically inert. Consequently, the osmotic balance is more likely to be maintained throughout the isolation period than when, for example, glucose or sucrose is used as an osmotic stabilizer. Protoplasts have also been successfully isolated in a low concentration of sucrose but with the addition of 2% polyvinylpyrrolidone to maintain stability of the protoplasts (Shepard and Totten, 1975).

Once the cell is plasmolyzed, the release of the protoplast by removal or disruption of the cell wall can be achieved by two fundamentally different approaches. Prior to 1960, when Cocking reported enzymatic digestion of the cell wall to release protoplasts, mechanical disruption of the cell wall was the method by which preparations of protoplasts were obtained. The procedure involved thinly slicing plasmolyzed tissue. Following slight deplasmolysis, protoplasts were released from those cells in which the cell wall had been cut but the protoplast remained undamaged. Needless to say, yields were very low. The method was also tedious and restricted to certain types of tissue, such as large parenchymatous cells of storage organs.

This mechanical method of isolation has now been largely superseded by the use of fungal hydrolytic enzymes. Although enzymatic digestion of the cell wall is capable of releasing high yields of protoplasts from many different plant tissues, it does present a disadvantage in that protoplasts will be exposed to the damaging effects of hydrolytic enzymes, some of which are likely to be derived from damaged cells, for considerable periods of time.

Because the primary plant cell wall is a highly complex structure made up of a number of components, crude enzyme preparations are likely to be more effective in wall digestion than those that have been highly purified. However, such crude preparations also contain toxic impurities, which on prolonged exposure will have a detrimental effect on the yield of viable protoplasts. A wide range of partially purified enzymes is now commercially available, for example, the cellulase Onozuka R10 and the potent pectinase Pectolyase Y23, and it is these that are most frequently used. Even so, further purification by desalting may be required in some instances to reduce variability in protoplast yield (Slabas *et al.*, 1980) and to improve subsequent plating efficiency (dos Santos *et al.*, 1980).

The actual procedure adopted for protoplast isolation will be dictated mainly by the plant and tissue selected as starting material. It may be an advantage with some material to isolate first a preparation of free cells, which can then be treated with a cellulase to degrade the cell wall and liberate the protoplasts. These free cells can be isolated by enzymatic digestion of the intercellular pectins (Takebe *et al.*, 1968; Otsuki and Takebe, 1969). Alternatively, using leaf material of some plant species, it has proved possible to isolate cells mechanically by gentle grinding in a glass homogenizer (Rossini, 1969; Jullian, 1970; Harada *et al.*, 1972) or by shearing in a vortex impinger (Schwenk, 1980, 1981). Free cells have also been obtained by gently brushing the leaf surface with sand (Oliver *et al.*, 1979).

In most cases protoplasts can be isolated using a combined pectinase and cellulase treatment. Higher yields of mesophyll protoplasts are obtained if the lower epidermis is first removed before exposure to enzyme. In situations in which this proves difficult, leaves may be feathered, sliced, or chopped to allow access of the enzyme to the mesophyll layers. Failing this, gently brushing the leaf surface with carborundum (Beier and Bruening, 1975) or alumina (Roscoe and Bell, 1981) may well damage the epidermis sufficiently to allow enzyme penetration. The epidermis of some leaves can be digested by incubation in a solution of Rohament P, a pectin glucosidase (Schilde-Rentschler, 1973). A short period under reduced pressure is sometimes used to promote penetration of the enzyme into the tissue (Evans and Cocking, 1975).

Experience has shown that it is now possible to isolate protoplasts from virtually every organ and structure of the plant provided that the walls of the constituent cells have remained in a primary condition and have not undergone any significant secondary changes such as lignification. Leaves are frequently used as a source of protoplasts because of the ample availability of material and the relative ease with which large numbers of protoplasts can be obtained. Suspension-cultured cells have also proved to be an ideal source of protoplasts provided they are selected at a particular stage in their culture cycle. To obtain high yields of protoplasts, cell cultures must be in a state of rapid cell proliferation (Kao *et al.*, 1970) and ideally used 4–5 days after subculture (Uchimiya and Murashige, 1974). Even then, yields will sometimes fluctuate after several subcultures, and it may prove necessary to initiate fresh suspension cultures from callus tissue.

If somatic hybridization is the reason for isolating protoplasts, high yields, good viability, and stability must be ensured. The various parameters of the isolation procedure must be optimized for the particular plant material used. Temperature and duration of enzyme incubation, constitution and pH of enzyme mixtures, and the use of membrane-stabilizing compounds such as potassium dextran sulfate (Takebe *et al.*, 1968) should be given consideration. In addition, it has been shown that the plant age and the conditions under which the plants have been grown can be critical for reproducible high yields of protoplasts (Watts *et al.*, 1974). The influence of light intensity, in particular, has been shown to be extremely important in the isolation of protoplasts from the leaves of many plant species. Incubation of plants under low light intensity or using a short period of darkness prior to protoplast isolation appears to be beneficial in some instances (Kao and Michayluk, 1980; Karunaratne and Scott, 1981). In a number of cases, growth of plants under controlled environmental conditions is preferential to growth in a glasshouse. Some workers have used axenically grown shoots for the isolation of mesophyll protoplasts (Binding, 1975). In addition to complete control over environmental conditions, material grown *in vitro* offers the advantage that no sterilant or antibiotics are required that may reduce the quality and quantity of protoplast yield.

Several methods have been employed to purify protoplasts following isolation. A protoplast preparation can frequently be freed of partially degraded cellular material and subcellular debris by passage through a series of stainless-steel or nylon screens of different mesh size. Alternatively, protoplasts may be purified by low-speed centrifugation in solutions with a relatively high density. Mesophyll protoplasts are frequently separated from cell debris by flotation on sucrose. High sucrose concentrations, however, may prove unsuitable for some protoplast preparations, particularly those isolated in a low-osmotic environment. To aid flotation of the protoplasts, the density of the solution can be increased by the inclusion of components that contribute little to the osmotic potential, such as Ficoll (Schenk and Hildebrandt, 1971) or Percoll (Fitzsimons and Weyers, 1983). On occasion, a two-phase system such as Lymphoprep-Ficoll (Larkin, 1976) or dextran–polyethylene glycol (Kanai and Edwards, 1973; Slabas *et al.*, 1980) has been used. However, since polyethylene glycol is known to be a fusogen (see later), use of it for protoplast purification is probably undesirable.

Once protoplasts have been fused (see Section III), it is important that conditions be established such that at least one of the parental protoplast systems is capable of successful culture leading ultimately to plant regeneration. The first step in this process is the adaptation of the protoplast to the imposed nutrient and physical culture environment. Experience has shown that nutrient media requirements of protoplasts are broadly similar to those of cultured cells, although during the initial period of culture the protoplasts are generally considered to be "leaky," with the danger of the loss of essential metabolites to the surrounding medium. A particular protoplast system may exhibit subtle differences in nutrient requirements compared with those derived from a related species, and for success it may be necessary to carefully formulate each component of the medium.

The mineral salt composition of Murashige and Skoog (1962) or Gamborg *et al.* (1968), or modifications thereof, are frequently used to provide inorganic salts, and the organic component is usually composed of several vitamins and is also frequently based on these two media. On occasion, however, improvements in growth and survival can be achieved by the addition of other organic components such as amino acids. The source of carbon and energy is usually in the form of sucrose, although glucose is sometimes preferred. Most protoplast systems require the provision of auxin and a cytokinin for maintenance of viability and continued development, and particular attention should be paid to the type and concentration of these growth regulators since they are often critical components of the medium.

Until the protoplasts have regenerated an adequate cell wall, it will be necessary to supply an osmotic stabilizer, usually in the form of mannitol. The level of this osmotic stabilizer should be gradually reduced in order to encourage rapid development, since conditions of high osmotic potential are known to retard cell division.

Optimum physical environmental conditions for protoplast culture must also be determined for each plant species. Initial culture in darkness or under very low light intensity is vital for the development of some protoplast systems (Banks and Evans, 1976). Incubation temperature, type of culture vessel, density of protoplasts per milliliter of culture medium, and total volume of culture medium are all important. Particular problems may be encountered in the culture of mechanically isolated heterokaryons following fusion. In this connection, the development of microculture techniques has proved useful for the culture of single or very low densities of protoplasts (see later).

Under suitable culture conditions, isolated protoplasts will rapidly reform a cell wall and embark upon cell division. Frequently, once division has begun it will continue to give rise, in due course, to a callus colony. Some protoplast systems, however, will cease division after progressing through a number of mitotic cycles. For continued division it may be necessary to transfer the small colonies to a medium with a different formulation, particularly with regard to the growth regulators. Once a macroscopic cell colony has been formed, conditions can be sought that will induce organized development leading to the recovery of shoots. It is at this point that problems have arisen. Currently, the major restriction on the application of somatic hybridization to crop improvement resides in the limited number of species that have so far been successfully regenerated to whole plants from protoplasts. Unfortunately, most of the species of commercial interest, notably the cereals and legumes, have proved particularly recalcitrant in this respect. Nonetheless, work has continued on the assumption that provided the right conditions or sequence of conditions can be found, shoots will be recovered. Experience suggests that a given species may require a critical endogenous hormone balance for shoot induction, and it is difficult to achieve such a balance with the supply of exogenous hormones in the medium. It may be necessary to pass the tissue through a sequence of different hormone levels to reach the required condition. In fact, gradual progress is being made and protocols are being reported for shoot recovery starting from isolated protoplasts derived from a few legumes and cereals (Table I).

III. Fusion

Fusion of mixed populations of isolated protoplasts, leading to the formation of a heterokaryon, requires the presence of a fusion-inducing agent (a fusogen). This requirement is due to the fact that isolated protoplasts carry a negative electrostatic charge (Grout *et al.*, 1972), originating mainly from the phosphate groups of the cell membrane (Nagata and Melchers, 1978), which prevents them from coming into proximity to each other. As a first requirement, a fusogen must therefore be able to negate or circumvent this charge to encourage protoplasts to aggregate and adhere together. A second requirement of the fusogen is that it should cause some change or instability in the bilayer structure of membrane lipids so that fusion of closely apposed protoplasts may take place.

Although it is only in recent years that techniques for the reproducible fusion of protoplasts have been developed, observations on protoplast fusion extend back to the work of Kuster in 1909. He was able to demonstrate that $Ca(NO_3)_2$ could induce fusion of mechanically isolated protoplasts, albeit at a very low frequency (Kuster, 1910).

Using sodium nitrate, Power *et al.* (1970) were able to induce inter- and intraspecific cell fusion of protoplasts derived from roots of several different cereals, although subsequent culture of these protoplasts was not possible. Carlson *et al.* (1972) did, however, manage to produce a somatic hybrid between two different species of tobacco using $NaNO_3$ as a fusogen. But, because of the low frequency of fusion and the adverse effect on viability of protoplasts using $NaNO_3$, attention was directed toward obtaining a more effective fusion-inducing agent. Many techniques were examined, including those known to induce fusion of animal cells, but with no, or only limited, success.

Considerably more success was achieved by Keller and Melchers (1973), who were able to produce large numbers of fused protoplasts by exposing them to conditions of high pH (10.5) in the presence of Ca^{2+} at 37°C. Binding (1974) also came to a similar conclusion that alkaline conditions and presence of Ca^{2+} favored fusion, but at the expense of a substantial decrease in the subsequent viability of the protoplasts. This method of fusion has been used successfully by several workers to fuse protoplasts that have subsequently given rise to somatic hybrids (Schieder, 1974; Melchers and Labib, 1974).

The way in which high pH and Ca^{2+} induce fusion is not entirely

TABLE I. Legumes and cereals cultured from protoplast to plant

Species	Source of protoplasts	Reference
Legumes		
Medicago sativa	Leaf mesophyll	Kao and Mickayluk (1980); dos Santos *et al.* (1980); Johnson *et al.* (1981)
	Cotyledon	Lu *et al.* (1982b)
	Root	Xu *et al.* (1982)
Medicago coerulea	Leaf; cell-suspension cultures	Arcioni *et al.* (1982)
Medicago glutinosa	Leaf; cell-suspension cultures	Arcioni *et al.* (1982)
Trifolium repens	Suspension cultures from seed, seedling root, or stem callus	Gresshoff (1980)
Trigonella corniculata	Leaf mesophyll; cell-suspension cultures	Lu *et al.* (1982a); dos Santos *et al.* (1983)
Lotus corniculatus	Seedling roots; hypocotyls; cotyledons	Ahuja *et al.* (1983)
Stylosanthes guyanensis	Cell-suspension culture from leaf and hypocotyl	Meijer and Steinbiss (1983)
Cereals		
Panicum maximum	Suspension culture from immature embryos and young inflorescences (plantlets failed to grow to maturity)	Lu *et al.* (1981)
Pennisetum americanum	Suspension culture from immature embryos (plantlets failed to grow to maturity)	V. Vasil and Vasil (1980)
Pennisetum purpureum	Suspension culture from immature embryos and inflorescences (plantlets failed to grow to maturity)	Vasil *et al.* (1983)

clear. Exposure to high pH in the absence of Ca^{2+} leads to rapid lysis of the protoplasts. Presumably the plasma membrane is destabilized by the high pH while Ca^{2+} prevents total membrane disruption.

The presence of a high concentration of $CaCl_2$ (50–100 m*M*) has been shown to nullify the negative surface charge on protoplasts and hence electrostatic repulsion. Aggregation of protoplasts in the presence of Ca^{2+} can, therefore, be attributed to van der Waals forces of attraction (Nagata and Melchers, 1978). Such neutralization of the protoplast surface charge is, however, insufficient to induce fusion. Experience using phospholipid vesicles has shown that exposure to relatively high levels of Ca^{2+} causes the outer phospholipid monolayer to become crystalline while the inner layer remains fluid. This resultant phase separation causes membrane instability, and conceivably two phospholipid bilayers in close apposition could be susceptible to fusion (Papahadjopoulos *et al.*, 1977). A similar decrease in fluidity of protoplast membranes has been observed in the presence of Ca^{2+} (Boss and Mott, 1980).

Another approach to protoplast fusion has been developed in which the fusion-inducing agent is polyethylene glycol (PEG) (Kao and Michayluk, 1974; Wallin *et al.*, 1974). This method of fusion has proved to be very successful. High fusion frequencies have been obtained, and at concentrations conducive to fusion PEG is generally nontoxic. Furthermore, the PEG technique appears to be universally applicable, as fusions between a wide range of organisms, including interkingdom fusion, have been achieved.

Exposure of protoplasts to PEG causes quite dramatic aggregation and protoplasts appear to adhere very closely together. The degree of protoplast aggregation is influenced by the concentration of PEG, the concentration of protoplasts, the temperature of incubation, and the presence of divalent cations (Wallin *et al.*, 1974). Kao and Michayluk (1974) demonstrated that high-molecular-weight PEG (PEG 6000) was more effective at causing adhesion than was low-molecular-weight PEG, such as that used by Wallin *et al.* (1974). They also noted that the actual fusion of the protoplasts occurred during gradual dilution of the PEG solution and not when the protoplasts were tightly aggregated. Fusion frequencies were substantially increased when the PEG solution was enriched with Ca^{2+} and when a high Ca^{2+}/pH solution was used to elute the fusogen (Kao *et al.*, 1974; Constabel *et al.*, 1976).

The means by which PEG causes aggregation and induces fusion has stimulated considerable interest over the past decade. The precise mechanism involved, however, has yet to be completely resolved. Since the PEG molecule has a slightly negative polarity, it has been suggested that it will form a molecular bridge between membranes of adjacent protoplasts by binding to positively charged proteins and/or glycoproteins in the outer bilayer, and so cause protoplast aggregation (Kao and Michayluk, 1974; Kao and Wetter, 1977). Evidence for this comes from the fact that high-molecular-weight PEG causes greater aggregation than does the shorter chain, low-molecular-weight molecule. Increased aggregation in the presence of Ca^{2+} may be explained by additional indirect binding of PEG to negatively charged membrane components via Ca^{2+} (Kao and Michayluk, 1974; Kao and Wetter, 1977).

Many workers have demonstrated that a fairly high concentration of PEG is required to induce fusion. Too high a concentration of PEG, however, can cause cell death. The PEG molecule has a strong affinity for water, which results in a reduction of the free-water content in an aqueous solution. A strong correlation has been found between the concentration of PEG required to produce a solution containing zero free water and that required to induce maximum fusion of fibroblasts (Blow *et al.*, 1978). Evidence suggests that PEG at high concentration, and therefore in a solution in which there is no free water present, will partially dehydrate the phospholipid bilayers of the membrane (Arnold *et al.*, 1983). Undoubtedly, exposure to very high concentrations of PEG would lead to irreversible cell damage due to dehydration. Based on their results using artificial phospholipid bilayers, Arnold and colleagues (1983) speculated that dehydration together with alterations in distribution of membrane molecules following PEG treatment could contribute to the destabilization of cell membranes and result in fusion. Many workers, however, have observed no, or very low, incidence of fusion when PEG treatment is applied in the absence of Ca^{2+} (Kao and Michayluk, 1974; Blow *et al.*, 1978). Indeed, evidence from the work of Ueda and co-workers (1978) suggests that PEG alone will promote phagocytosis rather than fusion.

As already discussed, Ca^{2+} has been shown to cause structural changes at the surface of the membrane bilayer that are independent of the action of PEG. PEG, however, is thought to enhance membrane destabilization and fusion by increasing the permeability of the membrane to Ca^{2+} (Aldwinckle *et al.*, 1982). Alteration of membrane permeability properties may be a result of the action of PEG on the water of hydration of the phospholipid polar groups in the cell membrane and/or changes in surface potential (Maggio *et al.*, 1976). Cell fusion of hen erythrocytes was always preceded by an abnormal entry of Ca^{2+} following PEG treatment (Blow *et al.*, 1978). In addition, application of EDTA to erythrocytes after treatment with PEG/Ca^{2+}

failed to prevent fusion. These results would indicate that entry of Ca^{2+} is responsible for triggering fusion and that fusion, once initiated, is independent of exogenous Ca^{2+}.

It is conceivable that an increased concentration of Ca^{2+} at the cytoplasmic surface of the bilayer could mediate drastic alterations of membrane structure. It has been suggested that Ca^{2+} may interact with membrane phospholipids, resulting in redistribution and aggregation of intramembranous proteins (Vos *et al.*, 1976). Such aggregation of protein molecules would lead to lipid-rich areas in the membrane. It is now generally believed that fusion occurs following the interaction of lipids of closely apposed membranes in areas depleted of protein. The involvement of Ca^{2+} in fusion could therefore be related to changes in the lateral organization of the membrane.

Protease pretreatment has been shown to enhance PEG-induced fusion (Hartmann *et al.*, 1976). Presumably, degradation of certain membrane proteins takes place, producing lipid domains and hence potential sites for fusion. The increased frequency of fusion obtained in early experiments by Kao *et al.* (1974) when Driselase was used to isolate protoplasts could be related to a protease contaminant of this enzyme. There is some evidence to suggest that Ca^{2+} may be involved in the activation or release of endogenous proteolytic activity, and it has been proposed that this may assist membrane fusion (Ahkong *et al.*, 1978).

Although actual membrane fusion is rapid, little fusion is obtained until PEG is eluted. One possible explanation for this may be that the presence of the PEG polymer structurally inhibits membrane coalescence. Alternatively, phospholipid interaction between adjacent membranes may require the disturbance created by rehydration.

An interesting observation has been made by Honda and associates (1981a,b) regarding the effect of impurities of commercial-grade PEG on the fusion of human erythrocytes. They demonstrated that the "fusogenicity" of purified PEG was substantially reduced, although the capacity to induce aggregation was not affected. The contaminating chemicals removed during the purification process were subsequently identified as antioxidants. The fusion activity of commercial-grade PEG was therefore attributed to the combination of the high-molecular-weight polymer plus the low-molecular-weight, fat-soluble additives. Furthermore, more efficient fusion could be achieved by combining purified PEG 6000 with selected, and possibly modified, components generally present in commercial-grade PEG.

However, subsequent investigations have shown that purified PEG is able to induce fusion. Smith *et al.* (1982) demonstrated that purification of PEG from four of five commercial sources had no effect on its fusogenic properties, provided a suitable protocol for fusion was followed. A lower frequency of fusion was obtained, however, following purification of PEG from a fifth source (Wako Pure Chemical Industries, Japan). Similarly, Boss (1983) showed that plant protoplasts can be fused equally well with recrystallized or nonrecrystallized PEG.

A combined PEG–dimethyl sulfoxide (DMSO) treatment (Haydu *et al.*, 1977) and use of certain other high-molecular-weight polymers, such as polyvinyl alcohol (Nagata, 1978) and dextran (Kameya, 1979), have also been reported to promote fusion.

Another promising technique for the fusion of protoplasts that has recently emerged involves electrical stimulation. Senda *et al.* (1979) demonstrated fusion of two adhering protoplasts by applying a short electrical impulse across two microelectrodes placed in contact with the surface of the protoplasts. On a slightly larger scale, Zimmermann and Scheurich (1981) and Vienken *et al.* (1981) were able to induce aggregation of protoplasts by subjecting them to a nonuniform alternating electrical field. Fusion of the protoplasts was subsequently achieved by the application of a single short, high-intensity electrical field pulse causing the dielectric breakdown of the cell membrane. This method of fusion appears to be highly efficient, producing up to 100% yield of fused cells, and avoids the use of extreme conditions such as those used in high pH/Ca^{2+} and PEG treatments. Although fused cells have been observed to remain intact for several days, the effect on subsequent culture and whole plant regeneration has yet to be examined.

Experience has now shown that exposure of protoplasts to a suitable fusion-inducing agent quickly leads to membrane fusion between protoplasts derived not only from closely related species, but also between protoplasts from quite diverse sources, which indicates that at the cell membrane level no problems of incompatibility exist. Similarly, following membrane fusion, cytoplasm from each parent will readily coalesce to form a heterokaryon. Cytoplasmic mixing can be observed by the use of a marker system, such as the fusion of mesophyll protoplasts containing green chloroplasts with protoplasts derived from cultured cells that lack chloroplasts but that may have a cytoplasm with a characteristic appearance.

The behavior of nuclei in the heterokaryon is of crucial importance. Nuclei of pea and soybean heterokaryons were observed to fuse during interphase and the chromatin of both nuclei mixed, albeit slowly (Constabel *et al.*, 1975). Likewise, fusion of interphase nuclei was observed in carrot and barley heterokaryons (Dudits *et al.,* 1976). Larger heterokaryons originating from multiple protoplast fusions generally deteriorated and died. It was also possible to witness mitotic activity in a considerable number of both pea and soybean and carrot and barley heterokaryons and, in general, the component nuclei of a heterokaryon passed through the phases of mitosis in synchrony. Furthermore, evidence was obtained that the chromosomes of closely associated nuclei could even come to lie on a common metaphase plate. In this situation the reconstitution of the nuclear membrane at telophase would effectively result in nuclear fusion with the formation of a hybrid cell or synkaryon. In contrast, synchronous mitosis (followed by cytokinesis) in nuclei that were not closely associated resulted in the breakdown of the heterokaryon and the formation of uninucleate cells (Constabel *et al.,* 1975; Kao *et al.,* 1974). This pattern of behavior would lead to the formation of chimeral cell colonies.

It has now been clearly established that fusion products will divide, and this is true even when the components are derived from protoplasts arising from very distantly related species. In addition, heterokaryon nuclei coordinate their mitotic activity. When soybean protoplasts derived from cultured cells were fused with mesophyll protoplasts of tobacco or pea, mitotic activity in the heterokaryon occurred 2 or 3 days after fusion, whereas unfused soybean protoplasts usually divided after 1 day in culture and the unfused mesophyll protoplasts not until 5 days of culture (Constabel *et al.,* 1976).

It has been observed that when a protoplast derived from an actively growing cell culture of either carrot or soybean is fused with a barley mesophyll protoplast, mitotic activity of both nuclei in the heterokaryon is recorded, even though unfused barley mesophyll protoplasts do not divide (Kao *et al.,* 1974; Dudits *et al.,* 1976). Similarly, Szabados and Dudits (1980) found that mitotic activation of nondividing rice protoplasts could be induced by fusion with mitotic wheat cultured-cell protoplasts.

In the majority of cases in which distantly related protoplasts have been hybridized, continued proliferation of the fusion product has been difficult to maintain. In a few instances, however, some success has been achieved, most notably with the hybrid cell line between *Nicotiana tabacum* and *Glycine max* (Kao, 1977) and between *Petunia hybrida* and *Vicia faba* (Binding and Nehls, 1978). In both of these cases, however, chromosome elimination occurred, which resulted in the loss of the majority of the chromosomes of one of the parents. This question of the stability of the chromosomes in somatic hybrids will be discussed in more detail later.

IV. Selection and Recovery of Hybrids

Once heterokaryon formation has taken place, it is usually necessary to develop some means of recovering the hybrid material from among the overwhelming majority of parental protoplasts. Even in those situations in which the fusion rates have been relatively high, experience has shown that only a fraction of these heterokaryons will accomplish nuclear fusion and embark upon sustained cell division. At first, those working on cell fusion looked for inspiration to the results that had been achieved with the selection of animal cell hybrids. Experience with cultured animal cells had clearly shown that very powerful selection procedures, allowing the recovery of rare hybrid cells, could be devised by exploiting the different physiological and biochemical properties of the cells. The classic example of this approach is the hypoxanthine–aminopterin–thymidine (HAT) selection system first used by Littlefield in 1964, which exploits mutant cell lines deficient in certain enzyme activities (Szybalski *et al.*, 1962). The method relies on the fact that both parental cell lines contain a different recessive mutation and are prevented from growing in a particular medium. But hybrids are able to grow since each parental genome contributes the appropriate wild-type allele, complementing the deficiency in the other. In the early 1970s, when the first attempts to produce somatic hybrids were being undertaken, it quickly became apparent that selection systems in plants based on gene complementation along the lines used with animal cells were not available by virtue of the lack of appropriate mutants. As a consequence, it was necessary to apply considerable ingenuity in the development of systems for hybrid recovery and a wide range of strategies have been adopted.

A selection system that could be termed generally applicable has been one of the major aims. For success such a system would not depend on any prior knowledge as to how the hybrid would behave under a particular nutrient environment and could be used to recover hybrids between plants for which no sexually derived counterpart existed. In the event, the various selection methods have often depended on a particular feature or idiosyncracy of the protoplast system under study and many are of limited applicability.

In fact, not all the selection systems that have been devised have ultimately resulted in the recovery of somatic hybrid plants. On a number of occasions the selection has led to hybrid cell isolation, but for various reasons, subsequent development of the hybrid has not been maintained or problems have been encountered in the recovery of organized shoots. Some consideration will be given to the operation of these selection systems, even though they did not lead to recovery of somatic hybrid plants.

A. TIMING OF SELECTION

The aim of a selection system is to isolate the hybrids from among a background of parental protoplasts, either by identifying the hybrids and then manually removing them from the parental population by a physical selection or, alternatively, by developing conditions whereby the hybrids proliferate but the parental protoplasts fail to thrive, namely, a physiological selection. Within these two basic approaches the actual timing of the selection can vary. Indeed, the time at which the selection operates, as measured by the development of the hybrids and the parental protoplasts, may be crucial for success. If a stringent physiological selection pressure is applied immediately after fusion such that the parental protoplasts die, it will probably result in the viable hybrid population being at such a low density as to render any further development impossible. The problem can be somewhat reduced by removing only one of the parental protoplast systems at this early stage, then applying a second selection when the cultures have developed further, i.e., in practice, by a two-stage selection system.

The problem of maintaining the viability of the remaining hybrids can be alleviated to a certain degree by the addition of conditioned medium or by culture in a medium enriched with organic compounds and formulated for the culture of protoplasts at low densities (Kao and Michayluk, 1975). Alternatively, the imposition of some form of nurse effect may sustain the growth of the hybrids. Coculture with viable nonparental protoplasts from which the hybrids can be readily recovered has been used (Menczel *et al.,* 1978). The culture of hybrids in the presence of a feeder layer made up of protoplasts rendered incapable of division either by X-irradiation or some form of chemical inhibition has also been suggested (Raveh *et al.,* 1973). However, such measures may not entirely solve the problem, since the presence of a large population of parental protoplasts with diminished viability may cause impaired viability of the hybrids themselves. It would, of course, be very useful in this connection if the parental protoplasts remained viable but did not divide. Clearly, the difficulties caused by the presence of a large population of degenerating protoplasts are not encountered when the hybrids are physically isolated, but it will still be necessary to provide nurse conditions, augmented culture media, or maintenance of the hybrids in small culture volumes in order to maximize their chances of further development. There is some merit, therefore, in delaying the application of the selection pressure at least until the protoplasts have begun to divide and possibly even until small colonies have developed. It would be particularly helpful if the parental material would cease further development at this stage (for example, see Gupta *et al.*, 1982). Where auxotrophic mutants are to be used, it has been found beneficial by some workers to culture the protoplast population initially in enriched medium until some division has taken place and then transfer the cells to deficient medium allowing only continued growth of the hybrids (Glimelius *et al.*, 1978).

On occasion, a two-stage selection system has been utilized wherein one parental protoplast population was unable to grow from the outset because of unfavorable nutrient conditions or the presence of an inhibitor, whereas the other parental line grew to produce small colonies which then failed to develop further, but the growth of the hybrids was unhindered by either the inhibitor or the composition of the medium. It has been suggested, however, that delaying the time of selection may result in the loss of some hybrids. It is possible that through chromosome instability at the time of the first few divisions, some genetic information essential for survival later in the selection system could be lost and some hybrid lines that might be of considerable interest would fail to be rescued. Nonetheless, on occasion selection has been successfully carried out at a time when the callus colonies have developed to quite an advanced stage. Frequently, the development of chlorophyll in callus colonies in which the parental material is derived from chlorophyll-deficient lines has served to identify hybrids. Alternatively, a combination of morphological markers possessed by a callus, each of which is attributable to one of the parental lines, has been used to recognize hybrid material. Sometimes the development of chlorophyll combined with another morophological feature has been used.

Finally, selection can be delayed until the point at which shoots have been produced on the callus colonies. Sometimes the actual ability to produce shoots has been exploited for selection—one of the parental lines being able to undergo organogenesis whereas the other is not. Indeed, there is some evidence that the ability to undergo shoot formation is expressed as a dominant feature in hybrid callus. Regenerated shoots are then examined for features that would identify them as hybrid. Conversely, both parental lines may possess the capacity to regenerate, and then it is necessary to screen the regenerated plantlets for a feature or a combination of features that would identify them as hybrid. Again, forms of chlorophyll deficiency or light sensitivity have been exploited. In those situations in which clearly discernible visual markers are not available, use has been made of other differences, such as isoenzyme patterns.

A difficulty in delaying selection to this late stage is that large numbers of colonies have to be individually manipulated. This may present a problem, particularly if it is necessary to transfer the colonies through several subcultures before organogenesis can be induced. In systems such as tobacco, in which shoots can be induced on quite small colonies, possibly only after one change of medium, this problem is minimized. It will still be necessary to culture the protoplasts at a relatively low plating density and also to pick out individual colonies when they are still small in order to be certain that each colony is derived from a single protoplast or single fusion event.

Handling and screening large numbers of regenerated plants presents its own special problems, particularly when characters other than chlorophyll deficiencies are used. In practice, for some systems, hybrids have been recovered from quite surprisingly low numbers of regenerated plants. This is particularly so when high levels of fusion have been achieved and when the parental protoplasts are derived from sexually compatible partners and especially from intraspecific fusions. Much more difficulty is likely to be experienced when the parents are sexually incompatible.

B. STRATEGIES FOR SELECTION

1. *Physical selection methods*

When the various techniques for protoplast fusion were being developed, it was necessary to monitor the amount of fusion obtained. The best way to achieve this and yet maintain the viability of the fusion products was to use two protoplast systems that differed markedly in appearance. The fusion products could then be identified visually by possession of the appropriate features. Fusion of protoplasts from leaf mesophyll with protoplasts derived from cultured cells offered the most convenient system, the hybrid being readily identified by the presence of chloroplasts in a protoplast rich in cytoplasm and with obvious cytoplasmic strands. It was natural, therefore, to continue to use such visual markers for the selection of the hybrid cells. One of the difficulties, however, of using visual markers of this type is that after a short period in culture (2–3 days), when the protoplasts have expanded and the chlorophyll has begun to degenerate, it becomes increasingly more difficult to recognize the hybrids. Consequently, selection has to be done soon after fusion. One approach to recognizing fused protoplasts, particularly when both parental protoplasts are derived from the same type of cell system, is to label the cells with a marker. Clearly, such markers should not reduce the viability of the protoplasts or leak out from the protoplast when the plasma membrane is destabilized during fusion. Suspension culture cells prior to protoplast isolation have been incubated with a fluorescent probe such as fluorescein isothiocyanate (FITC) conjugated to octadecylamine or rhodamine conjugated to octadecanol. These probes become associated with membranes; the isolated protoplasts fluoresce apple green when labeled with the former and reddish when labeled with the latter. Fused protoplasts fluoresce with peaks in the emission spectra at 538 and 592 nm and are readily identified (Galbraith and Galbraith, 1979). The same technique has been used to identify fused mesophyll and cultured-cell protoplasts (Galbraith and Mauch, 1980). Similarly, a combination of FITC and chlorophyll, which fluoresces red, has been used to identify fused mesophyll and cultured-cell protoplasts (Patnaik *et al.*, 1982).

Once the fused cells have been identified, they can be removed from the protoplast population with a fine pipet, or in those cases in which the protoplasts have been plated in agar, their location on the plate can be recorded. To facilitate removal only of fused cells, it has proved necessary to dilute the population density to a relatively low level. The isolated fusion products are then cultured individually in small volumes of medium, frequently in the wells of Cuprak dishes (Kao, 1977; Gleba and Hoffmann, 1978). As already discussed, it is important to pay particular attention to the composition of the medium for the culture of protoplasts at very low densities. Kao and Michayluk (1975) formulated a medium rich in organic components that would support the growth of single protoplasts of *Vicia hajastana.* Similarly, single tobacco mesophyll protoplasts could be cultured provided the volume of the culture droplet was reduced to 1 μl and the protoplasts were initially cultured at a high density (Gleba, 1978a).

After identifying the heterokaryons using fluorescence, they could be isolated manually with the aid of a specially constructed capillary pipet and syringe linked to a micromanipulator (Patnaik *et al.*, 1982). For this purpose it was found preferable to fuse the protoplasts with high pH and Ca^{2+} since this leads to less aggregation of the protoplasts after fusion than does PEG treatment and allows easier isolation of single heterokaryons. Only 20–30 heterokaryons/hr could be recovered using this procedure, clearly a laborious and painstaking exercise. An exciting possibility, however, is offered by the fact that it may be feasible to automate the selection and screen as many as 1000 protoplasts/sec. The technique of flow cytometry and cell sorting is already well advanced for animal cells (Melamed *et al.*, 1979). In principle, this system makes use of the ability to label cells with different fluorescent probes, although other characteristics can be used, such as light scattering. The emission spectra of these probes should be such that when excited by one wavelength of light, each fluorochrome should produce a clearly separable emission peak. Cells are made to flow individually in a stream through a sensory region in which they intercept a fine laser beam of the exciting radiation (Fig. 1). The emission from the fluorochromes is recorded such that each cell is monitored for possession of one or the other of the fluroescent markers, or both. Downstream from the sensory region, a vibrating piezoelectric transducer breaks the flow into small droplets. By adjustments in the cell density and the flow rate, it can be arranged that each droplet contains either a single cell or is without a cell. After a cell with the appropriate emission characteristics passes through the sensory region, there is a time delay such that, as the droplet containing that cell is formed, the droplet is electrically charged. Such droplets can be either positively or neg-

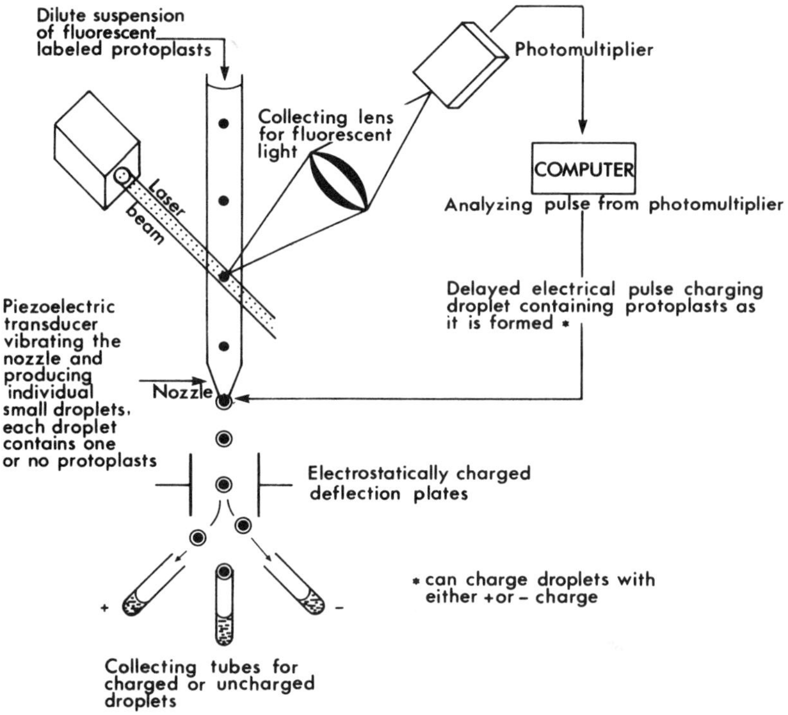

FIG. 1. Schematic diagram illustrating the mechanism of cell sorting by flow cytometry.

atively charged. The droplets then pass between two electrostatically charged plates and are either deflected to the right or left depending on the charge on the droplets. Uncharged droplets pass through undeflected. The droplets containing their cells can then be collected in vessels below the plates. In this way a single population of cells can be readily resolved from a mixture. The application of flow cytometry and cell sorting for the recovery of fused protoplasts looks very promising. As discussed already, fluorescent markers can be used to label protoplasts without impairing their viability. Furthermore, FITC and rhodamine isothiocyanate (RITC) can be used to label separate populations of protoplasts and the fused products will have a unique emission profile (Redenbaugh *et al.*, 1982). The use of a Becton Dickinson FACS IV cell sorter has allowed labeled and unlabeled *Euphorbia lathyres* protoplasts to be sorted. Similarly, *Petunia parodii* and albino *Petunia inflata* protoplasts could be sorted (Redenbaugh *et al.*, 1982). However, the instrument used could not directly select cells that were double labeled. There are still some technical difficulties to be overcome, particularly in relation to the size of the nozzle tip for the generation of the drops, the instrument being designed for the separation of animal cells, which are much smaller than plant protoplasts. Nevertheless, it does seem as if cell-sorting technology has considerable potential for fused-protoplast selection. Clearly, the speed of selection is a major advantage; in addition, a selection of this sort could be of general application, any two protoplast systems being readily labeled and the separation being independent of any physiological or genetic property of the protoplast system. Unfortunately, one drawback of this technique is the very considerable cost of the equipment.

Another physical technique for the recovery of hybrids has been suggested. The method exploits differences in buoyant density between different types of protoplasts and their fusion products. Density-gradient centrifugation using an isoosmotic gradient has led to the separation of a particular population of protoplasts enriched with fusion products (Harms and Potrykus, 1978).

In general, the physical selection of fused cells by the methods described is likely to be particularly valuable when wide crosses are undertaken or when chromosome instability is likely to be encountered. Because the selection does not depend on any physiological or genetic attribute of the cells, there is no danger of the capacity to express the particular features used for selection being lost, with consequent nonrecovery of the hybrid. It is, however, just such crosses, in which the lowest survival of fused cells is likely to occur, that necessitate the selection of large numbers of heterokaryons.

2. *Combined physiological and physical selection*

The principal feature of this type of selection is that, at the callus colony level, the hybrids should express a visible feature or a combination of features not expressed by either of the parental cell lines. Such visible markers should clearly characterize the hybrid material, enabling those callus colonies to be removed manually and cultured further in isolation. For this purpose the development of pigments in the hybrid, particularly chlorophyll, has been widely used in selection protocols ever since Melchers and Labib utilized light-sensitive mutants of tobacco for the recovery of somatic hybrids in 1974. In their system, protoplasts were isolated from haploid parental plants that contained one or the other of two nonallelic light-sensitive recessive mutations designated *s* and *v*. Under high light intensities the chlorophyll is bleached in these plants, but under relatively low light they can be grown to a stage sufficient to enable protoplasts to be isolated from the leaves. After fusion, the protoplasts were plated and proliferated to form callus colonies. They were then incubated under conditions of high light intensity and the green colonies that developed were removed and induced to regenerate plants. These green plants were unequivocably established as somatic hybrids since on selfing, some of the progeny expressed the *s* and *v* characteristics. This was an elegant demonstration that complementation would take place in the cell hybrids when two nonallelic genetic lesions were combined within one cell.

At much the same time, complementation was demonstrated between auxotrophic mutants in lower plants. Schieder (1974), using the liverwort *Sphaerocarpus,* isolated protoplasts from a green nicotinic acid-requiring female thallus ($n = 7 + X$) and from a pale green glucose-requiring male thallus ($n = 7 + Y$). After fusion the protoplasts were cultured in a medium lacking either glucose or nicotinic acid. A green plant developed that was diploid and contained both the X and Y sex chromosomes.

Clearly, a selection mechanism of this type depends not only on genetic complementation but also on the ability to induce unorganized callus colonies to produce sufficient chlorophyll for them to be identified on the culture plates. An appropriately formulated nutrient medium is required, which may necessitate alterations to the salt concentrations, levels of organic components, and the type and ratio of growth regulators.

Melchers extended the use of light-sensitive mutants to the complementation selection of interspecific somatic hybrids of *N. tabacum* and *Nicotiana sylvestris* (Melchers, 1977). Others have used the same principle for recovery of green colonies from colorless parental colonies but used instead mutants in which chlorophyll is not synthesized. Thus two yellow chlorophyll-deficient mutants of *Datura innoxia* complemented to allow the recovery of green colonies and subsequently wild-type plants (Schieder, 1977), whereas green callus could be selected after only 17 days culture following fusion between a chlorophyll-deficient mutant of *Nicotiana rustica* and an albino mutant of *N. tabacum* (Douglas *et al.*, 1981a). Similarly, four different chlorophyll-deficient mutants of *Nicotiana plumbaginifolia* were found to produce green callus colonies in all five of the combinations tested (Sidorov and Maliga, 1982).

It is perhaps significant that all of these successful pigment complementations involve either intraspecific hybridization or hybridization where sexual crossing is possible, although in some cases with difficulty. When complementation of this type was attempted between more distantly related species such as *Datura* and *Nicotiana,* and *Datura* and *Petunia,* no green colonies were recovered (Schieder, 1977).

Frequently in these selection schemes, use has been made of already existing and well-documented light-sensitive or chlorophyll-deficient mutations, whereas on other occasions these have been specifically isolated. Irradiation of pollen or of haploid somatic cells with ^{60}Co may easily generate such mutants in some species but much less so in others. A possibility does exist, however, that treatment of this kind will generate additional nonselected mutations in the plant material. There is some advantage, therefore, in minimizing the use of mutants and making use of a selection scheme wherein only one of the parents contains a chlorophyll mutation. A system in which the chlorophyll-containing partner is unable to grow at all in a particular nutrient environment or develops only to small cell clusters and consequently does not contribute any green colonies has been utilized. In a scheme of this sort, the majority of colonies that develop are white and are derived from a chlorophyll-deficient partner, and any green colonies are selected as possible hybrids. Such a selection system has led to the recovery of somatic hybrids between various *Petunia* spp. (Cocking *et al.*, 1977; Power *et al.*, 1979, 1980), *Datura* spp. (Schieder, 1978, 1980a), and *Nicotiana* spp. (Evans *et al.*, 1980). This selection system has also led to the recovery of fusion products between *Daucus carota* and another member of Umbelliferae, *Aegopodium podagraria.* In this case the *Daucus* protoplasts were albino and the *Aegopodium* protoplasts showed no development (Dudits *et al.*, 1977). The hybrids, however, although green and showing features of *Aegopodium* along with those of carrot, contained no *Aegopodium* chromosomes. In fact, in a subsequent experiment a positive attempt was made to produce such a situation in which only a part of the genome of one parent is present in a somatic hybrid. Wild-type parsley (*Petroselenium hortense*) protoplasts were exposed to X-irradiation, rendering them incapable of division, then fused with albino protoplasts from *D. carota*. Green colonies were selected and analysis of the plants recovered indicated the presence of parsley genes in a predominately carrot genome (Dudits *et al.*, 1980).

On occasion, protoplasts of an albino mutant have been fused with wild-type protoplasts capable of developing to produce callus colonies. Consequently, the development and isolation of green colonies is only half of the selection system and for recovery of somatic hybrids an additional feature has to be used. This type of selection scheme enabled the recovery of somatic hybrids between *D. carota* and *Daucus capillifolius*. The albino feature resided in the *D. carota* protoplasts and consequently in the green callus that developed with either the hybrid or *D. capillifolius*. The hybrid was identified by the morphology of the leaves when the shoots were produced (Dudits *et al.*, 1977). A similar scheme was utilized for the selection of somatic hybrids between *Nicotiana knightiana* and *N. tabacum*. In this case, the *N. tabacum* was albino and green colonies arising after fusion were either *N. knightiana* or hybrid in nature. However, *N. knightiana* callus colonies do not produce shoots; consequently, any green shoots produced were likely to be hybrid (Maliga *et al.*, 1978). In much the same way two visual markers were used in a selection method for the isolation of somatic hybrids between *D. innoxia* and *Atropa belladonna*. Both protoplast systems divided but the *Datura* protoplasts were albino. However, *Datura* callus colonies produce numerous hairs; consequently, by picking out green and "hairy" colonies, hybrids were selected (Krumbiegel and Schieder, 1979).

The chlorophyll-deficient and albino mutations that have been used have been recessive, but use has also been made of a semidominant chlorophyll mutation. *Nicotiana tabacum* protoplasts containing the mutation in a homozygous condition were fused with wild-type *N. rustica*. Both protoplast types were capable of further development and three differently pigmented callus colonies could be recognized: the white of *N. tabacum*, the green of *N. rustica*, and the greenish-white of the hybrid (Iwai *et al.*, 1980).

Sometimes, in addition to the use of chlorophyll-deficient mutation, the selection scheme has also involved a mutation in the other parent. Sidorov and Maliga (1982) fused a number of different auxotrophic mutants with a chlorophyll-deficient mutant and obtained complementation and hybrid recovery by selecting green prototrophic colonies.

Selection systems that still use chlorophyll development as a visual marker but do not involve any chlorophyll-deficient mutants have been devised. In one such scheme, an *N. tabacum* line with streptomycin-insensitive chloroplasts acted as one parent. Protoplasts prior to fusion were disabled by treatment with iodoacetate and were subsequently unable to divide. Wild-type untreated *N. sylvestris* protoplasts provided the other partner. After fusion, colonies developed either from *N. sylvestris* protoplasts or the fusion products. After 1 month the callus colonies were transferred to a medium that normally promotes chlorophyll synthesis, to which streptomycin was added. On this medium only streptomycin-resistant cells would develop chlorophyll and thus green colonies were selected for further study (Medgyesy *et al.*, 1980).

A slightly different approach but still one that utilizes chlorophyll development as one of the markers has led to the recovery of somatic hybrids between *N. sylvestris* and *N. knightiana* (Maliga *et al.*, 1977). After fusion, protoplasts of both parents proliferated and formed cell colonies. These were transferred to a different medium in which growth of most of the *N. knightiana* colonies ceased and the *N. sylvestris* colonies did not develop chlorophyll. Green colonies were selected and further tested for their ability to grow in the presence of kanamycin, a property of the *N. sylvestris* parent. Two of the 100 colonies selected were kanamycin resistant.

On occasion it has been observed that hybrid cells proliferate faster than do the parental protoplasts. This hybrid vigor has been particularly prominent in interspecific somatic hybrid calluses involving *Datura* species (Schieder, 1978, 1980a), but has also been recorded in *Nicotiana* hybrids (Smith *et al.*, 1976). It was pointed out by Schieder and Vasil (1980) that this phenomenon is not the result of high ploidy levels because intraspecific somatic hybrid *D. innoxia* cell lines do not exhibit this enhanced vigor. Although currently this property alone has not been used for selection, it seems reasonable to assume that by picking out the larger colonies developing on a culture plate a population enriched with hybrid material could be obtained.

3. *Physiological selection*

Selection of this type involves no visual markers since, in the final outcome, only hybrid colonies develop in the culture medium. To achieve this end, a range of different physiological properties of protoplasts have been exploited. Increasing use is being made of auxotrophic mutants and mutants possessing amino acid analog resistance or drug resistance. Use has been made of the differential sensitivity to drugs of wild-type protoplasts and the ability of a given protoplast population to proliferate under a particular nutrient regime.

a. *Selection without the use of mutants.* Experience has shown that in order to induce division of cultured protoplasts, the formulation of the nutrient medium is critical, particularly in regard to the level and composition of growth regulators. Furthermore, different species and even genotypes may have varying requirements. Indeed, Izhar and Power (1977), using leaf protoplasts of several highly inbred lines of *Petunia,* found substantial variations with respect to the ability of the protoplasts to grow on media containing specific hormone combinations. From results with F_1 and backcrosses to the parental lines it was concluded that only a few genes may control such differences. Even relatively small differences in levels of growth regulators can influence the capability of protoplasts to sustain division. This differential ability of protoplasts to maintain division in various nutrient media has formed the basis of a number of selection schemes. Indeed, the first reported somatic hybrids were recovered in this way. It was noted that *Nicotiana langsdorffii* and *Nicotiana glauca* protoplasts failed to divide in a medium in which protoplasts of the sexual hybrid would divide, albeit at a low frequency. After fusion and culture some colonies were recovered that, when transferred to a medium lacking growth regulators, continued to grow, an additional feature possessed by protoplasts derived from the sexual hybrids. Shoots recovered from these colonies had features intermediate between the parents and were identified as somatic hybrids (Carlson *et al.,* 1972). In subsequent experiments using the same parental species (Smith *et al.,* 1976; Chupeau *et al.,* 1978), the selection scheme was modified in that both parental protoplast populations, as well as the hybrid, were able to develop in the initial nutrient medium, but after transfer to a second medium lacking hormones only the hybrid continued to grow. In the genus *Petunia,* differing responses of *P. hybrida, P. parodii,* and their sexual hybrid to (2,4-dichlorophenoxy)acetic acid (2,4-D) have been exploited for the recovery of the somatic hybrids (Power *et al.,* 1977). Although selection systems of this type have proved valuable, they are of limited application since their development depends on knowledge of how the sexual hybrid will behave under the particular nutrient conditions.

In addition to differences in the ability of a protoplast population to survive in a particular medium, differences have also been found in their tolerance to the presence of various additives to the medium, such as drugs, amino acid analogs, and other antimetabolites (Cocking *et al.,* 1974). This differential sensitivity has been utilized in selection systems. Protoplasts of *P. hybrida* were found to be much more sensitive to the presence of actinomycin D in the medium than were those of *P. parodii.* At a particular concentration, division of the former was prevented whereas that of the latter appeared unaffected. This feature was combined with a difference exhibited in the ability of the two protoplast systems to grow in the medium; *P. hybrida* protoplasts normally formed large colonies whereas *P. parodii* colonies did not grow beyond about 50 cells. It was known that resistance to actinomycin D is a dominant drug-resistance feature of animal cells and conceivably the ability to continue growth possessed by the *P. hybrida* protoplasts might be expressed in the hybrid. In the event, some colonies grew and regenerated plants that were characterized as hybrids (Power *et al.*, 1976, 1977). More recently, a selection system based essentially on differential sensitivity has allowed the recovery of somatic hybrids between potato and tomato (Shepard *et al.*, 1983). At 24°C the tomato protoplasts grew with only a low plating efficiency, whereas this temperature was optimum for the culture of potato protoplasts. These potato protoplasts were derived from a cell suspension of a chlorophyll-deficient variant. In addition, growth of the potato colonies could be halted by the presence of abscisic acid at a concentration that allowed continued growth of tomato colonies. Further selection pressure was provided by the observations that the tomato colonies did not produce shoots under the conditions that allowed recovery of potato shoots. Consequently, any green shoots regenerated were screened for features characteristic of tomato.

It has also proved possible to design selection systems in which growth and development of protoplasts are prevented by disabling them with metabolic poisons. Nehls (1978) treated *P. hybrida* protoplasts with diethylpyrocarbonate and *Solanum nigrum* with iodoacetate, causing irreversible metabolic inhibition. After fusion, three protoplasts survived and one multicellular colony was identified as arising from a fusion product. The use of iodoacetate to prevent the growth of *N. tabacum* mesophyll protoplasts has formed part of a selection system that has led to the isolation of somatic hybrids of *N. tabacum* and *N. sylvestris* (Medgyesy *et al.*, 1980). Similarly, *N. plumbaginifolia* protoplasts treated with iodoacetate have been fused with protoplasts of *N. tabacum* rendered incapable of division by X-irradiation. Metabolic complementation between the disabled protoplasts took place and somatic hybrids were recovered (Sidorov *et al.*, 1981). This approach was further exploited for the recovery of intraspecific hybrids of carrot in which a cycloheximide-resistant (CH^r) line was fused with an albino cycloheximide-sensitive (CH^s) line. Iodoacetamide was used to disable the CH^r line and green colonies were selected that produce plants with dissected leaves, a feature of the albino CH^s line (Lázár *et al.*, 1981).

b. *Selection involving mutants.* When the first attempts were made to devise selection schemes, it was recognized that auxotrophic and drug-resistant mutants would be particularly useful, but at the time no satisfactory mutants were available. Such mutants are now being recovered, but the emphasis on their use, to a certain extent, has subtly shifted. Fusion and somatic hybridization are now being used to characterize the properties of the mutants rather than to act as a means of recovering a hybrid plant. As a result, an exciting area of plant cell genetics is now emerging in which cell fusion is used to determine complementation and recessive/dominant relationships, and frequently there is little interest in regenerating an entire plant. Nevertheless, various selection systems based on mutants have been devised for recovery of somatic hybrids. Work with animal cell hybrids has shown that auxotrophic mutants can be used for this selection. Unfortunately, as pointed out by Chaleff (1981), auxotrophs have proved to be the most difficult class of mutants to isolate in higher plants. They are, however, fairly readily isolated using the haploid cells of lower plants (Schieder, 1976), and consequently, they were first exploited for selection in these systems. After fusion of protoplasts from two auxotrophic mutants of the liverwort *Sphaerocarpus,* a prototrophic somatic hybrid was recovered (Schieder, 1974). In addition, auxotrophs have been isolated in the moss *Phycomitrella* (Ashton and Cove, 1977) and have been utilized in the selection of a number of somatic hybrids (Grimsley *et al.,* 1977). Recently, considerable progress has been made with techniques for the isolation of auxotrophic cell lines in higher plants, particularly in the recovery of mutants deficient in nitrate reductase activity (NR^-). Such mutants grow in media supplemented with reduced nitrogen compounds, but fail to grow on media containing nitrate as the sole nitrogen source (Müller and Grafe, 1978). These nitrate reductase-deficient mutants are proving particularly useful for hybrid selection, principally because a number of nonallelic mutants can be recovered, which, on fusion, will complement to allow the hybrids to use nitrate. In practice it has usually proved beneficial to culture the protoplasts after fusion for a time on media supplemented with amino acids and then apply the selection pressure by transferring to a culture media having nitrate as the sole nitrogen source. Using this approach, Glimelius *et al.* (1978) fused protoplasts derived from two NR^- mutants of *N. tabacum* and obtained a large number of prototrophic cell lines, many of which regenerated shoots. Similar complementation to wild type has been achieved with a range of NR^- mutants of *N. plumbaginifolia* with the recovery of plants. Apparently, the clones deficient in nitrate reductase do not normally undergo shoot regeneration (Márton *et al.,* 1982). In addition, complementation analysis of NR^- cell lines of *Hyoscyamus muticus* has been carried out using protoplast fusion, but in this instance no plants were regenerated from the hybrid clones (Lázár *et al.*, 1983).

Furthermore, restoration of nitrate reductase activity has been obtained following intergeneric protoplast fusion. Protoplasts derived from an NR^- line of *N. tabacum* were fused with mesophyll protoplasts of either *Physalis minima* or *D. innoxia* that had been rendered incapable of division by irradiation. Recovery of cell lines able to grow in medium containing nitrate as the only nitrogen source was used for selection (Gupta *et al.*, 1982). Nitrate reductase deficiency has also been used as part of a selection system. In one case protoplasts from the other parent, a male-sterile line of *N. tabacum,* were unable to grow in the nutrient medium (Glimelius *et al.*, 1981), and hybrids were selected on medium with nitrate as the nitrogen source. In another case, an NR^- line of *N. tabacum* was hybridized with a chlorophyll-deficient line of the same species, and green colonies capable of growth on selection medium were recovered and subsequently regenerated into plants (Glimelius and Bonnett, 1981). As well as the use of NR^- mutants, there are a few examples wherein other auxotrophic mutants have been shown to be recessive and that complement in somatic hybrid cell lines. In *H. muticus*, a histidine-requiring line and a cell line requiring tryptophan complemented to wild type after protoplast fusion (Gebhardt *et al.*, 1983; Shimamoto and King, 1983). Similarly, *N. plumbaginifolia* hybrid cell lines, and subsequently plants, have been recovered on "minimal media" after protoplast fusion between an isoleucine auxotroph and a uracil-requiring cell line, indicating complementation by these mutants (Sidorov and Maliga, 1982). In the same report, complementation was also demonstrated between uracil, isoleucine, and leucine auxotrophs and a series of chlorophyll-deficient mutants.

A number of amino acid analog mutants have now been obtained (Widholm, 1977). Clearly, for their successful use in a selection scheme it is necessary that they should be dominant or semidominant. It is also important that there should be no cross-feeding or cross-resistance. Mutants exhibiting resistance to *S*-2-aminoethylcysteine (AEC^r) and to 5-methyltryptophan ($5TM^r$) appear to have the required properties. Protoplasts from an AEC^r line of *N. sylvestris* were fused with those from a $5MT^r$ line and calluses were recovered from a culture medium containing both analogs and were characterized as hybrids (White and Vasil, 1979). A selection system using resistance to the same amino acid analog, but in *D. carota,* has led to the recovery of intraspecific hybrid cell lines (Harms *et al.*, 1981). In addition to selection on media containing both AEC and 5MT, fusion products were also recovered after culture in the presence of one analog and then exposure to both. They could also be recovered when selection was delayed for some time after fusion. There is, therefore, some flexibility in the way in which mutants of this type can be used. However, in neither of these examples were plants recovered from the hybrid cell lines, principally because regenerative capacity had been lost due to the extended period that the cell lines had been in culture. However, shoots were obtained when protoplasts of a *5MT^r* line of *D. carota* were fused with those derived from suspension-cultured cells of *D. capillifolius*. Culture on a medium containing 5MT selected against parental *D. capillifolius* protoplasts. But unlike *D. capillifolius*, the *5MT^r* carrot line does not produce green colonies. Consequently, green colonies were removed from the medium with 5MT and were cultured to produce shoots (Kameya *et al.*, 1981).

Drug-resistant mutants have been used extensively for selection of animal hybrid cells, but although a number of such mutants have now been recovered in plant cells, they have not featured in many selection schemes. Resistance to kanamycin has been used as part of a selection system in the hybridization of *N. sylvestris* and *N. knightiana*, the *N. sylvestris* line possessing the resistance. *Nicotiana knightiana* callus colonies were selected against by the fact that they failed to grow in a particular medium, whereas the *N. sylvestris* colonies failed to develop chlorophyll; any colonies that did were further selected by culture on a medium containing kanamycin (Maliga *et al.*, 1977). Streptomycin resistance, a cytoplasmically inherited trait in *N. tabacum*, has also been exploited for selection. Streptomycin-resistant protoplasts that had been disabled with a metabolic poison to prevent their development were fused with wild-type *N. sylvestris* protoplasts. Colonies that formed were transferred to a medium formulated to promote chlorophyll synthesis, but with the inclusion of streptomycin. Only streptomycin-resistant colonies became green (Medgyesy *et al.*, 1980). Streptomycin resistance has also been used to select intraspecific hybrids in *N. tabacum*. Mesophyll protoplasts of the streptomycin-resistant line were fused with protoplasts derived from a crown gall cell line that consequently exhibited autonomy for phytohormones. Colonies were selected first for streptomycin resistance and then any green colonies that grew without an exogenous supply of hormones were further selected. Shoots were recovered, a capacity not exhibited by the crown gall line, and these shoots had lysopine dehydrogenase activity, a crown gall feature (Wullems *et al.*, 1980). Recently, a dominant nuclear mutation conferring resistance to hydroxyurea in an *N. tabacum* cell line has been used for the recovery of intraspecific hybrids. The other parent possessed a mutation that allowed it to utilize glycerol as a carbon source. The hybrids were recovered from a medium that included hydroxyurea and contained glycerol as the sole carbon source. The plants subsequently recovered were characterized genetically as somatic hybrids (Evola *et al.*, 1983).

Doubtless, as time goes on, more drug-resistant and auxotrophic mutants will be exploited for hybrid selection. A particularly useful combination would be a cell line containing both a dominant drug-resistance mutation and a recessive auxotrophic feature. Protoplasts of this parent could then be fused with protoplasts of any wild-type partner and hybrids could be selected on a minimal medium to which is added the appropriate drug. Some success in producing such double mutants has recently been reported (Hamill *et al.*, 1983).

4. *Isolation of hybrids by screening regenerated plants*

Although selection systems at the cell and callus colony level have greatly facilitated hybrid recovery, it is now clear that it is also possible to isolate hybrids by screening the regenerated plants. Screening large numbers of plants is made relatively easy if a clearly discernible visual marker can be used. Perhaps the most obvious marker is offered by degrees of chlorophyll development. Gleba *et al.* (1975) made use of chlorophyll-deficient mutants for the recovery of intraspecific somatic hybrids of *N. tabacum*. Protoplasts were isolated from white areas of leaves of a variegated plastome mutant and from yellow seedling leaves of a chlorophyll-deficient mutant that was homozygous for a semidominant nuclear mutation. Parental protoplasts gave rise either to albino or to yellow plants. After fusion, plants were regenerated, some of which were green, some variegated, some yellow-green, and others yellow-green and variegated. Yellow-green plants were considered to be somatic hybrids, being heterozygous for the nuclear mutation. Variegation was caused by segregation of normal and defective chloroplasts. The green and green-variegated plants were taken to have arisen from cytoplasmic fusion of the parental protoplasts but without subsequent nuclear fusion, i.e., they were cytoplasmic hybrids. The same chlorophyll-deficient nuclear mutant of tobacco has also been used in a selection system that has led to the recovery of interspecific somatic hybrids with *N. tabacum* and *Nicotiana nesophila* and with *Nicotiana stocktonii*. The parental *N. tabacum* produced only albino plants, whereas the other parent produced only green plants. Since the mutation is heterozygous in the somatic hybrids, they were yellow-green (Evans *et al.*, 1981).

The experiment of Gleba *et al.* (1975) emphasized that somatic hybrids differed from sexual hybrids in that they receive nuclear and cytoplasmic components from both parents and also showed that it was possible to recover cytoplasmic hybrids (cybrids) in which the genome comes from one parent and the cytoplasm from both. Screening regenerated plants has in fact been used as a means of recovering cybrids as well as nuclear somatic hybrids. In a number of these experiments, male sterility has been used as the cytoplasmically inherited marker. Naturally, this necessitates not only plant regeneration but that the plants be grown to maturity before screening can be carried out. After the fusion of protoplasts of a male-sterile tobacco variety (var. *techne*) with those from a fertile variety (either var. *samsun* or *xanthi*), plants were recovered and nuclear hybrids could be identified by the morphology of the leaves, *samsun* and *xanthi* having petiolate leaves, *techne* having sessile leaves, and the hybrid being intermediate. Cytoplasmic hybrids were recognized by having petiolate leaves but with abnormal floral morphology. Screening was made somewhat easier when var. *samsun* was used because under the culture conditions no shoots were produced by this variety (Belliard *et al.*, 1977). In a subsequent experiment, almost 1000 plants were grown to the flowering stage and could be separated into three classes. Members of the largest group (654) were identified as one or the other of the parents. The second largest class (225) was composed of plants that had leaves identical to one or the other of the parents but with altered flowers and were considered to be cytoplasmic hybrids. The smallest class (57) consisted of plants with modified flowers and intermediate leaves and were nuclear hybrids (Belliard *et al.*, 1978). In contrast, screening as few as 21 plants allowed the recovery of both nuclear and cytoplasmic hybrids after protoplast fusion between a white-flowered fertile line of *P. hybrida* and a male-sterile line with pink flowers. Nuclear hybrids were identified on the basis of flower color and leaf shape and cytoplasmic hybrids by the conversion of the pink-flowered variety from male sterile to male fertile (Bergounioux-Bunisset and Perennes, 1980).

A selection system has been designed to recover specifically cybrids and to select against nuclear somatic hybrids. Using this approach Izhar and Power (1979) were able to transfer male sterility from one species of *Petunia* to another. Protoplasts from a cytoplasmic male-sterile (CMS) line of *P. hybrida* were fused with those of a male-fertile line of *Petunia axillaris*. Under the nutrient conditions, *P. hybrida* protoplasts failed to survive, as did any hybrids containing the *P. hybrida* genome. Consequently, any plants that were recovered were likely to be either normal *P. axillaris* or cytoplasmic hybrids containing the *P. axillaris* genome. Screening for cytoplasmic hybrids was, however, complicated by the presence of male fertility restoration alleles in *P. hybrida*. It was necessary to self the regenerated plants and screen the F_2 population for segregation of male sterility. Out of 110 plants recovered from two fusion experiments, 6 segregated for male sterility in the F_2.

Screening for features other than chlorophyll development and flower morphology has also led to the isolation of somatic hybrids. Screening has been eased in some systems because one of the parents has failed either to grow or to produce shoots. Melchers *et al.* (1978) fused mesophyll protoplasts of a chlorophyll-deficient mutant of tomato with protoplasts derived from cultured cells of potato. The tomato produced no shoots, and regenerated plants were screened for plants that differed from the normal potato. Some abnormal plants were recovered and were characterized as hybrids by chromosome analysis and fraction 1 protein composition. Scowcroft and Larkin (1981) regenerated plants after fusion of mesophyll protoplasts derived from two genotypes of *Nicotiana debneyi*. These genotypes differed in the nuclear-coded phosphoglucomutase (Pgm) isoenzyme. The characteristics of Pgm were examined in 225 regenerated plants and 6 exhibited Pgm isoenzyme patterns that contained characteristic bands attributable to each genotype.

There are further indications that interspecific hybrids can be recovered by screening regenerated plants. After protoplast fusion of *Solanum tuberosum* and *S. nigrum*, some 2705 clones were induced to produce shoots that were screened for abnormal features, particularly the morphology of the hairs. The majority resembled *S. nigrum* and no shoots of normal potato were observed. Shoots from 35 clones were sufficiently different to warrant further study. Shoots from 9 clones possessed features of both parents and it was suggested that these were somatic hybrids (Binding *et al.*, 1982).

At one time, recovery of hybrid cells following treatment of a mixed population of protoplasts with a fusogen presented a formidable problem. What is now clear, however, is that through care and ingenuity hybrids can be recovered and indeed the problem of selection has now, to a considerable extent, been reduced. There are, however, a number of studies which report that protoplasts from different sources have been fused, but, in spite of the application of selection pressure, no hybrid cell colonies have grown through (Schieder, 1977; Zenkteler and Melchers, 1978; Dudits *et al.*, 1980; Evans *et al.*, 1981). What is not established at present is whether this is the result of inadequacies in the cultural environment, with the hybrids being more demanding in their nutrient requirements than the parental protoplasts, or the result of inadequacies in the design of the selection procedure, or whether a real barrier to hybridization has been encountered at the cell level.

V. Identification of Somatic Hybrids

Although the recovery of plants from callus colonies that grow through a selection procedure, or the development of plants from manually isolated heterokaryons, strongly suggests that they are somatic hybrids, it is not conclusive proof. The selection system may break down for various reasons and allow parental material to grow through. Alternatively, a heterokaryon may fail to undergo nuclear fusion with subsequent formation of a chimeral callus. The possibility of a chimeral callus also necessitates that the evidence for hybridity should ideally be sought in the regenerated plants and not in the callus tissue from which the plants are derived. It is required, therefore, to have some other evidence that at least part of each parental genome is present in the regenerated plant. This evidence may come from a study of the karyotype or may be based on gene expression in the hybrid or the segregation and expression of parental features in the F_2.

Analysis of chromosome complements of the regenerated plants has virtually always been carried out but has not necessarily furnished conclusive evidence that the plants are hybrids. A chromosome number that is a sum of the parental species would provide supporting evidence, but frequently the parents have the same or similar chromosome numbers; experience has shown that plants regenerated from cultured cells may exhibit considerable variation in chromosome number, lessening the value of chromosome counts in establishing their hybrid nature. When the karyotypes of the two parents are sufficiently different, the presence of marker chromosomes in the hybrid, which are clearly attributable to each of the parents, can provide the necessary evidence (Krumbiegel and Schieder, 1979; Evans *et al.*, 1980).

Proof of the presence of genetic information from both parents in regenerated plants can be based upon gene expression and the appearance of phenotypic characters. In those species combinations in which sexual hybrids are obtainable, they have been useful for comparison with the putative hybrids. As a rule, these sexual hybrids tend to exhibit forms intermediate to those of the parents, indicative of the involvement of multiple genes, and this has also proved to be the case for somatic hybrids. Leaf shape and size (Carlson *et al.*, 1972), for example, as well as flower shape, size, and color (Power *et al.*, 1976) and plant height (Evans *et al.*, 1981) have all been found to be intermediate in plants recovered after selection as compared to the parental species. However, in view of the range of variant types that can be recovered from parental species after *in vitro* culture, the intermediate appearance of a small group of characters or of abnormal or altered morphology, on their own, is not sufficient evidence for considering the plants to be hybrid. In some species combinations, dominance has been exhibited by certain features such as leaf size and shape (Schieder, 1978) and growth habit (Power *et al.*, 1980). On several occasions the shape of hairs, particularly their branching patterns, and their distribution have been used as diagnostic features (Carlson *et al.*, 1972; Gleba and Hoffmann, 1980; Evans *et al.*, 1980; Binding *et al.*, 1982). In rare instances the sexual hybrids may possess a feature not expressed by either parent. *Nicotiana glauca* × *N. langsdorffii* hybrids are prone to produce tumerous outgrowths, and the appearance of this feature has been used as corroborative evidence for somatic hybrids of these species (Carlson *et al.*, 1972; Smith *et al.*, 1976; Chupeau *et al.*, 1978).

In addition to morphological features, use has also been made of biochemical markers. Parental species may possess a characteristic pattern of isoenzymes as determined after electrophoretic separation on polyacrylamide gels. The pattern of isoenzyme bands of the hybrid may be the sum of the two parents, or additional bands not present in either parent may be detected. A range of different enzymes has been used for this purpose, esterase and peroxidase being exploited most frequently but others such as aspartate aminotransferase, alanyl aminopeptidase, amylase, alcohol dehydrogenase, and phosphodiesterase proving useful on some occasions.

The makeup of fraction 1 protein has provided a very elegant means of characterizing both the nuclear and the cytoplasmic origin of somatic hybrids (Kung *et al.*, 1975). This protein is the major soluble protein of chloroplasts and possesses the dual enzyme activities of ribulose-1,5-biphosphate carboxylase–oxygenase. It dissociates into large and small subunits, with the small subunit encoded in the nuclear genome and the large subunit encoded in the chloroplast genome. Isoelectric focusing resolves the large unit into three polypeptides and the small unit into one or more polypeptides. The isoelectric points of these polypeptides may be characteristic of a genus or even of a species. In a hybrid, the genes coding for the small subunit of both parents are expressed, providing a valuable marker for the presence of the parental nuclear genome. Similarly, the presence of characteristic large-subunit polypeptides can be used to establish the presence of a particular chloroplast genome. This technique has been used to authenticate a number of somatic hybrids (Kung *et al.*, 1975; Chen *et al.*, 1977; Melchers *et al.*, 1978; Evans *et al.*, 1980; Power *et al.*, 1980).

In those somatic hybrids that prove to be fertile and self-compatible, a definitive way of establishing their hybrid nature is the segregation and recovery of parental characters in the F_2. Melchers and Labib (1974) recovered from the somatic hybrids progeny expressing the *v* and *s* light-sensitive mutations originally present in the two parental varieties of *N. tabacum*. Similarly, Power *et al.* (1978) reported the segregation for flower color in F_2 testcross and backcross populations using the *P. parodii* + *P. hybrida* somatic hybrids. More recently (Evola *et al.*, 1983), intraspecific somatic hybrids have been recovered after fusion of protoplasts in which one parent possessed two dominant mutant alleles and the other a single dominant mutation. Verification of the somatic hybrids was obtained by the segregation of each of the parental markers in the progeny of backcross to plants that were homozygous for the normal alleles at each marker locus.

There is clearly a range of techniques available to establish the hybrid nature of plants recovered after selection. Usually, evidence for hybridity is accumulated from a number of these sources and does not rest on any one feature. There can be no doubt now that protoplast fusion does lead to the bypassing of the sexual process and the generation of authentic hybrids from somatic cells.

VI. Properties of Somatic Hybrids

It is evident from the preceding discussion that somatic hybridization is a multistep technique. For hybrid recovery the processes of protoplast isolation, fusion, culture, hybrid selection, and plant regeneration must all be successfully negotiated. This has now been accomplished in a considerable number of cases. There are now, in fact, over 50 reports of somatic hybrid production (Table II). The actual number of hybrid plants produced from independent cell fusion events is probably in excess of several thousand. A proportion of these somatic hybrids have resulted from intraspecific protoplast fusion and have been used as model systems to establish the techniques. A further proportion involve interspecific hybridization. A number of these are derived from species combinations that show some degree of sexual incompatibility—either unilateral cross-incompatibility or full sexual incompatibility. There is also now a sizable group in which the somatic hybrids have arisen as a result of intergeneric fusion. Clearly, somatic hybridization has led to the production of plants containing a new gene pool

TABLE II. Somatic hybrid plants

Species	Reference
Intraspecific hybrids	
Nicotiana tabacum	Melchers and Labib (1974); Gleba *et al.* (1975); Kameya (1975); Belliard *et al.* (1977, 1978); Glimelius *et al.* (1978); Wullems *et al.* (1980); Glimelius and Bonnett (1981); Glimelius *et al.* (1981); Evola *et al.* (1983)
Nicotiana plumbaginifolia	Sidorov and Maliga (1982); Márton *et al.* (1982)
Nicotiana debneyi	Scowcroft and Larkin (1981)
Petunia hybrida	Bergounioux-Bunisset and Perennes (1980)
Datura innoxia	Schieder (1977)
Daucus carota	Lázár *et al.* (1981)
Interspecific hybrids	
In *Nicotiana*	
N. tabacum + *N. alata*	Nagao (1979)
N. tabacum + *N. glauca*	Evans *et al.* (1980)
N. tabacum + *N. glutinosa*	Nagao (1979); Uchimiya (1982)
N. tabacum + *N. knightiana*	Maliga *et al.* (1978); Menczel *et al.* (1981)
N. tabacum + *N. nesophila*[a]	Evans *et al.* (1981)
N. tabacum + *N. otophora*	Flick and Evans (1982)
N. tabacum + *N. plumbaginifolia*	Sidorov *et al.* (1981); Maliga *et al.* (1982)
N. tabacum + *N. repanda*[a]	Nagao (1982)
N. tabacum + *N. rustica*	Nagao (1978); Iwai *et al.* (1980); Douglas *et al.* (1981a)
N. tabacum + *N. stocktonii*[a]	Evans *et al.* (1981)
N. tabacum + *N. sylvestris*	Melchers (1977); Aviv *et al.* (1980); Medgyesy *et al.* (1980); Flick and Evans (1982)
N. glauca + *N. langsdorffii*	Carlson *et al.* (1972); Smith *et al.* (1976); Chupeau *et al.* (1978)
N. sylvestris + *N. knightiana*	Maliga *et al.* (1977)
In *Petunia*	
P. parodii + *P. hybrida*	Power *et al.* (1976); Cocking *et al.* (1977); Power *et al.* (1977)
P. parodii + *P. inflata*	Power *et al.* (1979)
P. parodii + *P. parviflora*[a]	Power *et al.* (1980)
In *Datura*	
D. innoxia + *D. discolor*[a]	Schieder (1978)
D. innoxia + *D. stramonium*[a]	Schieder (1978)
D. innoxia + *D. candida*[a]	Schieder (1980a)
D. innoxia + *D. sanguinea*[a]	Schieder (1980a)

(*Continued*)

TABLE II. (*Continued*)

Species	Reference
In *Solanum*	
S. tuberosum + *S. chacoense*[a]	Butenko *et al.* (1982)
S. tuberosum + *S. nigrum*[a]	Binding *et al.* (1982)
In *Brassica*	
B. oleracea + *B. campestris*[a]	Schenck and Röbbelen (1982)
In *Daucus*	
D. carota + *D. capillifolius*	Dudits *et al.* (1977); Kameya *et al.* (1981)
Intergeneric hybrids	
In Solanaceae	
Lycopersicon esculentum + *Solanum tuberosum*[a]	Melchers *et al.* (1978); Shepard *et al.* (1983)
Nicotiana tabacum + *Salpiglossis sinuata*[a]	Nagao (1982)
Datura innoxia + *Atropa belladonna*[a]	Krumbiegel and Schieder (1981)
In Cruciferae	
Arabidopsis thaliana + *Brassica campestris*[a]	Gleba and Hoffmann (1980); Hoffmann and Adachi (1981)
Other hybrids[b]	
Daucus carota + *Aegopodium podagraria*[a]	Dudits *et al.* (1979)
Daucus carota + *Petroselinium hortense*[a]	Dudits *et al.* (1980)

[a]Hybrids not obtainable by conventional crossing.
[b]Plants recovered after fusion that possessed one or more features attributable to each parent but apparently the chromosomes of only one.

and with totally novel gene combinations, which could not be produced in any other way. However, various advances in the techniques for the production of sexual hybrids such as bud pollination, fertilization of ovules *in vitro,* and the *in vitro* culture of fertilized ovules and embryos may mean that the limits to crossability have to be redefined. It is perhaps important to note that all the somatic hybrids recovered so far have been derived from only three families: Solanaceae, Umbelliferae, and Cruciferae. By far the largest number involves members of the Solanaceae, and even then members of only seven genera have been used. This is undoubtedly a reflection on the ease with which plants can be regenerated from protoplast-derived callus colonies from members of the Solanaceae as well as an indication of the difficulties encountered in this respect with members of other families. This problem of obtaining reproducible shoot regeneration, particularly in the major crop species, has already been emphasized. Currently, it is a major block to the production of somatic hybrids including a wider range of species. Nonetheless, sufficient somatic hybrids have now been produced to allow some appreciation of their properties.

As might be expected, somatic hybrids differ from sexually produced hybrids in a number of important respects. In the first place, the fusion of somatic cell protoplasts will result in the production of a tetraploid hybrid after an intraspecific fusion event and of an amphiploid hybrid following an interspecific fusion, unless, of course, steps are taken to isolate protoplasts from haploid parental plants. A second feature of somatic hybrids is their variability. On occasion, and when sexually derived hybrids have been available for comparison, it has been observed that there is a wider range of phenotypic variation in the somatic hybrids than in the sexual hybrids. In, for example, the *N. glauca* and *N. langsdorffii* combination, the somatic hybrid had a greater range of leaf shape, flower size, and pollen viability than did the sexual counterpart (Smith *et al.*, 1976). Similarly, the somatic hybrids of *N. glauca* and *N. tabacum* showed a greater range of petiole length than did the sexual cross (Evans *et al.*, 1980), and in somatic hybrids of *N. tabacum* and *N. knightiana*, a range of flower color shades was reported (Maliga *et al.*, 1978). In making such comparisons it is clearly important, if the somatic hybrids are tetraploid or amphiploid, to compare them with a sexual hybrid in which the chromosome number has doubled. Variegation, for example, was observed in the corolla of *N. tabacum* × *N. glauca* sexual hybrids that was absent both from the somatic hybrid and from the diploidized sexual hybrid (Evans *et al.*, 1980). Such appropriate comparisons have not always been made. These phenotypic variations recorded in somatic hybrids presumably reflect a variation in the genetic composition of the plants. Indeed, the chromosome composition of somatic hybrids has been found to exhibit considerable variability. In the majority of the reports in which a number of somatic hybrids have been recovered and chromosome numbers determined, plants have been found in which the chromosome numbers have departed from the simple sum of the two parental species. This is the case with somatic hybrids derived from both sexually compatible and incompatible species.

A further way in which somatic and sexual hybrids differ relates to the composition of the cytoplasm. Protoplast fusion results in the formation of a heterokaryon and in due course a synkaryon, in which the cytoplasm is also hybrid and may be derived more or less equally from both parents. By contrast, in a sexual cross the cytoplasmic components are, in a large number of species, almost entirely derived from the maternal side. This hybrid cytoplasm has important implications for the behavior of organelles and for nuclear-cytoplasmic interactions, and these will be discussed in greater depth later.

A. CHROMOSOMAL STABILITY OF SOMATIC HYBRIDS

The observed variation in chromosome composition of somatic hybrids may have arisen for a number of different reasons. If, for the moment, consideration is limited to intraspecific, interspecific, and intergeneric combinations between closely related species that may or may not show some degree of incompatibility, it is probable that the variation results as a consequence of the techniques employed for the production of the hybrids and not as a result of the interaction of the parental genomes.

One possible source for the high and variable chromosome counts may reside in the type of tissue from which the protoplasts are derived. When the protoplast preparation is isolated directly from mature tissue of the plant, it is possible that it will consist of a mixture of diploid and tetraploid protoplasts, since it is known that mature tissues of many species contain polyploid cells. A more likely source of the variability would arise from the use of cultured cells as a source of protoplasts. It is well established that *in vitro* culture leads to chromosome instability, with the generation of aneuploids as well as increases in ploidy level. In addition, chromosome breakage and translocations are often observed in cultured cells, particularly in those that have been in culture for a prolonged period.

The actual process whereby the protoplasts are isolated could also, on occasion, contribute to the high chromosome counts. Isolation of protoplasts from mesophyll tissue under conditions of relatively low osmotic stress, such that the cells are only weakly plasmolyzed, may result in a protoplast preparation containing binucleate or multinucleate protoplasts as a result of spontaneous fusion during cell wall degradation (Withers and Cocking, 1972), and these may become involved in a fusion event.

A further source of the variability could arise from the production of multiple fusions. Treatment with PEG leads to a high degree of aggregation, and subsequently, a proportion of the fusion events are found to involve more than two protoplasts. Some of the other fusion techniques such as high pH and Ca^{2+} and the much less efficient sodium nitrate treatment may produce far fewer multiple fusions. In this connection it is of interest that the somatic hybrids produced between *N. glauca* ($2n = 24$) and *N. langsdorffii* ($2n = 18$) by Carlson *et al.*, in 1972, using sodium nitrate, all had the amphidiploid chromosome complement of 42, whereas somatic hybrids produced between the same parents using PEG produced chromosome numbers ranging from 56 to 64, indicative of multiple fusion (Smith *et al.*, 1976). Similarly high chromosome numbers were observed by Chupeau and associates (Chupeau *et al.*, 1978) using PEG and the same two species.

The actual process whereby the nuclei of a heterokaryon fuse may be a source of some chromosome instability. As already discussed, the nuclei may fuse during interphase or may enter mitosis in synchrony and possibly form a common spindle upon which all the chromosomes align. Failure of one or more chromosomes to become aligned correctly or to be included within the nuclear membrane at telophase would result in aneuploidy.

Obviously, one necessary consequence of the present technique of somatic hybridization is that the hybrid cells will proliferate for a time as an unorganized mass of cells and this, too, could contribute to the observed variation. Phenotypic variation could occur not only through the tendency for gross chromosomal instability connected with *in vitro* culture, but also through more subtle genetic changes. Plants regenerated from protoplasts have been observed to exhibit considerable variation in the morphology of stems, leaves, and flowers as well as in response to pathogens and in yield. These variations were first described in plants regenerated from potato protoplasts (Shepard *et al.*, 1980) and have now been reported for other species and have come to be termed *somaclonal variation* (Larkin and Scowcroft, 1981).

All of the processes leading to chromosomal variation are likely to take place prior to shoot regeneration. Indeed, cells forming part of an organized meristem appear to be much less prone to chromosomal instability. Furthermore, there may be a positive selection through shoot regeneration for a particular chromosome complement, the majority of aneuploids present in the culture failing to give rise to organized tissues. It must be emphasized, however, that chromosome variation is not an inevitable consequence of protoplast culture or of somatic hybridization. All 25 somatic hybrids obtained after fusion between protoplasts of *N. glauca* and *N. tabacum* had the amphiploid chromosome number and no aneuploids were recovered (Evans *et al.*, 1980); a similar situation was reported with the hybrids between *N. tabacum* and *N. nesophila* and *N. stocktonii* (Evans *et al.*, 1981).

When somatic hybridization of more distantly related species takes place, other factors influencing chromosomal stability appear to operate. A characteristic of animal cell hybrids is the progressive elimination of chromosomes of one of the parental genomes. In fact, study of the unilateral loss of human chromosomes from rodent × human cell hybrids, with the concomitant loss of phenotypic features, is now providing a very powerful tool for analyzing the human genome (see Goss, 1978). It was not unexpected, therefore, when Kao (1977) reported the progressive loss of tobacco chromosomes from a cell line originating from a fusion event between soybean (*Glycine max*) and *N. glauca*. This chromosome elimination occurred randomly and was preceded by gross chromosomal abnormalities, whereas the soybean chromosome complement appeared unaffected. Evidence from isoenzyme banding patterns for aspartate aminotransferase and alcohol dehydrogenase indicated that both genomes were being expressed (Wetter, 1977), in agreement with the experience with animal cell hybrids. Although two bands possessed by *N. glauca* were never present in these cell lines, they were detected in later experiments (Wetter and Kao, 1980). After 6 months in culture, most of the *N. glauca* chromosomes had been lost, but some remained and the movement of these was in synchrony with the soybean chromosomes. The isoenzyme bands of *N. glauca* were also lost. After 3 years in culture, a few of the *N. glauca* chromosomes with modified structures were still present. "Back fusion" of protoplasts derived from the hybrid cell with mesophyll protoplasts of *N. glauca* was carried out 27 months after the original fusion and again chromosomes of *N. glauca* were progressively lost. Some 7 months later, protoplasts isolated from a cell line resulting from this first back fusion that contained only a few *N. glauca* chromosomes were fused again with mesophyll protoplasts of *N. glauca*. These *N. glauca* protoplasts were, however, derived from leaf tissue that had been cultured for 24 hr to induce cell division. Cell lines from this second back fusion retained more of the *N. glauca* chromosomes, and after 6 months numerous *N. glauca* chromosomes were still present (Wetter and Kao, 1980). Similar unilateral loss of tobacco chromosomes was observed in soybean + tobacco cell lines in which *N. tabacum* was used as one of the parents instead of *N. glauca* (Chien *et al.*, 1982). In this case, however, a larger number of tobacco chromosomes were retained, and after 7 months, more than half the tobacco genome was still present in some cell lines.

Highly asymmetric chromosome complements have also been observed in other hybrid combinations. In three hybrid cell lines arising from fusion between *P. hybrida* and *V. faba* protoplasts, a large number of chromosomes of one parent were lost (Binding and Nehls, 1978). Two cell lines appeared to retain the *Petunia* chromosomes, and in the other the tendency was for the *Vicia* chromosomes to be retained. The extreme condition in which apparently total elimination of one parental chromosome set has occurred and yet some phenotypic features of that parent were still expressed has also been recorded. Fusion of protoplasts derived from cultured crown gall cells of *Parthenocissus tricuspidata* and mesophyll protoplasts of *P. hybrida* resulted in a cell culture that expressed both *Petunia* and *Parthenocissus* isoperoxidases but appeared to have no *Petunia* chromosomes (Power *et al.*, 1975). A comparable situation was obtained after fusion of cultured cells of *D. carota* and mesophyll protoplasts of *A. podagraria,* chromosomes of the latter being eliminated. In this case, however, it was possible to recover plants, and they resembled the *Daucus* parent but had features such as root development, root carotenoids, and chloroplast and chlorophyll development attributable to *Aegopodium* genes (Dudits *et al.*, 1979).

The mechanism for this unilateral loss of chromosomes is not clear. Experience with animal cell hybrids indicates that the direction of chromosome loss depends both on the parent used and on the type of tissue from which the cells are derived. In the early experiments on the human × rodent hybrids, the human chromosomes were always eliminated. In these experiments, cells that had been in culture for some time were used. However, if freshly isolated rodent cells were fused with cultured human cells, the direction of loss could be changed and the rodent chromosomes eliminated (Minna and Gon, 1974). It is perhaps significant that in those situations in which unilateral chromosome loss occurs in plant somatic hybrids, the fusion has involved protoplasts derived from rapidly dividing cultured cells of one parent with nondividing mesophyll protoplasts of the other. It was the chromosomes of the latter parent that were eliminated. In the report of Binding and Nehls (1978), in which both parental protoplasts were from mesophyll tissue, loss of chromosomes occurred from either one or the other parent.

The actual timing of chromosome loss in animal hybrids appears to consist of two phases: rapid loss of chromosomes over the first few division cycles and then a slower progressive loss of the remaining chromosomes over a longer period of culture. Evidence suggests that chromosome elimination in plant cell hybrids proceeds in a similar fashion. It has been proposed that this early chromosome loss results from the fusion of cells in different stages of the cell cycle. Again, observations on animal cells have revealed that when cells in mitosis are fused with cells in other stages of the cell cycle, the chromosomes of the interphase cells are caused to condense prematurely. The actual morphology of the prematurely condensed chromosomes depends upon the stage in the cell cycle of the interphase partner. This premature chromosome condensation (PCC) leads to fragmentation of chromosomes and to their subsequent loss (Rao and Johnson, 1972). Similar premature chromosome condensation has been observed after the fusion of mitotic protoplasts with protoplasts in interphase (Szabados and Dudits, 1980). The fact that it is the chromosomes of the nonactively dividing partner that are lost in the various somatic hybrid cell lines (discussed above) lends support to the suggestion that PCC is a contributing factor. Clearly, if this is the case, then it does not really represent a basic incompatibility in the genomes. Fusion of cells at the same stage in interphase would result in no chromosome elimination; additionally, the direction of loss could be determined by the appropriate choice of parental protoplast type.

Once some chromosomes of one genome have been lost, the rest of that chromosome set is effectively rendered redundant. Further loss of these chromosomes would not alter the viability of the cells and might even lead to a shortening of the cell cycle and a more rapid proliferation, providing a competitive advantage to such cells in the population. Indeed, Wetter and Kao (1980) noted that those cells that retained a high number of *N. glauca* chromosomes in the *N. glauca* + *G. max* hybrid cell lines grew slower than did those with fewer *N. glauca* chromosomes.

It is possible that PCC may play only a minor role in chromosome elimination and that other mechanisms, which depend more on fundamental incompatibilities of the genomes, may operate. Kao and Puck (1970) drew attention to the tendency for chromosomes of the slower growing parental cell type to be eliminated in animal cell hybrids and to the possibility that the generation times of the parental cells influenced the direction of chromosome loss in the hybrids. Chromosome loss could result in a cell with a shorter generation time and this cell type would come to predominate in the population. Clearly, the observations of Wetter and Kao (1980) on the *N. glauca* + *G. max* hybrids could also be used to support this mechanism.

The unilateral loss of chromosomes is not an inevitable consequence of combining relatively distantly related genomes. No chromosome elimination was found in somatic hybrid plants obtained from fusion of tomato (*Lycopersicum esculentum*) and potato (*Solanum tuberosum*) protoplasts (Melchers *et al.*, 1978; Shepard *et al.*, 1983). In addition, no evidence of chromosome elimination was found in hybrid cell lines of *Arabidopsis thaliana* + *Brassica campestris* (Gleba and Hoffman, 1978) and *Atropa belladonna* + *Nicotiana chinensis* (Gleba *et al.*, 1982) after 6–7 months in culture. Similarly, Krumbiegel and Schieder (1979) found no unilateral chromosome elimination in somatic hybrid cell lines of *D. innoxia* + *A. belladonna,* although a range of chromosome numbers was recorded. After 3–4 months, organized structures in the form of thick and pulpy leaves developed on the calluses. These leaves did not resemble either the *Datura* or *Atropa* parent. These hybrid cell lines continued to produce the poorly developed pulpy leaves, which never developed further into expanded leaves and shoots, during $1\frac{1}{2}$ years in culture. At this point, one line began to produce numerous green shoots, which, when examined for chromosome composition, were found to have a reduced number attributable to *Atropa*. These shoots exhibited a range of different phenotypes, including albino sectors and total albino shoots (the *D. innoxia* parental protoplasts were albino). Shoots were also recovered that were stable morphologically and appeared to have a stable but asymmetric chromosome complement, having probably only six chromosomes from *A. belladonna* and the original number from *D. innoxia* (Krumbiegel and Schieder, 1981).

A parallel situation has also been observed in the *A. thaliana* + *B. campestris* hybrid system. One cell line produced two shoots that appeared intermediate in morphology between *Brassica* and *Arabidopsis*, and it was established that both *Brassica* and *Arabidopsis* chromosomes were present. These shoots were considered to be stable allopolyploid intertribal hybrids. Another cell line produced organized structures on three occasions. Two of these events resulted in highly abnormal leaf and shootlike structures, which did not develop further. The third regenerant produced shoots that had predominantly *Arabidopsis* features, and none of the *Brassica* marker chromosomes could be identified. These were considered to be asymmetric hybrid shoots (Gleba and Hoffmann, 1980). Subsequently, numerous shoots with drastically differing phenotypes were recovered from another cell line originating from a single fusion event. Some of these regenerants had predominantly *Arabidopsis*-like features, whereas others had predominantly *Brassica* features and intermediate forms were recovered. Some shoots could not be assigned to either category. Cytological analysis revealed the presence of both *Brassica* and *Arabidopsis* chromosomes in all of the shoots sampled. The karyotype in these regenerated shoots was reported to be essentially stable. These karyotypes did, however, contain altered chromosomes; in some shoots very extensive chromosomal recombination was observed, with strong indications that this recombination involved chromosomes of the two parents (Hoffmann and Adachi, 1981). What is particularly encouraging about the observations on shoot regeneration in both the *B. campestris* + *A. thaliana* and the *D. innoxia* + *A. belladonna* hybrids is that the chromosome elimination has led to a series of situations wherein a balance in the remaining genome is conducive to shoot regeneration. This is all the more surprising since no shoots could be recovered from the culture of protoplasts of either *A. thaliana* or *B. campestris*.

The original aim in producing somatic hybrids between distantly related species was to obtain novel amphiploid plants that would provide a new gene pool from which fresh variants could be recovered. Although this is still a valid objective, it presupposes that the somatic hybrids will be fertile and can be introduced into a breeding program. Currently, none of the intergeneric somatic hybrids recovered has been reported to be fertile. From the experience with asymmetric somatic hybrids, an alternative strategy is beginning to emerge. It may be possible to exploit the chromosomal elimination and recombination and to recover stable asymmetric hybrids that contain only small, alien chromosomal segments integrated into the surviving genome. Unfortunately, at present there is little control over which genetic information is eliminated and which is retained. However, as already pointed out, it may be possible to determine which chromosome set is eliminated by appropriate choice of the protoplast source. Alternatively, treatment of one genome prior to fusion may influence the direction of chromosome loss. Ionizing radiation has induced directional elimination of irradiated chromosomes in animal cell hybrids (Pontecorvo, 1971; Goss and Harris, 1975), and this approach has been adopted for plant protoplasts with some success. Fusion of X-irradiated *N. tabacum* protoplasts with protoplasts of *N. sylvestris* led to a series of somatic hybrids, of which some were considered to have a largely *N. sylvestris* genome with the inclusion of some *N. tabacum* genes (Zelcer *et al.*, 1978). Similar results were obtained by Dudits *et al.* (1980) when X-irradiated parsley (*P. hortense*) protoplasts were fused with carrot (*D. carota*) protoplasts. Although such treatments may determine which parental genome is eliminated, they provide no means of controlling which fragments of the genome are retained. It may be more advantageous, therefore, instead of causing rapid elimination of most of one genome, to attempt to produce cell lines that are essentially symmetric and then derive from them, after chromosome segregation, a series of asymmetric secondary lines capable of giving rise to shoots. These shoots, in which the karyotype may be stabilized to some extent, could then be screened both cytologically and morphologically for features of interest. Promising regenerant plants could then be returned to *in vitro* culture in order to stimulate and recover any further chromosome segregation and recombination. In the human × rodent system it has proved possible to select for the retention of a particular chromosome by providing culture conditions that require the retention of this chromosome for continued viability. In the future, when considerably more is known about the location of genes on plant chromosomes, it may be possible to adopt a similar approach to plant somatic hybrids. As a step in this direction, it has been reported (Gupta *et al.*, 1982) that a nitrate reductase-deficient cell line of tobacco has been corrected by the introduction, through protoplast fusion, of genes from either *Physalis minima* or *D. innoxia*. The donor protoplasts were treated with X-irradiation, and corrected tobacco cell lines were selected by their ability to grow on a medium with nitrate as the sole nitrogen source.

B. BEHAVIOR OF CYTOPLASMIC COMPONENTS

In somatic hybrids, in addition to the formation of a hybrid nucleus, the cytoplasm will also be hybrid. The presence of two sets of plastids and mitochondria within a common cytoplasm is a condition not normally encountered in sexual hybridization. These novel combinations of nuclear and cytoplasmic components are of interest both for the study of nuclear–cytoplasmic interactions and for the potential for transfer of cytoplasmically inherited characteristics. On occasion, protoplast fusion can also lead to a situation in which the cells of the regenerated plant have a cytoplasm that is hybrid and is derived from both parents, but in which the nucleus of only one of the parents is present. Such plants are known as cybrids. Cybrids are of particular value when the transfer of a given extrachromosomal trait is required.

1. *Cybrid production*

In order to produce cybrids, the nucleus of the donor protoplast must be eliminated, resulting in transfer of the cytoplasm only. Menczel *et al.* (1982) managed to obtain a very high frequency of chloroplast transfer using donor protoplasts in which the nuclei had been completely inactivated following a high dose of radiation. Lower doses of radiation have also been used to enhance chloroplast transfer, although in some instances total elimination of the donor protoplast nucleus was not achieved (Zelcer *et al.*, 1978; Aviv *et al.*, 1980; Sidorov *et al.*, 1981). However, this could prove useful for the production of cybrids that contain a few desired chromosomes of the irradiated parent in addition to the nuclear genome of the unirradiated parent.

Selection of cybrids following fusion may be achieved by the use of genetic markers such as streptomycin resistance (Medgyesy *et al.*, 1980; Menczel *et al.*, 1982, 1983). Alternatively, when such markers are not available, cybrids may be selected by metabolic complementation following prior treatment of parental protoplasts with irradiation (donor) and iodoacetate (recipient) (Sidorov *et al.*, 1981).

A potentially more efficient method of cytoplasmic transfer would be to fuse enucleated protoplasts (cytoplasts) with nucleated recipient protoplasts. Various techniques for the production of cytoplasts have been developed. Cytochalasin B combined with centrifugation has been used since the early 1970s to enucleate mammalian cells (Wise and Prescott, 1973; Bossart *et al.*, 1975). This technique has been modified for plant protoplasts by Wallin *et al.* (1978). These workers were able to enucleate protoplasts by exposing them to cytochalasin B under high-speed centrifugation on a density gradient. Under such conditions the nucleus is drawn out of the protoplast, resulting in the formation of a cytoplast. Cytoplasts and miniprotoplasts (nucleated protoplasts containing only a small cytoplasmic component) were recovered from separated bands on the gradient.

A high level of enucleation (60–65%) was achieved by Lörz *et al.* (1981) by high-speed centrifugation of suspension-cell protoplasts through a discontinuous, isoosmotic density gradient containing Percoll, $CaCl_2$, and mannitol. Cytoplast preparations recovered contained only 1–7% contamination with nucleated protoplasts. Miniprotoplasts were also recovered from the gradient, concentrating in a lower region of the gradient than the cytoplasts. This method was developed to avoid the use of cytochalasin B, which was found to reduce the viability and plating efficiency of isolated minprotoplasts.

Archer *et al.* (1982) observed that cytoplasts were often present in protoplast populations following enzymatic digestion of leaves of *Nicotiana* spp., particularly when mature leaves were used. Cytoplasts were also obtained from suspension cultures, provided a large proportion of the cells were elongated. Formation of cytoplasts in elongated cells is likely to occur during plasmolysis. Enrichment of cytoplasts was achieved using a two-step discontinuous Percoll gradient.

Large numbers of small enucleate subcellular units were obtained by Bilkey *et al.* (1982) by gently squeezing friable callus consisting of thin-walled, highly vacuolated cells. These subcellular units, termed *microplasts,* vary in degree of cytoplasmic content and are bounded by a membrane thought to be derived from the tonoplast. By fusion of these microplasts with nucleated recipient protoplasts, it may be possible to obtain a range of cybrids possessing different levels of cytoplasmic hybridity.

Many workers have observed the phenomenon of "budding" during protoplast isolation and/or culture. Budding refers to the formation of rounded protuberances from the surface of the protoplast or cell that can become detached, resulting in the formation of enucleate subprotoplasts. These subprotoplasts, containing a proportion of the cytoplasm of the original protoplast, could prove of value for the production of cybrids. Subprotoplast formation has been attributed to the development of a new cell wall with local areas of weakness that are insufficient to contain the expanding protoplast (Hanke and Northcote, 1974). Vatsya and Bhaskaran (1981) demonstrated that subprotoplast formation during protoplast isolation was dependent on the osmolarity of the enzyme solution. For the production of a large population of subprotoplasts, these workers suggest that a hypertonic enzyme solution should be used.

In a similar vein, Hoffmann (1981) reported the formation of cytoplasts from giant protoplasts in culture. Callus cell protoplasts of *N. plumbaginifolia* cultured in a defined medium and under 16-hr day length grew up to 65-fold in volume but failed to regenerate any substantial wall, even after several months. These giant protoplasts begin to release cytoplasts into the medium after 3 weeks in culture. Following separation from nucleated protoplasts, these cytoplasts could be used for cybrid production.

Methods for protoplast fusion appear to be applicable to the fusion of cytoplasts with protoplasts. Maliga *et al.* (1982) fused cytoplasts of *N. tabacum* with *N. plumbaginifolia* protoplasts using PEG and obtained approximately 10% efficiency of chloroplast transfer, i.e., plants possessing the nuclear genome of *N. plumbaginifolia* and chloroplasts of *N. tabacum*. However, a large proportion (80%) of the total regenerants following this fusion were interspecific somatic hybrids arising from the 2–7% contamination of the cytoplast preparation by *N. tabacum* protoplasts. Maliga and co-workers suggest, therefore, that *N. tabacum* cytoplasts are less stable during fusion induction than are their nucleated counterparts. This is obviously a problem that needs further investigation before cytoplast–protoplast fusion can be efficiently achieved.

Since miniprotoplasts have only a small cytoplasmic content, they could be used in fusion experiments with cytoplasts in order to obtain cells possessing a nucleus with an almost totally alien cytoplasm. Such a situation can take a considerable amount of time to achieve using conventional breeding methods. These fusion products would be equivalent to reconstituted cells obtained after the fusion of minicells and cytoplasts in animals (see Ringertz and Savage, 1976). In fact, the fusion of enucleated cytoplasts of onion with miniprotoplasts from the same species has been reported (Bracha and Sher, 1981), but the fusion products were not subsequently cultured.

2. *Behavior of chloroplasts*

In order to trace the fate of chloroplasts following protoplast fusion, it is important to have a marker system that will characterize a particular chloroplast population. The composition of the enzyme ribulose-1,5-bisphosphate carboxylase (RuBPCase), with its large subunit coded by cpDNA and its small subunit coded by nuclear DNA, has proved particularly useful for this purpose. As already discussed, each of these subunits consists of one or more polypeptides, and analysis of the banding pattern produced by these polypeptides following isoelectric focusing has allowed identification of both the nuclear and the chloroplast constitution of regenerated somatic hybrids. In the event of mixed populations of polypeptides, sensitivity of detection is in the order of 10% of the total RuBPCase protein.

Demonstration of resistance to streptomycin or tentoxin has also been used to follow chloroplast inheritance. It has been shown that tentoxin, a fungal toxin, inactivates chloroplasts of sensitive species by specifically binding to chloroplast coupling factor 1 (Steele *et al.*, 1976), causing chlorosis. Reaction to streptomycin, on the other hand, is governed by the presence of resistance factors thought to be carried on the chloroplast ribosomes (Yurina *et al.*, 1978). On occasion, one of the parent protoplast systems has carried a cytoplasmic albino mutation, which has not only aided hybrid selection, but has also allowed simple detection of the form of chloroplast inheritance.

Chloroplasts can also be characterized by electrophoretic analysis of cpDNA digests following treatment with various restriction endonucleases. By comparison with parental chloroplast types, heterogeneous chloroplast populations, as well as possible recombination of chloroplast DNA in a somatic hybrid plant, should be detected. This technique has an advantage in that it does not rely on the detection of a product of the chloroplast genome. It is conceivable that as a result of mixing of two alien cytoplasms, one or part of a chloroplast genome may not be expressed and therefore may go undetected.

Although the fusion products initially contain a mixed chloroplast population, somatic hybrid plants subsequently recovered have been found in most cases to possess only one chloroplast type (Chen *et al.*, 1977; Belliard *et al.*, 1978; Gleba, 1978b; Melchers *et al.*, 1978; Aviv *et al.*, 1980; Evans *et al.*, 1980; Maliga *et al.*, 1980; Scowcroft and Larkin, 1981; Douglas *et al.*, 1981b; Kumar *et al.*, 1981, 1982; Schiller *et al.*, 1982).

Evidence suggests that a sorting of chloroplast types takes place during the process of plant regeneration. In the majority of cases, complete segregation of chloroplast types is achieved, hybrid plants having either but not both parental-type chloroplasts. As far as can be determined, this segregation, in most cases, appears to be random. There is little evidence to suggest that there is any nuclear control over chloroplast segregation. No nuclear complementation was found necessary in a cross between cytoplasmic male-sterile (CMS) *N. sylvestris* and X-irradiated *N. tabacum* protoplasts (Aviv and Galun, 1980). Either type of chloroplast was found in combination with the *N. sylvestris* nucleus. Similarly, chloroplast dominance could not be demonstrated in the presence of either a homogeneous (Belliard *et al.*, 1978) or a heterogeneous nucleus (Douglas *et al.*, 1981b). Chloroplast segregation also appears to be unaffected by the degree of compatibility of fusion partners. Random sorting of chloroplasts has been reported in somatic hybrids resulting from intraspecific (Scowcroft and Larkin, 1981), interspecific (Chen *et al.*, 1977; Iwai *et al.*, 1980), and intergeneric (Melchers *et al.*, 1978) hybridizations. However, as pointed out by Schiller *et al.* (1982), complementary genetic information for chloroplast biogenesis may be lost due to individual chromosome elimination. This is particularly likely to occur as a result of fusion between distantly related species. Under such conditions, direction of chloroplast segregation may be predetermined. Only when true amphiploids are obtained can it be concluded that chloroplast segregation is completely random.

In some somatic hybrids, unidirectional chloroplast segregation has been recorded (Evans *et al.*, 1980; Maliga *et al.*, 1980; Kumar *et al.*, 1981, 1982). This unidirectional chloroplast inheritance could be explained by the use of stringent selection pressures against one of the parents (Kumar *et al.*, 1982) or by the use of protoplasts at different physiological levels, i.e., mesophyll and suspension-cultured cell protoplasts (Maliga *et al.*, 1980; Kumar *et al.*, 1981, 1982). It is noteworthy that uniparental chloroplast inheritance in each of those cases in which mesophyll protoplasts were fused with cultured cells was in favor of the differentiated mesophyll state rather than of the undifferentiated proplastid type of the suspension-cultured parent. It is conceivable that dominance of one chloroplast type may occur under certain circumstances.

It has been suggested (Flick and Evans, 1982) that nuclear–cytoplasmic incompatibilities may influence chloroplast inheritance following somatic hybridization between species that are unidirectionally sexually incompatible due to a postzygotic event. Three somatic hybrids, for example, produced from the fusion of *N. tabacum* and *N. glauca* protoplasts, contained exclusively *N. tabacum* chloroplasts. Sexual crosses between these two species is only possible if *N. tabacum* is the female parent. Similarly, only *N. knightiana* can act as the female in a sexual cross with *N. tabacum*. Only *N. knightiana* chloroplasts were found in regenerated somatic hybrid plants (Maliga *et al.*, 1980).

The precise timing of complete chloroplast segregation has not been determined. Menezel *et al.* (1981) have suggested that mixed populations of chloroplasts can exist in calluses, at least until a 500-cell stage. Evidence for this was obtained from hybrid cell lines between streptomycin-resistant *N. tabacum* and streptomycin-sensitive *N. knightiana*. Calluses were found to be composed of both resistant and sensitive sectors, as indicated by a characteristic coloring pattern on selective medium.

The fate of chloroplasts in fused protoplasts was observed using electron microscopy (Rennie *et al.*, 1980). Mesophyll protoplasts of *Vicia narbonensis* or *Vicia hajastana* were fused with suspension-cell protoplasts of *V. hajastana*. Chloroplasts were seen to dedifferentiate after 7 days following fusion between mesophyll and suspension-cell protoplasts. No dedifferentiation was observed in the nondividing unfused mesophyll protoplasts. Chloroplast dedifferentiation occurred following both interspecific and homospecific fusions and was therefore not due to an incompatibility problem. Rennie and co-workers suggested that chloroplast dedifferentiation was the result of mixing the cytoplasm of nondividing protoplasts with that of protoplasts from rapidly dividing cells. It is possible that, following fusion, proplastids may coexist until such time as they are stimulated to differentiate. Indeed, following the fusion of streptomycin-sensitive *N. plumbaginifolia* with streptomycin-resistant *N. tabacum*, Maliga and co-workers (1982) noted that sensitive as well as resistant plants were regenerated from calluses originally showing streptomycin resistance. This indicates that not only was the callus cytoplasmically chimeric but that complete chloroplast segregation was not obtained until the mature plant stage.

Plants having a mixture of chloroplast types have been obtained by some workers (Gleba, 1978b; Glimelius *et al.*, 1981; Kung *et al.*, 1975; Sidorov *et al.*, 1981). It is perhaps of interest to note that in three of these cases mesophyll protoplasts of a cytoplasmic albino *N. tabacum* mutant were used as one partner. Suspension-cell protoplasts derived from a variety of other sources were used as the second partner. In the fourth instance (Glimelius *et al.*, 1981), mesophyll protoplasts containing an *N. tabacum* nucleus combined with an alien cytoplasm derived from CMS *Nicotiana sauveolens* were fused with suspension-cell protoplasts of a nitrate reductase mutant of *N. tabacum*. Gleba (1978b) demonstrated that chloroplast heterogeneity of hybrid plants was also transmitted through subsequent sexual crossing.

Chen *et al.* (1977) found that one of nine regenerated somatic hybrid plants contained a mixture of both parental chloroplast types. Complete segregation was found, however, during subsequent vegetative proliferation. It was subsequently found that this plant was a chimera and that the two populations of chloroplasts resided in different cells (Uchimiya and Wildman, 1979).

Complete segregation of chloroplast types was obtained by Iwai and associates (1980) in somatic hybrid plants regenerated from the fusion of mesophyll protoplasts of *N. rustica* and *N. tabacum*. Anthers from one of these somatic hybrid plants, having large-subunit RuBPCase polypeptides characteristic of *N. tabacum* only, were subsequently used to produce androgenic plants (Iwai *et al.*, 1981). Surprisingly, two of nine of the regenerated androgenic plants contained large-subunit polypeptides of *N. rustica* chloroplasts. Both chloroplast types must therefore have been present in the original hybrid. Iwai and co-workers suggested that the original hybrid was perhaps a cytoplasmic chimera, in which *N. tabacum* chloroplasts were in great excess over *N. rustica*. Although the *N. rustica* chloroplast genome was not expressed in the original hybrid, predominance of this chloroplast type may occur in subsequent progeny. Because each of the androgenic plants was produced from anthers of different flowers, it is conceivable that during floral differentiation at the apical meristem some flowers may have developed from cell lineages in which *N. rustica* chloroplasts had become predominant.

Although mixed populations of chloroplasts obviously can be tolerated in the same tissue, no irrefutable evidence for recombination of chloroplast genomes in higher plants has been obtained.

3. *Behavior of mitochondria*

Naturally, protoplast fusion, in addition to production of a mixed population of chloroplasts, also leads to a mixed mitochondrial population. Unfortunately, at present there appear to be no marker proteins or polypeptides available to characterize the mitochondrial populations in the same way that the large-subunit polypeptides have been used with chloroplasts. Consequently, tracing the fate of mitochondria has relied on analysis of restriction endonuclease digests of mtDNA. Results with *Nicotiana* species indicate that the restriction digest patterns of mtDNA in the hybrids differ from those of either of the parental mitochondria (Belliard *et al.*, 1979; Nagy *et al.*, 1982; Galun *et al.*, 1982). Similar results have recently been reported for *Petunia* (Boeshore *et al.*, 1983). It has been suggested that these new restriction patterns result from mitochondrial recombination (Belliard *et al.*, 1979; Nagy *et al.*, 1981) or possibly also from the assortment of different DNA molecules in the mitochondria (Boeshore *et al.*, 1983). It was also noted (Galun *et al.*, 1982) that some of the mitochondrial populations in the cybrids appeared more like those from one parent than the other. Possibly, sorting of mitochondrial types took place that was independent of the nuclear genome. The mitochondria also assorted independently of the chloroplasts, resulting in new chloroplast–mitochondrial combinations.

4. *Male sterility*

In recent years considerable interest has developed in the phenomenon of male sterility, in the main because of its value for the production of hybrid seed. Some forms of male sterility are controlled by genetic elements in the cytoplasm (cytoplasmic male sterility) or by particular nuclear–cytoplasmic interactions (alloplasmic male sterility). Currently, there is some uncertainty as to whether the genetic elements controlling male sterility reside in the mitochondria or chloroplast genomes or elsewhere in the cytoplasm. Protoplast fusion, with the generation of a hybrid cytoplasm and the subsequent segregation of organelles in the regenerated somatic hybrid, offers a unique approach to the analysis of cytoplasmically determined male sterility. In *Nicotiana* it has proved possible to transfer, as a result of protoplast fusion, both male sterility and fertility between different varieties (Belliard *et al.*, 1978; Glimelius *et al.*, 1981) and also between different species (Zelcer *et al.*, 1978; Aviv and Galun, 1980; Menczel *et al.*, 1983). Similar intervarietal (Bergounioux-Bunisset and Perennes, 1980) and interspecific (Izhar and Power, 1979) transfer of male sterility and fertility has been achieved with *Petunia*. Interestingly, in *Nicotiana*, analysis of the cytoplasmic components of somatic hybrids has not found any direct link between the presence of a particular chloroplast type and male fertility or sterility (Belliard *et al.*, 1978; Aviv and Galun, 1980; Glimelius *et al.*, 1981; Galun *et al.*, 1982). This is at variance with the observations of Frankel *et al.* (1979), who analyzed the chloroplast composition of a range of isonuclear male-sterile lines of tobacco produced by sexual crossing. There was, however, some correlation between the mitochondria composition and male fertility or sterility (Belliard *et al.*, 1979; Galun *et al.*, 1982).

A heteroplasmic state with respect to cytoplasmic male sterility has been demonstrated in cytoplasmic hybrids of *Petunia* (Izhar and Tabib, 1980). Segregation into stable male-sterile and -fertile plants occurred in both the F_2 and F_3 generations following selfing of a fertile hybrid. Since plants of the F_2 were produced from a single zygotic cell, segregation could not be attributed to a chimeric situation. No such clear segregation for male sterility or fertility has been reported for *Nicotiana*. Different degrees of fertility have been observed, however, among hybrid plants of a cross between CMS *N. sylvestris* and X-irradiated, fertile *N. tabacum* (Aviv and Galun, 1980) and of fertile *N. tabacum* with a CMS alloplasmic *N. tabacum* (Belliard *et al.*, 1978). In addition, different types of plants, with respect to their degree of fertility, were obtained from individual calluses (Aviv and Glun, 1980).

Aviv *et al.* (1980) produced a single androgenic plant from a hybrid showing impaired male fertility. This androgenic plant was completely fertile. It is conceivable that expression of different levels of male fertility may be related to the presence of a heteroplasmic state regarding this factor. On the other hand, a homoplasmic condition is indicated in the case of completely sterile plants. For instance, due to a late abortion of pollen, it proved possible to raise androgenic plants from completely sterile cytoplasmic hybrids. All the androgenic plants produced proved to be identical to the hybrid in that they were completely male sterile (Aviv *et al.*, 1980). Further evidence suggesting that cytoplasmic male sterility is expressed only as a result of a homoplasmic condition comes from the fact that calluses that subsequently produced fully sterile plants did not produce any fertile or partially fertile plants (Aviv and Galun, 1980). Izhar *et al.* (1983), however, reported that a heteroplasmic state in *Petunia* may express male sterility. The progeny of the male-sterile plants segregated for male fertility and sterility, whereas male-fertile plants produced only male-fertile progeny and were assumed to be homoplasmic. This contrasts with the earlier report of Izhar and Tabib (1980) in which segregation was obtained from male-fertile plants. These experiments, however, were carried out with petunias with a different genetic constitution, and it was suggested that the nuclear composition might influence the behavior of the elements controlling male sterility (Izhar *et al.*, 1983).

The frequent sorting out into stable male-fertile and male-sterile lines in petunias and the lack of any clear correlation between mtDNA restriction endonuclease digestion patterns in either male-sterile somatic hybrids and those of the male-sterile parent or male-fertile hybrids and the male-fertile parent led Izhar *et al.* (1983) to suggest that the basis for male sterility in petunias is different from that in tobacco.

VII. Concluding Remarks

The original motivation for isolating protoplasts was to develop a technique that would be used to answer basic questions in plant cell biology. What was essentially an exercise in fundamental science has subsequently developed into a technology that, through the process of crop improvement, may have a far-reaching influence on world agriculture. Over the past 10 years or so a number of very significant advances in somatic hybridization have been made. Techniques for obtaining reproducibly high levels of fusion have been developed. Methods for selection have been developed allowing the recovery of somatic hybrids, first between sexually compatible species and then between sexually incompatible species. The fusion of somatic cells has therefore enabled the sexual process, with its attendant mechanisms for screening out unaccepted fertilizations, to be bypassed. Some of the novel interspecific hybrids produced have proved to be fertile and have been tentatively designated as new species (Schieder, 1980b). Therefore, one of the original aims of somatic hybridization—the combining of two genetically isolated genomes to produce a new gene pool from which fresh gene combinations can be retrieved—has been demonstrated as a practicality. The limits to hybridization by protoplast fusion are now being probed. Hybridization of more distantly related species has led to the recovery of a number of intergeneric somatic hybrids. Currently, none of these hybrids has proved to be fertile. Obviously, some degree of fertility is essential if somatic hybrids are to be fully exploited. It has frequently been stressed that in order to obtain any agronomic benefits from somatic hybridization, the technique has to form part of a broader based breeding program. Certainly it was never envisaged that somatic hybridization would immediately lead to a plant expressing superior characteristics to its parents. At present, experience with these intergeneric somatic hybrids is limited, but the unilateral loss of chromosomes from one parental genome witnessed in these hybrids does offer some interesting possibilities, particularly if chromosomal fragmentation, translocation, and rearrangements between the chromosomes of the parents also turn out to be regular occurrences during *in vitro* culture. It is possible to envisage these phenomena as a means of generating variability, the process operating as a very crude mimic of sexual recombination. The plants recovered could then be screened for improved performance. In time it may be possible to exert some more precise control over the behavior of chromosomes in intergeneric somatic hybrids. Clearly, in vegetatively propagated crops wherein the harvestable product is also a vegetative development, lack of fertility may not of itself be a major disadvantage. Obviously, the position is very different when the product is a fruit or seed or when the crop is seed propagated. In the longer term, there may even be ways of bypassing this problem. It has been suggested recently (Heslop-Harrison, 1983) that considerable agronomic advantages might accrue from agamospermous, apomictic reproduction of seed crops, if only ways could be found to induce apomixis at will.

Were this to be achieved, it might allow abundant seed and grain production from totally sterile somatic hybrids.

There are also advantages to be gained from somatic hybridization between sexually compatible species because of the opportunity it offers for generating a hybrid cytoplasm. When this is combined with the sorting of organelles during subsequent culture, it should allow the recovery of novel combinations of cytoplasmic components. In particular, the transfer of male sterility between species and varieties is likely to be facilitated by this technique.

Somatic hybridization is still essentially at the stage of using model systems to explore the possibilities of the technique. If progress continues to be made at the same pace as has been seen over the past few years, it is likely that we will see some of these possibilities realized in species of commercial interest. However, it is always difficult with biological systems to predict a time scale for obtaining particular objectives. Those supporting this research with a view of obtaining a commercial return may have to be patient.

REFERENCES

Ahkong, Q. F., Blow, A. M. J., Botham, G. M., Launder, J. M., Quirk, S. J., and Lucy, J. A. (1978). Proteinases and cell fusion. *FEBS Lett.* **95**, 147–152.

Ahuja, P. S., Haduizzaman, S., Davey, M. R., and Cocking, E. C. (1983). Prolific regeneration from protoplast-derived tissues of *Lotus corniculatus* L. (birdsfoot trefoil). *Plant Cell Rep.* **2**, 101–104.

Aldwinckle, T. J., Ahkong, Q. F., Bangham, A. D., Fisher, D., and Lucy, J. A. (1982). Effects of poly(ethylene glycol) on liposomes and erythrocytes: Permeability changes and membrane fusion. *Biochim. Biophys. Acta* **689**, 548–560.

Archer, E. K., Landgren, C. R., and Bonnett, H. T. (1982). Cytoplast formation and enrichment from mesophyll tissues of *Nicotiana* spp. *Plant Sci. Lett.* **25**, 175–185.

Arcioni, S., Davey, M. R., dos Santos, A. V. P., and Cocking, E. C. (1982). Somatic embryogenesis in tissues from mesophyll and cell suspension protoplasts of *Medicago coerulea* and *M. glutinosa*. *Z. Pflanzenphysiol.* **106**, 105–110.

Arnold, K., Pratsch, L., and Gawrisch, K. (1983). Effect of poly(ethylene glycol) on phospholipid hydration and polarity of the external phase. *Biochim. Biophys. Acta* **728**, 121–128.

Ashton, N. W., and Cove, D. J. (1977). The isolation and preliminary characterisation of auxotrophic and analogue resistant mutants of the moss, *Physcomitrella patens*. *Mol. Gen. Genet.* **154**, 87–95.

Aviv, D., and Galun, E. (1980). Restoration of fertility in cytoplasmic male sterile (CMS) *Nicotiana sylvestris* by fusion with X-irradiated *N. tabacum* protoplasts. *Theor. Appl. Genet.* **58**, 121–127.

Aviv, D., Fluhr, R., Edelman, M., and Galun, E. (1980). Progeny analysis of the interspecific somatic hybrids: *Nicotiana tabacum* (CMS) + *Nicotiana sylvestris* with respect to nuclear and chloroplast markers. *Theor. Appl. Genet.* **56**, 145–150.

Banks, M. S., and Evans, P. K. (1976). A comparison of the isolation and culture of mesophyll protoplasts from several *Nicotiana* species and their hybrids. *Plant Sci. Lett.* **7,** 409–416.
Beier, H., and Bruening, G. (1975). The use of an abrasive in the isolation of cowpea leaf protoplasts which support the multiplication of cowpea mosaic virus. *Virology* **64,** 272–276.
Belliard, G., Pelletier, G., and Ferault, M. (1977). Fusion de protoplastes de *Nicotiana tabacum* à cytoplasmes différents: Etude des hybrides cytoplasmiques néo-formes. *C. R. Hebd. Seances Acad. Sci., Ser. D* **284,** 749–752.
Belliard, G., Pelletier, G., Vedel, F., and Quétier, F. (1978). Morophologcial characteristics and chloroplast DNA distribution in different cytoplasmic parasexual hybrids of *Nicotiana tabacum. Mol. Gen. Genet.* **165,** 231–237.
Belliard, G., Vedel, F., and Pelletier, G. (1979). Mitochondrial recombination in cytoplasmic hybrids of *Nicotiana tabacum* by protoplast fusion. *Nature (London)* **281,** 401–403.
Bergounioux-Bunisset, C., and Perennes, C. (1980). Transfert de facteurs cytoplasmiques de la fertilité male entre 2 lignes de *Petunia hybrida* par fusion de protoplastes. *Plant Sci. Lett.* **19,** 143–149.
Bilkey, P. C., Davey, M. R., and Cocking, E. C. (1982). Isolation, origin and properties of enucleate plant microplasts. *Protoplasma* **110,** 147–151.
Binding, H. (1974). Fusionverusche mit isolierten protoplasten von *Petunia hybrida. Z. Pflanzenphysiol.* **72,** 422–426.
Binding, H. (1975). Reproducibly high plating efficiencies of isolated mesophyll protoplasts from shoot cultures of tobacco. *Physiol. Plant.* **35,** 225–227.
Binding, H., and Nehls, R. (1978). Somatic cell hybridisation of *Vicia faba* + *Petunia hybrida. Mol. Gen. Genet.* **164,** 137–143.
Binding, H., Jain, S. M., Finger, J., Mordhorst, G., Nehls, R., and Gressel, J. (1982). Somatic hybridisation of an atrazine resistant biotype of *Solanum nigrum* with *Solanum tuberosum.* Part 1. Colonal variation in morphology and in atrazine sensitivity. *Theor. Appl. Genet.* **63,** 273–277.
Blow, A. M. J., Botham, G. M., Fisher, D., Goodall, A. H., Tilcock, C. P. S., and Lucy, J. A. (1978). Water and calcium ions in cell fusion induced by poly(ethylene glycol). *FEBS Lett.* **94,** 305–310.
Boeshore, M. L., Lifshitz, I., Hanson, M. R., and Izhar, S. (1983). Novel composition of mitochondrial genomes in *Petunia* somatic hybrids derived from cytoplasmic male sterile and fertile plants. *Mol. Gen. Genet.* **190,** 459–467.
Boss, W. F. (1983). Poly(ethylene glycol)-induced fusion of plant protoplasts. A spin-label study. *Biochim. Biophys. Acta* **730,** 111–118.
Boss, W. F., and Mott, R. L. (1980). Effects of divalent cations and polyethylene glycol on the membrane fluidity of protoplasts. *Plant Physiol.* **66,** 835–837.
Bossart, W., Leoffler, H., and Bienz, K. (1975). Enucleation of cells by density gradient centrifugation. *Exp. Cell Res.* **96,** 360–366.
Bracha, M., and Sher, N. (1981). Fusion of enucleated protoplasts with nucleated miniprotoplasts in onion (*Allium cepta* L.). *Plant Sci. Lett.* **23,** 95–101.
Butenko, R., Kuchko, A., and Komarnitsky, I (1982). Some features of somatic hybrids between *Solanum tuberosum* and *S. chacoense* and its F_1 sexual progeny. *Plant Tissue Cult., Proc. Int. Congr. Plant Tissue Cell Cult., 5th, 1982* pp. 643–644.
Carlson, P. S., Smith, H. H., and Dearing, R. D. (1972). Parasexual interspecific plant hybridisation. *Proc. Natl. Acad. Sci. U.S.A.* **69,** 2292–2294.

Chaleff, R. S. (1981). "Genetics of Higher Plants. Application of Cell Culture." Cambridge Univ. Press, London and New York.

Chen, K., Wildman, S. G., and Smith, H. H. (1977). Chloroplast DNA distribution in parasexual hybrids as shown by polypeptide composition of fraction 1 protein. *Proc. Natl. Acad. Sci. U.S.A.* **74,** 5109–5112.

Chien, Y.-C., Kao, K. N., and Wetter, L. R. (1982). Chromosomal and isozyme studies of *Nicotiana tabacum-Glycine max* hybrid cell lines. *Theor. Appl. Genet.* **62,** 301–304.

Chupeau, Y., Missonier, G., Hommel, M.-C., and Goujard, J. (1978). Somatic hybrids of plants by fusion of protoplasts. *Mol. Gen. Genet.* **165,** 239–245.

Cocking, E. C. (1960). A method for the isolation of plant protoplasts and vacuoles. *Nature (London)* **187,** 927–929.

Cocking, E. C., Power, J. B., Evans, P. K., Safwat, F., Frearson, E. M., Hayward, C., Berry, S. F., and George, D. (1974). Naturally occurring differential drug sensitivities of cultured plant protoplasts. *Plant Sci. Lett.* **3,** 341–350.

Cocking, E. C., George, D., Price-Jones, M. J., and Power, J. B. (1977). Selection procedures for the production of interspecies somatic hybrids of *Petunia hybrida* and *Petunia parodii.* 2. Albino complementation selection. *Plant Sci. Lett.* **10,** 7–12.

Constabel, F., Dudits, D., Gamborg, O. L., and Kao, K. N. (1975). Nuclear fusion in intergeneric heterokaryons. A note. *Can. J. Bot.* **53,** 2092–2095.

Constabel, F., Weber, G., Kirkpatrick, J. W., and Pohl, K. (1976). Cell division of intergeneric protoplast fusion products. *Z. Pflanzenphysiol.* **79,** 1–7.

dos Santos, A. V. P., Outka, D. E., Cocking, E. C., and Davey, M. R. (1980). Organogenesis and somatic embryogenesis in tissues derived from leaf protoplasts and leaf explants of *Medicago sativa. Z. Pflanzenphysiol.* **99,** 261–270.

dos Santos, A. V. P., Davey, M. R., and Cocking, E. C. (1983). Cultural studies of protoplasts of *Trigonella corniculata* and *T. foenum-graecum. Z. Pflanzenphysiol.* **109,** 227–234.

Douglas, G. C., Keller, W. A., and Setterfield, G. (1981a). Somatic hybridisation between *Nicotiana rustica* and *N. tabacum.* II. Protoplast fusion and selection and regeneration of hybrid plants. *Can. J. Bot.* **59,** 220–227.

Douglas, G. C., Wetter, L. R., Keller, W. A., and Setterfield, G. (1981b). Somatic hybridisation between *Nicotiana rustica* and *N. tabacum.* IV. Analysis of nuclear and chloroplast genome expression in somatic hybrids. *Can. J. Bot.* **59,** 1509–1513.

Dudits, D., Kao, K. N., Constabel, F., and Gamborg, O. L. (1976). Fusion of carrot and barley protoplasts and division of heterokaryocytes. *Can. J. Genet. Cytol.* **18,** 263–269.

Dudits, D., Hadlaczky, G., Lévi, E., Fejér, O., Haydu, Z., and Lázár, G. (1977). Somatic hybridization of *Daucus carota* and *D. capillifolius* by protoplast fusion. *Theor. Appl. Genet.* **51,** 127–132.

Dudits, D., Hadlaczky, G., Bajszár, G. Y., Koncz, C., Lázár, G., and Horváth, G. (1979). Plant regeneration from intergeneric cell hybrids. *Plant Sci. Lett.* **15,** 101–112.

Dudits, D., Fejér, O., Hadlaczky, C., Koncz, G., Lázár, G. B., and Horváth, G. (1980). Intergeneric gene transfer mediated by plant protoplast fusion. *Mol. Gen. Genet.* **179,** 283–288.

Evans, D. A., Wetter, L. R., and Gamborg, O. L. (1980). Somatic hybrid plants of *Nicotiana glauca* with *Nicotiana tabacum* obtained by protoplast fusion. *Physiol. Plant.* **48,** 225–230.

Evans, D. A., Flick, C. E., and Jensen, R. A. (1981). Disease resistance: Incorporation into sexually incompatible somatic hybrids of the genus *Nicotiana*. *Science* **213**, 907-909.

Evans, P. K., and Cocking, E. C. (1975). The techniques of plant cell culture and somatic cell hybridization. *New Tech. Biophys. Cell Biol.* **2**, 127-158.

Evola, S. V., Earle, E. D., and Chaleff, R. S. (1983). The use of genetic markers selected *in vitro* for the isolation and genetic verification of intraspecific somatic hybrids of *Nicotiana tabacum* L. *Mol. Gen. Genet.* **189**, 441-446.

Fitzsimons, P. J., and Weyers, J. D. B. (1983). Separation and purification of protoplast types from *Commelina communis* L. leaf epidermis. *J. Exp. Bot.* **34**, 55-66.

Flick, C. E., and Evans, D. A. (1982). Evaluation of cytoplasmic segregation in somatic hybrids of *Nicotiana:* Tentoxin sensitivity. *J. Hered.* **73**, 264-266.

Frankel, R., Scowcroft, W. R., and Whitfeld, P. R. (1979). Chloroplast DNA variation in isonuclear male-sterile lines of *Nicotiana. Mol. Gen. Genet.* **169**, 129-135.

Galbraith, D. W., and Galbraith, J. E. C. (1979). A method for identification of fusion of plant protoplasts derived from tissue cultures. *Z. Pflanzenphysiol.* **93**, 149-158.

Galbraith, D. W., and Mauch, T. J. (1980). Identification of fusion of plant protoplasts. II. Conditions for the reproducible fluorescence labelling of protoplasts derived from mesophyll tissue. *Z. Pflanzenphysiol.* **98**, 129-140.

Galun, E. (1981). Plant protoplasts as physiological tools. *Annu. Rev. Plant Physiol.* **32**, 237-266.

Galun, E., Arzee-Gonen, P., Fluhr, R., Edelman, M., and Aviv, D. (1982). Cytoplasmic hybridisation in *Nicotiana:* Mitochondrial DNA analysis in progenies resulting from fusion between protoplasts having different organelle constitutions. *Mol. Gen. Genet.* **186**, 50-56.

Gamborg, O. L., Miller, R. A., and Ojima, K. (1968). Nutrient requirements of suspension cultures of soybean root cells. *Exp. Cell Res.* **50**, 151-158.

Gebhardt, C., Shamamoto, K., Lázár, G., Schnebli, V., and King, P. J. (1983). Isolation of biochemical mutants using haploid mesophyll protoplasts of *Hyoscyamus muticus*. III. General characteristics of histidine and tryptophan auxotrophs. *Planta* **159**, 18-24.

Gleba, Y. Y. (1978a). Microdroplet culture: Tobacco plants from single mesophyll protoplasts. *Naturwissenschaften* **65**, 158-159.

Gelba, Y. Y. (1978b). Extranuclear inheritance investigated by somatic hybridization. *Front. Plant Tissue Cult., Proc. Int. Congr., 4th, 1978* pp. 95-102.

Gleba, Y. Y., and Hoffmann, F. (1978). Hybrid cell lines *Arabidospsis thaliana* + *Brassica campestris:* No evidence for specific chromosome elimination. *Mol. Gen. Genet.* **165**, 257-264.

Gleba, Y. Y., and Hoffmann, F. (1980). "Arabidobrassica": A novel plant obtained by protoplast fusion. *Planta* **149**, 112-117.

Gleba, Y. Y., Butenko, R. G., and Sytnik, K. M. (1975). Fusion of protoplasts and parasexual hybridization in *Nicotiana tabacum* L. *Dokl. Biol. Sci. (Engl. Transl.)* **221**, 117-119.

Gleba, Y. Y., Momot, V. P., Cherep, N. N., and Skarzynskaya, M. V. (1982). Intertribal hybrid cell lines of *Atropa belladonna* (X) *Nicotiana chinensis* obtained by cloning individual protoplast fusion products. *Theor. Appl. Genet.* **62**, 75-79.

Glimelius, K., and Bonnett, H. (1981). Somatic hybridisation in *Nicotiana:* Restoration of photoautotrophy to an albino mutant with defective plastids. *Planta* **153**, 497-503.

Glimelius, K., Eriksson, T., Grafe, R., and Müller, A. J. (1978). Somatic hybridization of nitrate reductase-deficient mutants of *Nicotiana tabacum* by protoplast fusion. *Physiol. Plant.* **44,** 273–277.

Glimelius, K., Chen, K., and Bonnett, H. T. (1981). Somatic hybridisation in *Nicotiana:* Segregation of organellar traits among hybrid and cybrid plants. *Planta* **153,** 504–510.

Goss, S. J. (1978). Gene mapping by cell fusion. *Int. Rev. Cytol., Suppl.* **8,** 127–169.

Goss, S. J., and Harris, H. (1975). New method for mapping genes in human chromosomes. *Nature (London)* **255,** 680–684.

Gresshoff, P. M. (1980). *In vitro* culture of white clover: Callus, suspension, protoplast culture, and plant regeneration. *Bot. Gaz. (Chicago)* **141,** 157–164.

Grimsley, N. H., Ashton, N. W., and Cove, D. J. (1977). The production of somatic hybrids by protoplast fusion in the moss, *Physcomitrella patens. Mol. Gen. Genet.* **154,** 97–100.

Grout, B. W. W., Willison, J. H. M., and Cocking, E. C. (1972). Interactions at the surface of plant cell protoplasts; an electrophoretic and freeze-etch study. *J. Bioenerg.* **4,** 311–328.

Gupta, P. P., Gupta, N., and Schieder, O. (1982). Correction of nitrate reductase defect in auxotrophic plant cells through protoplast-mediated intergeneric gene transfers. *Mol. Gen. Genet.* **188,** 378–383.

Hamill, J. D., Pental, D., Cocking, E. C., and Müller, A. J. (1983). Production of a nitrate reductase deficient streptomycin resistant mutant of *Nicotiana tabacum* for somatic hybridisation studies. *Heredity* **50,** 197–200.

Hanke, D. E., and Northcote, D. H. (1974). Cell wall formation by soybean callus protoplasts. *J. Cell Sci.* **14,** 29–50.

Harada, H., Ohyama, K., and Cheruel, J. (1972). Effects of coumarin and other factors on the modification of form and growth of isolated mesophyll cells. *Z. Pflanzenphysiol.* **66,** 307–324.

Harms, C. T., and Potrykus, I. (1978). Enrichment for heterokaryocytes by the use of iso-osmotic density gradients after plant protoplast fusion. *Theor. Appl. Genet.* **53,** 49–55.

Harms, C. T., Potrykus, I., and Widholm, J. M. (1981). Complementation and dominant expression of amino acid analogue resistance markers in somatic hybrid clones from *Daucus carota* after protoplast fusion. *Z. Pflanzenphysiol.* **101,** 377–390.

Hartmann, J. X., Galla, J. D., Emma, D. A., Kao, K. N., and Gamborg, O. L. (1976). The fusion of erythrocytes by treatment with proteolytic enzymes and polyethylene glycol. *Can. J. Genet. Cytol.* **18,** 503–512.

Haydu, Z., Lázár, G., and Dudits, D. (1977). Increased frequency of polyethylene glycol induced protoplast fusion by dimethylsulfoxide. *Plant Sci. Lett.* **10,** 357–360.

Heslop-Harrison, J. (1984). Clonal propagation: Hopes and hazards. *In* "Improvement of Vegetatively-propagated Plants." Academic Press, New York. In press.

Hoffmann, F. (1981). Formation of cytoplasts from giant protoplasts in culture. *Protoplasma* **107,** 387–391.

Hoffmann, F., and Adachi, T. (1981). "Arabidobrassica": Chromosomal recombination and morphogenesis in asymmetric intergeneric hybrid cells. *Planta* **153,** 586–593.

Honda, K., Maeda, Y., Sasakawa, S., Ohno, H., and Tsuchida, E. (1981a). Activities of cell fusion and lysis of the hybrid type of chemical fusogens. I. Structure and function of the promotor of cell fusion. *Biochem. Biophys. Res. Commun.* **100,** 442–448.

Honda, K., Maeda, Y., Sasakawa, S., Ohno, H., and Tsuchida, E. (1981b). The components contained in polyethylene glycol of commercial grade (PEG-6,000) as cell fusogen. *Biochem. Biophys. Res. Commun.* **101,** 165–171.

Iwai, S., Nagao, T., Nakata, K., Kawashima, N., and Matsuyama, S. (1980). Expression of nuclear and chloroplastic genes coding for fraction-1 protein in somatic hybrids of *Nicotiana tabacum* + *N. rustica. Planta* **147,** 414–417.

Iwai, S., Nakata, K., Nagao, T., Kawashima, N., and Matsuyama, S. (1981). Detection of the *Nicotiana rustica* chloroplast genome coding for the large subunit of fraction-1 protein in a somatic hybrid in which only the *N. tabacum* chloroplast genome appeared to have been expressed. *Planta* **152,** 478–480.

Izhar, S., and Power, J. B. (1977). Genetical studies with *Petunia* leaf protoplasts. I. Genetic variation to specific growth hormones and possible genetic control on stages of protoplast development in culture. *Plant Sci. Lett.* **8,** 375–383.

Izhar, S., and Power, J. B. (1979). Somatic hybridization in *Petunia:* A male sterile cytoplasmic hybrid. *Plant Sci. Lett.* **14,** 49–55.

Izhar, S., and Tabib, Y. (1980). Somatic hybridization in *Petunia.* Part 2. Heteroplasmic state in somatic hybrids followed by cytoplasmic segregation into male sterile and male fertile lines. *Theor. Appl. Genet.* **57,** 241–245.

Izhar, S., Schlicter, M., and Swartzberg, D. (1983). Sorting out of cytoplasmic elements in somatic hybrids of *Petunia* and the prevalence of the heteroplasmon through several meiotic cycles. *Mol. Gen. Genet.* **190,** 468–474.

Johnson, L. B., Stuteville, D. L., Higgins, R. K., and Skinner, D. Z., (1981). Regeneration of alfalfa plants from protoplasts of selected Regen S clones. *Plant Sci. Lett.* **20,** 297–304.

Jullian, M., (1970). Sur l'aptitude à la division *in vitro* des cellules séparées du parenchyme foliaire d'*Archis hypogaea* L. *C. R. Hebd. Seances Acad. Sci.* **270,** 3051–3054.

Kameya, T. (1975). Induction of hybrids through somatic cell fusion with dextran sulphate and gelatin. *Jpn. J. Genet.* **50,** 235–246.

Kameya, T. (1979). Studies on plant cell fusion: Effects of dextran and pronase E on fusion. *Cytologia* **44,** 449–456.

Kameya, T., and Uchimiya, H. (1972). Embryoids derived from isolated protoplasts of carrot. *Planta* **103,** 356–360.

Kameya, T., Horn, M. E., and Widholm, J. M. (1981). Hybrid shoot formation from fused *Daucus carota* and *D. capillifolius* protoplasts. *Z. Pflanzenphysiol.* **104,** 459–466.

Kanai, R., and Edwards, G. E. (1973). Purification of enzymatically isolated mesophyll protoplasts from C_3 and C_4 and crassulacean acid metabolism plants using an aqueous dextran-polyethylene glycol two-phase system. *Plant Physiol.* **52,** 484–490.

Kao, F.-T. and Puck, T. T. (1970). Genetics of somatic mammalian cells: Linkage studies with human-chinese hamster cell hybrids. *Nature (London)* **228,** 329–332.

Kao, K. N. (1977). Chromosomal behaviour in somatic hybrids of soybean-*Nicotiana glauca. Mol. Gen. Genet.* **150,** 225–230.

Kao, K. N., and Michayluk, M. R. (1974). A method for high-frequency intergeneric fusion of plant protoplasts. *Planta* **115,** 355–367.

Kao, K. N., and Michayluk, M. R. (1975). Nutritional requirements for growth of *Vicia hajastana* cells and protoplasts at a very low population density in liquid media. *Planta* **126,** 106–110.

Kao, K. N., and Michayluk, M. R. (1980). Plant regeneration from mesophyll protoplasts of alfalfa. *Z. Pflanzenphysiol.* **96,** 135–141.

Kao, K. N., and Wetter, L. R. (1977). Advances in techniques of plant protoplast fusion and culture of heterokaryocytes. *In*"International Cell Biology 1976–1977" (B. R. Brinkley and K. R. Porter, eds.), pp. 216–224. Rockefeller Univ. Press, New York.

Kao, K. N., Keller, W. A., and Miller, R. A. (1970). Cell division of newly formed cells from protoplasts of soybean. *Exp. Cell Res.* **62,** 338–340.

Kao, K. N., Constabel, F., Michayluk, M. R., and Gamborg, O. L. (1974). Plant protoplast fusion and growth of intergeneric hybrid cells. *Planta* **120,** 215–227.

Karunaratne, S. M., and Scott, K. J. (1981). Mitotic activity in protoplast isolated from *Sorghum bicolor* leaves. *Plant Sci. Lett.* **23,** 11–16.

Keller, W. A., and Melchers, G. (1973). The effect of high pH and calcium on tobacco leaf protoplast fusion. *Z. Naturforsch.* **28,** 737–741.

Klercker, J. (1892). Eine methode zur isolierung lebender protoplasten. *Oefvers. Vetenskaps Akad. Foerh, Stockholm* **9,** 463–471.

Krumbiegel, G., and Schieder, O. (1979). Selection of somatic hybrids after fusion of protoplasts from *Datura innoxia* Mill. and *Atropa belladonna* L. *Planta* **145,** 371–375.

Krumbiegel, G., and Schieder, O. (1981). Comparison of somatic and sexual incompatibility between *Datura innoxia* and *Atropa belladonna. Planta* **153,** 466–470.

Kumar, A., Wilson, D., and Cocking, E. C. (1981). Polypeptide composition of fraction 1 protein of the somatic hybrid between *Petunia parodii* and *Petunia parviflora. Biochem. Genet.* **19,** 255–261.

Kumar, A., Cocking, E. C., Bovenberg, W. A., and Kool, A. J. (1982). Restriction endonuclease analysis of chloroplast DNA in interspecies somatic hybrids of *Petunia. Theor. Appl. Genet.* **62,** 377–383.

Kung, S. D., Gray, J. C. Wildman, S. G., and Carlson, P. S. (1975). Polypeptide composition of fraction 1 protein from parasexual hybrid plants in the genus *Nicotiana. Science* **187,** 353–355.

Kuster, E. (1909). Uber die verschmelzung nackter protoplasten. *Ber. Dtsch. Bot. Ges.* **27,** 589–598.

Kuster, E. (1910). Eine method zur gewinnung abnorm grosser protoplasten. *Arch. Entwicklungsmech. Org.* **30,** 351–355.

Larkin, P. J. (1976). Purification and viability determination of plant protoplasts. *Planta* **128,** 213–216.

Larkin, P. J., and Scowcroft, W. R. (1981). Somaclonal variation—A novel source of variability from cell cultures for plant improvement. *Theor. Appl. Genet.* **60,** 197–214.

Lázár, G. B., Dudits, D., and Sung, Z. R. (1981). Expression of cyclohexamide resistance in carrot somatic hybrids and their segregants. *Genetics* **98,** 347–356.

Lázár, G. B., Frankhauser, H., and Potrykus, I. (1983). Complementation analysis of a nitrate reductase deficient *Hyoscyamus muticus* cell line by somatic hybridisation. *Mol. Gen. Genet.* **189,** 359–364.

Littlefield, J. W. (1964). Selection of hybrids from matings of fibroblasts *in vitro* and their presumed recombinants. *Science* **145,** 709–710.

Lörz, H., Paszkowski, J., Dierks-Ventling, C., and Potrykus, I. (1981). Isolation and characterisation of cytoplasts and miniprotoplasts derived from protoplasts of cultured cells. *Physiol. Plant.* **53,** 384–391.

Lu, C., Vasil, V., and Vasil, I. K. (1981). Isolation and culture of protoplasts of *Panicum maximum* Jacq. (Guinea grass). Somatic embryogenesis and plant formation. *Z. Pflanzenphysiol.* **104,** 311–318.

Lu, D. Y., Davey, M. R., and Cocking, E. C. (1982a). Somatic embryogenesis from mesophyll protoplasts of *Trigonella corniculata*. Leguminosae. *Plant Cell Rep.* **1**, 278-280.

Lu, D. Y., Pental, D., and Cocking, E. C., (1982b). Plant regeneration from seedling cotyledon protoplasts. *Z. Pflanzenphysiol.* **107**, 59-63.

Maggio, B., Ahkong, Q. F., and Lucy, J. A. (1976). Polyethylene glycol, surface potential and cell fusion. *Biochem. J.* **158**, 647-650.

Maliga, P., Lázár, G., Joó, F., Nagy, A. H., and Menczel, L. (1977). Restoration of morphogenetic potential in *Nicotiana* by somatic hybridization. *Mol. Gen. Genet.* **157**, 291-296.

Maliga, P., Kiss, Z. R., Nagy, A. H., and Lázár, G. (1978). Genetic instability in somatic hybrids of *Nicotiana tabacum* and *Nicotiana knightiana*. *Mol. Gen. Genet.* **163**, 145-151.

Maliga, P., Nagy, F., Xuon, L. T., Kiss, Z. R., Menczel, L., and Lázár, G. (1980). Protoplast fusion to study cytoplasmic traits in *Nicotiana*. *In* "Advances in Protoplast Research" (L. Ferenczy and G. L. Farkas, eds.) pp. 341-348. Akadémiai Kiadó, Budapest.

Maliga, P., Lörz, H., Lázár, G., and Nagy, F. (1982). Cytoplast-protoplast fusion for interspecific chloroplast transfer in *Nicotiana*. *Mol. Gen. Genet.* **185**, 211-215.

Márton, L., Sidorov, V., Biasini, G., and Maliga, P. (1982). Complementation in somatic hybrids indicates four types of nitrate reductase deficient lines in *Nicotiana plumbaginifolia*. *Mol. Gen. Genet.* **187**, 1-3.

Medgyesy, P., Menczel, L., and Maliga, P. (1980). The use of cytoplasmic streptomycin resistance: Chloroplast transfer from *Nicotiana tabacum* into *Nicotiana sylvestris*, and isolation of their somatic hybrids. *Mol. Gen. Genet.* **179**, 693-698.

Meijer, E. G. M., and Steinbiss, H. H. (1983). Plantlet regeneration from suspension and protoplast cultures of the tropical pasture legume *Stylosanthes guyanensis* (Aubl.) SW. *Ann. Bot. (London)* [N. S.] **52**, 305-310.

Melamed, M. R., Mullaney, P. F., and Mendelsohn, M. L. (1979). "Flow Cytometry and Sorting." Wiley, New York.

Melchers, G. (1977). Microbial techniques in somatic hybridization by fusion of protoplasts. *In* "International Cell Biology 1976-1977" (B. R. Brinkley and K. R. Porter, eds.), pp. 207-215. Rockefeller Univ. Press, New York.

Melchers, G., and Labib, G. (1974). Somatic hybridisation of plants by fusion of protoplasts. I. Selection of light resistant hybrids of "haploid" light sensitive varieties of tobacco. *Mol. Gen. Genet.* **135**, 277-294.

Melchers, G., Sacristan, M. D., and Holder, A. A. (1978). Somatic hybrid plants of potato and tomato regenerated from fused protoplasts. *Carlsberg Res. Commun.* **43**, 203-218.

Menczel, L., Lázár, G., and Maliga, P. (1978). Isolation of somatic hybrids by cloning *Nicotiana* heterokaryons in nurse cultures. *Planta* **143**, 29-32.

Menczel, L., Nagy, F., Kiss, Z. R., and Maliga, P. (1981). Streptomycin resistant and sensitive somatic hybrids of *Nicotiana tabacum* + *Nicotiana knightiana*: Correlation of resistance to *N. tabacum* plastids. *Theor. Appl. Genet.* **59**, 191-195.

Menczel, L., Galiba, G., Nagy, F., and Maliga, P. (1982). Effect of radiation dosage on efficiency of chloroplast transfer by protoplast fusion in *Nicotiana*. *Genetics* **100**, 487-495.

Menczel, L., Nagy, F., Lázár, G., and Maliga, P. (1983). Transfer of cytoplasmic male sterility by selection for streptomycin resistance after protoplast fusion in *Nicotiana*. *Mol. Gen. Genet.* **189**, 365-369.

Meyer, Y., and Abel, W. O. (1975). Importance of the wall for cell division and in the activity of the cytoplasm in cultured tobacco protoplasts. *Planta* **123**, 33–40.

Minna, J. D., and Coon, H. G. (1974). Human × mouse hybrid cells segregating mouse chromosomes and isozymes. *Nature (London)* **252**, 401–404.

Müller, A. J., and Grafe, R. (1978). Isolation and characterization of cell lines of *Nicotiana tabacum* lacking nitrate reductase. *Mol. Gen. Genet.* **161**, 67–76.

Murashige, T., and Skoog, F. (1962). A revised medium for rapid growth and bioassays with tobacco tissue cultures. *Physiol. Plant.* **15**, 473–497.

Nagao, T. (1978). Somatic hybridisation by fusion of protoplasts. I. The combination of *Nicotiana tabacum* and *Nicotiana rustica*. *Jpn. J. Crop Sci.* **47**, 491–498.

Nagao, T. (1979). Somatic hybridisation by fusion of protoplasts. II. The combinations of *Nicotiana tabacum* and *N. glutinosa* and of *N. tabacum* and *N. alata*. *Jpn. J. Crop Sci.* **48**, 385–392.

Nagao, T. (1982). Somatic hybridisation by fusion of protoplasts. III. Somatic hybrids of sexually incompatible combinations *Nicotiana tabacum* + *Nicotiana repanda* and *Nicotiana tabacum* + *Salpiglossis sinuata*. *Jpn. J. Crop Sci.* **51**, 35–42.

Nagata, T. (1978). A novel cell fusion method of protoplasts by polyvinyl alcohol. *Naturwissenschaften* **65**, 263–264.

Nagata, T., and Melchers, G. (1978). Surface charge of protoplasts and their significance in cell-cell interaction. *Planta* **142**, 235–238.

Nagy, F., Török, I., and Maliga, P. (1981). Extensive rearrangements in the mitochondrial DNA in somatic hybrids of *Nicotiana tabacum* and *Nicotiana knightiana*. *Mol. Gen. Genet.* **183**, 437–439.

Nehls, R. (1978). The use of metabolic inhibitors for the selection of fusion products of higher plants protoplasts. *Mol. Gen. Genet.* **166**, 117–118.

Oliver, D. J., Thorne, J. H., and Poincelot, R. P. (1979). Rapid isolation of mesophyll cells from soybean leaves. *Plant Sci. Lett.* **16**, 149–155.

Otsuki, Y., and Takebe, I. (1969). Isolation of intact mesophyll cells and their protoplasts from higher plants. *Plant Cell Physiol.* **10**, 917–921.

Papahadjopoulos, D., Vail, W. J., Newton, C., Nir, S., Jacobson, K. Poste, G., and Lazo, R. (1977). Studies on membrane fusion. III. The role of calcium-induced phase changes. *Biochim. Biophys. Acta* **465**, 579–598.

Patnaik, G., Cocking, E. C., Hamill, J., and Pental, D. (1982). A simple procedure for the manual isolation and identification of plant heterokaryons. *Plant Sci. Lett.* **24**, 105–110.

Pontecorvo, G. (1971). Induction of directional chromosome elimination in somatic cell hybrids. *Nature (London)* **230**, 367–369.

Power, J. B., Cummins, S. E., and Cocking, E. C. (1970). Fusion of isolated plant protoplasts. *Nature (London)* **225**, 1016–1018.

Power, J. B., Frearson, E. M., Hayward, C., and Cocking, E. C. (1975). Some consequences of the fusion and selective culture of *Petunia* and *Parthenocissus* protoplasts. *Plant Sci. Lett.* **5**, 197–207.

Power, J. B., Frearson, E. M., Hayward, C., George, D., Evans, P. K., Berry, S. F., and Cocking, E. C. (1976). Somatic hybridization of *Petunia hybrida* and *P. parodii*. *Nature (London)* **263**, 500–502.

Power, J. B., Berry, S. F., Frearson, E. M., and Cocking, E. C. (1977). Selection procedures for the production of interspecies somatic hybrids of *Petunia hybrida* and *Petunia parodii*. I. Nutrient media and drug sensitivity complementation selection. *Plant Sci. Lett.* **10**, 1–6.

Power, J. B., Sink, K. C., Berry, S. F., Burns, S. F., and Cocking, E. C. (1978).

Somatic and sexual hybrids of *Petunia hybrida* and *Petunia parodii*. A comparison of flower colour segregation. *J. Hered.* **69,** 373-376.

Power, J. B., Berry, S. F., Chapman, J. V., Cocking, E. C., and Sink, K. C. (1979). Somatic hybrids between unilateral cross-incompatible *Petunia* species. *Theor. Appl. Genet.* **55,** 97-99.

Power, J. B., Berry, S. F., Chapman, J. V., and Cocking, E. C. (1980). Somatic hybridization of sexually incompatible *Petunias: Petunia parodii, Petunia parviflora. Theor. Appl. Genet.* **57,** 1-4.

Rao, P. N., and Johnson, R. T. (1972). Cell fusion and its application to studies on the regulation of cell cycle. *Methods Cell Physiol.* **5,** 76-126.

Raveh, D., Huberman, E., and Galun, E. (1973). *In vitro* culture of tobacco protoplasts: Use of feeder techniques to support division of cells plated at low densities. *In Vitro* **9,** 216-222.

Redenbaugh, K., Ruzin, S., Bartholomew, J., and Bassham, J. A. (1982). Characterization and separation of plant protoplasts via flow cytometry and cell sorting. *Z. Pflanzenphysiol.* **107,** 65-80.

Rennie, P. J., Weber, G., Constabel, F., and Fowke, L. C. (1980). Dedifferentiation of chloroplasts in interspecific and homospecific protoplast fusion products. *Protoplasma* **103,** 253-262.

Ringertz, N. R., and Savage, R. E. (1976). "Cell Hybrids." Academic Press, New York.

Roscoe, D. H., and Bell, G. M. (1981). Use of a pH indicator in protoplast culture medium. *Plant Sci. Lett.* **21,** 275-279.

Rossini, L. (1969). Une nouvelle méthode de culture *in vitro* de cellules parenchymateuses séparées des feuilles de *Calystegia sepium* L. *C. R. Hebd. Seances Acad. Sci.* **268,** 683-685.

Schenck, H. R., and Röbbelen, G. (1982). Somatic hybrids by fusion of protoplasts from *Brassica oleracea* and *B. campestris. Z. Pflanzenzuecht* **89,** 278-288.

Schenk, R. U., and Hildebrandt, A. C. (1971). Production, manipulation and fusion of plant cell protoplasts as steps toward somatic hybridization. *Coll. Int. C.N.R.S.* **193,** 319-331.

Schieder, O. (1974). Selektion einer somatischen hybride nach fusion von protoplasten auxotropher mutanten von *Sphaerocarpos donnellii* Aust. *Z. Pflanzenphysiol.* **74,** 357-365.

Schieder, O. (1976). The spectrum of auxotrophic mutants from the liverwort *Sphaerocarpos donnellii* Aust. *Mol. Gen. Genet.* **144,** 63-66.

Schieder, O. (1977). Hybridization experiments with protoplasts from chlorophyll-deficient mutants of some Solanaceous species. *Planta* **137,** 253-257.

Schieder, O. (1978). Somatic hybrids of *Datura innoxia* Mill. + *Datura discolor* Bernh. and of *Datura innoxia* Mill. + *Datura stramonium* L. var. tatula L. I. Selection and characterisation. *Mol. Gen. Genet.* **162,** 113-119.

Schieder, O. (1980a). Somatic hybrids between a herbaceous and two tree *Datura* species. *Z. Pflanzenphysiol.* **98,** 119-127.

Schieder, O. (1980b). Somatic hybrids of *Datura innoxia* Mill. + *Datura discolor* Bernh. and *Datura innoxia* Mill. + *Datura stramonium* L. var. tatula L. II. Analysis of progenies of three sexual generations. *Mol. Gen. Genet.* **139,** 1-4.

Schieder, O., and Vasil, I. K. (1980). Protoplast fusion and somatic hybridization. *Int. Rev. Cytol. Suppl.* **11B,** 21-46.

Schilde-Rentschler, L. (1973). Preparation of protoplasts for infection with *Agrobacterium tumefaciens. Coll. Int. C.N.R.S.* **212,** 479-483.

Schiller, B., Herrmann, R. G., and Melchers, G. (1982). Restriction endonuclease analysis of plastid DNA from tomato, potato, and some of their somatic hybrids. *Mol. Gen. Genet.* **186,** 453-459.
Schwenk, F. W. (1980). Callus formation from mechanically isolated soybean cotyledonary cells. *Plant Sci. Lett.* **17,** 437-442.
Schwenk, F. W. (1981). Callus formation from mechanically isolated mesophyll cells of soybean and sweet potato. *Plant Sci. Lett.* **23,** 147-151.
Scowcroft, W. R., and Larkin, P. J. (1981). Chloroplast DNA assorts randomly in intraspecific somatic hybrids of *Nicotiana debneyi. Theor. Appl. Genet.* **60,** 179-184.
Senda, M., Takeda, J., Abe, S., and Nakamura, T. (1979). Induction of cell fusion of plant protoplasts by electrical stimulation. *Plant Cell Physiol.* **20,** 1441-1443.
Shepard, J. F., and Totten, R. E. (1975). Isolation and regeneration of tobacco mesophyll cell protoplasts under low osmotic conditions. *Plant Physiol.* **55,** 689-694.
Shepard, J. F., Bidney, D., and Shahin, E. (1980). Potato protoplasts in crop improvement. *Science* **208,** 17-24.
Shepard, J. F., Bidney, D., Barsby, T., and Kemble, R. (1983). Genetic transfer in plants through interspecific protoplast fusion. *Science* **219,** 683-688.
Shimamoto, K., and King, P. J. (1983). Isolation of a hisitidine auxotroph of *Hyoscyamus muticus* during attempts to apply BUdR enrichment. *Mol. Gen. Genet.* **189,** 69-72.
Sidorov, V. A., and Maliga, P. (1982). Fusion-complementation analysis of auxotrophic and chlorophyll-deficient lines isolated in haploid *Nicotiana plumbaginifolia* protoplast cultures. *Mol. Gen. Genet.* **186,** 328-332.
Sidorov, V. A., Menczel, L., Nagy, F., and Maliga, P. (1981). Chloroplast transfer in *Nicotiana* based on metabolic complementation between irradiated and iodoacetate treated protoplasts. *Planta* **152,** 341-345.
Slabas, A. R., Powell, A. J., and Lloyd, C. W. (1980). An improved procedure for the isolation and purification of protoplasts from carrot suspension culture. *Planta* **147,** 283-286.
Smith, C. L., Ahkong, Q. F., Fisher, D., and Lucy, J. A. (1982). Is purified poly(ethylene glycol) able to induce cell fusion? *Biochim. Biophys. Acta* **692,** 109-114.
Smith, H. H., Kao, K. N., and Combatti, N. C. (1976). Interspecific hybridization by protoplast fusion in *Nicotiana J. Hered.* **67,** 123-128.
Steele, J. A., Uchytil, T. F., Durbin, R. D., Bhatnager, P., and Rich, D. H. (1976). Chloroplast coupling factor-1: A species specific receptor for tentoxin. *Proc. Natl. Acad. Sci. U.S.A.* **73,** 2245-2248.
Szabados, L., and Dudits, D. (1980). Fusion between interphase and mitotic plant protoplasts. Induction of premature chromosome condensation. *Exp. Cell Res.* **127,** 442-446.
Szybalski, W., Szybalska, E. H., and Ragni, G. (1962). Genetic studies with human cell lines. *Natl. Cancer Inst. Monogr.* **7,** 75-89.
Takebe, I., Otsuki, Y., and Aoki, S. (1968). Isolation of tobacco mesophyll cells in intact and active state. *Plant Cell Physiol.* **9,** 115-124.
Uchimiya, H. (1982). Somatic hybridisation between male sterile *Nicotiana tabacum* and *N. glutinosa* through protoplast fusion. *Theor. Appl. Genet.* **61,** 69-72.
Uchimiya, H., and Murashige. T. (1974). Evaluation of parameters in the isolation of viable protoplasts from cultured tobacco cells. *Plant Physiol.* **54,** 936-944.
Uchimiya. H., and Wildman, S. G. (1979). Nontranslation of foreign genetic information for fraction 1 protein under circumstances favourable for direct transfer of

Nicotiana gossei isolated chloroplasts into *N. tabacum* protoplasts. *In Vitro* **15,** 463-468.

Ueda, K., Tan, K., Sato, F., and Yamada, Y. (1978). Phagocytosis in plant protoplasts. *Cell Struct. Funct.* **3,** 25-30.

Vasil, I. K., and Vasil, V. (1980). Isolation and culture of protoplasts. *Int. Rev. Cytol., Suppl.* **11B,** 1-19.

Vasil, V., and Vasil, I. K. (1980). Isolation and culture of cereal protoplasts. 2. Embryogenesis and plantlet formation from protoplasts of *Pennisetum americanum. Theor. Appl. Genet.* **56,** 97-99.

Vasil. V., Wang, D-Y., and Vasil, I. K. (1983). Plant regeneration from protoplasts of napier grass (*Pennisetum purpureum* Schum.). *Z. Pflanzenphysiol.* **111,** 233-239.

Vatsya, B., and Bhaskaran, S. (1981). Production of subprotoplasts in *Brassica oleracea* var. *capitata*—a function of osmolarity of the media. *Plant Sci. Lett.* **23,** 277-282.

Vienken, J., Ganser, R., Hampp, R., and Zimmermann, U. (1981). Electric field-induced fusion of isolated vacuoles and protoplasts of different developmental and metabolic provenience. *Physiol. Plant* **53,** 64-70.

Vos, J., Ahkong, Q. F., Botham, G. M., Quirk, S. J., and Lucy, J. A. (1976). Changes in the distribution of intramembranous particles in hen erythrocytes during cell fusion induced by the bivalent-cation ionophore A23187. *Biochem. J.* **158,** 651-653.

Wallin, A., Glimelius, K., and Eriksson, T. (1974). The induction of aggregation and fusion of *Daucus carota* protoplasts by polyethylene glycol. *Z. Pflanzenphysiol.* **74,** 64-80.

Wallin, A., Glimelius, K., and Eriksson, T. (1978). Enucleation of plant protoplasts by cytochalasin B. *Z. Pflanzenphysiol.* **87,** 333-340.

Watts, J. W., Motoyoshi, F., and King, J. M. (1974). Problems associated with the production of stable protoplasts of cells of tobacco mesophyll. *Ann. Bot. (London)* [N. S.] **38,** 667-671.

Wetter, L. R. (1977). Isoenzyme patterns in soybean-*Nicotiana* somatic hybrid cell lines. *Mol. Gen. Genet.* **150,** 231-235.

Wetter, L. R., and Kao, K. N. (1980). Chromosome and isoenzyme studies on cells derived from protoplast fusion *Nicotiana glauca* with *Glycine max-Nicotiana glauca* cell hybrids. *Theor. Appl. Genet.* **57,** 272-276.

White, D. W. R., and Vasil, I. K. (1979). Use of amino acid analogue-resistant cell lines for selection of *Nicotiana sylvestris* somatic cell hybrids. *Theor. Appl. Genet.* **55,** 107-112.

Widholm, J. M. (1977). Selection and characterisation of biochemical mutants. *In* "Plant Tissue Culture and its Bio-technical Application" (W. Barz, E. Reinard, and M. H. Zenk, eds.), pp. 112-122. Springer-Verlag, Berlin and New York.

Wise, G. E., and Prescott, D. M. (1973). Ultrastructure of enucleated mammalian cells in culture. *Exp. Cell Res.* **81,** 63-72.

Withers, L. A., and Cocking, E. C. (1972). Fine-structural studies on spontaneous and induced fusion of higher plant protoplasts. *J. Cell Sci.* **11,** 59-75.

Wullems, G. J., Molendijk, L., and Schilperoot, R. A. (1980). The expression of tumour markers in intraspecific somatic hybrids of normal and crown gall cells from *Nicotiana tabacum. Theor. Appl. Genet.* **56,** 203-208.

Xu, Z. -H., Davey, M. R., and Cocking, E. C. (1982). Organogensis from root protoplasts of the forage legumes *Medicago sativa* and *Trigonella foenum-graecum. Z. Pflanzenphysiol.* **107,** 231-235.

Yurina, N. P., Odintsova, M. S., and Maliga, P. (1978). An altered chloroplast ribosomal protein in a streptomycin resistant tobacco mutant. *Theor. Appl. Genet.* **52,** 125–128.

Zelcer, A., Aviv, D., and Galun, E. (1978). Interspecific transfer of cytoplasmic male sterility by fusion between protoplasts of normal *Nicotiana sylvestris* and X-ray irradiated protoplasts of male sterile. *N. tabacum. Z. Pflanzenphysiol.* **90,** 397–407.

Zenkteler, M., and Melchers, G. (1978). *In vitro* hybridization by sexual methods and by fusion of somatic protoplasts. *Theor. Appl. Genet.* **52,** 81–90.

Zimmermann, U., and Scheurich, P. (1981). High frequency fusion of plant protoplasts by electric fields. *Planta* **151,** 26–32.

Incompatibility in Angiosperms: Significance in Crop Improvement*

D. C. SASTRI

ICRISAT Centre, Patancheru, Andhra Pradesh, India

I. INTRODUCTION

There is a continuous need for modifying crop plants to suit changing human needs in existing environments and to fit the crops into new environments. Most often such modifications are achieved by hybridization. The objective for modification, such as alteration of a character or introduction of a new character into a cultivar, dictates the choice of parents in any breeding program. Most often the parents are close to each other taxonomically and usually belong to the same species. However, there are instances when the parents are only distantly related and may also be reproductively isolated. Such situations are growing in number, for desired characters are not (and need not be) always available in closely related taxa. In such cases the choice of parents may be limited and is governed primarily by the availability of character(s) in a taxon; but the taxon in which the character is avail-

*Submitted as Journal Article No. 273 by the International Crops Research Institute for the Semi-Arid Tropics (ICRISAT).

ISBN 0-12-040910-0

able may be distantly related, and the hybrid may not be produced at all, and even if produced it may not be viable or fertile.

In this article an account of the problems usually encountered in such situations and the methods to circumvent them are discussed. Incompatibility in angiosperms has been known for about 200 years. The very existence of these barriers between taxa has been used as a criterion for taxonomic delimitations, but has been the cause of frustration to plant breeders interested in transfer of character(s) from one taxon to another, as well as to evolutionary biologists interested in the phylogeny of a group of taxa. The solution to this problem has often come from geneticists, physiologists, and cytologists who have repeatedly attacked this problem. Commendable progress has been made, as is evident by two full-length discussions on the subject by the Royal Society, London—"Incompatibility in Angiosperms" in 1975 and "Manipulations of Genetic Systems in Plants" (Rees *et al.*, 1981)—in addition to a 300-page monograph by Professor de Nettancourt (1977) and a large number of research and review papers on the topic.

II. Incompatibility

Incompatibility is defined as the inability of the functional male and female gametes to fuse with each other to form a viable zygote and a hybrid (Arasu, 1968). Incompatibility is used here to refer to failure of seed set after either self- or cross-pollinations. Temporal and/or geographic separation (or isolation) of two taxa to be hybridized sometimes occur, but incompatibility should not be assumed in these cases. Such problems have been solved by low-temperature storage of pollen until required or by transporting pollen to overcome geographical separation. There are instances when certain genetic changes may lead to incompatibility between two taxa. Incompatibility between taxa, referred to as interspecific incompatibility (or cross-incompatibility) in the literature, prevents promiscuous hybridization, whereas incompatibility within a taxon, referred to as intraspecific (or self-) incompatibility, is an evolutionary strategy to promote outcrossing.

For convenience, therefore, incompatibility can be discussed under two broad titles: intraspecific and interspecific. In the context of crop improvement, however, incompatibility between taxa is of greater concern as it prevents the desired transfer of genes. But investigations on several aspects of self-incompatibility, and some on interspecific incompatibility, have revealed that inhibition of pollen germination and pollen tube growth are similar in both. There may also be a common genetic control; for instance, in *Nicotiana*, Pandey (1976) observed that alleles governing self-incompatibility are effective in interspecific incompatibility also.

A. SELF-INCOMPATIBILITY (INTRASPECIFIC)

About half of the flowering plant species investigated so far have been found to be self-incompatible (de Nettancourt, 1977). Self-incompatibility is the rejection by a plant of its own pollen, or pollen from the same genotype, before or after it has germinated on the stigma, but mostly before fertilization. It is believed to be the result of an interaction between the male gametophyte (pollen grain) and the sporophytic tissue of the pistil. Geneticists have recognized taxa with either a sporophytic or a gametophytic type of self-incompatibility depending on whether self-incompatibility is controlled by the genotype of the sporophyte (pollen parent) or that of the gametophyte (pollen grain), respectively, Brewbaker (1957, 1967) found that in taxa with the sporophytic type of self-incompatibility, the pollen grain is usually three celled at anthesis and is inhibited on the stigma, whereas in taxa with gametophytic self-incompatibility, pollen grains are two celled at anthesis and it is the pollen tubes that are inhibited in the style. This seems to be the general trend, but there are a few exceptions (Brewbaker, 1967).

During the last two decades there has been a great interest in structural and functional aspects of the incompatibility reaction. In spite of concerted efforts by physiologists and biochemists, a precise interactive model is still to be defined.

1. *Sporophytic self-incompatibility*

Brassica campestris, Brassica oleracea, Raphanus sativus, Eruca sativa, Iberis amara (Brassicaceae), *Cosmos bipinnatus, Helianthus annuus* (Asteraceae), and *Ipomoea* spp. (Convolvulaceae) are well-known examples of the sporophytic system of self-incompatibility, and in these cases incompatible pollen is invariably inhibited on the stigma. A phenomenon correlated with this is the characteristic synthesis and accumulation of callose in the form of lenticular deposits in the stigma cells in direct contact with the pollen grain (Dickinson and Lewis, 1973; Heslop-Harrison and Heslop-Harrison, 1975), and this has been suggested as a bioassay. This phenomenon is strongly suggestive of the fact that the pollen and the pistil do communicate with each other. Cytochemical investigations have revealed that there are certain proteinaceous substances on the surface of the pollen grains (Heslop-Harrison *et al.*, 1973, 1974; Dickinson and Lewis, 1973; Howlett *et al.*, 1975) as well as on stigma cells (Mattsson *et al.*, 1974; Heslop-Harrison *et al.*, 1975; Knox *et al.,* 1976; Heslop-Harrison and Shivanna, 1977; Heslop-Harrison, 1981). The pollen wall proteins are labile and diffuse within minutes on the moist substratum of the stigma or on agar gel (Heslop-Harrison *et al.,* 1974). These diffusates from incompatible pollen are potentially capable of inducing callose synthesis in the stigma papillae (Dickinson and Lewis, 1973; Heslop-Harrison *et al.,* 1973, 1974). On the other hand, incubation of the stigma in a protein-digesting enzyme (Heslop-Harrison and Heslop-Harrison, 1975; Heslop-Harrison and Shivanna, 1977) or coating the stigma with concanavalin (a lectin) (Heslop-Harrison, 1976; Knox *et al.,* 1976) has been found to disturb the behavior of even compatible pollen grains, i.e., preventing the entry of pollen tubes into the stigmatic tissue. Serological and electrophoretic investigations on *B. oleracea* stigma proteins have led to the identification of the self-incompatibility allele (*S* allele) specific proteins (Nasrallah and Wallace, 1967; Nasrallah *et al.,* 1970; Sedgley, 1974; Nishio and Hinata, 1977, 1978, 1980). The most likely source of these proteins is the stigma surface, as shown for *Brassica* (Heslop-Harrison *et al.,* 1975). Furthermore, it has also been reported that *Brassica* stigmas have a factor that inhibits self-incompatible pollen *in vitro* (Ferrari and Wallace, 1975, 1976).

The nature of the pollen grain in contact with the stigma papillae determines the direction of the events leading to either pollen acceptance or rejection. The first event, viz., adhesion of self-incompatible pollen, is slower than that of the compatible pollen grains in *B. oleracea* (Roggen, 1975; Stead *et al.,* 1979; Roberts *et al.,* 1980). This is followed by the diffusion of the pollen wall proteins onto the stigma accompanied by imbibition by the pollen grains of moisture from stigma. Stead *et al.* (1979, 1980) and Roberts *et al.* (1980) have proposed that hydration of compatible pollen is different from that of incompatible pollen. They have also suggested that there is a protein fraction responsible for pollen grain adhesion, and Ferrari *et al.* (1981a) have shown that a hydrophilic stigmatic factor is involved in pollen hydration. The next discernible change is the germination of the pollen grain and the growth of the pollen tubes, which are different in compatible and incompatible pollinations (see reviews by Heslop-Harrison, 1975a,b, 1978a,b).

2. *Gametophytic self-incompatibility*

In taxa with gametophytic self-incompatibility, the genotype of the pollen (gametophyte) is responsible for the incompatibility (see de Nettancourt, 1977). The first observation of this kind of incompatibility was in *Nicotiana* (East and Mangelsdorf, 1925). Subsequently, other taxa, such as *Petunia hybrida, Lilium longiflorum, Trifolium pratense,* and *Oenothera organensis,* have also been found to have gametophytic self-incompatibility. In these taxa the site of inhibition is usually the style, and the stigma is usually covered with a copious exudate at the time when pollination normally takes place; these are thus referred to as wet-type stigmas. Lipids, sugars, phenols, proteins, and water have been identified in the stigmatic exudate of some taxa, and a role has been proposed for each of these components in stigma receptivity and pollen germination. In comparing the self-incompatible taxa having dry-type stigmas, proteins in the stigmatic exudate of the taxa with wet stigmas have not been attributed with specific roles in pollen recognition and pollen germination. But proteins on the stigma surface have been identified; these are extracellular and are present on the stigma papillae during early stages of development. The fact that the inhibition of incompatible pollen tubes in these taxa is in the style led East (1934) to suggest that the inhibition is in some way analogous to the antigen–antibody reaction found in animals. This assumption has prompted several investigators to propose hypotheses on incompatibility assuming that proteins are indeed the interacting molecules involved in rejection or acceptance of the pollen tubes (see discussion in Ferrari and Wallace, 1977; de Nettancourt, 1977; Heslop-Harrison, 1978a,b; Ferrari *et al.,* 1981b). Whatever the mechanism, it has been amply clarified that pollination triggers a reaction characteristic of the nature of the pollination. This is evident from structural, ultrastructural, physiological, and biochemical comparisons of the compatibly and incompatibly pollinated pistils.

In *P. hybrida* no apparent distinctions have been found between the behavior of the compatible and incompatible pollen grains on the stigma, or even of the pollen tubes within it. The differences are apparent only when the pollen tubes have come in contact with the stylar tissue (Sastri and Shivanna, 1980a; Shivanna and Sastri, 1981; Herrero and Dickinson, 1980b). In incompatible pollinations there may be a reduction in the number of pollen tubes deeper in the styles, slower rates of growth of incompatible pollen tubes and heavy callose deposits along the pollen tube lengths, and abnormalities at the tube tips such as swelling, bursting, or branching of the pollen tubes. Incompatible pollen tube walls are much thicker than those of compatible pollen tubes (vander Pluijm and Linskens, 1966). Differences have been found in the pistil also. In *P. hybrida,* for instance, Herrero and Dickinson (1979) observed that in a compatibly pollinated pistil, starch and lipid reserves are mobilized in the style faster than after incompatible pollination. In the incompatibly pollinated pistil of *Lycopersicon peruvianum,* it was found that self-incompatible pollen tube tips revealed a concentric organization of the rough endoplasmic reticulum (de Nettancourt *et al.,*

1973a,b, 1974; Cresti *et al.*, 1980), which is inhibitory for protein synthesis. A similar observation was also made in *P. hybrida* (Cresti *et al.*, 1979).

van der Donk (1974a,b, 1975) reported differences in protein and RNA synthesis in compatibly and incompatibly pollinated pistils. In *Nicotiana alata* there are differences in peroxidase patterns corresponding to the kind of pollination (Bredemeijer, 1974). Around 18 hr after self-pollination in *P. hybrida,* floral metabolites flow away from the flowers, whereas in compatible pollination the ovary continues to be the major sink (Linskens, 1975). Deurenberg (1976, 1977) observed that ovaries of crossed and selfed flowers revealed differences in proteins 12 hr after pollination.

B. INTERSPECIFIC INCOMPATIBILITY

During speciation and evolution, populations differentiate to such an extent that morphologically, physiologically, and/or genetically each one becomes a distinct entity warranting a unique taxonomic status. Reproductive isolation at some stage prevents gene flow among them, and the taxa are then described as incompatible with each other. Interspecific incompatibility has not been studied as extensively as intraspecific incompatibility. However, it is known that there is some similarity between the two kinds of incompatibility. Pollen tube growth may be inhibited in the style, as can be seen in a self-pollinated pistil of a taxon with the gametophytic type of self-incompatibility. In addition to the types of pollen inhibition met within self-incompatible systems, the incompatible taxa may reveal other phenomena. In spite of a normal pollen germination and pollen tube growth, fertilization between the two gametes may not occur; in the event of a normal fertilization the resulting hybrid zygote may collapse any time before it develops into an embryo or a seedling. Such a phenomenon may be due to lethality [e.g., *Gossypium davidsonii* when used as a parent in crosses with most *Gossypium* taxa (Lee, 1981)], genic disharmony, inefficient endosperm as in several cases, or the failure of the embryo. In a few cases the hybrid seeds and seedlings are formed, which then develop into plants, but these are sterile due to meiotic irregularities, do not produce gametes, and so do not form fruits and seeds.

Sometimes species can be crossed in one direction only and not in the reciprocal direction. Such observations have led to the concept of "unilateral incompatibility" as suggested by Harrison and Darby (1955). In such instances it is often found that the pistil of a self-compatible plant did not have any inhibitory effect on the pollen of the self-incompatible plant; the reciprocal cross, however, was not a successful one. Investigations on interspecific crosses in *Nicotiana* by Anderson and de Winton (1931), followed up by Pandey (1964, 1976), revealed that incompatibility in such cases was governed by a gene that also effected the self-incompatibility of the female parent. Martin (1968) concluded that unilateral incompatibility and self-incompatibility are under the same genetic control.

There is now another school of thought that considers interspecific incompatibility as a separate function with no interference by the factors controlling self-incompatibility. Hogenboom (1973), based on crosses between *L. peruvianum* × *Lycopersicon esculentum*, suggested that the inhibition of *L. esculentum* pollen tubes in *L. peruvianum* pistils was governed by loci different from those governing self-incompatibility. From the same crosses de Nettancourt *et al.* (1974) arrived at a different inference—that loci inhibiting pollen tube growth in this cross are either closely linked to or are allelic to the *S* locus.

Interspecific incompatibility is believed to be controlled by one gene or a group of genes and is often accompanied by zygotic and postzygotic inviability. Therefore, based on time and site of incompatibility, one or more of the following methods have to be critically selected for creation of new hybrids, as has been done in several cases in the past. It has to be emphasized that the determination of the cause of incompatibility is an essential prerequisite for deciding upon or developing a method for combining the two parental genomes. Some of these methods are indicated in Tables I–IV for some well-known crosses attempted in the past.

III. Circumvention of Barriers

A. The Early Methods

The early realization that the stigma or the style acted as the barrier to foreign pollen prompted certain surgical methods. These surgical methods evolved from the observation by Jost (1907) that transversely cut styles of two species, when placed end to end in the form of a graft, did permit the growth of pollen tubes. With refinements, this method was successfully applied to crosses that involved heterostylous parents. It is believed that pollen grains of long-styled plants have potentiality for longer growth (Rangaswamy, 1963). For example, pollen grains of *Nicotiana paniculata* (whose styles are 2–3 mm long) are not successful when dusted on the styles (~10 mm) of *Nicotiana rustica*, whereas the reciprocal cross was successful (see Rangaswamy, 1963). Such incompatibility was overcome by grafting by Gardella (1950) in *Datura* and by Davies (1957) in *Lathyrus*. Elegant grafting experiments by Hecht (1960, 1964), in *O. organensis* revealed that self-incompatibility in this taxon could be overcome by grafting a stigmatic part (compatible with pollen grains) onto a stylar part (incompatibile with pollen grains). Fortunately, the flowers and pistils in *Oenothera* are large enough for such manipulations to be feasible. Similar experiments by Straub in *Petunia violacea* indicated that in a graft of compatible–incompatible stylar tissues, length of the compatible partner determined the extent of pollen tube growth in the incompatible partner (Straub, 1946, 1947).

These methods achieved a little more refinement in the experiments of Swaminathan (1955), who recommended the substitution of the natural stigma (causing incompatibility) with an agar–sucrose–gelatin medium on the cut end of the pistil. Swaminathan and Murty (1957) succeeded in making crosses in otherwise incompatible combinations in *Nicotiana* and *Solanum*. It was later realized that surgical operations are not always necessary; in *Brassica* and *Petunia* the stigma alone, or with some style, can be simply removed and self-pollen dusted on the cut ends to obtain fruits and seeds (see Maheswari, 1950; Frankel and Galun, 1977). In fact, in *B. oleracea* injury of the stigma by a steel wire brush is enough to break self-incompatibility (Roggen and van Dijk, 1972).

B. BUD POLLINATION

The idea of bud pollination probably arose from the realization that stigmatic secretion in mature flowers of some plants is inhibitory to self-pollen. The fact that in some taxa the mature stigmas are secretory and that the younger ones are not possibly prompted investigations on receptivity of immature pistils to incompatible pollen grains. One of the earliest of these was that of Yasuda (1934), who overcame self-incompatibility in *P. violacea* by self-pollinating the buds; Attia (1950) also succeeded in this way with *B. oleracea*. Linskens (1964) repeated the experiments of Yasuda with *P. hybrida* and found that the inhibition of incompatible pollen tubes was directly proportional to the age of the bud. Similar results were obtained when buds of *Petunia axillaris* were incompatibly pollinated (Shivanna and Rangaswamy, 1969). It was also found that smearing the stigmas of buds with stigmatic exudate from compatible mature flowers increased the success of bud self-pollination (Shivanna and Rangaswamy, 1969). In all these studies and in those on *Nicotiana alata* (Pandey, 1963; Bredemeijer, 1976) it must be noted that the developmental stage of the pistil is critical for optimum results. Pandey (1963) found that in *N. alata*, only buds at half the length of the mature flower responded to self-incompatible pollination; younger or older buds failed to do so. In the same species, Bredemeijer (1976) investigated pollen tube growth and pollen tube length in different stages of the pistils and found that in 3.5- to 5.5-cm-long buds the growth and length of compatible and incompatible pollen tubes were comparable. It was only in the later stages of development that the pistil was able to discriminate between the two kinds of pollen tubes. The results were similar when pollinated buds were analyzed for seed number per fruit (Bredemeijer, 1976). Investigations on *R. sativus*, *Cheiranthus cheiri*, and *Brassica* spp. led to similar observations (Haruta, 1966; Shivanna *et al.*, 1978; Shivanna and Sastri, 1981).

There have been some attempts to explain these results. Bredemeijer (1976) attributed the success of bud pollination in *N. alata* to the absence of a peroxidase isoenzyme (number 10) in the self-pollinated buds; this particular isoenzyme has been observed in self-pollinated mature flowers, suggesting that it is involved in the rejection of the incompatible pollen tubes (see also Bredemeijer and Blaas, 1975). It was suggested earlier that substances causing incompatibility are either absent or are not effective in immature pistils (Linskens, 1964). Nasrallah found that in immature stigmas of *Brassica oleracea,* proteins responsible for incompatibility either were absent or were present in very low concentrations (Nasrallah, 1974; Nasrallah and Wallace, 1967). The absence from buds of *S*-gene specific antigens being responsible for the success of bud pollination was also supported by studies of Shivanna *et al.* (1978) from their studies on *Raphanus* and *Cheiranthus*. Fractionation of stigmatic extracts by isoelectric focusing also revealed that there are indeed some fractions present in the mature stigmas that are absent from the buds of *B. oleracea* and *B. campestris* (Nishio and Hinata, 1977; Hinata and Nishio, 1978; Roberts *et al.*, 1979). Such differences were also apparent in *P. hybrida* (Sastri and Shivanna, 1980a; Herrero and Dickinson, 1980a; Sastri, 1981). Sastri and Shivanna (1980a) found that the pistils of buds showed some protein bands that were absent in the mature pistils.

Most of these studies have been on taxa that respond to bud pollination, and in all instances only self-incompatibility has been overcome. A question that emerges is whether bud pollination can also be extended to interspecific crosses. At the moment it is difficult to answer this because receptivity of buds in several taxa has yet to be investigated. In some taxa it is known that buds are incapable of accepting even compatible pollen, for example, *Sinapis alba* (Shivanna *et al.*, 1978), *L. longiflorum* (Ascher and Peloquin, 1966a), *Crinum defixum, Amaryllis vittata* (Shivanna and Sastri, 1981), *Saccharum bengalense* (Sastri and Shivanna, 1979), and *Arachis hypogaea* (D. C. Sastri, unpublished). In these and other taxa in which buds are not receptive or are poorly receptive, it has to be seen whether smearing the bud stigma with a medium such as exudate from mature stigmas (Shivanna and Rangaswamy, 1969), another extract (Frimmel, 1956), or a synthetic medium that is known to stimulate pollen germination can be of any help. However, Knott and Dvorak (1976) have suggested the possibility of using bud pollination in interspecific incompatible pollination.

C. APPLICATION OF PLANT GROWTH REGULATORS

It is a well-recognized and accepted fact that, like other morphogenetic phenomena, the postfertilization changes leading to fruit formation are also under the influence of plant growth regulators, either in a sequence, independently, or in combination (Nitsch, 1952). Elucidation of hormonal regulation of fruit and seed development has been largely an academic interest. Also, the knowledge of these aspects is limited to such a small number of taxa that it is impossible to conceive a widely applicable hypothesis. Diversity in fruits is too great to warrant a general concept on hormonal regulation of fruit and seed development. However, a careful investigation of the postpollination events does reveal that these are under hormonal control. For example, Gilissen (1976) suggested that in *P. hybrida* differences in the floral wilting rates between compatible and incompatible pollinations are due to the style, which causes pollination-specific changes in the hormone metabolism. Sastri and Shivanna (1978) further showed that such changes in *Petunia* can be reversed by altering the kind of pollination. Self-incompatibly pollinated pistils of *P. hybrida*, when pollinated compatibly up to a certain time, can form pods and seeds (Sastri and Shivanna, 1978). Incidentally, Hall and Forsyth (1967) observed that among all the floral parts, the stigma and style released the greatest amount of ethylene, a gaseous hormone closely linked with wilting and ripening processes of flowers and fruits. It is also known that the changes in the flower due to incompatible pollinations are similar to those of senescence and abscission. In fact, in some of the early attempts, hormones were used to prolong the life of the flower, thereby effecting fertilization and preventing the floral abscission (see Rangaswamy, 1963). It is therefore necessary to find which hormones promote fruit development in compatibly pollinated flowers, how they operate, and whether they can promote fruit formation in incompatibly pollinated flowers.

In spite of the lack of specific information on these aspects, there are successful reports on the use of this group of chemicals in overcoming both intraspecific and interspecific incompatiblity in angiosperms. The major postpollination phenomena affected by hormones are discussed below.

1. *Pollen germination and pollen tube growth*

Recognition of requirements for pollen germination and pollen tube growth, such as humidity, a sugar, and other factors (see Johri and Vasil, 1961), resulted in the formulation of a medium suitable for a large number of taxa (Brewbaker and Kwack, 1963). This stimulated a number of workers to use pollen as a model system for various purposes, including the study of the effect of growth hormones. This aspect has been exhaustively covered by Stanley and Linskens (1974), Johri *et al.* (1977), and Shivanna *et al.* (1979). All these investigations conclude that hormones stimulate *in vitro* pollen germination and pollen tube growth in much the same way as they do for other processes of growth and development.

In contrast to the large volume of information on the behavior of pollen *in vitro*, there is very little on the effect of hormones on pollen germination and pollen tube growth in the pistil, though the latter information is definitely of greater application than the former. In one investigation, indoleacetic acid (IAA) was injected into the hollow styles of *L. longiflorum*, a taxon with gametophytic self-incompatibility, and these pistils were pollinated with compatible or incompatible pollen. By doing so, Henny and Ascher (1973) found that while incompatible pollen tubes were not affected, the compatible pollen tubes were inhibited in the styles. The inference was that compatible and incompatible pollen tubes differed from each other in their sensitivities to the injected IAA. It is noteworthy that compatible pollen tube inhibition occurred at a concentration (1000 ppm) that is indeed inhibitory for any other physiological process.

Kendall (1968) saw no positive effect of gibberellin on compatible and incompatible matings of *T. pratense.* Flook and Williams (1978) observed increased pollen tube growth in apple after spraying a mixture of gibberellic acid, 1,3-diphenylurea, and 1-naphthaleneacetic acid (NAA) onto self-pollinated flowers. Self-incompatibility in *L. longiflorum* was overcome by naphthalene acetamide and potassium gibberellate (Emsweller and Stuart, 1948; Emsweller *et al.*, 1960; Emsweller and Uhring, 1965) and cytokinin (Matsubara, 1973, 1978).

2. *Hormones and interspecific incompatibility*

Achievement of pear × apple hybridization due to hormone application marked the first step (Crane and Marks, 1952; Brock, 1954) and stimulated a series of other investigations, many successful but some unsuccessful. β-Naphthoxyacetic acid applied to the stigma promoted successful germination of incompatible pollen in interspecific crosses in *Trifolium* (Evans and Denward, 1955). Dionne (1958) applied a drop of (2,4-dichlorophenoxy)acetic acid (3–6 ppm) to ovaries 24 hr after interspecific pollination in *Solanum* and obtained normal fruits and seeds. Incompatibility between *Phaseolus vulgaris* and *Phaseolus acutifolius* was overcome by applying a mixture of naphthalene acetamide and potassium gibberellate (Al Yasiri and Coyne, 1964). *Nicotiana repanda* was crossed with *Nicotiana tabacum* by applying a lanolin paste of IAA (Pittagelli and Stavely, 1975). Hybrid in the cross *Corchorus capsularis* × *Corchorus olitorius* was not obtained until 300 ppm of IAA was applied to the pedicels of flowers (Islam, 1964).

Hormone application was also used successfully for certain intergeneric crosses. By an application of 2,4-dimethylamine followed by an application of gibberellin, Kruse (1974) demonstrated that *Hordeum* species could be crossed with species of *Avena, Phleum, Dactylis, Alopecurus, Triticum, Lolium,* and *Festuca*. Bajaj *et al.* (1980) obtained culturable embryos in the cross *Hordeum vulgare* × *Secale cereale* by bathing pollinated spikes in a solution of a mixture of gibberellin (25 ppm) and kinetin (0.5 ppm) solution. Larter and Enns (1960) had found that gibberellic acid promoted better development of hybrid barley embryos *in vivo*. It was also found that a combination of gibberellic acid (25 ppm) and IAA (1 ppm) promoted pollen tube growth and ovary development in barley (4*x*) × rye (2*x*) crosses (Larter and Chaubey, 1965). Successful use of gibberellic acid (75 ppm) in an *H. vulgare* × *Hordeum bulbosum* cross (Subrahmanyam and Kasha, 1971) was demonstrated in a range of interspecific crosses in *Hordeum* (Subrahmanyam, 1979). Pickering (1979, 1980), however, was not successful in getting hybrids in an *H. vulgare* × *H. bulbosum* cross. Postpollination treatments of gibberellic acid (75 ppm) gave successful results in *Agropyron junceum* × *Triticum aestivum* (Alonso and Kimber, 1980), barley × wheat (Fedak, 1978; Islam *et al.*, 1976), *T. aestivum* × *Elymus giganteus* (Mujeeb-Kazi and Rodriguez, 1980), and *H. vulgare* × *T. aestivum* (Mujeeb-Kazi, 1981). Mujeeb-Kazi and Rodriguez (1982) consider that in addition to a postpollination treatment, a prepollination application of 2,4-dimethylamine as given by Kruse (1974) could help in obtaining seeds from backcrosses in *H. vulgare* × *Elymus can-*

adensis hybrids. The author's recent experience has shown that hormones, particularly gibberellin and kinetin, can be used in intersectional incompatible crosses in the genus *Arachis* (Singh *et al.*, 1980; Sastri and Moss, 1982; Sastri *et al.*, 1981, 1982). These studies, along with others (Table I), therefore indicate that hormones have

TABLE I. Use of hormones for hybridization in incompatible crosses

Cross	Hormone used	References
Agropyron × *Triticum aestivum*	Gibberellic acid	Alonso and Kimber (1980)
Arachis hypogaea × *Arachis* sp. P.I. No. 276233		Sastri and Moss (1982); Sastri *et al.* (1981)
A. hypogaea × *Arachis glabrata*	Gibberellic acid, kinetin, 1-naphthylacetic acid, indoleacetic acid, 1-naphthylacetic acid	Singh *et al.* (1980)
A. hypogaea × *Arachis pusilla*		Sastri *et al.* (1982)
A. hypogaea × *Arachis* sp. Coll. No. 9649		
Arachis monticola × *Arachis* sp. P.I. No. 276233		
Corchorus olitorius × *Corchorus capsularis*	Indoleacetic acid	Islam (1964)
Hibiscus cannabinus × *Hibiscus sabdariffa*	Indoleacetic acid	Kuwada and Mabuchi (1976)
Hordeum × *Alopecurus, Hordeum* × *Avena, Hordeum* × *Dactylis, Hordeum* × *Festuca, Hordeum* × *Lolium, Hordeum* × *Phleum*	2,4-Dimethylamine	Kruse (1974)
Hordeum × *Triticum*	Gibberellic acid	Larter and Chaubey (1965)
Hordeum vulgare × *Secale cereale*	Gibberellic acid + kinetin	Bajaj *et al.* (1980)
H. vulgare × *T. aestivum*	Gibberellic acid	Fedak (1978); Islam *et al.* (1975)
Nicotiana repanda × *Nicotiana tabacum*	Indoleacetic acid	Pittagelli and Stavely (1975)
Phaseolus vulgaris × *Phaseolus acutifolius*	Naphthalene acetamide + potassium gibberellate	Al Yasiri and Coyne (1964)
Pyrus × *Malus*		Brock (1954); Crane and Marks (1952)
Solanum (interspecific)	(2,4-Dichlorophenoxy)-acetic acid	Dionne (1958)
Trifolium (interspecific)	β-Naphthoxyacetic acid	Evans and Denward (1955)

profitably been used in some interspecific and intergeneric incompatible crosses. It is not yet clear as to what is the precise role of the hormone used in such investigations. There are suggestions that in instances of retarded pollen tube growth and prefertilization abscission of the flower, hormones maintain the flower until the pollen tubes have grown long enough to discharge the male gametes in the vicinity of the female gametes; it is also suggested that hormones may stimulate the incompatible pollen tube growth in the pistils so that fertilization can take place before the flower has abscissed, but the hybrid zygote obtained this way may not develop any further or may not develop fully. In such cases embryos from immature fruits have to be excised and cultured for raising hybrid plants. Islam (1964) had to combine hormone treatment with embryo culture for interspecific hybridization in *Corchorus*. Similarly, Bajaj *et al.* (1980) had to culture embryos from a few developing ovaries on *Hordeum* spikes after they were pollinated with *Secale* and treated with hormones. Napier and Walton (1981) sprayed the spikes of *Agropyron* species with an aqueous solution of gibberellic acid (50 ppm), naphthaleneacetic acid (50 ppm), and 6-(γ,γ-dimethylallyamino)purine on alternate days until harvest and obtained less than 10% fruits from 15 interspecific crosses, and embryos from them had to be cultured to obtain the hybrid plants. In some interspecific incompatible crosses in *Arachis,* hormone treatments stimulate normal postpollination changes but only to a certain extent and not to maturity; in fact, ovules develop very slowly and from them embryos have to be cultured to obtain hybrid plants (Sastri *et al.*, 1981, 1982; Sastri and Moss, 1982).

Different methods of hormone application were used. A hormone may be applied as a spray (as an aqueous solution, with or without a wetting agent), injected, or applied in lanolin, or a solution may be applied to cotton wrapped around the ovary. More than one application may be necessary. Islam (1964) observed for *Corchorus* crosses that lanolin application was better than wrapping the pedicel with a cotton piece soaked in a hormone solution. In contrast to this Bajaj *et al.* (1980) found that wrapping spikes of *Hordeum* with hormone-wetted cotton led to fungal infection and therefore was inferior to the method of bathing the spikes in hormone solution.

Obviously, fruit and seed morphogenesis is a complex process and is under a complex regulation, and it is still too early to attribute precise roles to hormones in such a process. However, there has recently been great interest in the role of hormones in fruit development. It has long been known that certain hormones are produced in developing fruits and seeds of many species and that seeds are the major sources of these hormones (Nitsch, 1952). Cytokinins, for example (Burrows and Carr, 1970; Smith and van Staden, 1979), are suggested to stimulate both the cell division and the assimilate demand in growing embyronic tissues. In developing *Lupinus albus* seeds, the endosperm is rich in cytokinin, and this led Davey and van Staden (1979) to suggest that the embryo depends upon this cytokinin for its growth. Bennici and Cionini (1979) also suggested that there was a cytokinin requirement by young embryos of *Phaseolus coccineus*. It has also been shown that in interspecific crosses in *Phaseolus,* endosperm does not develop normally and has much lower levels of cytokinins than does endosperm from self-pollinations (Nessling and Morris, 1979). Cytokinin levels seem to be critical for a normal embryo development. However, whether an exogenous supply of cytokinin in this cross can prevent the embryo degeneration and promote its growth is a matter still to be investigated.

D. TEMPERATURE AND INCOMPATIBILITY

Temperature is known to be an important factor in induction of flowering in a large number of taxa (Wareing and Phillips, 1978), but relatively little is known about its role in floral changes leading to fruit formation. High temperatures are known to reduce pollen viability (see Shivanna *et al.,* 1979; Stanley and Linskens, 1974; Johri and Vasil, 1961; Johri *et al.,* 1977), and low temperatures have been known to prolong the life of pollen grains. High or low temperatures also cause poor pollen germination and poor pollen tube growth (Savitri *et al.,* 1980; Kuo *et al.,* 1981).

In the context of incompatibility, and self-incompatibility in particular, there have been some reports in which excised flowers were pollinated and incubated at different temperatures for investigations of pollen behavior. Later, intact flowers on the plants were also subjected to temperature effects. Although there is a lack of knowledge of the mechanisms of the effect of temperature either on the pollen or on the pistil, high temperatures have been shown in a few instances to weaken or break down self-incompatibility, particularly gametophytic self-incompatibility.

In *O. organensis* and *Prunus avium,* self-incompatible tubes grew well at 15°C, but were inhibited above this temperature (Lewis, 1942). In *Oenothera rhombipetala,* however, incompatible pollen tubes were not affected by the range of temperatures investigated (10–39°C), but compatible tubes grew faster at higher temperatures (Bali and Hecht, 1965).

Oenothera organensis pistils pretreated with hot water at 50°C for 5 min failed to discriminate compatible from incompatible pollen tubes (Hecht, 1964). Bali (1963) made similar observations on *O. rhombipetala* and also found that for the inactivation of the incompatibility reaction, the pollinations had to be done immediately after treatment, otherwise the treated pistils would gradually recover the ability to discriminate between compatible and incompatible pollen tubes. Kwack (1965) showed that similar pretreatment of *O. organensis* pistils for even 3 min weakened the incompatibility reaction but pretreatment for 5 min was more effective. *Lilium longiflorum* pistils (both detached and intact) reacted similarly. With increase in temperatures, detached pistils of *L. longiflorum* supported better growth of self-incompatible pollen, so much so that above 39°C incompatible and compatible pollen tubes were indistinguishable (Ascher and Peloquin, 1966b), but incubation at 39°C did not overcome interspecific incompatibility (Ascher and Peloquin, 1970). A pretreatment for 6 min in hot water at 50°C was found to be optimum for the best growth of self-incompatible pollen tubes, and higher temperatures (even 55°C) adversely affected both the compatible and incompatible pollen tubes (Hopper *et al.*, 1967). *Trifolium hybridum* showed self-incompatibility at lower temperatures (Townsend, 1968). Self-incompatibility in *Trifolium* was also weakened at 40°C (Kendall, 1968). It was found that incompatible pollen tubes grew longer in styles of *T. pratense* flowers that were developed at 40°C than in those developed at 25°C (Kendall and Taylor, 1969).

In *Petunia* self-incompatibility was overcome by higher temperatures (Straub, 1958; Takahashi, 1973; Linskens, 1975). Furthermore, in *P. hybrida* it was shown that incompatible pollen grains that were developed at higher temperatures prior to pollination produced longer pollen tubes than those that were developed at lower temperatures (van Herpen and Linskens, 1981). Incubations of fresh anthers in petri dishes at 40°C for 60 to 90 min, or at 50 °C for 30 and 60 min, with or without a prior subzero temperature treatment (−20°C for 24 hr) were effective in breaking self-incompatibility in *Lilium longiflorum* (Matsubara, 1980). Matsubara found that treatment for a shorter duration was more effective in producing seed. Coupling high-temperature treatment with −20°C treatment for 24 hr produced a high percentage of fruits whose seeds were heavier than those formed in fruits after compatible pollinations. The temperature treatments were found to be more efficacious than application of a floral organ extract to the stigma (Matsubara, 1981).

Temperature is therefore an important factor that can alter incompatibility. For some reasons thermal inactivation of incompatibility has largely been confined to self-incompatibility in *Brassica* spp. (Visser, 1977), *Chrysanthemum* sp. (Ronald and Ascher, 1975), *Nemesia strumosa* (Campbell and Ascher, 1972), *Oenothera* spp., *Petunia* sp., *R. sativus* (Matsubara, 1980), and *Trifolium* spp. Even in these taxa, genotypes sensitive or insensitive to temperature treatments have been recognized. In some instances of interspecific incompatibility, heat treatments have been given but the results have not been encouraging. In some interspecific crosses in *Brassica,* Robbelen (1960) found 15°C to be the optimum temperature for pollen germination. But investigations on crosses between *B. campestris* and *B. oleracea* revealed that 25°C was better than 15°C not only for pollen germination, but also for growth of the pollen tubes, some of them even reaching ovules (Matsuzawa, 1977).

E. RECOGNITION POLLEN AND INCOMPATIBILITY

The "recognition pollen effect," also called the mentor pollen effect, has evolved in principle from Michurin's (1950) work. A mixture of compatible and incompatible pollen on a stigma had a stimulatory effect on incompatible pollen. This phenomenon was also observed by Glendinning (1960), Wu (1955), Tsitsin (1962), Sarashima (1964), and others (see Ramulu *et al.,* 1979). A definite role of mentor pollen in incompatible crosses was clarified when Stettler (1968) produced hybrids between incompatible poplar species by mixing live incompatible pollen with γ-irradiated (killed) compatible pollen. The realization that the pollen wall is a physiologically active structure (Tsinger and Petrovskaya-Baranova, 1961) led Knox *et al.* (1972a,b) to propose a workable hypothesis for overcoming incompatibility and to illustrate this by repeating Stettler's (1968) hybridization experiments on the cross, *Populus deltoides* × *Populus alba.*

In this method, pollen grains of a compatible parent are killed and mixed with live incompatible pollen grains before pollination. The inviable pollen is called recognition (or mentor) pollen. The killing of the compatible pollen has been achieved in various ways. The pollen grains have been stored (Knox *et al.,* 1972a,b; Sastri and Shivanna, 1976a, 1980b), frozen and thawed repeatedly (Knox *et al.,* 1972b), treated with anhydrous methanol (Knox *et al.,* 1972b; Sastri and Shivanna, 1976a,b, 1980b; Taylor *et al.,* 1980), or irradiated with lethal doses of γ rays (Stettler, 1968; Knox *et al.,* 1972a; Stettler and Guries, 1976; Guries, 1978; Ramulu *et al.,* 1979; Howlett *et al.,* 1975; Stettler *et al.,* 1980).

The success of γ-irradiated pollen as mentor pollen was first demonstrated by Stettler (1968) in the interspecific cross between *P. deltoides* and *P. alba*. *Populus alba* pollen does not even germinate on the stigma of *P. deltoides*, hence the incompatibility between the two species. γ-Irradiated pollen grains of *P. deltoides* mixed with live pollen grains of *P. alba* apparently stimulate the incompatible pollen grains to germinate on the stigma, leading finally to formation of fruits and seeds in this interspecific and otherwise incompatible cross (Stettler, 1968). Knox *et al.* (1972a, 1972b) repeated this cross and obtained hybrids not only by the use of γ-irradiated compatible pollen mixed with live incompatible pollen, but also by the use of other methods to inactivate the compatible pollen. They found that storage at normal temperature, or repeatedly freezing and thawing the compatible pollen, was also an effective means of preparing mentor pollen (Knox *et al.*, 1972b). *Cosmos bipinnatus* and *R. sativus*, taxa with the sporophytic type of self-incompatibility, are examples wherein the incompatible pollen is inhibited on the stigma.

Subsequently, it was shown that gametophytic self-incompatibility could also be overcome by using methanol-treated compatible pollen as mentor pollen in *P. hybrida* (Sastri and Shivanna, 1976a, 1980b) and by using γ-irradiated pollen in *N. alata* (Ramulu *et al.*, 1979). Dayton (1974) had demonstrated that this method could be successfully adopted for overcoming gametophytic self-incompatibility in apple also. However, in apple, pear, and their crosses, mentor pollen prepared either by methanol treatment or by γ irradiation was found to be ineffective (Visser, 1981). It should be mentioned that in *P. hybrida*, self-pollination of buds produced a higher percentage of fruits with a larger number of seeds than were produced by the mentor pollen method (see Shivanna and Rangaswamy, 1969; Sastri and Shivanna, 1980b). Furthermore, in a strictly self-incompatible plant such as *P. hybrida*, mentor pollen prepared by methanol treatment was found to be ineffective, but its leachate, when applied to the stigma before self-incompatible pollination, gave a low percentage of fruits and the number of seeds set per capsule was comparable to that obtained by self-pollination of buds (Sastri and Shivanna, 1980b). In another taxon, *N. alata*, with gametophytic self-incompatibility, the number of seeds formed per fruit was much greater after bud pollination (see Bredemeijer, 1976) than was obtained by pollinating the mature stigmas with a mixture of mentor pollen and incompatible pollen (see Ramulu *et al.*, 1979).

Efficacy of this method has been examined in some interspecific incompatible crosses. In *Cucumis,* in each of the crosses investigated, about 50% of flowers pollinated with pollen mixture produced fruits. In all but one cross combination, ovules were larger, with well-formed embryo sacs and globular embyros, in contrast to untreated incompatible pollinations, which did not set any fruits (den Nijs and Oost, 1980). In *Sesamum indicum* × *Sesamum mulayanum,* recognition pollen prepared by methanol treatment of compatible pollen stimulated germination of incompatible pollen on the stigma as well as penetration into the stigmatic tissues (Sastri and Shivanna, 1976a). In this cross, however, no fruits were obtained because the incompatible pollen tubes that entered and the stylar tissues were not normal and were soon inhibited (Sastri and Shivanna, 1976a).

There are reports that mentor pollen was ineffective in overcoming self-incompatibility in *B. campestris* (Sastri and Shivanna, 1980b), *O. organensis,* and a hybrid between *L. esculentum* × *L. peruvianum* (Ramulu *et al.*, 1979) and in overcoming interspecific incompatibility in eight crosses of *Ipomoea* (Guries, 1978), *Trifolium* (Taylor *et al.*, 1980), and *Festuca arundinacea* × *Dactylis glomerata* (Matzk, 1981).

Although there are only a few cases in which different methods of preparing mentor pollen have been used in the same species, there are instances in which use of a specific method is crucial to the success in overcoming incompatibility. Self-incompatibility in *R. sativus* can be overcome by using the mentor pollen prepared by storage but not that obtained by methanol treatment (Sastri and Shivanna, 1980b). The mentor pollen prepared either by storage or by methanol treatment was not efficacious in overcoming self-incompatibility in *B. campestris* (Sastri and Shivanna, 1980b), but Roggen (1975) succeeded with a related species, *B. oleracea*, by using compatible pollen leachate on the stigma before self-pollination. Differences in the efficacy of methods for preparing recognition pollen were also evident in *P. hybrida*. In a strongly self-incompatible plant, methanol-treated mentor pollen was not effective, but the compatible pollen leachates were effective in overcoming self-incompatibility (Sastri and Shivanna, 1980b). The compatible pollen leachates were as effective as the mentor pollen prepared by storage, by repeated freezing and thawing, by γ irradiation, or by methanol treatment in overcoming interspecific incompatibility in *Populus* (Knox *et al.*, 1972a,b) and self-incompatibility in *C. bipinnatus* (Howlett *et al.*, 1975). It may be mentioned here that the incompatible pollen leachates were able to elicit rejection reaction in *Iberis* stigma papillae (in the form of callose deposits) just as the incompatible pollen grains do (Heslop-Harrison *et al.*, 1974). It is therefore suggested that for mentor pollen to be effective in overcoming incompatibility, the methods for its production have to be judiciously selected. In instances in which only one method has been tried and found unsuccessful, mentor pollen prepared by other methods should be tried.

When there has been success (Table II), it has been attributed to the early interaction between pollen and pistil (Knox *et al.*, 1972a). Stettler *et al.* (1980) reexamined the mentor pollen effects in some incompatible crosses of species belonging to three of the five sections of the genus *Populus*. They suggested that the success is due also to the fact that ovule and ovary are somehow stimulated by killed compatible pollen but not by incompatible pollen. That pollination provides a stimulus is evident from experiments of Illies (1974), who obtained haploids from pollinated pistils of *Populus* treated with toluidine blue. This dye arrested the pollen tube growth halfway through the styles and still the ovaries developed.

The strength of incompatibility and the extent of crossability of a parent that is the source of mentor pollen are other critical factors for

TABLE II. Successes and failures in overcoming incompatibility using recognition pollen

Intraspecific		
Sporophytic	Gametophytic	Interspecific
Successes		
Cosmos bipinnatus (Howlett *et al.*, 1975)[a,d,e]	*Malus* (Dayton, 1974)[a] *Petunia hybrida* (Sastri and Shivanna, 1976b)[c,e]	*Populus* (Stettler, 1968; Stettler and Guries, 1976; Stettler *et al.*, 1980; Knox *et al.*, 1972a,b)[a,c,d,e]
Raphanus sativus (Sastri and Shivanna, 1980b)[b,c]	*Nicotiana alata* (Pandey, 1975, 1977; Ramulu *et al.*, 1979)[a]	*Sesamum* (Sastri and Shivanna, 1976a)[c]
Brassica oleracea (Roggen, 1975)[c]	*Arachis* (D. C. Sastri, unpublished)[c]	*Cucumis* (den Nijs and Oost, 1980)[a]
Failures		
Brassica campestris (Sastri and Shivanna, 1980b)[b,c]	*Oenothera organensis* (Ramulu *et al.*, 1979)[a] *Lycopersicon* (Ramulu *et al.*, 1979)[a]	*Ipomoea* (Guries, 1978)[a] *Trifolium* (Taylor *et al.*, 1980)[c]

[a]Recognition pollen prepared by γ irradiation.
[b]Recognition pollen prepared by storage.
[c]Recognition pollen prepared by methanol treatment.
[d]Recognition pollen prepared by repeated freezing and thawing.
[e]Recognition pollen substituted by its leachates.

success. Pandey (1977, 1979) reported that mentor pollen had a promotive effect in individuals with weak incompatibility but not in individuals with strong incompatibility.

γ-Irradiated pollen and gene transfer

Attempting to overcome incompatibility in *N. alata* by the use of γ-irradiated pollen (100 krad Co), Pandey (1975, 1978, 1980) obtained some unusual results in addition to overcoming self-incompatibility. He observed that certain characters were transferred by mentor pollen and this process has been called a specialized form of "sexual transgenosis." Pandey (1975, 1979) suggested that a high dose of ionizing radiation transforms the generative nucleus into a number of small chromatin fragments, and this was confirmed by Grant *et al.* (1980). It was also shown that there is a lack of metaphase orientation and the failure of division of the generative nucleus during *in vitro* germination of the irradiated pollen grains. By using this method a small number of diploid progeny were obtained that resembled the female parent in a majority of characters but showed a few characters from the parent of the irradiated pollen. Jinks *et al.* (1981) have repeated Pandey's experiments in the same species and have arrived at similar conclusions, suggesting a novel method for *in vivo* transgenosis. These observations have opened a new method for incorporation of segments of paternal chromosomes into the maternal genome, thereby transforming the latter.

F. IMMUNOSUPPRESSANTS AND INCOMPATIBILITY

Bates and co-workers pioneered a novel concept in the light of possibilities of wide hybridization. Based on other reports that there are some organ-specific antigens (Wright, 1960) and on the existence of phytohemagglutinins in plants, Bates and Deyoe (1973) suggested the existence of an immune reaction analogous to that occurring in animal systems. They called this "stereospecific inhibition reaction" (SIR), but there is still no direct evidence for the existence of SIR in plants. However, they initiated wide hybridization experiments in which certain animal-effective immunosuppressants were used. These were ε-aminocaproic acid (εACA), chloramphenicol, acriflavin, salicylic acid, and gentisic acid. Success rates varied among immunosuppressants, εACA being the most effective. The results obtained have not only supported the hypothesis upon which these trials were initiated, but have also suggested new ways of breaking the interspecific crossability barriers. The crosses in which embryos were obtained were durum wheat × rye, barley × rye, barley × triticale, barley × oats, and maize × sorghum (Bates *et al.*, 1974). In the untreated controls even fertilization was not observed. Bates *et al.* also reported that progeny from barley × rye, durum wheat × barley, and bread wheat × barley have been advanced to F_2 generations.

The results (see Bates, 1974) with this novel group of chemicals did stimulate a few other workers, and a few reports published to date are encouraging. Tiara and Larter (1977a,b) observed that εACA stimulated embryo development in *Triticum turgidum* × *S. cereale* crosses. In all these experiments the immunosuppressant solution was applied to the leaf axils a few weeks before pollination.

In the interspecific cross between *Vigna radiata* and *Vigna umbellata,* εACA (100 ppm) applied as a foliar spray to the seed parent was twice as effective as the untreated controls (Asian Vegetable Research and Development Center, 1976). In the same cross Baker *et al.* (1975) found that an injection of 250 ppm of εACA into the internode of maternal plants gave optimum results. Foliar spray of εACA (100 ppm) applied for 14 days starting at, or earlier than, the premeiotic stage of flower development to two cultivars of *Vigna radiata* delayed but did not prevent embryo abortion in *V. radiata* × *V. umbellata* crosses (Chen *et al.*, 1978). Embryo abortion could also be prevented by defoliating the plants 4–6 days after pollination (Chen *et al.*, 1978), a procedure developed for *P. coccineus* × *P. vulgaris* crosses by Ibrahim and Coyne (1975). More recently, Mujeeb-Kazi (1981) has shown that in *Triticum timopheevii* × *S. cereale* crosses, εACA treatment (concentration not given) of *T. timopheevii* florets for 4 days after pollination reduced embryo recovery from 30.5 to 18.9%, but increased the number of ovaries with both embryo and endosperm formation from 11.4 to 18%. In this particular cross Mujeeb-Kazi has also shown that crossability is affected by the environment in which the female parents are grown and maintained. In *F. arundinacea* × *D. glomerata* cross, however, εACA treatment (concentration not given) was not effective (Matzk, 1981). These chemicals will probably repay the effort of testing on a larger number of taxa, with gametic incompatibility; chemicals with similar effects can be tried. A better understanding of the mode of action of these chemicals must be obtained to increase the effectiveness of their use in promoting other desirable but incompatible crosses.

G. MISCELLANEOUS METHODS

In addition to the preceding methods, each of which has been shown to be effective in more than one taxon, there are certain other methods that have been developed and applied to one taxon only (Table III).

TABLE III. Miscellaneous methods in overcoming intraspecific (SI) or interspecific (ISI) incompatibility

Method	Taxon/cross	Type of incompatibility	References
Organic solvents	*Brassica oleracea*	SI	Ockenden (1978)
	Populus	ISI	Willing and Pryor (1976)
Humidity	*Brassica oleracea*	SI	Ockenden (1978)
Electric-aided pollination	*Brassica* sp.	SI	Roggen *et al.* (1972)
Immunosuppressants	Maize × sorghum	ISI	Bates (1974); Bates and Deyoe, (1973)
	Vigna	ISI	Bates *et al.* (1974); Chen *et al.* (1978)
	Lycopersicon, Triticum timopheevi	ISI	Kesicki (1979)
N-m-Tolyphthalmic acid, *P-m*-tolyphthalmic acid	*Brassica pekinensis* × *B. oleracea*	ISI	Honma and Hecht (1960)
CO_2	*Brassica* spp.	SI	Nakanishi *et al.* (1969); Nakanishi and Hinata (1973)

Freshly opened flowers of *Brassica* spp., when exposed to 3–5% CO_2, behaved as self-compatible to a certain extent, although there were differences according to the genotype or the species investigated (Nakanishi *et al.*, 1969; Nakanishi and Hinata, 1973). In *B. oleracea*, self-incompatibility was also overcome by "electric-aided pollination" in which an electric potential difference of 100 V was applied between pollen and stigma (Roggen *et al.*, 1972). The efficacy of this method in this taxon, expressed as seed number per pollination, is comparable to that obtained by other methods, such as decapitated pistil pollination, bud pollination, chemical treatments, and temperature treatment. In interspecific crosses in *Populus,* certain organic solvents (ethyl acetate and hexane being the most effective ones) were applied to stigmas and hybrids were obtained (Willing and Pryor, 1976).

H. GENETIC AND CYTOLOGICAL MANIPULATION

Adverse pollen and stigma interactions are not the sole causes of incompatibility, and there are a number of genetic or cytological reasons for failure to produce hybrids or to achieve successful gene transfer. These will be mentioned briefly before considering *in vitro* methods, which have become important techniques for interspecific transfer.

Differences in number of chromosomes and/or ploidy differences in two species to be crossed can be strong factors, preventing hybridization between them. The taxa involved may have the same chromosome number, such as *Trifolium repens* and *Trifolium ambiguum* ($2n = 32$) (Williams, 1980), yet they cannot normally be crossed.

In many diploid × tetraploid crosses within or between species, the endosperm collapses, causing early embryo abortion (Brink and Cooper, 1947). Johnston *et al.* (1980) proposed that in such instances ploidy per se is not the problem. According to them, an abnormal endosperm is due to a deviation of maternal:paternal genome ratios from 2:1 in the endosperm. In this hypothesis the genome of each species has to be assigned a specific value for the endosperm, irrespective of the ploidy levels of the parental species. By manipulating these numbers, Johnston and Hanneman (1982) have succeeded in producing hybrids between some diploid species of *Solanum* that cannot be crossed otherwise, It appears that results from a few interspecific crosses, such as *Solanum, Gossypium, Lycopersicon, Datura,* and *Avena,* can be explained by this hypothesis (Johnston *et al.,* 1980).

Elimination of chromosomes of one of the parents is another problem often encountered in wide crosses, and this has been profitably employed in production of haploids in *Hordeum* (Subrahmanyam, 1979).

These problems have been tackled largely by strategic manipulation of chromosome numbers and ploidy level. Increase in ploidy level has often been achieved by using colchicine and certain other chemicals, whereas reduction in ploidy has been achieved by haploid parthenogenesis and/or by anther and pollen culture or by some chemical treatments (Illies, 1974).

When two taxa cannot be hybridized, a third taxon crossable with one of them has often been used as a bridge for transfer of character(s). Examples of such bridge crosses are found in *Nicotiana, Triticum, Cucurbita, and Solanum* (see reviews by Hadley and Openshaw, 1980; Stalker, 1980). The search for genetic control of crossability and chromosome pairing as found in *Triticum* should continue in other plant taxa. Crosses should be attempted with as many accessions as possible; possibly the different cultivars may show varying crossability with another species. Such differences have been observed in *N. tabacum* cultivars (Pittagelli and Stavely, 1975), *Trifolium nigrescens* (Hoven, 1962), *Tripsacum dactyloides* (Harlan and de Wet, 1977), and so on. *Triticum aestivum* genes controlling crossability have been identified as *Kr1* and

Kr2 and are located on the 5B chromosome. The dominant alleles of these genes in genotypes such as in the variety Hope interfere with the pollen tube growth in the micropyle in *T. aestivum* × *S. cereale* (Jalani, and Moss, 1980, 1981) and *T. aestivum* × *H. bulbosum* (Snape *et al.*, 1980) crosses. The 5B chromosome of wheat also carries a gene (*Ph*) that restricts pairing. By eliminating this chromosome (Cauderon, 1979; Thomas, 1981) or by suppressing the activity of the *Ph* gene by *Aegilops speltoides* genotypes (Riley *et al.*, 1968), it has been possible to increase pairing and enhance recombination between genomes.

Details of these and other aspects of genetic and cytological manipulations have been listed and discussed often and are not presented here. The papers of Stalker (1980), Rees *et al.* (1981), Peloquin (1981), Hadley and Openshaw (1980), Thomas (1981), Riley *et al.* (1981), and Driscoll (1981) are suggested for consultation.

I. THE *in Vitro* METHODS

The *in vitro* methods are increasingly being recognized as regular techniques for the plant breeder interested in interspecific hybridization and in overcoming incompatibility. Advances in *in vitro* techniques have been providing opportunities for sexual hybridization and, more recently, for parasexual hybridization by protoplast fusion or for gene transfer by plasmids, liposomes, viruses, chromosomes, or otherwise.

Sexual hybridization by these methods encompasses culture of embryos, ovules, or ovaries from incompatible crosses in which embryos or ovules do not develop fully after wide hybridization by conventional means. The first successful culture of embryos was from the cross *Linum perenne* × *Linum austriacum* (Laibach, 1929); there are now over 40 crosses in which hybrids have been obtained by culture of embryos (see Raghavan, 1977, and Table IV). In many instances, however, the embryo degenerates when it is too small to be dissected out for culture. In these instances, ovule or ovary culture facilitates hybrid production (Stewart, 1981). Takeshita *et al.* (1980) have compared the effectiveness of embryo culture, ovary culture, and ovule culture from some interspecific crosses involving species of *Brassica* and *R. sativus*. They found that in some crosses ovule culture was better than either embryo culture or ovary culture; this was particularly true when *B. oleracea* was one of the parents (Takeshita *et al.*, 1980). Ovules from interspecific crosses in *Gossypium* (Stewart and Hsu, 1978) and ovaries from interspecific crosses in *Brassica* (Inomata, 1978, 1979) have been cultured and hybrids obtained.

TABLE IV. Some interspecific hybrids by embryo culture[a]

Cross	References
Aegilops squarrosa × *Triticum boeoticum*	Gill *et al.* (1981)
Agropyron tsukushiense (6*x*) × *Hordeum bulbosum* (4*x*)	Shigenobu and Sakamoto (1981)
Arachis hypogaea × *Arachis* sp. P.I. No. 276233	Sastri and Moss (1982); Sastri *et al.* (1981)
Elymus canadensis × *Hordeum vulgare*	Mujeeb-Kazi and Rodriguez (1982)
Festuca arundinacea × *Dactylis glomerata*	Matzk (1976)
Hibiscus asper × *Hibiscus cannabinus*	Kuwada and Mabuchi (1976)
H. asper × *Hibiscus sabdariffa*	Kuwada and Mabuchi (1976)
Hordeum jubatum × *Secale cereale*	Brink *et al.* (1944)
Impatiens hookerina × *Impatiens campanulata*	Arisumi (1980)
Lolium perenne × *Festuca rubra*	Nitzsche and Henning (1976)
Lotus pedunculatus × *Lotus tenuis*	De La Tour *et al.* (1978)
Lycopersicon esculentum × *Lycopersicon peruvianum*	Thomas and Pratt (1981)
Ornithopus sp. × *Ornithopus compressus*	Williams and De La Tour (1980, 1981)
Solanum melongena × *Solanum khasianum*	Sharma *et al.* (1980)
Trifolium ambiguum × *Trifolium hybridum*	Williams (1980)
T. ambiguum × *Trifolium repens* and reciprocal	Williams (1978, 1980)
T. repens × *T. ambiguum*	Williams and Verry (1981)
Trifolium pratense × *Trifolium sarosiense*	Phillips *et al.* (1982)

[a]In addition to those listed by Raghavan (1977).

Both female and male gametophytes have been cultured together *in vitro*, so that pollination, fertilization, and postfertilization changes leading to formation of hybrid seed or seedlings are all achieved in the test tube (Rangaswamy, 1977; Zenkteler and Melchers, 1978; Zenkteler, 1980; Stewart, 1981). Of 22 intergeneric or interspecific combinations, 5 formed seeds with viable embryos, 13 with immature embryos, 2 showed only endosperm formation, and 2 only fertilization (Zenkteler, 1980). The test-tube fertilization is a refinement of the experiments of Kanta and associates on successful intraovarian pollinations in some members of Papaveraceae (Kanta, 1960; Maheshwari and Kanta, 1961).

Another approach to exploit the *in vitro* methods is to force the fusion of somatic protoplasts and provide conditions for the growth and differentiation of the heterokaryocyte, leading to somatic hybrids. Numerous attempts, encouraged by the initial success in fusing protoplasts in the sexually compatible taxa in *Petunia* (Power *et al.*, 1970) and *Nicotiana* (Carlson *et al.*, 1972), have been made to produce somatic hybrids from sexually incompatible species (see Schieder and Vasil, 1980). Significant among these is the creation of "*Arabidobrassica*" by fusing the protoplasts of *Arabidopsis* and *Brassica*, genera of two different taxonomic tribes. Equally significant is the fact that the methods, so far exploratory in nature and confined to well worked out model systems, are now being extended to hybridization and improvement of crop species (Wenzel *et al.*, 1979). In several other attempts at interspecific and intergeneric and protoplast fusion, hybrid callus lines have been obtained (see Schieder and Vasil, 1980; Gamborg *et al.*, 1981; Cocking, 1981). Krumbiegel and Schieder (1981) have observed that hybrids between *Datura innoxia* and *Atropa belladonna* can be produced only by somatic hybridization and not by other *in vitro* methods suggested by Rangaswamy (1977) and Zenkteler (1980). Hybrids between *N. tabacum* and *Nicotiana nesophila*, impossible to obtain by conventional means, were produced by *in vitro* sexual methods (Reed and Collins, 1978) and by somatic fusion (Evans *et al.*, 1981). Evans *et al.* (1982) compared these hybrids and observed that somatic hybrid clones showed a greater range of variability for certain morphological characters than did the sexual hybrids. A commonly observed problem in such wide somatic hybridization is the gradual loss of a part of or a full genome of one of the parents (Dudits *et al.*, 1980). Experiments of Szabados *et al.* (1981) and Griesbach *et al.* (1981) suggest chromosome uptake by protoplasts as another alternative to transfer of the full genome by somatic fusion. Uptake of chromosomes or of their segments can also be facilitated by encapsulating them in liposomes before fusing the latter with the recipient protoplasts. This has been shown by Matthews and Cress (1981), Lurquin (1981), and Giles (1983). Alternatively, the desired segments of DNA can be tagged to certain vectors such as *Agrobacterium tumefaciens* Ti plasmid or cauliflower mosaic virus DNA, which may transfer the DNA to the host cell for integration by its nuclear DNA. This has been demonstrated recently by Chilton *et al.* (1982) and Krens *et al.* (1982; see also reviews by Cocking *et al.*, 1981; Kado and Kleinhofs, 1980).

IV. Concluding Remarks

There is a growing interest in the use of wild relatives for reversing genetic erosion and for genetic improvement of crops. Wild species have always been of concern to students of biosystematics, but now they are of equal concern to plant breeders. A knowledge of evolution and speciation has helped our understanding of the reasons for failures of wide crosses and vice versa. A deeper search into these failures has provided methods for converting some of these into successes. It is hoped that these methods, with modifications and improvement as necessary, will stimulate new ideas for the creation of hybrids that have so far eluded us.

It is certainly not easy to pick one of the methods as the best one, but self-incompatibility was said to be overcome best by high-temperature treatments (Townsend, 1971). To break interspecific barriers, a range of parents have to be screened for the most crossable one, and the nature of incompatibility—whether pre- or postfertilization—has to be determined. Fluorescence microscopy has been a convenient method for determining this. This method (Martin, 1959) facilitates the observation of pollen tube growth through the pistil, which is generally not easy by light miscroscopic staining methods. Having determined the site of the barrier, a range of suitable methods has to be adopted. The most common of these methods have been discussed in this article, and with greater understanding of the phenomena involved more techniques are bound to emerge.

ACKNOWLEDGMENTS

I am grateful to Dr. J. P. Moss and Dr. D. McDonald for their comments on the article and Miss C. Sashikala for help in preparation of the typescript.

REFERENCES

Alonso, L. C., and Kimber, G. (1980). A haploid between *Agropyron junceum* and *Triticum aestivum*. *Cereal Res. Commun.* **8**, 355–358.

Al Yasiri, A., and Coyne, D. P. (1964). Effects of growth regulators in delaying pod abscission and embryo abortion in the interspecific cross *Phaseolus vulgaris* × *P. acutifolius*. *Crop Sci.* **4**, 433–435.

Anderson, E., and de Winton, D. (1931). The genetic analysis of unusual relationship between self-sterility and self-fertility in *Nicotiana*. *Ann. Mo. Bot. Gard.* **18**, 97–116.

Arasu, N. T. (1968). Self-incompatibility in angiosperms: A review. *Genetica (The Hague)* **39**, 1–24.

Arisumi, T. (1980). *In vitro* culture of embryos and ovules of certain incompatible selfs and crosses among *Impatiens* species. *J. Am. Soc. Hortic. Sci.* **105**, 629–631.

Ascher, P. D., and Peloquin, S. J. (1966a). Effect of floral ageing on the growth of compatible and incompatible pollen tubes in *Lilium longiflorum*. *Am. J. Bot.* **53**, 99–102.

Ascher, P. D., and Peloquin, S. J. (1966b). Influence of temperature on incompatible and compatible pollen tube growth in *Lilium longiflorum*. *Can. J. Genet. Cytol.* **8**, 661–664.

Ascher, P. D., and Peloquin, S. J. (1970). Temperature and self-incompatibility reaction in *Lilium longiflorum*. Thunb. *J. Am. Soc. Hortic. Sci.* **95**, 586–588.

Asian Vegetable Research and Development Center (1976). "Progress Report for 1975 (Mungbean)," pp. 35–40. AVRDC, Shanhua, Taiwan, Republic of China.

Attia, M. S. (1950). The nature of incompatibility in cabbage. *Proc. Am. Soc. Hortic. Sci.* **56,** 369-371.

Bajaj, Y. P. S., Verma, M. M., and Dhanju, M. S. (1980). Barley × rye hybrids (Hordecale) through embryo culture. *Curr. Sci.* **49,** 362-363.

Baker, L. R., Chen, N. C., and Park, H. G. (1975). Effect of an immunosuppressant on an interspecific cross of the genus *Vigna. Hort. Science* **70,** 325-333.

Bali, P. N. (1963). Some experimental studies on the self-incompatibility of *Oenothera rhombipetala* Nutt. *Phyton (Buenos Aires)* **20,** 97-103.

Bali, P. N., and Hecht, A. (1965). The genetics of self-incompatibility in *Oenothera rhombipetala. Genetics* **36,** 159-171.

Bates, L. S. (1974). Wide crosses. *In* "Proceedings of The Worldwide Maize Improvement in the 70s and the Role for CIMMYT," Vol. 5, pp. 1B-7B.

Bates, L. S., and Deyoe, C. W. (1973). Wide hybridization and cereal improvement. *Econ. Bot.* **27,** 401-412.

Bates, L. S., Campos, V. A., Rodriguez, R. R., and Anderson, R. G. (1974). Progress towards novel cereal grains. *Cereal Sci. Today* **19,** 283-284, 286.

Bennici, A., and Cionini, P. G. (1979). Cytokinins and *in vitro* development of *Phaseolus coccineus* embryos. *Planta* **147,** 27-29.

Bredemeijer, G. M. M. (1974). Peroxidase activity and peroxidase isoenzyme composition in self-pollinated, cross-pollinated and unpollinated styles of *Nicotiana alata. Acta Bot. Neerl.* **23,** 149-157.

Bredemeijer, G. M. M. (1976). Effect of bud pollination and delayed self-pollination on the induction of possible rejection peroxidase in styles of *Nicotiana alata. Acta Bot. Neerl.* **25,** 107-116.

Bredemeijer, G. M. M., and Blaas, J. (1975). A possible role of stylar peroxidase gradient in the rejection of incompatible growing pollen tubes. *Acta Bot. Neerl.* **24,** 37-48.

Brewbaker, J. L. (1957). Pollen cytology and incompatibility systems in plants. *J. Hered.* **48,** 271-277.

Brewbaker, J. L. (1967). The distribution and significance of binucleate and trinucleate pollen grains in the angiosperms. *Am. J. Bot.* **54,** 1069-1083.

Brewbaker, J. L., and Kwack, B. H. (1963). The essential role of calcium ion in pollen germination and pollen tube growth. *Am. J. Bot.* **50,** 859-865.

Brink, R. A., and Cooper, D. C. (1947). The endosperm in seed development. *Bot. Rev.* **13,** 423-541.

Brink, R. A., Cooper, D. C., and Ausherman, L. E. (1944). A hybrid between *Hordeum jubatum* and *Secale cereale. J. Hered.* **35,** 67-75.

Brock, R. D. (1954). Hormone-induced pear-apple hybrids. *Heredity* **8,** 421-429.

Burrows, W. J., and Carr, D. J. (1970). Cytokinin content of pea seeds during their growth and development. *Physiol. Plant.* **23,** 1064-1070.

Campbell, R. J., and Ascher, P. D. (1972). High temperature removes self-incompatibility in *Nemesia strumosa. Incompatibility Newsl.* **1,** 3-5.

Carlson, P. S., Smith, H. H., and Dearing, R. D. (1972). Parasexual interspecific plant hybridization. *Proc. Natl. Acad. Sci. U.S.A.* **69,** 2292-2294.

Cauderon, Y. (1979). Use of *Agropyron* species for wheat improvement. *In* "Broadening the Genetic Base of Crops" (A. C. Zeven and A. M. van Harten, eds.), pp. 175-186. Centre for Agricultural Publishing and Documentation, Wageningen.

Chen, N. C., Parrott, J. F., Jacobs, T., Baker, L. R., and Carlson, P. S. (1978). Interspecific hybridization of food grain legumes by unconventional methods of breeding. *In* "International Mungbean Symposium," pp. 247-252. Asian Vegetable Research and Development Center, Shanhua, Taiwan, Republic of China.

Chilton, M. D., Tepfer, D. A., Petit, A., David, C., Casse-Delbart, F., and Tempe,

J. (1982). *Agrobacterium* rhizogenes insert T-DNA into the genomes of host plant root cells. *Nature (London)* **295,** 432–434.

Cocking, E. C. (1981). Opportunities from the use of protoplasts. *Philos. Trans. R. Soc. London, Ser. B* **292,** 557-568.

Cocking, E. C., Davey, M. R., Pental, D., and Power, J. B. (1981). Aspects of plant genetic manipulation. *Nature (London)* **293,** 265–270.

Crane, M. B., and Marks, E. (1952). Pear-apple hybrids. *Nature (London)* **170,** 1017.

Cresti, M., Ciampolini, F., Pacini, E., Sarfatti, G., van Went, J. L., and Willemse, M. T. M. (1979). Ultrastructural differences between compatible and incompatible pollen tubes in the stylar transmitting tissue of *Petunia hybrida*. *J. Submicrosc. Cytol.* **11,** 209–219.

Cresti, M., Ciampolini, F., and Sarfatti, G. (1980). Ultrastuctural investigations on *Lycopersicum peruvianum* pollen activation and pollen tube organization after self- and cross-pollination. *Planta* **150,** 211–217.

Davey, J., and van Staden, J. (1979). Cytokinin in *Lupinus albus*. III. Distribution in fruits. *Physiol. Plant.* **43,** 87–93.

Davies, A. J. S. (1957). Successful crossing in the genus *Lathyrus* through stylar amputation. *Nature (London)* **180,** 612.

Dayton, D. F. (1974). Overcoming self-incompatibility in apple with killed compatible pollen. *J. Am. Soc. Hortic. Sci.* **99,** 190–192.

De La Tour, G., Jones, W. T., and Ross, M. D. (1978). Production of interspecific hybrids in *Lotus* aided by endosperm transplants. *N. Z. J. Bot.* **16,** 61–68.

de Nettancourt, D. (1977). "Incompatibility in Angiosperms." Springer-Verlag, Berlin and New York.

de Nettancourt, D., Devreux, M., Bozzini, A., Cresti, M., Pacini, E., and Sarfatti, G., (1973a). Ultrastructural aspects of self-incompatibility mechanism in *Lycopersicum peruvianum* Mill. *J. Cell Sci.* **12,** 403–419.

de Nettancourt, D., Devreux, M., Laneri, Y., Pacini, E., Cresti, M., and Sarfatti, G. (1973b). Ultrastructural aspects of unilateral interspecific incompatibility between *Lycopersicum peruvianum* and *L. esculentum*. *Caryologia, Suppl.* **25,** 207–219.

de Nettancourt, D., Devreux, M., Laneri, U., Cresti, M., Pacini, E., and Sarfatti, G. (1974). Genetical and ultrastructural aspects of self- and cross-incompatibility in interspecific hybrids between self-compatible *Lycopersicum esculentum* and self-incompatible *L. peruvianum*. *Theor. Appl. Genet.* **44,** 278–288.

den Nijs, A. P. M., and Oost, E. H. (1980). Effect of mentor pollen on pollen pistil incongruities among species of *Cucumis* L. *Euphytica* **29,** 267–272.

Deurenberg, J. J. M. (1976). *In vitro* protein synthesis with polysomes from unpollinated, cross- and self-pollinated *Petunia* ovaries. *Planta* **128,** 29–33.

Deurenberg, J. J. M. (1977). Differentiated protein synthesis with polysomes from *Petunia* ovaries before fertilization. *Planta* **133,** 201–206.

Dickinson, H. G., and Lewis, D. (1973). Cytochemical and ultrastructural differences between intraspecific compatible and incompatible pollinations in *Raphanus*. *Proc. R. Soc. London, Ser. B* **183,** 21–28.

Dionne, L. A. (1958). A survey of methods for overcoming cross incompatibility between certain species of the genus *Solanum*. *Am. Potato J.* **35,** 422–423.

Driscoll, C. J. (1981). Perspectives in chromosome manipulation. *Philos. Trans. R. Soc. London* **292,** 535–546.

Dudits, D., Fejer, O., Hadlaczky, G., Koncz, C., Lazar, G., and Horvath, G. (1980). Intergeneric gene transfer mediated by plant protoplast fusion. *Mol. Gen. Genet.* **179,** 283–288.

East, E. M. (1934). Norms of pollen tube growth in incompatible matings of self-sterile plants. *Proc. Natl. Acad. Sci. U.S.A.* **11,** 166–171.

East, E. M., and Mangelsdorf, A. J. (1925). A new interpretation of the hereditary behaviour of self-sterile plants. *Proc. Natl. Acad. Sci. U.S.A.* **11,** 166–171.

Emsweller, S. L., and Stuart, N. W. (1948). Use of growth regulating substances to overcome incompatibilities in *Lilium. Am. Soc. Hortic. Sci.* **51,** 581.

Emsweller, S. L., and Uhring, J. (1965). Interaction of temperature and growth regulator in overcoming self-incompatibility in *Lilium longiflorum* Thunb. *Hereditas* **52,** 295–306.

Emsweller, S. L., Uhring, J., and Stuart, N. W. (1960). The roles of naphthalene acetamide and potassium gibberellate on overcoming self-incompatibility in *Lilium longiflorum. Proc. Am. Soc. Hortic. Sci.* **75,** 720–725.

Evans, A. M., and Denward, T. (1955). Grafting and hybridization experiments in the genus *Trifolium. Nature (London)* **175,** 687–688.

Evans, D. A., Flick, C. E., and Jensen, R. A. (1981). Disease resistance: Incorporation into sexually incompatible somatic hybrids of the genus *Nicotiana. Science* **313,** 907–909.

Evans, D. A., Flick, C. E., Kut, S. A., and Reed, S. M. (1982). Comparison of *Nicotiana tabacum* and *N. nesophila* hybrids produced by ovule culture and protoplast fusion. *Theor. Appl. Genet.* **62,** 193–198.

Fedak, G. (1978). Barley-wheat hybrids. *Interspecific Hybrid. Plant Breed, Proc. Congr. EUCARPIA, 8th 1977,* pp. 261–267.

Ferrari, T. E., and Wallace, D. H. (1975). Germination of *Brassica* pollen and expression of incompatibility *in vitro. Euphytica* **24,** 757–765.

Ferrari, T. E., and Wallace, D. H. (1976). Pollen protein synthesis and control of incompatibility in *Brassica. Theor. Appl. Genet.* **148,** 243–249.

Ferrari, T. E., and Wallace, D. H. (1977). Incompatibility in *Brassica* stigmas is overcome by treating pollen with cycloheximide. *Science* **196,** 436–438.

Ferrari, T. E., Bruns, D., and Wallace, D. H. (1981a). Isolation of a plant glycoprotein involved with control of intercellular recognition. *Plant Physiol.* **67,** 270–277.

Ferrari, T. E., Lee, S. S., and Wallace, D. H. (1981b). Biochemistry and physiology of recognition in pollen-stigma interactions. *Phytopathology* **71,** 752–755.

Flook, V., and Williams, R. R. (1978). *Rep.—Long Ashton Res. Stn.* p. 24 (cited by Pickering, 1980).

Frankel, O., and Galun, E. (1977). "Pollination Mechanisms, Reproduction and Plant Breeding." Springer-Verlag, Berlin and New York.

Frimmel, G. (1956). Uber Hormone in Kartoffelpollen. *Bodenkultur* **8,** 349–351 (cited by Rangaswamy, 1963).

Gamborg, O. A., Shyluk, J. P., and Shahin, E. A. (1981). Isolation, fusion and culture of plant protoplasts. *In* "Plant Tissue Culture: Methods and Applications in Agriculture" (T. A. Thorpe, ed.), pp. 115–158. Academic Press, New York.

Gardella, C. (1950). Overcoming barriers to crossability due to style length. *Am. J. Bot.* **27,** 219–224.

Giles, K. L. (1983). Mechanisms of uptake into plant protoplasts. *In* "Plant Cell Culture in Crop Improvement" (S. K. Sen and K. L. Giles, eds.), pp. 227–235. Plenum, New York.

Gilissen, L. J. W. (1976). The role of style as a sense organ in relation to wilting of the flower. *Planta* **131,** 201–202.

Gill, B. S., Waines, J. G., and Sharma, H. C. (1981). Endosperm abortion and the production of viable *Aegilops squarrosa* × *Triticum boeticum* hybrids by embryo culture. *Plant Sci. Lett.* **23,** 181–187.

Glendinning, D. R. (1960). Selfing of self-incompatible cocoa. *Nature (London)* **187,** 170.

Grant, J. E., Pandey, K. K., and Williams, E. G. (1980). Pollen nuclei after ionising irradiation for egg transformation in *Nicotiana N. Z. J. Bot.* **18,** 339–341.

Griesbach, R. J., Koivuniemi, P. J., and Carlson, P. S. (1981). Extending the range of plant genetic manipulation. *BioScience* **31,** 754–756.

Guries, R. P. (1978). A test of the mentor pollen technique in the genus *Ipomoea. Euphytica* **27,** 825–830.

Hadley, H. H., and Openshaw, S. J. (1980). Interspecific and intergeneric hybridization. *In* "Hybridization of Crop Plants" (W. R. Fehr and H. H. Hadley, eds), pp. 133–159. Am. Soc. Agron. and Crop Sci. Soc. Am., Madison, Wisconsin.

Hall, I. V., and Forsyth, F. R. (1967). Production of ethylene by flowers following pollination and treatments with water and auxin. *Can. J. Bot.* **45,** 1163–1166.

Harlan, J. R., and de Wet, J. M. J. (1977). Pathways of genetic transfer from *Tripsacum* to *Zea mays. Proc. Natl. Acad. Sci. U.S.A.* **74,** 3494–3497.

Harrison, B. J., and Darby, L. (1955). Unilateral hybridization. *Nature (London)* **176,** 982.

Haruta, T. (1966). "Studies on the Genetics of Self- and Cross-incompatibility in Cruciferous Vegetables." Northrop King & Co., Minneapolis, Minnesota (cited by Frankel and Galun, 1977).

Hecht, A. (1960). Growth of pollen tubes of *Oenothera organensis* through otherwise incompatible styles. *Am. J. Bot.* **47,** 32–36.

Hecht, A., (1964). Partial inactivation of incompatibility substance in the stigmas and styles of *Oenothera. In* "Pollen Physiology and Fertilization" (H. F. Linskens, ed.), pp. 237–243. North-Holland Publ., Amsterdam.

Henny, R. J., and Ascher, P. D. (1973). Effect of auxin (3-indole acetic acid) on *in vivo* compatible and incompatible pollen tube growth in detached styles of *Lilium longiflorum* Thunb. *Incompatibility Newsl.* **3,** 14–17.

Herrero, M., and Dickinson, H. G. (1979). Pollen–pistil incompatibility in *Petunia hybrida:* Changes in the pistil following compatible and incompatible interspecific crosses. *J. Cell Sci.* **36,** 1–18.

Herrero, M., and Dickinson, H. G. (1980a). Ultrastructural and physiological differences between buds and mature flowers of *Petunia hybrida* prior to and following pollination. *Planta* **148,** 138–145.

Herrero, M., and Dickinson, H. G. (1980b). Pollen tube growth following compatible and incompatible intraspecific pollinations in *Petunia hybrida. Planta* **148,** 217–221.

Heslop-Harrison, J. (1975a). Incompatibility and pollen stigma interactions. *Annu. Rev. Plant Physiol.* **26,** 403–425.

Heslop-Harrison, J. (1975b). The physiology of the pollen-grain surface. *Proc. R. Soc. London, Ser. B* **190,** 275–299.

Heslop-Harrison, J. (1978a). Genetics and physiology of angiosperm incompatibility systems. *Proc. R. Soc. London, Ser. B* **202,** 73–92.

Heslop-Harrison, J. (1978b). Recognition and response in the pollen–stigma interaction. *Symp. Soc. Exp. Biol.* **32,** 121–138.

Heslop-Harrison, J., and Heslop-Harrison, Y. (1975). Enzymic removal of proteinaceous pellicle of the stigma papillae prevents pollen tube entry in the Caryophyllaceae. *Ann. Bot. (London)* [N. S.] **39,** 163–165.

Heslop-Harrison, J., Heslop-Harrison, Y., Knox, R. B., and Howlett, B. J. (1973). Pollen wall proteins: "Gametophytic" and "sporophytic" fractions in the pollen wall of the Malvaceae. *Ann. Bot. (London)* [N. S.] **37,** 403–412.

Heslop-Harrison, J., Knox, R. B., and Heslop-Harrison, Y. (1974). Pollen-wall proteins: Exine-held fractions associated with incompatibility responses in Cruciferae. *Theor. Appl. Genet.* **44,** 133–137.

Heslop-Harrison, J., Heslop-Harrison, Y., and Barber, J. T. (1975). The stigma surface in incompatibility responses. *Proc. R. Soc. London, Ser. B* **183,** 287–297.

Heslop-Harrison, Y. (1976). Localisation of concanavalin A binding sites on the stigma surface of grass species. *Micron* **7,** 33–36.

Heslop-Harrison, Y. (1981). Stigma characteristics and angiosperm taxonomy. *Nord. J. Bot.* **1,** 401–420.

Heslop-Harrison, Y., and Shivanna, K. R. (1977). The receptive surface of the angiosperm stigma. *Ann. Bot. (London)* [N. S.] **41,** 1233–1258.

Hinata, K., and Nishio, T. (1978). S-allele specificity of stigma proteins in *Brassica oleracea* and *B. campestris. Heredity* **41,** 93–100

Hogenboom, N. G. (1973). A model for incongruity in intimate partner relationships. *Euphytica* **22,** 219–233.

Honma, S., and Hecht, O. (1960). *Euphytica* **9,** 243–246.

Hopper, J. E., Ascher, P. D., and Peloquin, S. J. (1967). Inactivation of self-incompatibility following temperature pretreatments of styles in *Lilium longiflorum. Euphytica* **16,** 215–220.

Hoven, A. W. (1962). Interspecific hybridization between *Trifolium repens* L. and *T. nigrescens* Viv. and analysis of hybrid meiosis. *Crop Sci.* **2,** 251–254.

Howlett, B. J., Knox, R. B., Paxton, J. B., and Heslop-Harrison, J. (1975). Pollen-wall proteins: Physico-chemical characterization and role in self-incompatibility in *Cosmos bipinnatus. Proc. R. Soc. London, Ser. B* **188,** 167–182.

Ibrahim, A. M., and Coyne, D. P. (1975). Genetics of stigma shape, cotyledon position and flower colour in reciprocal crosses between *Phaseolus vulgaris* L. and *Phaseolus coccineus* (Lam.) and implications in breeding. *J. Am. Soc. Hortic. Sci.* **100,** 622–626.

Illies, Z. M. (1974). Experimentally induced haploid parthenogenesis in the *Populus* section Leuce after late inactivation of the male gamete with toluidine blue. *In* "Fertilization in Higher Plants" (H. F. Linskens, ed.), pp. 335–340. North-Holland Publ., Amsterdam.

Inomata, M. (1978). Production of interspecific hybrids in *Brassica campestris* × *B. oleracea* by culture *in vitro* of excised ovaries. I. Development of excised ovaries in the crosses of various cultivars. *Jpn. J. Genet.* **53,** 161–173.

Inomata, N. (1979). Production of interspecific hybrids in *Brassica campestris* × *B. oleracea* by culture *in vitro* of excised ovaries. II. Development of excised ovaries on various culture media. *Jpn. J. Breed.* **29,** 115–120.

Islam, A. K. M. R., Shepherd, K. W., and Sparrow, D. H. B. (1976). Addition of individual barley chromosomes to wheat. *Barley Genet., Proc. Int. Barley Genet. Symp., 3rd, 1975,* pp. 260–270.

Islam, A. S. (1964). A rare hybrid combination through application of hormone and embryo culture. *Nature (London)* **201,** 320.

Jalani, B. S., and Moss, J. P. (1980). The site of action of crossability genes (*Kr1, Kr2*) between *Triticum* and *Secale.* I. Pollen germination, pollen tube growth and number of pollen tubes. *Euphytica* **29,** 571–579.

Jalani, B. S., and Moss, J. P. (1981). The site of action of crossability genes (*Kr1, Kr2*) between *Triticum* and *Secale.* II. Proportion of pollen tubes containing pollen tubes and effects of alternate pollination on seed set. *Euphytica* **30,** 105–112.

Jinks, J. L., Caligari, P. D. S., and Ingram, N. R. (1981). Gene transfer in *Nicotiana rustica* using irradiated pollen. *Nature (London)* **291,** 586–588.

Johnston, S. A., and Hanneman, R. E., Jr. (1982). Manipulations of endosperm balance number overcome crossing barriers between *Solanum* species. *Science* **217,** 446–448.

Johnston, S. A., den Nijs, T. P. M., Peloquin, S. J., and Hanneman, R. E., Jr. (1980). The significance of genic balance to endosperm development in interspecific crosses. *Theor. Appl. Genet.* **57,** 5-9.

Johri, B. M., and Vasil, I. K. (1961). Physiology of pollen. *Bot. Rev.* **27,** 325-381.

Johri, B. M., Sastri, D. C., and Shivanna, K. R. (1977). Pollen viability, storage and germination. *Adv. Pollen-Spore Res.* **2,** 120-139.

Jost, L. (1907). Uber die Selbststerilitat eininger Bluten. *Bot. Ztg.* **65,** 77-117.

Kado, C. I., and Kleinhofs, A. (1980). Genetic modification of plant cell through uptake of foreign DNA. *Int. Rev. Cytol., Suppl.* **11B,** 47-80.

Kanta, K. (1960). Intra-ovarian pollination in *Papaver rhoeas* L. *Nature (London)* **188,** 683-684.

Kendall, W. A. (1968). Growth of *Trifolium pratense* L. pollen tubes in compatible and incompatible styles of excised pistils. *Theor. Appl. Genet.* **38,** 351-354.

Kendall, W. A., and Taylor, N. L. (1969). Effects of temperature on pseudocompatibility in *Trifolium pratense* L. *Theor. Appl. Genet.* **39,** 123-126.

Kesicki, E. (1979). New hybrids between *Lycopersicum esculentum* and *L. peruvianum*. *Rep. Tomato Genet. Coop.* **29,** 28 (cited by Taylor and Al-Kumma, 1982).

Knott, D. R., and Dvorak, J. (1976). Alien germplasm as a source of resistance to disease. *Annu. Rev. Phytopathol.* **14,** 211-215.

Knox, R. B., Willing, R. R., and Ashford, A. E. (1972a). Role of pollen wall proteins as recognition substances in interspecific incompatibility in poplars. *Nature (London)* **237,** 381-383.

Knox, R. B., Willing, R. R., and Pryor, L. D. (1972b). Interspecific hybridization in poplars using recognition pollen. *Silvae Genet.* **21,** 65-69.

Knox, R. B., Clarke, A., Harrison, S., Smith, P., and Marchalonis, J. J. (1976). Cell recognition in plants: Determinants of stigma surface and their pollen interactions. *Proc. Natl. Acad. Sci. U.S.A.* **73,** 2788-2792.

Krens, F. A., Molendijk, L., Wullems, G. J., and Schilperoort, R. A. (1982). *In vitro* transformation of plant protoplasts with Ti-plasmid DNA. *Nature (London)* **296,** 72-74.

Krumbiegel, G., and Schieder, O. (1981). Comparison of somatic and sexual incompatibility between *Datura innoxia* and *Atropa belladonna*. *Planta* **153,** 466-470.

Kruse, A. (1974). A 2,4-D treatment prior to pollination eliminates the haplontic (gametic) sterility in wide intergeneric crosses with 2-rowed barley, *Hordeum vulgare* ssp. *distichum* as maternal species. *Hereditas* **78,** 319.

Kuo, C. G., Peng, J. S., and Tsay, J. S. (1981). Effect of high temperature on pollen grain germination, pollen tube growth, and seed yield of Chinese cabbage. *HortScience* **16,** 67-68.

Kuwada, H., and Mabuchi, T. (1976). Ovule and embryo culture of the seeds obtained from the crosses between *Hibiscus asper, H. cannabinus* and *H. sabdariffa*. *Jpn. J. Breed.* **26,** 298-306.

Kwack, B. H. (1965). Stylar culture of pollen and physiological studies of self-incompatibility in *Oenothera organensis*. *Physiol. Plant.* **18,** 297-305.

Laibach, F. (1929). Ectogenesis in plants. *J. Hered.* **20,** 200-208.

Larter, E., and Chaubey, C. (1965). Use of exogenous growth substances in promoting pollen tube growth and fertilization in barley-rye crosses. *Can. J. Genet. Cytol.* **7,** 511-518.

Larter, E. N., and Enns, H. (1960). The influence of gibberellic acid on the development of hybrid barley ovules *in vivo*. *Can. J. Genet. Cytol.* **2,** 435-441.

Lee, J. A. (1981). Genetics of D_3 complementary lethality in *Gossypium hirsutum* and *G. barbadense*. *J. Hered.* **72,** 299-300.

Lewis, D. (1942). The physiology of incompatibility in plants. I. The effect of temperature, *Proc. R. Soc. London, Ser. B* **131,** 13-26.

Linskens, H. F. (1964). The influence of castration of pollen tube growth after self-pollination. *In* "Pollen Physiology and Fertilization" (H. F. Linskens, ed.), pp. 230-236. North-Holland Publ., Amsterdam.

Linskens, H. F. (1975). Incompatibility in *Petunia. Proc. R. Soc. London, Ser. B* **188,** 299-311.

Linskens, H. F., and Kroh, M. (1967). Incompatibilitat der Phanerogamen. *In* "Handbuch der Pflanzenphysiologie" (W. Ruhland, ed.), Vol. 18, pp. 506-530. Springer-Verlag, Berlin and New York.

Lurquin, P. F. (1981). Binding of plasmid loaded liposomes to plant protoplasts: Validity of biochemical methods to evaluate the transfer of exogenous DNA. *Plant Sci. Lett.* **21,** 31-40.

Maheshwari, P. (1950). "An Introduction to the Embryology of Angiosperms." McGraw-Hill, New York.

Maheshwari, P., and Kanta, K. (1961). Intraovarian pollination in *Eschscholzia californica* Cham., *Argemone mexicana* L. and *A. ochroleuca* Sweet. *Nature (London)* **191,** 304.

Martin, F. W. (1959). Staining and observing pollen tubes in the style by means of fluorescence. *Stain Technol.* **34,** 125-128.

Martin, F. W. (1968). Behaviour of *Lycopersicum* incompatibility alleles in an alien genetic milieu. *Genetics* **56,** 101-109.

Matsubara, S. (1973). Overcoming self-incompatibility by cytokinin treatment on *Lilium longiflorum. Bot. Mag.* **86,** 43-46.

Matsubara, S. (1978). Overcoming self-incompatibility of *Lilium longiflorum* by chemical and high temperature treatments and endogenous levels of plant growth regulators after pollination. *Proc. Int. Palynol. Conf., 4th, 1978,* pp. 359-368.

Matsubara, S. (1980). Overcoming self-incompatibility in *Raphanus sativus* L. with high temperature. *J. Am. Soc. Hortic. Sci.* **105,** 842-846.

Matsubara, S. (1981). Overcoming self-incompatibility of *Lilium longiflorum* Thunb. by application of flower organ extract or by temperature treatment of pollen. *Euphytica* **30,** 97-104.

Matsuzawa, Y. (1977). Pollen germination and pollen tube growth at different pollination temperatures in interspecific crosses in the genus *Brassica. Bull. Coll. Agric., Utsunomiya Univ.* **10,** 1-10.

Matthews, B. F., and Cress, D. E. (1981). Liposome-mediated delivery of DNA to carrot protoplasts. *Planta* **153,** 90-94.

Mattsson, O., Knox, R. B., Heslop-Harrison. J. and Heslop-Harrison, Y. (1974). Protein pellicle of the stigma papillae as a probable recognition site in incompatibility reactions. *Nature (London)* **247,** 298-300.

Matzk, F. (1976). Attempts to overcoming of incompatibilities in interspecific and intergeneric crosses with grasses. *Incompatibility Newsl.* **7,** 65-74.

Matzk, F. (1981). Successful crosses between *Festuca arundinacea* Schreb. and *Dactylis glomerata* L. *Theor. Appl. Genet.* **60,** 119-122.

Michurin, L. V. (1950). "Selected Works." Moscow (cited by Ramulu *et al.,* 1979).

Mujeeb-Kazi, A. (1981). *Triticum timopheevii* × *Secale cereale* crossability. *J. Hered.* **72,** 227-228.

Mujeeb-Kazi, A., and Rodriguez, R. (1980). Some intergeneric hybrids in the Triticeae. *Cereal Res. Commun.* **8,** 469-475.

Mujeeb-Kazi, A., and Rodriguez, R. (1982). Cytogenetics of hybrids of *Elymus canadensis* × *Hordeum vulgare. J. Hered.* **73,** 77-79.

Nakanishi, T., and Hinata, K. (1973). An effective time for CO_2 gas treatment in overcoming self-incompatibility in *Brassica. Plant Cell Physiol.* **14,** 873–879.

Nakanishi, T., Esahi, Y., and Hinata, K. (1969). Control of self-incompatibility by CO_2 gas in *Brassica. Plant Cell Physiol.* **10,** 925–927.

Napier, K. V., and Walton, P. D. (1981). New interspecific hybrids in the genus *Agropyron. Euphytica* **30,** 459–466.

Nasrallah, M. E. (1974). Genetic control of quantitative variation in self-incompatibility proteins detected by immunodiffusion. *Genetics* **76,** 45–50.

Nasrallah, M. E., and Wallace, D. H. (1967). Immunogenetics of self-incompatibility in *Brassica oleracea* L. *Heredity* **22,** 519–527.

Nasrallah, M. E., Barber, J. T., and Wallace, D. H. (1970). Self-incompatibility proteins in plants: Detection, genetics and possible mode of action. *Heredity* **25,** 23–27.

Nessling, F. A. V., and Morris, D. A. (1979). Cytokinin levels and embryo abortion in interspecific *Phaseolus* crosses. *Z. Pflanzenphysiol.* **91,** 345–358.

Nishio, T., and Hinata, K. (1977). Analysis of S-specific proteins in stigma of *Brassica oleracea* L. by isoelectric focussing. *Heredity* **38,** 391–396.

Nishio, T., and Hinata, K. (1978). S-allele specificity of stigma proteins in *Brassica oleracea* and *B. campestris. Heredity* **41,** 93–100.

Nishio, T., and Hinata, K. (1980). Rapid detection of S-glycoproteins of self-incompatibile crucifers using con-A reaction. *Euphytica* **29,** 217–221.

Nitsch, J. P. (1952). Plant hormones in the development of fruits. *Q. Rev. Biol.* **27,** 33–57.

Nitzsche, W., and Hennig, L. (1976). Ovule culture in grasses. *Z. Pflanzenzuecht.* **77,** 80–82.

Ockenden, D. J. (1978). Effect of hexane and humidity on self-incompatibility in *Brassica oleracea. Theor. Appl. Genet.* **52,** 113–119.

Pandey, K. K. (1963). Stigmatic secretion and bud pollination in self- and cross-incompatible plants. *Naturwissenschaften* **50,** 408–409.

Pandey, K. K. (1964). Elements of the S-gene complex. I. The SF1 alleles in *Nicotiana. Genet. Res.* **2,** 397–409.

Pandey, K. K. (1975). Sexual transfer of specific genes without gametic fusion. *Nature (London)* **256,** 311–312.

Pandey, K. K. (1976). The genus *Nicotiana:* Evolution of incompatibility in flowering plants. *Linn. Soc. Symp. Ser.* **7,** 421–434.

Pandey, K. K. (1977). Mentor pollen: Possible role of wall-held pollen growth substances in overcoming intra- and inter-specific incompatibility. *Genetica (The Hague)* **47,** 219–229.

Pandey, K. K. (1978). Gametic gene transfer by means of irradiated pollen. *Genetica (The Hague)* **49,** 53–69.

Pandey, K. K. (1979). Overcoming incompatibility and promoting genetic recombination in flowering plants. *N.Z.J. Bot.* **17,** 645–663.

Pandey, K. K. (1980). Further evidence for egg transformation in *Nicotiana. Heredity* **45,** 15–29.

Peloquin, S. J. (1981). Chromosomal and cytoplasmic manipulations. *Plant Breed. 2 [Two] [Proc. Plant Breed. Symp.], 2nd, 1979,* pp. 117–150.

Phillips, G. C., Collins, G. B., and Taylor, N. L. (1982). Interspecific hybridization of red clover (*Trifolium pratense* L.) with *T. sarosiense* Hazsl. using *in vitro* embryo rescue. *Theor. Appl. Genet.* **62,** 17–24.

Pickering, R. A. (1979). Further investigations on partial incompatibility in crosses between *Hordeum vulgare* L. and *H. bulbosum. In* "Broadening Genetic Base of

Crops" (A. C. Zeven and A. M. van Harten, eds.), pp. 319–325. Centre for Agricultural Publishing and Documentation, Wageningen.

Pickering, R. A. (1980). Attempts to overcome partial incompatibility between *Hordeum vulgare* L. and *H. bulbosum* L. *Euphytica* **29**, 369–377.

Pittagelli, G. W., and Stavely, J. R. (1975). Direct hybridization of *Nicotiana repanda* × *N. tabacum*. *J. Hered.* **66**, 281–284.

Power, J. B., Cummins, S. E., and Cocking, E. C. (1970). Fusion of isolated plant protoplasts. *Nature (London)* **225**, 1016–1018.

Raghavan, V. (1977). Applied aspects of embryo culture. *In* "Applied and Fundamental Aspects of Plant Cell, Tissue and Organ Culture" (J. Reinert and Y. P. S. Bajaj, eds.), pp. 375–397. Springer-Verlag, Berlin and New York.

Ramulu, K. S., Bredemeijer, G. M. M., Dijkhuis, P., de Nettancourt, D., and Schibilla, H. (1979). Mentor pollen effects on gametophytic incompatibility in *Nicotiana, Oenothera* and *Lycopersicum*. *Theor. Appl. Genet.* **54**, 215–218.

Rangaswamy, N. S. (1963). Control of fertilization and embryo development. *In* "Recent Advances in the Embryology of Angiosperms" (P. Maheshwari, ed.), pp. 327–353. Int. Soc. Plant Morphol., University of Delhi, Delhi.

Rangaswamy, N. S. (1977). Applications of *in vitro* pollination and *in vitro* fertilization. *In* "Applied and Fundamental Aspects of Plant Cell, Tissue and Organ Culture" (J. Reinert and Y. P. S. Bajaj, eds.), pp. 412–425. Springer-Verlag, Berlin and New York.

Reed, S. M., and Collins, G. B. (1978). Interspecific hybrids in *Nicotiana* through *in vitro* culture of fertilised ovules. *J. Hered.* **69**, 311–315.

Rees, H., Riley, R., Breese, E. L., and Law, C. N. eds. (1981). The manipulation of genetic systems in plant breeding. *Philos. Trans. R. Soc. London, Ser. B* **292**, 401–609.

Riley, R., Chapman, V., and Johnson, R. (1968). The incorporation of alien disease resistance in wheat by genetic interference with the regulation of meiotic chromosome synapsis. *Genet. Res.* **12**, 199–219.

Riley, R., Law, C. N., and Chapman. V. (1981). The control of recombination. *Philos. Trans. R. Soc. London, Ser. B* **292**, 529–534.

Robbelen, G. (1960). Uber die kreuzungsunvertraglichkeit verschiedener *Brassica*-Arten als folge eines gehemmten Pollenschlauchwachstums. *Zuechter* **30**, 300–312.

Roberts, I. N., Stead, A. D., Ockendon, D. J., and Dickinson, H. G. (1979). A glycoprotein associated with the acquisition of self-incompatibility system by maturing stigmas of *Brassica oleracea*. *Planta* **146**, 179–183.

Roberts, I. N., Stead, A. D., Ockendon, D. J., and Dickinson, H. G. (1980). Pollen stigma interactions in *Brassica oleracea*. *Theor. Appl. Genet.* **58**, 241–246.

Roggen, H. P. (1975). Stigma application of an extract from rape pollen (*Brassica napus* L.) effects self-incompatibility in Brussels sprout (*Brassica oleracea* var. "gemmifera"). *Incompatibility Newsl.* **6**, 80–84.

Roggen, H. P., and van Dijk, A. J. (1972). Breaking incompatibility in *Brassica oleracea* L. by steel-brush pollination. *Euphytica* **21**, 48–51.

Roggen, H. P., van Dijk, A. J., and Dosman, C. (1972). Electric aided pollination: A method of breaking incompatibility in *Brassica oleracea* L. *Euphytica* **21**, 181–184.

Ronald, W. G., and Ascher, P. D. (1975). Effects of high temperature treatments and seed yield and self-incompatibility in *Chrysanthemum*. *Euphytica* **24**, 317–322.

Sarashima, M. (1964). Studies on the breeding of artificially synthesized rape (*Brassica napus*). I. F_1 hybrids between *B. campestris* group and *B. oleracea* group and the derived F_2 plants. *Jpn. J. Breed.* **14**, 226–237.

Sastri, D. C. (1981). Some aspects of self-incompatibility in *Petunia hybrida. Plant Mol. Biol. Newsl.* **2,** 110–111.
Sastri, D. C., and Moss, J. P. (1982). Effects of growth regulators on incompatible crosses in the genus *Arachis* L. *J. Exp. Bot.* **33,** 1293–1301.
Sastri, D. C., and Shivanna, K. R. (1976a). Attempts to overcome interspecific incompatibility in *Sesamum* using recognition pollen. *Ann. Bot. (London)* [N. S.] **41,** 891–893.
Sastri, D. C., and Shivanna, K. R. (1976b). Recognition pollen alters incompatibility in *Petunia. Incompatibility Newsl.* **7,** 22–24.
Sastri, D. C., and Shivanna, K. R. (1978). Seed set following compatible pollination in incompatibly pollinated flowers of *Petunia. Incompatibility Newsl.* **9,** 91–93.
Sastri, D. C., and Shivanna, K. R. (1979). Role of pollen wall proteins in intraspecific incompatibility in *Saccharum bengalense. Phytomorphology* **29,** 324–330.
Sastri, D. C., and Shivanna, K. R. (1980a). Electrophoretic patterns of proteins and isozymes in developing pistils of *Petunia hybrida. Incompatibility Newsl.* **12,** 24–29.
Sastri, D. C., and Shivanna, K. R. (1980b). Efficacy of mentor pollen in overcoming intraspecific incompatibility in *Petunia, Raphanus* and *Brassica. J. Cytol. Genet.* **15,** 107–112.
Sastri, D. C., Nalini, M. S., and Moss, J. P. (1981). Tissue culture and prospects of crop improvement in *Arachis hypogaea* and other oilseeds crops. *In* "Tissue Culture of Economically Important Plants in Developing Countries" (A. N. Rao, ed.), pp. 42–57. National University of Singapore, Singapore.
Sastri, D. C., Moss, J. P., and Nalini, M. S. (1982). The use of *in vitro* methods in groundnut improvement. *In* "Plant Cell Culture in Crop Improvement" (S. K. Sen and K. L. Giles, eds.), pp. 365–370. Plenum, New York.
Savitri, K. S., Ganapathy, P. S., and Sinha, S. K. (1980). Sensitivity to low temperature in pollen germination and fruit set in *Cicer arietinum* L. *J. Exp. Bot.* **31,** 475–481.
Schieder, O., and Vasil, I. K. (1980). Protoplast fusion and somatic hybridization. *Int. Rev. Cytol., Suppl.* **11B,** 21–46.
Sedgley, M. (1974). Assessment of serological techniques for S-allele identification in *Brassica oleracea. Euphytica* **23,** 543–551.
Sharma, D. R., Chowdhury, J. B., Ahuja, U., and Dhankhar, B. S. (1980). Interspecific hybridization in genus *Solanum.* A cross between *S. melongena* and *S. khasianum* through embryo culture. *Z. Pflanzenzuecht.* **85,** 248–253.
Shigenobu, T., and Sakamoto, S. (1981). Intergeneric hybridization between *Agropyron tsukushiense* and *Hordeum bulbosum. Jpn. J. Genet.* **56,** 505–515.
Shivanna, K. R., and Rangaswamy, N. S. (1969). Overcoming self-incompatibility in *Petunia axillaris.* I. Delayed pollination, pollination with stored pollen, and bud pollination. *Phytomorphology* **19,** 372–380.
Shivanna, K. R., and Sastri, D. C. (1981). Stigma surface esterase activity and stigma receptivity in some taxa characterized by wet stigma. *Ann. Bot. (London)* [N. S.] **47,** 53–64.
Shivanna, K. R., Heslop-Harrison, Y., and Heslop-Harrison, J. (1978). The pollen stigma interaction: Bud pollination in the Cruciferae. *Acta. Bot. Neerl.* **27,** 107–119.
Shivanna, K. R., Johri, B. M., and Sastri, D. C. (1979). "Development and Physiology of Angiosperm Pollen." Today and Tomorrow Printers and Publishers, New Delhi.
Singh, A. K., Sastri, D. C., and Moss, J. P. (1980). Utilisation of wild *Arachis* species at ICRISAT. *Proc. Int. Groundnut Workshop* (R. W. Gibbons, ed.), pp. 82–90. ICRISAT, Patancheru.

Smith, A. R., and van Staden, J. (1979). Cytokinins in excised embryos and endosperm of *Zea mays* grown under aseptic conditions. *Z. Pflanzenphysiol.* **93,** 95-103.

Snape, J. W., Bennett, M. D., and Simpson, E. (1980). Post-pollination events in crosses of hexaploid wheat with tetraploid *Hordeum bulbosum*. *Z. Pflanzenzuecht.* **85,** 200-204.

Stalker, H. T. (1980). Utilisation of wild species for crop improvement. *Adv. Agron.* **33,** 111-147.

Stanley, R. G., and Linskens, H. P. (1974). "Pollen: Biology, Biochemistry and Management." Springer-Verlag, Berlin and New York.

Stead, A. D., Roberts, A. D., and Dickinson, H. G. (1979). Pollen pistil interaction in *Brassica oleracea;* events prior to pollen germination. *Planta* **146,** 211-216.

Stead, A. D., Roberts, A. D., and Dickinson, H. G. (1980.). Pollen-stigma interaction in *Brassica oleracea:* The role of stigmatic proteins in pollen grain adhesion. *J. Cell Sci.* **42,** 417-423.

Stettler, R. F. (1968.). Irradiated mentor pollen: Its use in remote hybridization of black cottonwood. *Nature (London)* **219,** 746-747.

Stettler, R. F., and Guries, R. P. (1976). The mentor pollen phenomenon in black cottonwood. *Can. J. Bot.* **54,** 820-830.

Stettler, R. F., Koster, R., and Steenackers, V. (1980). Interspecific crossability studies in poplars. *Theor. Appl. Genet.* **58,** 273-282.

Stewart, J. M. (1981). *In vitro* fertilization and embryo rescue. *Environ. Exp. Bot.* **21,** 301-305.

Stewart, J. M., and Hsu, C. L. (1978). Hybridization of diploid and tetraploid cottons through *in-ovulo* embryo culture. *J. Hered.* **69,** 404-408.

Straub, J. (1946). Zur Entwicklungsphysiologie der Selbsterilitat von *Petunia*. *Z. Naturforsch.* **1,** 287-291.

Straub, J. (1947). Zur Entwicklungsphysiologie der Selbststerilitat von *Petunia*. II. Das Prinzip des Hemmungs-mechanismus. *Z. Naturforsch. B: Anorg. Chem., Org. Chem., Biochem., Biophys., Biol.* **2B,** 433-444.

Straub, J. (1958). Das uberwinden der Selbsterilitat. *Z. Bot.* **46,** 98-111.

Subrahmanyam, N. C. (1979). Haploidy from *Hordeum* interspecific crosses. Part 2. Dihaploids from *H. branchyantherum* and *H. depressum*. *Theor. Appl. Genet.* **55,** 139-144.

Subrahmanyam, N. C., and Kasha, K. J. (1971). Increased barley haploid production following gibberellic acid treatment. *Barley Genet. Newsl.* **1,** 47-50.

Swaminathan, M. S. (1955). Overcoming cross-incompatibility among some Mexican diploid species of *Solanum*. *Nature (London)* **176,** 23-26.

Swaminathan, M. S., and Murty, B. R. (1957). One way incompatibility in some species crosses in the genus *Nicotiana*. *Indian J. Genet. Plant. Breed.* **17,** 23-26.

Szabados, L., Hadlaczky, G. Y., and Dudits, D. (1981). Uptake of isolated plant chromosomes by plant protoplasts. *Planta* **151,** 141-145.

Takahashi, H. (1973). Genetic and physiological analysis of pseudo-self-compatibility in *Petunia hybrida*. *Jpn. J. Genet.* **48,** 27-33.

Taekshita, M., Kato, M., and Tokomasu, S. (1980). Application of ovule culture to production of intergeneric or interspecific hybrids in *Brassica* and *Raphanus*. *Jpn. J. Genet.* **55,** 373-387.

Taylor, I. B., and Al-Kummer, M. K. (1982). The formation of complex hybrids between *Lycopersicon esculentum* × *L. peruvianum* and their potential use in promoting intergeneric gene transfer. *Theor. Appl. Genet.* **61,** 59-64.

Taylor, N. L., Quarles, R. F., and Anderson, M. K. (1980). Methods of overcoming interspecific barriers in *Trifolium*. *Euphytica* **29,** 441-450.

Thomas, B. R., and Pratt, D. (1981). Efficient hybridization between *Lycopersicum esculentum* and *L. peruvianum* via embryo callus. *Theor. Appl. Genet.* **59,** 215–220.
Thomas, H. (1981). Interspecific manipulation of chromosomes. *Philos. Trans. R. Soc. London, Ser. B* **292,** 519–528.
Tiara, T., and Larter, E. N. (1977a). Effects of ϵ-amino-*n*-caproic acid and L-lysine on the development of hybrid embryo of triticale (×-triticale-Secale). *Can. J. Bot.* **55,** 2330–2334.
Tiara, T., and Larter, E. N. (1977b). The effects of variation in ambient temperature alone and in combination with ϵ-amino-*n*-caproic acid on development of embryos from wheat rye crosses (*Triticum turgidum* var. *durum* cv. *gora* × *Secale cereale. Can. J. Bot.* **55,** 2335–2337.
Townsend, C. E. (1968). Self-compatibility studies with diploid alsike clover, *Trifolium hybridum* L. III. Response to temperature. *Crop Sci.* **8,** 269–272.
Townsend, C. E. (1971). Advances in the study of incompatibility. *In* "Pollen: Development and Physiology" (J. Heslop-Harrison, ed.), pp. 281–309. Butterworth, London.
Tsinger, N. V., and Petrovskaya-Baranova, T. P. (1961). The pollen grain wall: A living physiologically active structure. *Dokl. Akad. Nauk SSSR* **138,** 466–496.
Tsitsin, N. V., ed. (1962). "Wide Hybridization in Plants." Isr. Program Sci. Transl., Jerusalem.
van der Donk, J. A. W. M. (1974a). Differential synthesis of RNA in self- and cross-pollinated styles of *Petunia hybrida* L. *Mol. Gen. Genet.* **131,** 1–8.
van der Donk, J. A. W. M. (1974b). Synthesis of RNA and protein as a function of pollen tube-style interaction in *Petunia hybrida* L. *Mol. Gen. Genet.* **134,** 93–98.
van der Donk, J. A. W. M. (1975). Recognition and gene expression during the incompatibility reaction in *Petunia hybrida* L. *Mol. Gen. Genet.* **141,** 305–316.
van Herpen, M. M. A. and Linskens, H. R. (1981). Effect of season, plant age and temperature during plant growth on compatible and incompatible pollen tube growth in *Petunia hybrida. Acta Bot. Neerl.* **30,** 209–218.
van der Pluijm, J., and Linskens, H. F. (1966). Feinstruktur der Pollenschlauche in Griffel von *Petunia. Zuechter* **36,** 220–224.
Visser, D. L. (1977). The effect of alternating temperatures on the self-incompatibility of some clones of Brussels sprout (*Brassica oleracea* L. var. Gemmifera (D.C.) Schulz). *Euphytica* **26,** 273–277.
Visser, T. (1981). Pollen and pollination experiments. IV. 'Mentor pollen' and 'pioneer pollen' technique regarding incompatibility and incongruity in apple and pear. *Euphytica* **30,** 363–369.
Wareing, P. F., and Phillips, I. D. J. (1978). "The Control of Growth and Differentiation in Plants." Pergamon, Oxford.
Wenzel, G., Schieder, O., Prezwozny, T., Sopory, S. K., and Melchers, G. (1979). Comparison of single cell culture derived from *Solanum tuberosum* L. plants and a model for their application in breeding programs. *Theor. Appl. Genet.* **55,** 49–55.
Williams, E. E. (1978). A hybrid between *Trifolium repens* and *T. ambiguum* with the aid of embryo culture. *N. Z. J. Bot.* **16,** 499–506.
Williams, E. E. (1980). Hybrids between *Trifolium ambiguum* and *T. hybridum* obtained with the aid of embryo culture. *N. Z. J. Bot.* **18,** 215–200.
Williams, E. G., and de La Tour, G. (1980). The use of embryo culture with transplanted nurse endosperm for the production of interspecific hybrids in pasture legumes. *Bot. Gaz. (Chicago)* **141,** 252–257.
Williams, E. G., and de La Tour, G. (1981). Production of tetraploid hybrids between *Ornithopus pinnatus* and *O. sativus* using embryo culture. *N. Z. J. Bot.* **19,** 23–30.

Williams, E. G., and Verry, I. M. (1981). A partially fertile hybrid between *Trifolium repens* and *T. ambiguum*. *N. Z. J. Bot.* **19,** 1-7.

Willing, R. R., and Pryor, R. D. (1976). Interspecific hybridization in poplar. *Theor. Appl. Genet.* **47,** 141-151.

Wright, S. T. C. (1960). Occurrence of an organ specific antigen associated with the microsome fraction of plant cells and its possible significance in the process of cellular differentiation. *Nature (London)* **185,** 82-85 (cited by Bates and Deyoe, 1973).

Wu, F. (1955). An interspecific cross of *Brassica pekinensis* Rupr. × *B. oleracea* var. *fimbriata* Mill. *Acta Bot. Sin.* **4,** 63-69.

Yasuda, S. (1934). Physiological researches on self-incompatibility in *Petunia violacea*. *Bull. Coll. Agric. For. Morioka* **20,** 1-95.

Zenkteler, M. (1980). Intraovarian and *in vitro* pollination. *Int. Rev. Cytol., Suppl.* **11B,** 137-156.

Zenkteler, M., and Melchers, G. (1978). *In vitro* hybridization by sexual methods and by fusion of somatic protoplasts. *Theor. Appl. Genet.* **52,** 81-90.

Cytoplasmic Male Sterility in Pearl Millet [*Pennisetum americanum* (L.) Leeke]—A Review*

K. ANAND KUMAR

Pearl Millet Improvement Program, ICRISAT Sahelian Centre, Niamey, Niger

and

D. J. ANDREWS

Pearl Millet Improvement Program, ICRISAT Centre, Patancheru, Andhra Pradesh, India

I. Introduction

Pearl millet [*Pennisetum americanum* (L.) Leeke] is a staple food for millions of people in several African countries and in the Indian subcontinent. It is grown on an estimated 26 million ha in these two regions with an annual production of about 13 million metric tons (Food

*Submitted as ICRISAT Journal Article No. 303.

ISBN 0-12-040910-0

and Agriculture Organization, 1978). The average grain yields of traditional cultivars (open-pollinated landrace varieties) are between 400 and 550 kg/ha.

In 1962, seed of the first cytoplasmic-genic male-sterile [or cytoplasmic male sterility (CMS), as it is normally termed] line of pearl millet developed in the United States was used by breeders in India to identify, and 3 years later to release, the first successful commercial grain hybrid. The floral biology and the resulting mating system facilitates the production of F_1 hybrids in this wind-pollinated crop (Burton and Powell, 1968; Duvick, 1966).

The history of development of CMS in pearl millet, and the foreseen need for it, has involved many scientists in two continents. While the application of CMS to crop production in India has been a success story, it has been beset by epidemics of downy mildew on successive hybrids, which remain a continuing threat. Cytoplasmic male sterility remains to be utilized in Africa, where the largest amount of pearl millet is grown in a wide range of diverse environments. There are regions, however, where, through the breeding of adapted seed parents, CMS has the potential to increase food production.

It is the purpose of this article to trace the discovery and use of CMS in pearl millet, but before reviewing the subject a description of the characteristics of flowering, the basis for cytoplasmic male sterility, and a summary of early breeding work are given.

A. CHARACTERISTICS OF FLOWERING

Pearl millet is protogynous; that is, the stylar branches are exerted from the florets 1 to several days before the anthers. Spikelets generally consist of two florets: one perfect and the other staminate. Stylar branches are usually first exerted from the florets in the upper half of the head, and by the third day nearly all styles will have emerged on the head. Generally, anthers emerge from the same florets that exerted styles first, beginning at least 1 day after complete stylar emergence. A head will normally shed pollen 4 to 6 days after first style emergence. A second flush of anthers may then emerge if the staminate florets are functional. Stigmas will remain receptive if not pollinated for up to 10 days, depending on weather conditions. Fertilization occurs within a few hours after pollination, and the stylar branches wilt and dry usually 24 hr after pollination (Burton, 1980). Thus the mating system of pearl millet encourages, but does not enforce, cross-pollination. Cross-pollination is observed to be around 70 to 80%, but some self-pollination occurs because tillers may flower in succession (Rao *et al.*, 1951; Burton, 1974).

B. BASIS FOR CYTOPLASMIC MALE STERILITY

Cytoplasmic male sterility in pearl millet, where anthers fail to dehisce and pollen may not be properly formed or may be empty, results from the interaction of a "sterile" cytoplasm (termed A cytoplasm) with homozygous recessive alleles of nuclear genes causing male sterility, e.g., ms_c ms_c (Burton and Athwal, 1967, 1968). Lines with such a constitution are termed A lines. When in "normal" (N) cytoplasm, the same recessive homozygote ms_c ms_c does not cause male sterility since its genetic effect is not expressed in normal cytoplasm. Lines with this constitution are called maintainers, or B lines, since, when they are used to pollinate A lines, the result will again be all male-sterile plants (hence male sterility has been maintained). Large quantities of seed that will give all male-sterile plants can be produced this way and this method forms the basis for commercial hybrid seed production. The presence of a dominant Ms_c allele will cause male fertility regardless of the type of cytoplasm. Lines of the constitution Ms_c Ms_c are termed restorers (R lines—as are all male or "pollen parents" of hybrids) because, when they are used to pollinate A lines, resulting plants will be ms_c Ms_c and will therefore have male fertility restored.

C. EARLY BREEDING WORK

In India two breeding approaches were used prior to 1965 to develop high-yielding and stable genotypes taking advantage of the mating system. These were, first, to develop improved open-pollinated varieties, and, second, to breed single-cross hybrids without the use of CMS.

Mass selection has been the principal method used in the development of varieties. A few improved strains have been evolved by pureline selection, but owing to the predominantly cross-pollinated nature of this crop, the chances of obtaining superior varieties by this approach were poor. Individual plant selections in Akola Bajri led to the development of three improved cultivars, Nos. 37, 54, and 59 (Pandya *et al.*, 1955). Selections in the local populations were made on the basis of well-filled, compact, long panicles; high grain weight; and uniformity in ripening. In this manner several improved varieties were evolved from local materials, notably CO2, CO3, AKP1, AKP2, RSJ, RSK, Punjab type 55, and A1/3 (Ahluwalia and Vittal Rao, 1964;

Khan *et al.*, 1958; Utkhede, 1972). In addition to using indigenous variability, introductions from African material were also used in developing varieties; for example, Babapuri and Jamnagar giant in Gujarat, AF-3 in Maharashtra, Improved Ghana (renamed Pusa Moti) in Delhi, and S-530 (an outcross of an African introduction with local varieties in the Punjab) were developed and released for cultivation (Joshi *et al.*, 1961; Athwal and Rachie, 1963). These improved open-pollinated varieties had, however, a low yield potential, giving average yields of 900–1200 kg/ha, and could not be maintained because of extensive outcrossing with local landraces.

The second approach of producing hybrids (without the use of CMS) was started in India in the early 1940s (Rao *et al.*, 1951; Chavan *et al.*, 1955). In 1943, at the Millet Breeding Station in Coimbatore, India, 15 F_1 crosses were made between eight different types of pearl millet. Evaluations showed that three of these F_1 hybrids gave 16–163% more grain yield than did the best parents. Between 1944 and 1946 an additional 86 F_1 hybrids were evaluated, of which 34 were superior to the best parent. Between 1946 and 1950 a further 743 F_1 hybrids were tested, of which 25 gave yields significantly superior to both the best parent and the check CO.1. Of these, two hybrids, X.1 and X.2 were multiplied by planting the respective parents in rows and harvesting and mixing the seed from both the parental rows. In 21 trials conducted in nine districts on farmers' fields of the then Madras presidency during 1949 and 1950, hybrids X.1 and X.2 yielded 48 and 44 % more grain, respectively, over the local check and were released for cultivation (Rao *et al.*, 1951). Similar attempts were made in the former Bombay state (Chavan *et al.*, 1955).

The principal constraint in the development and seed production of a good hybrid was the lack of a practical and easy method to produce 100% hybrid seed. This fact was recognized in 1951 by Rao *et al.*, who emphasized that

> The method of large scale production of hybrid seeds for distribution is a problem demanding particular attention in this crop due to the peculiar floral mechanism of the plant. *Perhaps induction of male-sterility in female rows (similar to detasseling in maize) may assure complete cross pollination.* But attempts so far made to induce male-sterility have not been successful.

Other limitations were the narrow adaptability and limited superiority of hybrids over the local varieties (Athwal, 1966).

During the same time that breeders in India were trying to develop hybrids in this crop, Burton (1948), with studies that began in 1936, reported that maximum forage yields (the principal use of pearl millet in the United States) could be obtained from the F_1 hybrid of two lines possessing high combining ability. He realized that most forage crops—with their small perfect flowers, few seeds per flower, and high seedling rates—do not lend themselves to controlled hybridization on the extensive scale required for commerical hybrid production; consequently, the economical production of commercial F_1 hybrid seed was seen as a major obstacle. Results from his experiments, with mixtures of parent and hybrid millet seed containing 90, 80, 50, and 20% hybrid seed together with pure seed of the parents, indicated that the mean forage production of the 90, 80, and 50% hybrid mixtures over 6 years did not differ significantly from that of pure hybrids. The use of a high seed rate, with consequent natural elimination of the weaker parental seedlings or by selective thinning, increases the proportion of hybrid seedlings to be established, and over a period of years, any seed mixture within the range of 50–90% was expected to yield as much as pure hybrid seed (Burton, 1948).

Burton (1948) realized the importance of CMS for the commercial production of hybrids, as did the workers in India (Rao *et al.*, 1951). Burton detected self-sterility in many lines but commented that the *"difficulties associated with maintaining and using such lines in a commercial seed production program of an annual grass were so great as to make their use seem impractical."*

To circumvent the difficulty of providing pure hybrid seed to farmers, Athwal (1961) suggested the use of the xenia effect using a yellow seed color or some other marker gene for eliminating nonhybrid seed or seedlings.

To summarize, research during this period clearly indicated that large yield increases were possible with F_1 hybrids and that there was an absolute need for a system such as CMS to exploit heterosis on a commercial scale.

III. Cytoplasmic and Other Types of Male Sterility

A. Discovery and Development of CMS Lines

As early as 1940 Kadam *et al.* observed various forms of male sterility when inbreeding local millet from Nasik in the Bombay presidency, but did not conceive of the sterility as useful in hybrid production.

Kajjari and Patil (1956) reported the occurrence of spikes producing shriveled anthers without pollen in crossbred progenies. On bagging some of these spikes, no seed was obtained in those left unpollinated, but those that were dusted with pollen from normal spikes set seed fully. These researchers suggested, but did not establish, that the observed male sterility could be of a cytoplasmic type and realized that it could be used to produce 100% hybrid seed.

Burton (1958) observed CMS in the winter of 1955–1956, in a cross designated 556 × 23, where 2 of the 4 selected F_2 plants failed to shed pollen or set seed when selfed. When these 2 male-sterile plants were again pollinated (backcrossed) by 23, the F_1 progeny again failed to shed pollen or to set seed when selfed. However, when pollen from other lines was used, seed set was complete, thus suggesting CMS. When a range of 41 inbreds were used as pollen parents on these male-sterile plants [(556 × 23) × 23], 6 of the resulting F_1 progeny were male sterile, 8 others were partially male sterile, and 27 were male fertile, proving conclusively that CMS in pearl millet had been found and at the same time showing that male fertility could easily be restored. Thus the first CMS line, Tift 23A, which was developed by repeated backcrossing with Tift 23B (maintainer), was released in 1965 (Burton, 1965a, 1969). Burton (1969) also developed dwarf versions of Tift 23A and B, called Tift 23DA and Tift 23DB, by transferring the recessive *d2* gene through a series of backcrosses into Tift 23A and Tift 23B. He also observed that since the tall and dwarf versions are near isogenic, similar heterogenic responses should be found in hybrid combinations. A dwarf male-sterile line such as 23DA with a tall male pollinator should produce more hybrid seed and should make better quality forage compared with tall sister hybrids (Burton, 1969).

Madhava Menon (1958), at the Millets Breeding Station, Coimbatore, observed in 1949 a high frequency of male-sterile plants showing underdeveloped, nondehiscent anthers in an open-pollinated population, PT819, originating from the Bellary district of Mysore state. No seed was set in selfed spikes of male-sterile plants, whereas in open-pollinated or artificially pollinated spikes, seed set was total, indicating normal female fertility. Two of seven crosses made with PT819 male-sterile plants in 1950 gave male-sterile F_1 hybrids, whereas the three testcrosses with male-fertile PT819 plants gave both male-sterile and male-fertile plants. The 2 male-sterile F_1 hybrids (PT819 × PT732/5 and PT819 × PT837/7) were backcrossed to the male parents (PT732/5 and PT837/7) using individual plants. Of the 22 hybrids evaluated, 13 were male-sterile, 2 were male-fertile, and 7 segregated in a 1:1 proportion for male-sterile and male-fertile plants. These results led Madhava Menon (1959) to conclude that "male-sterility observed in PT819 is dependent on an interaction between nuclear and cytoplasmic factors." Though this CMS source was found and backcrossed again in 1951, unfortunately these lines were subsequently left out of further maintenance and were eventually lost (Appadurai and Sambathkumar, 1976). Work on new crosses of PT819 × PT732 reported by Appadurai *et al.* (1982) indicates that this CMS source may have been rediscovered and that it differs from several other male-sterile lines and their maintainers on which it was tested.

Athwal (1961) identified CMS in the late-maturing genetic stock IP189 (a selfed progeny of an African variety) at Ludhiana. The CMS plants were pollinated with pollen from different sources for maintenance and the line developed was designated as CMS 66A (also referred to as L66A). During 1962, male-sterile plants noticed in a segregating population from a natural cross (outcross) in a stock possessing pearly amber-colored grains were used to develop CMS 67A (L67A) (Athwal, 1966).

Burton (1965b) developed Tift 18A and Tift 18B inbreds by repeatedly backcrossing CMS Tift 23A with Tift 18, which carries a dormancy factor that inhibits premature germination.

Athwal (1966) reported the development of 11 new CMS lines at Ludhiana. These are L101, L102, L104, L105, L106, L107, L110, and L111, which incorporate Tift 23A sterile cytoplasm; L103 incorporates the sterile cytoplasm of L66A, and L108 and L109 incorporate the sterile cytoplasm of L67A. In each case sterile cytoplasm was introduced by repeated backcrossing into the identified maintainer starting in 1962. The distinguishing morphological characters of these CMS lines are described by Athwal *et al.* (1976).

In 1968, Burton and Athwal (1969) released a dwarf maintainer Tift 239DB (an inbred derived by introducing the *d2* dwarf gene into Tift 13) and its corresponding sterile Tift 239DA, which incorporates the sterile cytoplasm of L103A.

A number of other CMS lines have been developed since the late 1960s. D202A was developed at the Indian Agricultural Research Institute (IARI), New Delhi, in 1966, as a selection in the tall CMS line Tift 18B (Utkhede, 1972). Vohra (1969) isolated a dwarf CMS line designated as 18D2A from the tall Tift 18B at Jamnagar. Four CMS lines, 28A, 330A, 558A, and 628A, were developed at the Regional Research Center of IARI at Kanpur (Utkhede, 1972). Pokhriyal *et al.* (1976), at IARI, New Delhi, bred 5071A (an induced downy-mildew-resistant mutant from Tift 23B), 5054A (a Nigerian line, Kano 2457, incorporating sterile cytoplasm of Tift 23A), and 5141A (an inbred of Indian origin from Baroda 4, which also incorporates the sterile cytoplasm of Tift 23A). Gill *et al.* (1979), at Ludhiana, developed Pb 304A and Pb 405A as induced downy-mildew-resistant mutants from

Tift 239DB and L110B, respectively. Gill *et al.* (1981) reported the isolation of a natural downy-mildew-resistant mutant of Tift 23A—designated as Pb 204A—from a population of Tift 23A and Tift 23B. At the International Crops Research Institute for the Semi-Arid Tropics (ICRISAT) an induced downy-mildew-resistant mutant was isolated from an irradiated Tift 23DB population with rigorous screening at each selection and backcross generation in the downy mildew nursery (Williams *et al.*, 1981). This was designated as ICM ms81A and B and was distributed to research workers in 1981 (Andrews and Anand Kumar, 1982).

Burton (1981a,b) reported the development of Tift 23DAE and Tift 23DBE, which are early and photoperiod-insensitive versions of Tift 23DA and Tift 23DB. The early gene was transferred by repeated backcrossing from a weak, spindly, very early-maturing plant discovered in a field of "Katherine" pearl millet growing in Queensland, Australia. Powell and Burton (1973) introduced a recessive trichomeless gene (*tr*) into the normally pubescent Tift 23B that, when homozygous, suppresses all trichomes. The near-isogenic lines Tift 23B Tr Tr and Tift 23B tr tr have been used in studies to compare the pleiotropic effects of the *Tr* gene on several characters (Burton *et al.*, 1977).

A list of all the CMS lines that have been mentioned in the literature, irrespective of whether they have been used for commercial exploitation of hybrid vigor, appears in Table I. Reference will be made to some of these CMS lines in subsequent discussions.

B. COMMERCIAL UTILIZATION OF CMS LINES IN F_1 HYBRID PRODUCTION

The discovery of CMS fulfilled a historical need for a viable and economic method of producing high-yielding grain hybrids in pearl millet on a commercial scale.

Mahadevappa and Ponnaiya (1966) crossed four inbred lines having good combining ability with four CMS stocks developed by Madhava Menon (1958). The range of grain yield increases from 15 hybrids was from 4.4 to 157% over the check variety CO.1, and four were significantly superior to the check.

Seed of male-sterile Tift 23A and its maintainer Tift 23B was made available to breeders in India in 1962 (Athwal, 1966); seed of Tift 23DA and B and Tift 18A and B was made available in 1964 [Indian Council of Agricultural Research (ICAR), 1966; Utkhede, 1972].

The first five grain hybrids to be made on CMS Tift 23A, by the millet botanist at Ludhiana, were evaluated at six locations in 1963 and

TABLE I. Cytoplasmic male-sterile lines in pearl millet

Cytoplasmic male-sterile line	Remarks	Reference[a]
Tift 23A	Carries A1 cytoplasm	Burton (1965a)
Tift 23DA	Dwarf version of Tift 23A	Burton (1969)
Tift 23DA tr tr	Trichomeless, dwarf	Powell and Burton (1973)
Tift 23DEA	Early, photoperiod insensitive	Burton (1981a,b)
Tift 239DA	Carries A2 cytoplasm of L103A	Burton and Athwal (1969)
Tift 18A	Carries dormancy factor in seed	Burton (1965b)
L66A	Carries A2 cytoplasm	Athwal (1961, 1966)
L67A	Carries A3 cytoplasm	Athwal (1961, 1966)
L101A	Carries Tift 23A cytoplasm	Athwal *et al.* (1976)
L102A	Carries Tift 23A cytoplasm	Athwal *et al.* (1976)
L104A	Carries Tift 23A cytoplasm	Athwal *et al.* (1976)
L105A	Carries Tift 23A cytoplasm	Athwal *et al.* (1976)
L106A	Carries Tift 23A cytoplasm	Athwal *et al.* (1976)
L107A	Carries Tift 23A cytoplasm	Athwal *et al.* (1976)
L110A	Carries Tift 23A cytoplasm	Athwal *et al.* (1976)
L111A	Carries Tift 23A cytoplasm	Athwal *et al.* (1976)
L103A	Carries L66A cytoplasm	Athwal *et al.* (1976)
L108A	Carries L67A cytoplasm	Athwal *et al.* (1976)
L109A	Carries L67A cytoplasm	Athwal *et al.* (1976)
D202A	Selection in Tift 18A	Utkhede (1972)
18DA (126DA?)	Dwarf selection in Tift 18A	Vohra (1969)
28A	—	Utkhede (1972)
330A	—	Utkhede (1972)
558A	—	Utkhede (1972)
628A	—	Utkhede (1972)
5071A	Induced downy-mildew-reisistant mutant of Tift 23B	Pokhriyal *et al.* (1976)
5054A	A Nigerian line incorporating Tift 23A cytoplasm	Pokhriyal *et al.* (1976)
5141A	An Indian inbred incorporating Tift 23A cytoplasm	Pokhriyal *et al.* (1976)
5094A	A Nigerian line incorporating Tift 23A cytoplasm	Pokhriyal *et al.* (1976)
Pb 304A	Induced downy-mildew-resistant mutant of Tift 239DB	Gill *et al.* (1979)
Pb 405A	Induced downy-mildew-resistant mutant of L110B	Gill *et al.* (1979)
Pb 204A	Spontaneous downy-mildew-resistant mutant of Tift 23A and Tift 23B	Gill *et al.* (1981)
ICM ms81A	Induced downy-mildew-resistant mutant from Tift 23DB	Andrews and Anand Kumar (1982)
PT732A	An Indian inbred incorporating PT819 (Bellary, India) cytoplasm	Appadurai *et al.* (1982)

[a]Not necessarily report of development of a male-sterile line.

gave yields of 40 to 113% more than did the checks. In addition, 256 hybrids, also on Tift 23A, were evaluated in a preliminary trial at six locations in which several hybrids showed significant yield superiority over the check. However, restoration of pollen fertility was far from satisfactory (ICAR, 1964). In 1964, new hybrid combinations were evaluated at 7 or 20 locations (Table II) and yield as percentage of check ranged from 175 to 200. One of these hybrids, Tift 23A × Bil 3B, was released under the name HB-1 (HB, Hybrid Bajra; "Bajra," pearl millet) for commercial cultivation in 1965. Another hybrid, Tift 23A × J15, was recommended for cultivation in the state of Gujarat.

In advanced hybrid Bajra Class I trials (with adequate moisture) and Class II trials (under limited moisture) conducted by the All India Coordinated Millets Improvement Project (AICMIP) during 1965–1966, HB-1 yielded 77% more grain than the check (1191 kg/ha) over 17 locations and 73% more grain than the check (1179 kg/ha) over 14 locations in the respective trials (ICAR, 1966).

The spectacular yield advances that were achieved as predicted (Burton, 1948; Athwal and Rachie, 1963) stimulated several breeders to make and test other new hybrid combinations using CMS Tift 23A, Tift 18A, Tift 23DA, and L101A among those available. This increased activity led to the identification of four more hybrid combinations, named HB-2 (Tift 23A × J88), HB-3 (Tift 23A × J104), HB-4 (Tift 23A × K560), and HB-5 (Tift 23A × K559), between 1967 and 1972 (Table III). As the number of superior hybrids bred increased, the area planted to these also significantly increased. Of an estimated 12 million ha planted annually to pearl millet in India, the percentage of total area planted to hybrids increased from 3.3 in 1967–1968 to about 16 by 1971–1972 (Table IV). With the adoption of hybrids, production

TABLE II. Performance of some promising pearl millet hybrids, AICMIP, rainy season, 1964[a,b]

Pedigree	Grain yield (as % of checks)	Number of locations
Tift 18A × Bil 2A	200	7
Tift 23A × S 350	185	7
Tift 23A × Bil 3B	188	20
Tift 23A × CM63	175	20
L111A × Bil 3B	177	20
Check 1 (yield kg/ha)	735	7
Check 2 (yield kg/ha)	898	20

[a]AICMIP, All India Coordinated Millets Improvement Project.
[b]From the Indian Council of Agricultural Research (1966).

TABLE III. Pedigree of pearl millet hybrids released in India, 1965-1972, by AICMIP[a]

Hybrid	Pedigree	Year of release	Breeding site
HB-1	Tift 23A × Bil 3B	1965	Ludhiana
HB-2	Tift 23A × J88	1967	Jamnagar
HB-3	Tift 23A × J104	1968	Jamnagar
HB-4	Tift 23A × K560	1968	Kanpur
HB-5	Tift 23A × K559	1972	Kanpur/Delhi

[a]All India Coordinated Millets Improvement Project.

increased from 2.6 million metric tons in 1950–1951 to nearly 8 million metric tons during 1970–1971, with a corresponding increase in per hectare yields from 288 to 622 kg (Safeeulla, 1977). Among the hybrids released, HB-3 was by far the most popular hybrid because of its early maturity, bolder grains, and good performance under moisture-stress conditions.

India's pearl millet production then suffered a severe setback in the early 1970s due to epidemics of downy mildew caused by the fungus *Sclerospora graminicola* (Sacc.) Schroet, and by 1974 the production dropped to 3.6 million metric tons largely due to the effects of this disease (Jain and Pokhriyal, 1975; Murty, 1980). It became obvious that the epidemics were because of the common CMS line Tift 23A that was used in the production of all hybrids popular up to that time (Table

TABLE IV. Adoption of pearl millet hybrids in India, 1966–1967 to 1977–1978[a]

Cropping year	Total cropped area[b]	Hybrid adoption (%)
1966–1967	12,239	0.5
1967–1968	12,808	3.3
1968–1969	12,052	6.2
1969–1970	12,493	10.2
1970–1971	12,913	15.9
1971–1972	11,773	15.9
1972–1973	11,817	21.2
1973–1974	13,934	23.6
1974–1975	11,285	22.4
1975–1976	11,571	25.0
1976–1977	10,751	21.1
1977–1978	11,035	23.8

[a]From Swindale (1981).
[b]In millions of hectares.

III), which became so susceptible to downy mildew that it was no longer possible to grow it (Jain and Pokhriyal, 1975).

Efforts were directed initially at inducing resistance to downy mildew in Tift 23A and B through irradiation of Tift 23B seeds with 25 krad of γ rays, generating large numbers of plant(A) × plant(B) pairs and screening them for downy mildew resistance. At the sixth generation after irradiation, three A-line progenies were found that recorded no downy mildew incidence and were stable for CMS (Murty, 1973, 1974). One of these, named 5071A, showed a high degree of field resistance to downy mildew (Raut *et al.*, 1973; Pokhriyal and Jain, 1974), and with this line it became possible to reconstitute the original commercial hybrids. For example, HB-3 (Tift 23A × J104) was reconstituted and called NHB-3 (new HB-3; 5071A × J104). Likewise, the other hybrids, HB-4 and HB-5, were reconstituted and were named, respectively, NHB-4 (5071A × K560) and NHB-5 (5071A × K559). Seed of the reconstituted hybrids was multiplied for distribution to farmers; for example, Jain and Pokhriyal (1975) reported the multiplication of 600 metric tons of seed of hybrid NHB-5 (seed rate of 4 kg/ha) during 1974 to replace some of the then-existing downy-mildew-susceptible hybrids.

CMS line 111A (Table II) was found at the Punjab Agricultural University to show a high degree of resistance to downy mildew, and two resistant hybrids, PHB-10 (also called HB-6; 111A × PIB-115) and PHB-14 (also called HB-7; 111A × PIB-228), were released in 1975 (Gill *et al.*, 1975).

Thus the reconstituted versions of the "first-generation" hybrids (i.e., NHB-3, NHB-4, and NHB-5) and the two new hybrids (PHB-10 and PHB-14) developed on 111A were multiplied and successfully introduced into cultivation, thereby reducing downy mildew incidence considerably.

However, the success of the reconstituted hybrids was short-lived because CMS 5071A became rapidly susceptible to downy mildew, as did the reconstituted hybrids made with it. Sain Dass and Kanwar (1977) recorded, for instance, 29 and 39% downy mildew incidence on 5071A under natural and epiphytotic conditions, respectively, at the Haryana Agricultural University in Hissar, India. Further breeding efforts made at the IARI in New Delhi (Pokhriyal *et al.*, 1976) resulted in two new downy-mildew-resistant CMS lines—5141A and 5054A.

Two of the successful hybrids, HB-3 and HB-4 (which became NHB-3 and NHB-4 with 5071A as the female parent), were again reconstituted and renamed BJ104 (5141A × J104) and BK 560 (5141A

× BK560-230), respectively, and were released for cultivation throughout India in 1976. Hybrid CJ104 (5054A × J104) and a dwarf hybrid, GHB-1399 (126D2A × J1399), were released for the state of Gujarat (Pokhriyal, 1977). Of these, BJ104, an early, high-tillering, and downy-mildew-resistant hybrid, has stability of yield and performs well under moisture-stress situations (Pokhriyal, 1977). In India, currently hybrids BJ104 and BK560 are widely grown, whereas CJ104 and PHB-14 are restricted to specific areas.

Of the limited number of commercially available CMS lines in India, 5141A is used in about 60% of the new hybrid combinations that are evaluated each year in AICMIP multilocational hybrid trials (Table V).

Research continues to develop other downy-mildew-resistant CMS lines in order to breed diversified hybrids to minimize future disease epidemics. Gill *et al.* (1977) were able to select for residual variation for downy mildew resistance in populations of Tift 23A (in a total population of 4000 plants) and Tift 23B (1000 plants) under natural conditions. One of the three CMS lines selected for downy mildew resistance resembles Tift 23A and has been designated as Pb 204A (Gill *et al.*, 1981). Andrews and Anand Kumar (1982) isolated an induced downy-mildew-resistant version of the highly susceptible dwarf CMS line Tift 23DA by irradiating seed of Tift 23DB. This was designated as ICM ms81A. (see Section II,A).

C. BREAKDOWN OF CMS

There are four reports (Vittal Rao, 1969; Reddi and Reddi, 1970; Thakare 1977; Saxena and Chaudhary, 1977) in which the stability of

TABLE V. Relative use of male-sterile lines in new hybrids tested by AICMIP, 1977–1979[a,b]

Male-sterile line	No. of hybrids/year			Total	Percentage
	1977	1978	1979		
5141A	18	17	15	50	59
111A	5	3	2	10	12
5054A	2	3	2	7	8
5071A	1	—	2	3	4
Others	4	6	5	15	17
Total	30	29	26	85	100

[a]AICMIP, All India Coordinated Millets Improvement Project.
[b]From Coordinator's Report, AICMIP 1979–1980 (ICAR, 1980).

CMS lines has been compared in different seasons or years. In three studies it was found that environmental effects, principally temperature and humidity, can influence the frequency of plants shedding pollen. Thakur (1977), however, found no differences due to seasonal effects. It was also concluded that there may be genetic effects in which modifier genes can restore partial pollen fertility in an otherwise purely CMS line.

Pollen shedders in CMS 111A were eliminated by making plant(A) × plant(B) crosses and selecting in their progeny for stable male sterility (Gill *et al.*, 1977, 1979). The success achieved in breeding stable 111A indicates that modifier genes that restore fertility are present in certain male-sterile backgrounds and selection against them is possible.

Burton (1972) showed that fertile sectors discovered in heads of Tift 23A were a result of the occurrence of a dominant male-fertility-restoring mutation where one recessive ms_{c1} allele had mutated to Ms_{c1}. He also put forward the alternative hypothesis that fertile sectors could result because of the "mutation of A (sterile) to N (normal) cytoplasm."

Clement (1975), using four different CMS lines [ASM-3, derived from African material; LMS-1A (Tift 23A); and two sterile F_1 hybrids, ASM-5 (LMS-1A × male-fertile nonrestorer) and ASM-7 (LMS-1A × male-fertile nonrestorer)], observed several sectors of fertile anthers. ASM-3 showed the lowest rate of 0.03 fertile sectors/1000 heads, ASM-7 was highest with 1.17/1000, whereas ASM-5 and LMS-1A were intermediate, having rates of 0.26 and 0.15/1000, respectively. Hybrids obtained by crossing normal CMS plants × pollen from male-fertile sectors were all sterile, but selfed seed obtained from the fertile sectors produced fertile progeny, thereby indicating that the fertile sectors observed were due to cytoplasmic (plasmon) mutations.

Burton (1977) provided further evidence for the cytoplasmic nature of the fertile-sector mutants in sterility maintainers using CMS Tift 23A and Tift 239DA. He observed 103 male-fertile mutants that were the result of the cytoplasmic mutation that changed sterile (A) cytoplasm to normal (N) cytoplasm and hence made them male-fertile maintainers. These B (maintainer) lines resulting from such mutations appeared to be stable and identical to normal B lines in appearance and performance. The frequency of male-fertile mutations from CMS plants ranged from 1:431 to 1:737. In Tift 239DA, 219 plants with one or more heads were found that shed pollen in a population of 10,600 plants (slightly over 2%).

The evidence provided by Burton (1972, 1977) and Clement (1975) indicates that male-fertile plants or CMS plants with fertile sectors originate because of nuclear or cytoplasmic (plasmon) mutations. Obviously the gradual increase of male-fertile plants in a CMS line in a hybrid-seed-increase program would reduce the percentage of hybrid seed produced. Limited generation increase from breeders' seed and strict roguing offers the best methods of preventing both cytoplasmic- and nuclear-fertile mutants affecting the hybrid seed industry (Burton, 1977).

D. SOURCES OF CMS

Burton and Athwal (1967) reported the relationship between Tift 23A (Burton, 1965a) and L66A and L67A (Athwal, 1966) sterile cytoplasms. Genetic cytoplasmic interactions for fertility restoration or sterility maintenance as observed in the F_1 hybrids, originating from all possible reciprocal crosses between the sterile and maintainer lines, showed that the sterile cytoplasms carried by L66A and L67A are different from Tift 23A. L66B and L67B maintain sterility in Tift 23A, but Tift 23B restores fertility in both L66A and L67A. L66B restores fertility in L67A, and L67B is a partial fertility restorer for L66A. The ability of male lines to maintain sterility or restore fertility was visually estimated on the basis of percentage seed set by selfed heads and number of seeds per centimeter of head of the hybrid. The CMS Tift 23A, L66A, and L67A sources, since they carry different cytoplasms, were designated as S1, S2, and S3, respectively (Burton and Athwal, 1967), but the letter *S* was later substituted by the letter *A* because S1, S2, and S3 are normally used to describe the selfing generations (Burton and Powell, 1968). Burton and Athwal (1967) have also presented genetic models suggesting the relationship between different sources.

Aken'Ova and Chheda (1981) reported a CMS plant in a population of ex-Bornu "gero" (early) millet in northern Nigeria. To determine the relationship between the ex-Bornu CMS source and the three known sources in pearl millet, two plants (named Gero-1 and Gero-2) that were good maintainers for the CMS ex-Bornu were each crossed to Tift 23A1, 239A2, and 426A3. Gero-1 and Gero-2 were good maintainers for 426A3 and 239A2, respectively, but neither was a good maintainer for all three sources. The authors, however, suggest that the CMS source found in ex-Bornu may be different from the three previously known sources. Unfortunately, the maintainer lines are presently not available.

As noted earlier, crosses made with PT732A and B (Appadurai *et al.*, 1982) on other A and B lines indicate that PT732 may be a new CMS source.

Burton and Athwal (1967) found that L103B (maintainer of L103A developed from the same African source of cytoplasms as L66A) was a good fertility restorer for Tift 23A, in contrast to L66B, which maintained sterility in Tift 23A. Clement (1975), investigating the plasmon (cytoplasmic) mutations to male fertility on CMS lines, stated that the common assumption that the cytoplasm is the same for all stocks possessing the same maternal parentage is open to question and that there is likely to be considerable cytoplasmic variability in divergent lines originating from the same cytoplasmic source. The classification of male-sterile cytoplasms carried in different genetic backgrounds, if based only on the source of sterile cytoplasm (Athwal *et al.*, 1976), may therefore be erroneous when data on reciprocal relationships of restoration of fertility and maintenance of sterility are not included.

Burton and Athwal (1968), based on the reciprocal maintainer relationship that exists between A1 and A2 sterile cytoplasms, have proposed a scheme where population *Y* containing plants with A1 cytoplasm, and population *Z* containing plants with A2 cytoplasm and their maintainers, are used in a reciprocal recurrent selection program that facilitates the development of superior F_1 hybrids.

E. COMBINING-ABILITY TESTS WITH CMS LINES

Several studies were carried out to assess the general combining ability (GCA) of CMS lines in pearl millet (Table VI). The number of CMS lines involved in these studies ranged from 2 (Murty *et al.*, 1967; Appadurai *et al.*, 1980) to 7 (Kapoor *et al.*, 1979) and the testers from 9 (Ramadass *et al.*, 1974) to 184 (Murty *et al.*, 1967). Table VI indicates that though the same common CMS lines are involved in several studies, their combining-ability rating differs from researcher to researcher. For example, whereas Kapoor *et al.* (1979) and Yadav *et al.* (1981) have rated 5141A to be the best general combiner, Pokhriyal *et al.* (1976) rated 5054A better than 5141A. Likewise, Badwal *et al.* (1973) and Ramadass *et al.* (1974) found 111A to be best general combiner, but it was not rated as such by Kapoor *et al.* (1979) or Yadav *et al.* (1981). Pokhriyal *et al.* (1974) observed, contrary to predictions (Burton, 1969), that Tift 23A and Tift 23DA, which are near isogenic, showed wide differences in their combining ability.

Several of these researchers commented that the actual cross performance is decidedly more important when the development of the F_1 hybrids is the ultimate objective. This is because a CMS line, though rated as a good general combiner, may produce hybrids that are unacceptable for other reasons. This was illustrated clearly by Phul *et al.*

TABLE VI. Reports on combining ability of cytoplasmic male-sterile lines of pearl millet

CMS line involved[a]	No. of testers used	Better combiners (in descending order)	Reference
Tift 23A, Tift 18A (2)	184	Tift 23A (for tiller number), Tift 18A (ear length and girth)	Murty *et al.* (1967)
Tift 23A, L101A, L103A (3)	18	101A, Tift 23A, 103A	Gupta and Gupta (1971)
Tift 23A, L101A, L107A, L110A, and L111A (5)	10	111A, 110A, Tift 23A, 101A, 107A	Badwal *et al.* (1973)
Tift 23DA, Tift 18DA, Tift 18A, L110A, L111A (5)	10	110A, Tift 18DA, 111A, Tift 23DA, Tift 18A	Singh *et al.* (1974)
Tift 23A, Tift 18A, D202A, and L111A (4)	9	111A, Tift 18A, D202A, Tift 23A	Ramadass *et al.* (1974)
126D2A, 628A, Tift 23DA, 202A, and Tift 23A (5)	9	628A, Tift 23A	Pokhriyal *et al.* (1974)
L101A, L103A, L111A (3)	18	101 (forage characteristics)	Tyagi *et al.* (1974)
L101A, L103A, L111A, Tift 23A, Tift 23DA (5)	21	101A, Tift 23DA, Tift 23A	Tyagi *et al.* (1975)
5054A, 5094A, 5141A, Tift 23A, 5071A (5)	12	5054A, 5094A, 5141A, Tift 23A, 5071A	Pokhriyal *et al.* (1976)
67A, L111A, Tift 239DA, 628A (4)	19	628A, 111A, 67A, Tift 239DA	Phul *et al.* (1976)
Tift 23DA, L111A, 126DA, 5071A, 5054A, 5141A, and 5094A (7)	12	5141A, 5054A	Kapoor *et al.* (1979)
5141A and Tift 23DA (2)	40	No differences	Appadurai *et al.* (1980)
5141A, 5054A, L111A (3)	35	5141A, 5054A	Yadav *et al.* (1981)
5141A, 5054A, L111A (3)	16	5141A, 111A	Singh *et al.* (1982)

[a]Numbers in parentheses donote number of lines used.

(1976) and Pokhriyal *et al.* (1974), who found the CMS line 628A to be the best combiner, but the hybrids were tall, susceptible to downy mildew, and late in maturity. Murty *et al.* (1967) advocated individual performance of hybrids as the practical way of judging superiority, and Tyagi *et al.* (1974) also commented that a line with good general combining ability may not necessarily be better in all cross combinations. Ramandass *et al.* (1974) found that though 111A was the best general combiner for grain yield, the resultant hybrids were late in maturity, and those with Tift 18A, the second best combiner, were tall, with prolonged maturity.

The question that arises is whether the choice of testers used to evaluate the combining ability among CMS lines is appropriate. In some cases in which the objective is the replacement of a line (for example, the change of Tift 23A with 5141A to reconstitute hybrid BJ104) in a particular combination, obviously specific combining ability is of prime importance, and the most appropriate tester is the opposite inbred (J104 in the example cited) parent of a single cross (Matzinger, 1953). Development of new CMS lines is a time-consuming and laborious task, and ways are needed to determine at an early stage the worth of the newly developed CMS lines in hybrid combinations. During the process of CMS development it is a common practice to discard lines that have obvious morphological defects, unstable sterility, or susceptibility to diseases such as downy mildew. Phenotypic elimination of lines is effective for many traits that influence the commercial acceptance of hybrids, but to our knowledge effective elimination of poor combining lines by phenotype has not been achieved. Breeders test to identify unique hybrid combinations with high yields and stable performance, and it is here that the specific combining ability is expressed and capitalized.

F. INDUCTION OF CMS

Burton and Hanna (1976) reported the induction of CMS in pearl millet Tift 23DB using ethidium bromide. Male-sterile mutants (whole heads, sectored heads, or heads with sterile and fertile florets intermingled) occurred at frequencies of 1 in 30,100, 1 in 515, and 1 in 274 plants treated with 0, 250, and 100 ppm of ethidium bromide, respectively. The occurrence of sterile mutants in the generation that was treated, which set seed when pollinated and gave rise to CMS progenies, proved that the mutants were cytoplasmic in nature. They suggested that by this treatment the time and effort required to create and have CMS mutants in production would be much less than that required for the five or more generations of backcrossing now currently used. Furthermore, the utility of this approach would be in such cases as corn, in which the T cytoplasm carried by the CMS line conditions susceptibility to *Helminthosporium maydis* and the isogenic maintainer is resistant (Hooker, 1978). However, in pearl millet, Anand Kumar *et al.* (1983) have shown that the A1 type of male-sterile cytoplasm does not condition susceptibility to downy mildew and that it is the nuclear genes that are responsible for imparting resistance to CMS lines.

Burton and Hanna (1982) reported that treatment of Tift 23DB seed with aqueous solutions of streptomycin and mitomycin resulted in stable CMS mutants. Furthermore, the induced mutants were found to have sterility maintainer and fertility restorer requirements similar to Tift 23DA.

Hanna and Powell (1974) described a female-sterile mutant in Tift 23B subjected to thermal neutron treatment. This could be used to produce an obligate apomict, and they suggested a scheme for the production of hybrid seed, which presupposes a chromosomal rearrangement in which the female sterile segregates to give a 3:1 female-sterile to female-fertile ratio.

G. GENETIC MALE STERILITY

Genetic male sterility in pearl millet was reported by Gill *et al.* (1973) and Rao and Koduru (1978a) in which the male-sterile gene had no other effect except to cause abortion of the male germ cells. Rao and Koduru (1978b) showed that homozygosity for the gene *ms-2* produces, in addition to pollen abortion, plasmodial tapetum, plasmodial pollen mother cells, delayed and asynchronous meiotic development, desynapsis, and blockage of meiosis. Rao and Devi (1983) reported male sterility in lines Vg272 and IP482 that is controlled by a single recessive gene.

Genetic male sterility is the factor least used commercially of all the systems of sterility discovered in crop plants (Duvick, 1966), and this is also true for pearl millet. At the moment, genetic male sterility is of academic interest in pearl millet and may not be used because of the breeding system of the crop.

H. INDUCTION OF FUNCTIONAL MALE STERILITY

Hanna (1977) found that DPX 3778 (a methoxy triazine complex), prevented both anther exertion and dehiscence in pearl millet, but the pollen remained stainable and plump. A 7.43 kg/ha application at the mid- to late-boot leaf stage, followed by a second application at the same rate 5–6 days later, reduced the selfed seed set to 2, 13, 5, and 30% respectively, in inbreds Tift 23DB, Tift 239DB, Tift 13, and Tift 18DB. Hanna (1977) suggested that DPX 3778 could be used for producing hybrids in pearl millet.

Sharma (1979) reported that a single foliar spray of 0.5% FW-450 solution was effective in inducing functional male sterility in a local strain (Bichpuri) of pearl millet. In the treated plants the emergence of anthers was delayed by a few days, and those anthers that emerged did not dehisce. Pollen and ovular fertility were not affected.

The availability of adapted CMS lines, though limited in range for maturity and height, has permitted new hybrids to be discovered in India. However, for areas in Africa where the Indian- or United States-bred CMS lines succumb to the high downy mildew pressure and CMS is not available in local backgrounds, the method of using male gametocides for producing hybrids may be feasible in the short term.

I. SCHEMES TO INCREASE THE FREQUENCY OF CMS MAINTAINER LINES

In recent years there have been proposals to develop "gene pools" of maintainer lines in pearl millet. These include the schemes to develop B-line synthetics (Andrews, 1976), maintainer or B-line complexes (Gill, 1979), and B composites (Rai and Andrews, 1980). All these proposals envisage the identification of superior maintainers and subsequent conversion through conventional backcrossing into CMS lines.

III. DEVELOPMENT OF CMS LINES AT ICRISAT

A. BREEDING DOWNY-MILDEW-RESISTANT CMS LINES

At ICRISAT, breeding of CMS lines was initiated in 1978 with a view to develop and distribute the lines to breeders in India and Africa as a support function in terms of providing them with means of identifying new hybrid combinations.

Conventional backcrossing is the technique (Allard, 1960; House 1980; Sharma, 1980) that has been used to incorporate sterile cytoplasm. The scheme that is routinely used for the development of new CMS lines involves (1) the grow-out of identified male-sterile testcrosses in two contrasting seasons, rainy and dry, to check the stability of sterility, (2) breeding operations, at least from second or third backcross generations in the downy mildew nursery, and (3) generation of a large number of plant(A) × plant(B) crosses to allow selection for total male sterility, uniformity, and downy mildew resistance. It has been found that the frequency of maintainer lines is low: only 41 maintainers were identified after screening over 6000 testcrosses (about 0.6%) using the three standard CMS lines, 5141A, 5054A, and 111A (Table VII). These are at different backcross stages when a large number of plant(A) × plant(B) pairs are being handled for each CMS source under development.

In an effort to induce downy mildew resistance in susceptible Tift 23D2B, its seed was irradiated with 30 krad of γ rays in the rainy season of 1975. All the plants from the treated seed were selfed and planted as "head-to-rows" in the next generation. Each generation was grown in the downy mildew nursery where disease-free plants in the B line were crossed onto individual plants in the A line on a plant-to-plant basis. This process of pedigree selection and backcrossing was carried out to the sixth backcross generation in the rainy season of 1979, which corresponded to the eighth generation from the irradiation (Table VIII). At this stage three downy-mildew-resistant A and B pairs were identified based on uniformity, stable sterility, and other characters such as seed set and exertion, and their seed was increased in isolations. One of these CMS pairs was named ICM ms81A and its maintainer as ICM ms81B and was released to breeders in India through AICMIP in 1981.

The evaluation of a large number of plant(A) × plant(B) pairs in

TABLE VII. Frequency of maintainer lines in testcrosses on 5141A, 5054A, and 111A

Year	No. of testcrosses screened[a]	No. initially identified[b]	No. of maintainers confirmed[c]
1977	1655	168	5
1978	1513	78	0
1979	1266	102	27
1980	2000	9	9
Total	6434	357 (5.5%)	41 (0.63%)

[a]Rainy season.
[b]Based on rainy season observations.
[c]Based on rainy season and dry season observations.

TABLE VIII. Downy mildew incidence on sterile and fertile sixth-backcross progenies derived from mutagen-treated Tift 23D2B

	Relative frequency (%)		
Incidence class (%)	A lines (sterile cytoplasm)	B lines (normal cytoplasm)	Indicator[a]
0–10	61.5	62.8	0
11–20	27.6	28.6	0
21–30	7.3	5.3	4.5
31–40	2.4	1.3	4.5
41–50	0.5	1.0	0
51–60	0.3	1.0	9.1
61–70	0.3	0	13.6
71–80	0.1	0	27.3
81–90	0	0	18.2
91–100	0	0	22.7
Chi-square value	3.76[b]		
Probability range	0.75–0.50		
No. of progenies	1142	301	22

[a]Susceptible hybrid NHB-3.
[b]Numbers of progenies in the 41–60% incidence range were combined, as were those in the 61–80% range.

the downy mildew screening nursery provided data showing that the downy mildew incidence on A- and B-line progenies is not significantly different. This observation, coupled with the data provided elsewhere (Anand Kumar *et al.*, 1983), indicates that sterile cytoplasm has probably no role to play in determining downy mildew susceptibility. In

TABLE IX. Morphological characteristics of the three standard male-sterile lines and ICM ms81A[a]

	Male-sterile line			
Character	5054A	5141A	111A	ICM ms81A
Days to 50% bloom	50.7 ± 0.2	49.2 ± 0.1	57.8 ± 0.1	56.7 ± 0.2
Plant height (cm)	129 ± 0.7	131 ± 0.6	117 ± 0.7	82.7 ± 1.2
Ear length (cm)	17.4 ± 0.1	17.1 ± 0.1	28.1 ± 0.2	14.7 ± 0.2
Ear girth (cm)	5.5 ± 0.03	5.4 ± 0.03	6.3 ± 0.03	5.9 ± 0.05
No. of tillers/plant	2.7 ± 0.08	3.3 ± 0.08	1.4 ± 0.08	1.1 ± 0.02

[a]Recorded in rainy season 1980 at ICRISAT Center. Observations represent mean ± SEM and based on 100 plants for all except ICM ms81A (based on 72).

Table IX a summary of some of the morphological characteristics of the three standard CMS lines that are currently in use in India and ICM ms81A are presented.

Observations from many crosses with a wide range of diverse material indicate that the maintainer discovery rate is four times higher (around 2.5%) in crosses on ICM ms81A than that observed with the three standard CMS lines, which substantially increases the rate at which new CMS sources can be found. Experience in making hybrids using this dwarf male-sterile line indicated that it is a good combiner (in empirical terms), and the range of hybrid phenotypes that can be obtained is extensive.

B. INCORPORATING ERGOT RESISTANCE

All existing CMS lines are susceptible to ergot (*Claviceps fusiformis* Lov.) and smut (*Tolyposporium penicillariae* Bref.). In Table X ergot and smut reactions of two CMS lines and their respective maintainers are presented. ICRISAT millet pathologists have been able to identify and build up high levels of ergot resistance through selection in crosses between lines with low levels of resistance (since high levels of resistance could not be found in the world germplasm collection of pearl millet)

TABLE X. Ergot and smut reactions of two male steriles and their maintainers[a]

Head	Ergot severity (%)				Smut severity (%)			
no.	5141A	5141B	5054A	5054B	5141A	5141B[b]	5054A	5054B[b]
1	65	75	85	65	50	45	35	40
2	50	60	95	85	80	60	30	15
3	45	85	90	50	85	50	45	35
4	75	90	95	60	85	35	70	70
5	80	85	85	75	95	50	80	85
6	80	90	90	80	98	45	90	60
7	75	85	95	75	98	40	65	75
8	70	65	95	90	98	45	60	40
9	75	60	90	60	95	65	60	65
10	85	80	70	85	60	75	85	60
$\overline{X}$	70	77	89	72	84	51	62	54

[a]Recorded in the rainy season of 1981 at ICRISAT Center. Data courtesy of R. J. Williams and R. P. Thakur.

[b]In B lines (maintainer lines) individuals heads with low smut severity scores also had poor seed set.

(Thakur *et al.*, 1982). Evidence from this process and from crosses between resistant and susceptible lines indicates that the identified resistance is controlled by several recessive genes with cumulative effects.

The work on incorporation of ergot resistance into CMS lines has been carried out in two phases. In the first phase (dry season, 1980), 14 F_2 populations were derived using 10 ergot-resistant lines and 2 B lines, 5141B and 5054B. Over all the F_2 populations, the frequency of 0–10% ergot severity class (desirable) ranged from 0.5 to 62%. Though the frequency of ergot-resistant plants was relatively high (Table XI), from all the 14 F_2 populations only 73 plants (out of 5600 inoculated; 1.3% frequency) could be selected that combined good seed set and low ergot severity. These 73 were planted as F_3 progenies in the rainy season of 1981 and 10 heads were inoculated/progeny. In all, 52 individual plants could be selected that showed ergot resistance and good seed set. Progenies from these will be used for crossing onto the respective male sterile of the maintainer from which they were derived to assess their maintenance ability, for backcrossing to their respective B lines, and for intercrossing if necessary to increase the level of ergot resistance.

In the second phase, 66 new F_2 populations were generated, of which 22 involved two lines (ICMPE 134-6-9 and ICMPE 134-6-18) rated as "consistent" for ergot resistance. Fortunately, these two consistent ergot-resistant lines were found to be maintainers on ICM ms81A, thus opening up the possibility of converting these into CMS lines.

TABLE XI. Ergot severity in four F_2 populations from crosses between B line (maintainer) × ergot-resistant lines[a]

Ergot severity (%) class	Relative frequency (%) in F_2 populations[b]			
	Cross 3	Cross 7	Cross 8	Cross 9
0–10	62	8	45	45
11–20	8	1	10	10
21–30	8	7	8	10
31–40	7	12	12	11
41–50	6	10	7	11
51–60	3	5	6	4
61–70	3	11	8	5
71–80	3	24	4	3
81–90	0	14	0	1
91–100	0	8	0	0

[a]400 plants/F_2 population inoculated by millet pathologists.
[b]Based on observations on 200 plants.

C. INCORPORATING SMUT RESISTANCE

When the progenies derived from mutagen-treated 23D2B were grown at Hissar (a hot spot for smut) in the rainy season of 1977, it was observed that these, like all other CMS lines, were highly susceptible. To incorporate resistance, crosses were made between downy-mildew-resistant progenies of 23D2B and five smut-resistant lines in the 1978 dry season. Eighteen F_2 populations were grown at Hissar in the rainy season of 1980, and only those plants that were dwarf and had less than 10% smut severity were selected. Fifty-seven such F_3 progenies were grown in the 1980 dry season and testcrosses were made onto ICM ms81A to evaluate their maintenance ability. In the rainy season of 1981, the testcrosses and their corresponding F_4 progenies were planted at Hissar in the smut nursery. It was observed that the smut severity on F_4 progenies was much less compared to the testcrosses (Table XII). Of the 57 testcrosses, 16 scored for their fertile and sterile reactions at both Hissar and ICRISAT Center, were male sterile, and 14 of the remainder were partially sterile. The mean smut incidence was 47% on male-sterile testcrosses, which was significantly different from 33% observed on fertile testcrosses. From the data recorded it is evident that male fertility, i.e., pollination, has some effect on smut severity.

TABLE XII. Smut severity (%) on (23D2B-I × smut-resistant lines) F_4 progenies and their testcrosses, rainy season, 1981, Hissar[a,b]

Smut severity (%) class	Test cross		F_4 progenies	
	Number	Frequency (%)	Number	Frequency (%)
0–10	1	1.8	50	87.7
11–20	5	8.8	3	5.2
21–30	15	26.3	1	1.8
31–40	11	19.3	0	0
41–50	5	8.8	1	1.8
51–60	14	24.6	1	1.8
61–70	4	7.0	1	1.8
71–80	1	1.8	0	0
81–90	1	1.8	0	0
91–100	0	0	0	0
Total	57	—	57	—

[a]Ten heads were inoculated per entry by millet pathologists of ICRISAT Center.
[b]Testcrosses made on ICM ms81A.

D. Hybrids for Africa

As previously mentioned, CMS lines that are bred in either India or the United States are not suitable for most of Africa because they tend to be too early and are susceptible to downy mildew, ergot, and smut, in addition to insect pests.

At ICRISAT we have been able to identify maintainers in ex-Bornu (an improved landrace population from Nigeria), in Souna millets (from Mali), and in a Togo population (an early, large-grained variety); the latter two involve ICM ms81A cytoplasm. These and others such as a derivative of the cross J1623 × 3/4 ex-Bornu hold promise in the African situation for the development of adapted hybrids. Conducting further backcrossing during CMS line development in locations in Africa will aid in identifying disease resistances and other adaptation requirements.

IV. Conclusion and Summary

This article on cytoplasmic male sterility has largely concentrated on work carried out in India. The notable aspect of the history of the development and utilization of CMS in pearl millet is the simultaneous need that was felt in both the United States and India for a male-sterility mechanism for the production of commercial hybrids to exploit hybrid vigor. The discovery of male sterility was also almost simultaneous, and the first CMS line was made available in 1962. This made the production of pearl millet grain hybrids possible in India, which dramatically increased production. The downy mildew epidemic that ravaged the Indian pearl millet hybrid crop had its lessons, though not as much publicized as was the blight epidemic of maize in the United States. Breeders soon realized the need to replace Tift 23, which was highly susceptible to downy mildew, and they were eventually successful in finding replacements. Pearl millet production through the use of downy-mildew-resistant hybrids has again risen in India, and we consider this a remarkable achievement in such a short time.

Pearl millet hybrids in India are still based on the Tift 23A sterile cytoplasm, and efforts are being made both by breeders in Indian institutes and at ICRISAT to develop and use other CMS sources.

Work in progress at ICRISAT indicates the possibility of breeding and evaluating pearl millet hybrids using CMS lines that are adapted to Africa. If this leads to a positive outcome, the phenomenon of heterosis in specific combinations can be further exploited to increase grain production in another major region of the semiarid tropics.

REFERENCES

Ahluwalia, M., and Vittal Rao, S. (1964). Pusa Moti bajra shows better adaptability in Andhra Pradesh. *Andhra Agric. J.* **11,** 160–161.

Aken'Ova, M. E., and Chheda, H. R. (1981). A new source of cytoplasmic-genic male-sterility in pearl millet. *Crop Sci.* **21,** 984–985.

Allard, R. W. (1960). "Principles of Plant Breeding." Wiley, New York.

Anand Kumar, K., Jain, R. P., and Singh, S. D. (1983). Downy mildew reaction of pearl millet lines with and without cytoplasmic male-sterility. *Plant Dis.* **67,** 663–665.

Andrews, D. J. (1976)., Multilocational breeding. *Pap., AICMIP Workshop, Gwalior, March, 1976* (mimeo).

Andrews, D. J., and Anand Kumar, K. (1982). Induction of downy mildew resistance in pearl millet male-sterile Tift 23d2 *Mutat. Breed. Newsl.* No. 20, pp. 1–3.

Appadurai, R., and Sambathkumar, S. (1976). Diversification of cytoplasmic-genic male-sterile lines in pearl millet. *Indian J. Agric. Sci.* **46,** 451–452.

Appadurai, R., Natarajan, U. S., and Raveendran, T. S. (1980). Fertility restoration capacity of high combining pollinators in pearl millet. *Indian J. Genet. Plant Breed.* **40,** 505–511.

Appadurai, R., Raveendran, T. S., and Nagarajan, C. (1982). A new male-sterility system in pearl millet. *Indian J. Agric. Sci.* **52,** 832–834.

Athwal, D. S. (1961). Recent developments in the breeding and improvement of bajra (pearl millet) in the Punjab. *Madras Agric. J.* **48,** 18–19 (abstr.).

Athwal, D. S. (1966). Current plant breeding research with special reference to *Pennisetum. Indian J. Genet. Plant Breed.* **26A,** 73–85.

Athwal, D. S., and Rachie, K. O. (1963). Potentialities and future breeding for the improvement of *bajra. Indian J. Genet. Plant Breed.* **23,** 155–157.

Athwal, D. S., Gill, B. S., and Minocha, J. L. (1976). Diversification of the sources of male-sterility in pearl millet. *Crop Improv.* **3,** 96–100.

Badwal, S. S., Luthra, R. C., Gill, B. S., and Ajit Singh (1973). Combining ability on newly developed male-sterile lines in pearl millet. *Indian J. Genet. Plant Breed.* **33,** 7–12.

Burton, G. W. (1948). The performance on various mixtures of hybrid and parent inbred pearl millet *Pennisetum glaucum* (L) R.Br. *J. Am. Soc. Agron.* **40,** 908–915.

Burton, G. W. (1958). Cytoplasmic male-sterility in pearl millet *Pennisetum glaucum* (L.) R.Br. *Agron. J.* **50,** 230.

Burton, G. W. (1965a). Pearl millet Tift 23A released. *Crops Soils* **17,** 19.

Burton, G. W. (1965b). Cytoplasmic male-sterile pearl millet Tift 18A released. *Crops Soils* **18,** 19.

Burton, G. W. (1969). Registration of pearl millet inbreds Tift 23B1, Tift 23A1, Tift 23DB1 and Tift 23DA1. *Crop Sci.* **9,** 397.

Burton, G. W. (1972). Natural sterility maintainer and fertility restorer mutants in Tift 23A1 cytoplasmic male-sterile pearl millet, *Pennisetum typhoides* (Burm.) Stapf. & Hubb. *Crop Sci.* **12,** 280–282.

Burton, G. W. (1974). Factors affecting pollen movement and natural crossing in pearl millet. *Crop Sci.* **14,** 802–805.

Burton, G. W. (1977). Fertile sterility maintainer mutants in cytoplasmic male-sterile pearl millet. *Crop Sci.* **17,** 635–637.

Burton, G. W. (1980). Pearl millet *In* "Hybridization of Crop Plants" (W. R. Fehr and H. H. Hadley, eds.), pp. 457–469. Am. Soc. Agron. and Crop Sci. Soc. Am., Madison, Wisconsin.

Burton, G. W. (1981a). A gene for early maturity and photoperiod insensitivity in pearl millet. *Crop Sci.* **21,** 317–318.

Burton, G. W. (1981b). Registration of pearl millet inbreds Tift 23DBE, Tift 23DAE and Tift 756. *Crop Sci.* **21,** 804.

Burton, G. W., and Athwal, D. S. (1967). Two additional sources of cytoplasmic male-sterility in pearl millet and their relationship to Tift 23A. *Crop Sci.* **7,** 209–211.

Burton, G. W., and Athwal, D. S. (1968). Reciprocal maintainer–restorer relationship between A1 and A2 sterile cytoplasms facilitates millet breeding. *Crop Sci.* **8,** 632–634.

Burton, G. W., and Athwal, D. S. (1969). Registration of pearl millet inbreds Tift 239DB2 and Tift 239DA2. *Crop Sci.* **9,** 398.

Burton, G. W., and Hanna, W. W. (1976). Ethidium bromide induced male-sterility in pearl millet. *Crop. Sci.* **16,** 731–732.

Burton, G. W., and Hanna, W. W. (1982). Stable cytoplasmic male-sterile mutants induced in Tift 23 DBE pearl millet with mitomycin and streptomycin. *Crop Sci.* **22,** 651–652.

Burton, G. W., and Powell, J. B. (1968). Pearl millet breeding and cytogenetics. *Adv. Agron.* **20,** 49–89.

Burton, G. W., Hanna, W. W., Johnson, J. C., Jr., Leuck, D. B., Monson, W. G., Powell, J. B., Wells, H. D., and Widström, N. W. (1977). Pleiotropic effects of the *tr* trichomeless gene in pearl millet on transpiration, forage quality and pest resistance. *Crop Sci.* **17,** 613–616.

Chavan, V. M., Patil, J. A., and Chowdhary, B. B. (1955). Hybrid bajri in Bombay State. *Poona Agric. Coll. Mag.* **46,** 148–150.

Clement, W. M., Jr. (1975). Plasmon mutations in cytoplasmic male-sterile pearl millet, *Pennisetum typhoides. Genetics* **79,** 583–588.

Duvick, D. N. (1966). Influence of morphology and sterility on breeding methodology. *In* "Plant Breeding I" (K. J. Frey, ed), pp. 85–138. Iowa State Univ. Press, Ames.

Food and Agriculture Organization (1978). "Production Yearbook," No. 32 FAO, Rome.

Gill, K. S. (1979). Advances in the improvement of pearl millet in India. *Pap. UNDP-CIMMYT-ICRISAT Policy Advis. Comm. Meet. March 6–9, 1979,* CIMMYT, El Batan, Mexico.

Gill, K. S., Harjinder Singh, and Singh, N. B. (1973). Inheritance of genetic male-sterility in pearl millet. *J. Res. (Punjab Agric. Univ.)* **10,** 4–10.

Gill, K. S., Phul, P. S., and Jindla, L. N. (1975). The new bajra hybrids PHB 10 and PHB 14 are resistant to downy mildew/greenear disease. *Seeds & Farms* **1,** 3–4.

Gill, K. S., Phul, P. S., and Jindla, L. N. (1977). Improved bajra male-sterile line Pb 111A. *Seed Tech. News* **7,** 3,6.

Gill, K. S., Phul, P. S., and Bharadwaj, B. L. (1979). Induction of resistance to downy mildew by irradiation in male-sterile lines of pearl millet. *Symp. Role Induced Mutat. Crop Improve., 1979.,* Hyderabad, India.

Gill, K. S., Phul, P. S., Jindla, L. N., and Singh, N. B. (1981). Pb 204A—A new downy mildew resistant male-sterile line in pearl millet. *Seeds & Farms* **7,** 19–20.

Gupta, S. P., and Gupta, V. P. (1971). Combining ability for green fodder characters in pearl millet. *Indian J. Genet. Plant Breed.* **31**, 36–42.

Hanna, W. W. (1977). Effect of DPX3778 on anther dehiscence in pearl millet. *Crop Sci.* **17**, 965–967.

Hanna, W. W., and Powell, J. B. (1974). Radiation induced female-sterile mutant in pearl millet. *J. Hered.* **65**, 247–249.

Hooker, A. L. (1978). Genetics of disease resistance in maize. *In* "Maize Breeding and Genetics" (D. B. Walden, ed.), pp. 319–332. Wiley, New York.

House, L. R. (1980). "A Guide to Sorghum Breeding." ICRISAT, Hyderabad, India.

Indian Council of Agricultural Research (ICAR) (1964). "Progress Report of the All India Coordinated Millet Improvement Project—1963-64." ICAR, New Delhi (mimeo).

Indian Council of Agricultural Research (ICAR) (1966). "Progress Report of the All India Coordinated Millet Improvement Project—1965-66." ICAR, New Delhi (mimeo).

Indian Council of Agricultural Research (ICAR) (1980). "Coordinators Report of the All India Coordinated Millet Improvement Project—1979–1980." ICAR, New Delhi (mimeo).

Jain, H. K., and Pokhriyal, S. C. (1975). Improved pearl millet hybrids. *Mutat. Breed. Newsl.* **6**, 11–12.

Joshi, A. B., Ahluwalia, M., and Shankar, K. (1961). Improved Ghana is a better bajra. *Indian Farming* **11**, 12–13.

Kadam, B. S., Patel, S. M., and Kulkarni, R. K. (1940). Consequences of inbreeding in bajri. *J. Hered.* **31**, 201–207.

Kajjari, N. B., and Patil, J. P. (1956). A male-sterile bajri. *Indian J. Genet. Plant Breed.* **16**, 146.

Kapoor, R. L., Sain Dass, and Batra, S. R. (1979). Combining ability of some newly developed lines of pearl millet. *Indian J. Agric. Sci.* **49**, 253–256.

Khan, A. R., Misra, K. P., and Mathur, B. P. (1958). A promising bajra variety for Delhi State. *Indian J. Agric. Sci.* **28**, 57–60.

Madhava, Menon, P. M. (1958). Studies on cytoplasmic inheritance in *Pennisetum typhoides* Stapf. & Hubb. Ph.D. Thesis, Madras University.

Madhava Menon, P. M., (1959). Occurrence of cytoplasmic male-sterility in pearl millet *Pennisetum typhoides* Stapf. & Hubb. *Curr. Sci.* **28**, 165–167.

Mahadevappa, M., and Ponnaiya, B. W. X. (1966). A note on utilizing male-sterility lines in single crosses of pearl millet. *Madras Agric. J.* **53**, 510–513.

Matzinger, D. F. (1953). Comparison of three types of testers for the evaluation of inbred lines of corn. *Agron. J.* **45**, 493–495.

Murty, B. R. (1973). Mutation breeding for resistance to downy mildew in *Pennisetum. Mutat. Breed. Newsl.* **2**, 2.

Murty, B. R. (1974). Mutation breeding for resistance to downy mildew and ergot in *Pennisetum* and to *Ascochyta* in chickpea. *In* "Induced Mutations for Disease Resistance in Crop Plants," pp. 89–100. IAEA Vienna.

Murty, B. R. (1980). Breakthrough in breeding for resistance to downy mildew in pearl millet. *Bull. OEPP* **10**, 311–315.

Murty, B. R., Tiwari, J. L., and Harinarayana, G. (1967). Line × tester analysis of combining ability for yield factors in *Pennisetum typhoides* (Burm.) S. & H. *Indian J. Genet. Plant Breed.* **27**, 238–245.

Pandya, P. S., Chavan, V. M., and Shendge, P. Y. (1955). A brief review of the improvement of bajri in Bombay State. *Poona Agric. Coll. Mag.* **46**, 142–147.

Phul, P. S., Girgla, K. S., and Gill, K. S. (1976). The evaluation of new inbreds by using diverse sources of cytoplasmic male-sterility in pearl millet. *Crop Improv.* **3,** 86–95.

Pokhriyal, S. C. (1977). Revamping bajra seed. *Seeds & Farms* **3,** 25, 28.

Pokhriyal, S. C., and Jain, H. K. (1974). Breeding for disease resistance in pearl millet. *Mutat. Breed. Newsl.* **3,** 8–9.

Pokhriyal, S. C., Patil, R. R., Ramadass, and Balzor Singh. (1974). Combining ability of new male-sterile lines in pearl millet. *Indian J. Genet. Plant Breed.* **34,** 208–215.

Pokhriyal, S. C., Unnikrishnan, K. V., Balzor Singh, Ramadass, and Patil, R. R. (1976). Combining ability of downy mildew resistant lines in pearl millet. *Indian J. Genet. Plant Breed.* **36,** 403–409.

Powell, J. B., and Burton, G. W. (1973). Registration of Tift 23B *tr* pearl millet germplasm (Reg. No. GP4). *Crop Sci.* **13,** 586.

Rai, K. N., and Andrews, D. J. (1980). "Inter-population Improvement in Pearl Millet at ICRISAT," PM-50. Pearl Millet Imrovement Program, ICRISAT, Hyderabad, India (mimeo).

Ramadass, Patil, R. R., and Pokhriyal, S. C. (1974). Note on combining ability of some male-sterile lines of pearl millet. *Indian J. Agric. Sci.* **44,** 626–627.

Rao, M. K., and Devi, U. (1983). Variation in expression of genic male sterility in pearl millet. *J. Hered.* **74,** 34–38.

Rao, M. K., and Koduru, P. R. K. (1978a). Inheritance of genetic male-sterility in *Pennisetum americanum* (L.) Leeke. *Euphytica* **27,** 777–783.

Rao, M. K., and Koduru, P. R. K. (1978b). Cytogenetics of a factor for syncyte formation and male-sterility in *Pennisetum americanum. Theor. Appl. Genet.* **53,** 1–7.

Rao, P. K., Nambiar, A. K., and Madhava Menon, P. (1951). Maximization of production by the cultivation of hybrid strains with special reference to Cumbu (Pearl Millet). *Madras Agric. J.* **38,** 95–100.

Raut, R. N., Sharma, B., Pokhriyal, S. C., Singh, M. P., and Jain, H. K. (1973). Induced mutations: Some basic findings and applied results. *Indian J. Genet. Plant Breed.* **34A,** 311–315.

Reddy, B. B., and Reddi, M. V. (1970). Studies on the breakdown of male-sterility and other related aspects in certain cytoplasmic male-sterile lines of pearl millet *(Pennisetum typhoides* Stapf. and Hubb.). *Andhra Agric. J.* **17,** 173–180.

Safeeulla, K. M. (1977). Genetic vulnerability. The basis of recent epidemics in India. *In* "The Genetic Basis of Epidemics in Agriculture" (P. R. Day, ed.), Part 1, pp. 72–85. *Ann. N.Y. Acad. Sci.,* **287.**

Sain Dass, and Kanwar, Z. S. (1977). Screening and evaluation of pearl millet male-sterile lines, pollinators and their F1's for downy mildew resistance. *Indian J. Agric. Sci.* **47,** 296–298.

Saxena, M. B. L., and Chaudhary, B. S. (1977). Breakdown of male-sterility in some male-sterile lines of pearl millet. *(Pennisetum typhoides)* under conditions of arid zone. *Ann. Arid Zone* **16,** 427–432.

Sharma, J. R. (1980). A note on conversion of new male-sterile lines by limited back-crossing in pearl millet *(Pennisetum typhoides* (Burm.) S. & H.). *Curr. Sci.* **49,** 513–514.

Sharma, Y. P. (1979). Note on functional male-sterility induced by growth regulators in pearl millet. *Indian J. Agric. Sci.* **49,** 294–295.

Singh, F., Singh, R. K., and Singh, V. P. (1974). Combining ability studies in pearl millet *Pennisetum typhoides* (Burm.) S & H. *Theor. Appl. Genet.* **44,** 106–110.

Singh, F., Kapoor, R. L. and Dahiya, B. N. (1982). Combining ability analysis for yield and its attributes in pearl millet. *Haryana Agric. Univ. J. Res.* **12**, 644–648.

Swindale, L. D. (1981). "A Time for Rainfed Agriculture," 11th Coromandel Lect. at New Delhi. Sponsored by Coromandel Fertilisers Ltd., India.

Thakare, R. B. (1977). Breakdown of male-sterility in pearl millet CMS line Tift-23A. *Crop. Improv.* **4**, 117–118.

Thakur, R. P., Williams, R. J., and Rao, V. P. (1982). Development of resistance to ergot in Pearl Millet. *Phytopathology* **72**, 406–408.

Tyagi, C. S., Arora, N. D., and Singh, K. P. (1974). A line × tester study of some male-sterile and pollinator parents for forage character in pearl millet. *Indian J. Hered.* **6**, 99–108.

Tyagi, C. S., Arora, N. D., Singh, R. K., and Singh, K. P. (1975). Combining ability analysis in *Pennistum typhoides* (Burm.) S & H. *Haryana Agric. Univ. J. Res.* **5**, 15–24.

Utkhede, R. S. (1972). Some breeding procedures used for improvement of pearl millet (*Pennisetum typhoides* (Burm. f.) Stapf & C.E. Hubb.). *Indian J. Agric. Sci.* **42**, 452–456.

Vittal Rao, S. (1969). An unusual occurrence of breakdown of male-sterility in bajra *(Pennisetum typhoides* (Burm.) Stapf. and Hubb.). *Andhra Agric. J.* **16**, 15.

Vohra, R. R. (1969). Development of dwarf seed parent 18D2A. *Proc. All-India Millets Workshop ICAR.*

Williams, R. J., Singh, S. D., and Pawar, M. N. (1981). An improved field screening technique for downy mildew resistance in pearl millet. *Plant Dis.* **65**, 239–241.

Yadav, H. P., Kapoor, R. L., and Sain Dass (1981). A study on combining ability and gene effects in pearl millet *(Pennisetum typhoides* (Burm.) Stapf. *et* Hubb.). *Haryana Agric. Univ. J. Res.* **11**, 172–176.

The *Chenopodium* Grains of the Andes: Inca Crops for Modern Agriculture

J. RISI C. and N. W. GALWEY

Department of Applied Biology, University of Cambridge, Cambridge, England

ISBN 0-12-040910-0

I. Introduction

Quinoa (*Chenopodium quinoa* Willd) and cañihua (*Chenopodium pallidicaule* Aellen) are grain crops that were domesticated in the Andes and whose cultivation is still confined to that region. Cañihua has always been a minor crop, but in pre-Columbian times quinoa was used for agricultural and culinary purposes similar to those of barley in the Old World. In the Colonial and Republican eras (since about 1530 AD) the cultivation of both crops has declined, and they are now mainly confined to marginal areas. However, quinoa is overdue for fuller exploitation. It contains more protein than do the major cereals, and the protein has a better balanced amino acid composition. It is cold and drought tolerant and therefore has potential for many highland-tropical and temperate regions, including Britain. It can be combine harvested and would be a suitable break crop for use in rotation with cereals. The main problem in its utilization is the bitter saponins that the grains of most varieties contain. These protect the plant from birds, but must be removed by vigorous washing in cold water before processing or consumption.

In Peru, the area under quinoa cultivation declined particularly rapidly, from 47,000 to 15,000 ha between 1947 and 1975 (Tapia, 1979a), partly because of a series of droughts in the Altiplano region, partly because of a policy of subsidizing imported foodstuffs, and partly because of the disdain that people in the urban areas felt for the products of indigenous culture. However, in recent years the acreage of quinoa has increased, as economic pressures are encouraging Peruvians and Bolivians to change their dietary habits and as the nutritional value of the crop has become more widely recognized. Cañihua, which has smaller grains and produces lower yields and in which no white-seeded genotypes exist, has remained much less important.

The agronomy, physiology, genetics, and nutritional value of quinoa and cañihua have been fairly extensively investigated, but most of this literature is in Spanish and is not widely available. In view of the potential of quinoa for cultivation in many parts of the world, we have attempted to summarize this information and make it available in English. Field plots of quinoa were grown in Cambridge, England, in 1982, and we have also included results from these experiments.

II. Evolution and Distribution

A. RELATIONSHIPS WITH WILD SPECIES

The genus *Chenopodium* has a worldwide distribution and comprises about 250 species (Giusti, 1970). It is the principal genus of the family Chenopodiaceae, which also includes sugar beet, mangold and beetroot (*Beta vulgaris*), and spinach (*Spinacia oleracea*). Three species of *Chenopodium* are cultivated as food plants, namely, *C. quinoa* and *C. pallidicaule* in South America, and huauzontle [*Chenopodium berlandieri* ssp. *nutalliae* (Safford) Wilson and Heiser] in Mexico. Like their more distant relatives buckwheat (*Fagopyrum* spp.) and the grain amaranths (*Amaranthus* spp.), these chenopods are often called pseudocereals, though huauzontle is mainly used as a vegetable (Heiser and Nelson, 1974). Morphologically, quinoa and huauzontle are rather similar to each other, cañihua being quite distinct (Nelson, 1968). The genus *Chenopodium* also includes a weed species of worldwide distribution, *Chenopodium album,* known as fat hen in England and as lamb's quarters in North America. South American weed species include *Chenopodium hircinum* (known as quinua silvestre, "wild quinoa"), *Chenopodium murale* (yerba de gallinazo, "vulture herb"), and *Chenopodium ambrosioides* (paico).

The basic chromosome number of the genus is $x = 8$ or $x = 9$ (Kawatani and Ohno, 1956, reported by Nelson, 1968). The number $x = 8$ may be restricted to the section Ambrina (Uotila, 1973). The somatic chromosome numbers of the cultivated species and some weed species are shown in Table I. *Chenopodium album* was reported to have varying ploidy levels by Winge (1917), Kjellmark (1934), Cooper (1935), and Witte (1947). However, a survey of chromosome number of *C. album* in Britain and elsewhere has shown that intraspecific variation in this respect is probably absent, all the determinations giving the hexaploid $2n = 54$ (Cole, 1962). This discrepancy could be due to the fact that *C. album* has often been a "convenient taxonomic receptacle" for material not readily assigned to other species of the genus (Wilson, 1980).

The somatic chromosome number of quinoa is $2n = 36$, and the chromosomes can be arranged into nine groups or four homologs on

TABLE I. Somatic numbers of cultivated and weed species of *Chenopodium*

Section	Subsection	Species	Diploid number	Reference
Chenopodia	Cellulata (alveolate grains)	*C. quinoa*	$2n = 4x = 36$	Kjellmark (1934), Cárdenas and Hawkes (1948), Heiser (1963), Simmonds (1965), Gandarillas and Luizaga (1967), Giusti (1970), Catácora (1977)
		C. berlandieri ssp. *nutalliae*	$2n = 4x = 36$	Singh (1961), Simmonds (1965)
		C. hircinum	$2n = 4x = 36$	Giusti (1970)
	Lejosperma (smooth grains)	*C. pallidicaule*	$2n = 2x = 18$	Simmonds (1965), Gandarillas and Gutiérrez (1973), Giusti (1970) Lescano (1976), Chimpén (1979)
		C. album	$2n = 6x = 54$	Cole (1962)
	Undata	*C. murale*	$2n = 2x = 18$	Winge (1917), Cole (1962), Giusti (1970)
Ambrina	—	*C. ambrosioides*	$2n = 2x = 16$	Lorz (1937), Woroschilov (1942), Suzuka (1950), Giusti (1970)

the basis of length and long arm/short-arm ratio (Catácora, 1977). This indicates that quinoa is a tetraploid, but genetical studies have indicated disomic inheritance of major gene characters (Gandarillas, 1974; Simmonds, 1971). Ovules are rarely aborted and pollen production in hermaphrodite flowers is good, suggesting that meiosis is regular, and hence that quinoa is an allotetraploid but contains genes that suppress pairing between homoeologous chromosomes and make it functionally diploid, like durum wheat, cotton, and tobacco. This raises the question of which species contributed their genomes. Gandarillas (1974) has suggested that allotetraploidy could have occurred in the Andes, with cañihua contributing a genome, since cañihua has saponin-free grains and a loose pericarp, characteristics that are found in some varieties of quinoa. On the other hand, the similarities of *C. quinoa* and

C. hircinum to *C berlandieri* var. *zschackei,* a North American tetraploid alveolate weed, and the fact that alveolate-fruited diploids are confined to North America, suggest that the tetraploids may have originated in the North (Wilson and Heiser, 1979). In this case the dispersion of a *C. berlandieri* var. *zschackei*-like ancestor into South America probably preceded human occupation of the area. Whatever its origin, the tetraploid progenitor of quinoa probably resembled *C. hircinum,* originally classified as *C. quinoa* ssp. *milleanum* (Aellen, 1929), which has great morphological similarity with quinoa and which when growing in favorable environments shows unusually large fruit and condensed inflorescence branches (Wilson and Heiser, 1979). A spontaneous form of quinoa, *C. quinoa* var. *melanospermum* Hunziker, known as "aspha quinua," which has small, black deciduous fruits and is common throughout the range of the cultivated quinoa, may represent the progenitor of the crop or a reversion from the domesticated form (Heiser and Nelson, 1974). *Chenopodium quinoa* var. *melanospermum* and *C. hircinum* are probably companion weeds that maintain some genetic contact with the crop, a situation that occurs in many other species (Harlan, 1965). Both of these types can easily be crossed with cultivated quinoa (Nelson, 1968; Wilson and Heiser, 1979), and the F_1 hybrids are fully fertile (Nelson, 1968).

Genetical studies in cañihua indicate that it is a diploid with $2n = 18$ (Gandarillas and Gutiérrez, 1973; Lescano, 1976), and it shows disomic inheritance of major gene characters (Simmonds, 1966; Paca, 1970).

B. CLASSIFICATION OF DOMESTICATED TYPES

Like other crop plants in their area of origin, cultivated quinoa is so diverse as to defy classification into botanical varieties. Early attempts were made by Humboldt, Bonpland and Kunth, and Moquin (reported by Hunziker, 1943) and by Gonzales (1917, reported by Lescano, 1981). Hunziker's (1943) discrimination between the spontaneous variety of *C. quinoa, melanospermum,* and the cultivated varieties *viridescens, rubescens,* and *lutescens* appears valid. The most detailed classification is that of Gandarillas (1968), who described 17 races of cultivated quinoa collected in Ecuador, Peru, and Bolivia, and classified on the basis of seed, inflorescence, leaf, and whole-plant characteristics, but who warned that his catalog was unlikely to be exhaustive. The most useful classification is probably that of Tapia *et al.* (1980), who distinguished the following ecotypes:

1. Valley type. From Andean valleys at altitudes between 2000 and 4000 m in Central Peru and places further north. Plants 2–3 m tall, most varieties branched, with growth periods of more than 7 months. This group includes the varieties Blanca de Junín, Rosada de Junín, Amarilla de Maranganí, Dulce de Quitopamba, and Dulce de Lazo.

2. Altiplano type. From the area around Lake Titicaca, at an altitude of about 4000 m. Plants 1–1.8 m tall, most varieties not branched, with growth periods from 4 to 7 months. This group includes Chewecca, Kanccolla, and Blanca de Julí.

3. Salar type. From the "salares," the salt flats of the southern altiplano in Bolivia, at an altitude of about 4000 m. The plants are grown in soils with a pH above 8.0, and most varieties have black seeds with a very high saponin content and sharp edges. In other respects they resemble varieties of the altiplano type. One of the parents of Sajama, a white-seeded, low-saponin variety, was a salar ecotype. There are some white-seeded salar varieties, the most important of which is Real.

4. Sea level type. From southern Chile, at latitudes about 40°S. The plants grow about 2 m tall in Cambridge, England, are mostly not branched, and will flower in long days. They produce small, yellow translucent seeds with a high saponin content.

5. Subtropical type. Tapia (1982) reports that a plant was found in the subtropical Yungas region of Bolivia. It had intense green coloration that turned orange at maturity, and produced very small yellow-orange grains. This plant may be considered to constitute a fifth group.

Cañihua was classified by Hunziker (1943) into the intensely pigmented, black-seeded form *melanospermum,* similar to his quinoa variety *melanospermum,* and the lighter colored forms *purpureum* and *typicum.* Paredes (1966) distinguished a wild variety of cañihua, prostrate and highly ramified with black seeds, named "machu cañihua" and probably corresponding to Hunziker's *melanospermum.* Paredes suggested a factorial classification of the cultivated types, shown in Table II.

TABLE II. Classification of cultivated cañihua types

Plant type	Seed color	Quechua name
Erect, little branched	Brown	Saihua cañihua
Erect, little branched	Black	Ccoito saihua
Semierect, branched	Brown	Lasta cañihua
Semierect, branched	Black	Ccoito lasta

C. HISTORY IN DOMESTICATION

The altiplano around Lake Titicaca is an ancient center of civilization as well as a center of diversity of several crops including quinoa and cañihua, and it is likely that these plants were domesticated there. Archaeological remains of quinoa have been dated to 5000 BC in Ayacucho, Peru (Uhle, 1919, reported by Tapia, 1979a), to 3000 BC in Chinchorro, Chile (Nunez, 1970, reported by Tapia, 1979a), and to 750–0 BC in Chiripa on the south shore of Lake Titicaca. Quinoa seeds have also been preserved at archaeological sites in the Peruvian coastal desert (Towle, 1961, reported by Nelson, 1968). It seems that no archaeological remains of cañihua have been found.

By the time of the Spanish conquest, quinoa was an important crop. Garcilazo de la Vega in his "Comentarios Reales" in 1609 states that it was called "mijo" (millet) or "arroz pequeno" (little rice) by the Spaniards. Spanish chroniclers such as Pedro de Valdivia in 1551, Cortez Hogea in 1558, Cieza de Leon in 1560, Pedro Sotelo in 1583, and Ulloa Mogollón in 1586 reported that quinoa was cultivated in an area extending from Peru and Bolivia north to Pasto in Colombia, south to the island of Chiloe in Chile, and southeast to Cordoba in Argentina (Tapia, 1979a). Mechoni reported in 1747 that it was cultivated even further south by the Araucano Indians (Tapia, 1979a), a tribe who fiercely resisted Spanish encroachment and who are probably responsible for the survival of quinoa in southern Chile today. The Spaniards introduced European crops such as barley, and the cultivation of quinoa was socially discouraged (Cardozo and Tapia, 1979), but in the late eighteenth and early nineteenth centuries, quinoa was still grown on a small scale even as far north as Cundinamarca near Bogota by the Chibcha Indians. Humboldt, reported by Pulgar Vidal (1954), made the surprising statement that it was as closely identified with that region as maize was with the Aztecs or the potato with the Peruvians. The names given to the crop included "kiuna" in Quechua and "jupha" or "juira" in Aymara. The Aymara people distinguished different quinoa types: "ppfique," white; "cami," purple; "kana llapi," red; "cchusllunca," yellow; and "isualla," wild quinoa (Tapia, 1979a). In the Chibcha language quinoa was called "suba," meaning "for grain" (Pulgar Vidal, 1954).

Cañihua was probably always much less widespread than quinoa. Diego Cabeza made the first mention of cañihua in 1586 in his "Description of the City of La Paz"; other chroniclers refer to it as a plant grown in the altiplano (Tapia, 1979b), and it may also have been cultivated in the highlands of northeast Argentina (Hunziker, 1943). The names for the crop include "kañiwa" in Quechua and "kañawa" (Tapia, 1979b) and "isualla hupa" (Hunziker, 1952) in Aymara. The names "cañihua" and "cañahua" are both commonly used in Spanish.

Chenopodium species are used worldwide for the identification of viruses, since they have characteristic reactions to inoculation. Apart from this modern development, their main use outside South America has been as green vegetables, but both in North America and in Europe they went some way down the road toward domestication as grain crops. Grains of *C. berlandieri* may have formed part of the annual tribute in the Aztec empire mentioned by the first viceroy of Mexico, Antonio Mendoza (reported by Hunziker, 1952), and the seeds of *C. album* were used as food by the former inhabitants of Russia, Denmark, Greece, and northern Italy. Considerable quantities of *C. album* seeds were found in the stomachs of corpses preserved in the Danish peat bogs (Renfrew, 1973).

D. PRESENT DISTRIBUTION

1. *Overall pattern*

Quinoa and cañihua are still found in nearly all the regions from which they were reported at the time of the conquest, but they are confined to marginal lands except in the altiplano and a few other parts of Peru. Their distributions are shown in Figs. 1 and 2. The average areas cultivated in the Andean countries over the period 1974–1979 are shown in Table III.

2. *Distribution of quinoa production*

a. *Colombia.* In a few districts in the Department of Narino, near the border with Ecuador, quinoa is still cultivated in backyards or in multiple-crop systems (Pulgar Vidal, 1954; Romero, 1976). Near Bo-

TABLE III. Hectares of *Chenopodium* crops cultivated in the Andean countries in the years of 1974–1979[a]

Crop	Colombia	Ecuador	Peru	Bolivia	Total
Quinoa	1000	1500	25,000	12,000	39,500
Cañihua	—	—	6000	3000	9000

[a]Data from Tapia (1981).

FIG. 1. Past and present distribution of quinoa. Area in Argentina and Chile and also in northern Peru and southern Ecuador (widely spaced dot pattern) shows presumed preconquest distribution. Regions denoted by closely spaced dots represent growth mainly in backyards, field margins, and intercropped. Crosshatching represents cultivation as a sole crop.

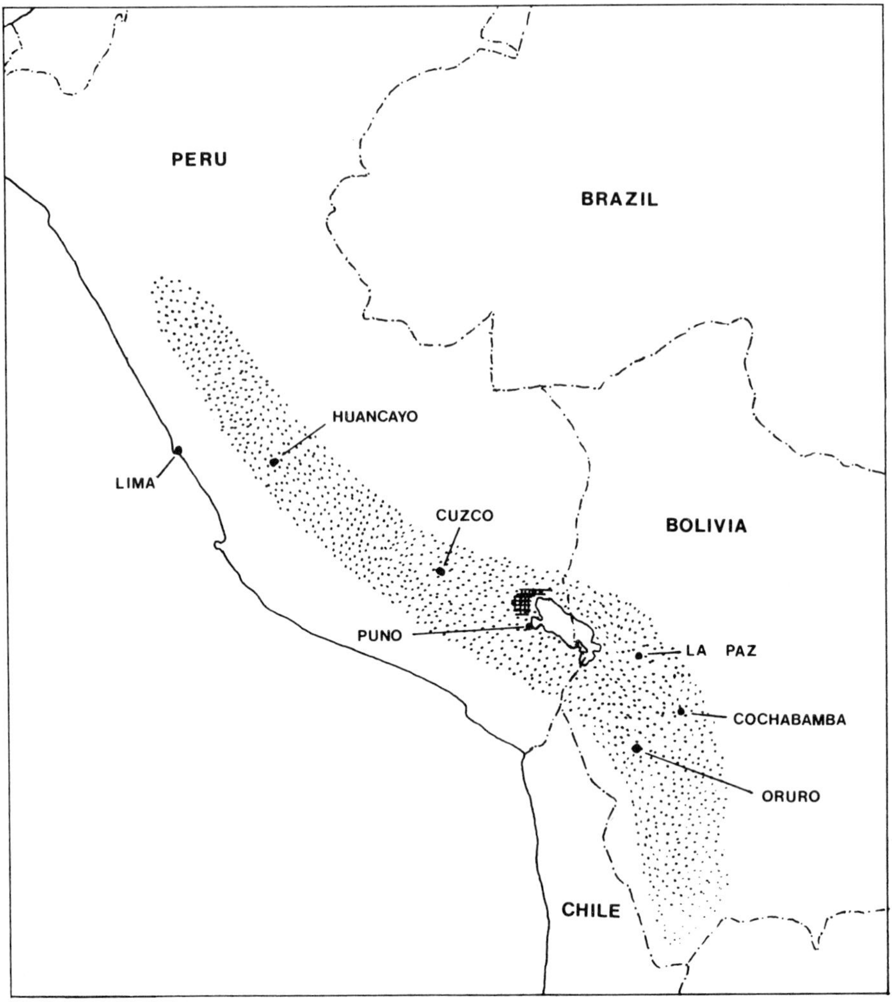

FIG. 2. Present distribution of cañihua. Dots denote region of growth on marginal land, mainly at altitudes over 3800 m. Crosshatching denotes area (near Lake Titicaca) of growth in arable rotations.

gota quinoa is found only very rarely, though the "Comite Interinstitucional Colombiano" has produced a type that yields up to 5000 kg/ha in that region (Romero, 1976).

b. *Ecuador.* Quinoa has persisted among the inhabitants of the provinces of Canchi, Imbabura, Pichincha, Cotopaxi, Chimborazo, and Loja, where it is grown between 1800 and 3800 m above sea level on acid soils. Ecuadorian varieties are of the valley type, and some of them have a low saponin content (Romero, 1976).

c. *Peru.* The country in which quinoa retains greatest importance is Peru. In the Andean valleys it is intercropped with maize or *Vicia* beans or grown as a border crop in potato fields. It acquires greater importance in the highest cultivated regions, where maize cannot be grown (Narrea, 1976b).

The two main quinoa-producing areas are the Mantaro Valley around Huancayo and the altiplano around Puno. In the Mantaro Valley quinoa is grown as a sole crop in mechanized agricultural systems, with fertilizers and pesticides, in fields of up to 5 ha. About 800 ha were sown in this region in 1976–1977, with an average yield of 2500 kg/ha (Narrea, 1977). The varieties used are white-seeded, low-saponin valley types such as Blanca de Junín, Rosada de Junín, and the selection UNC 20, and there is little genetic diversity. Quinoa is also grown in high valleys elsewhere in Peru, including the Callejón de Huaylas, Department of Ancash, and the valley between Cuzco and Sicuani, where the variety Amarilla de Maranganí is used. However, about 70% of the quinoa produced in Peru is grown around Puno, mostly in sole-crop systems. Altiplano types of diverse seed colors are cultivated, from which varieties such as Chewecca (white seeded and almost sweet), Kanccolla, and Blanca de Julí have been selected (Tapia, 1979a).

d. *Bolivia.* Quinoa is cultivated on the Bolivian side of Lake Titicaca as well as on the Peruvian side. Its importance diminishes in the southern part of the altiplano, except in the salt flats. At altitudes of 4000 m in Bolivia, the plants are exposed to temperatures as low as −18°C and receive as little as 86 mm of precipitation. These extreme conditions are reflected in low yields, from 276 to 1380 kg/ha. A law in Bolivia requires that bread must contain 5% and biscuits 7% of quinoa flour, and there is a commercial quinoa processing plant in Oruro (Ferrari, 1976). However, this law is not widely observed. Most Bolivian varieties are altiplano or salar types with a high saponin content, but the variety Sajama, containing almost no saponins, was selected in Bolivia in the 1960s and is now also grown in Peru (Romero, 1976).

e. *Chile.* Quinoa is grown in two distinct areas in Chile. In the small Chilean sector of the altiplano, conditions and cultivation methods are similar to those on the Bolivian altiplano (Lanino, 1976), whereas around Concepcion in central Chile quinoa is grown at sea level. Genotypes from these high latitudes will flower in long days, unlike many tropical types, and hence are of particular interest to breeders in other temperate countries. There is variation in stem color and compactness of inflorescence, but the seeds are uniformly small, yellow, and translucent. Varieties named Baer, Faro, Pichamán, Valdivia, and Litú have been selected (Etchevers and Avila, 1979).

f. *Argentina.* In the highlands of Jujuy and of northeastern Argentina, quinoa is grown in backyards and in small plots of about 50–100 m^2, giving yields of 400–800 kg/ha. It is also sometimes intercropped with maize or potatoes. The crop is declining in Argentina, but cannot be replaced completely in some environments (Vorano and García, 1976).

3. *Distribution of cañihua production*

Cañihua is grown only in Peru and Bolivia, mainly in the altiplano and near Cochabamba, but to a very small extent at high altitudes in Ancash, Apurímac, Cuzco, and elsewhere (Anonymous, 1976; Vargas, 1938). The major concentration of cañihua fields occurs around Puno, where about 5000 ha are cultivated (Tapia, 1979b), and around La Paz, at elevations above 4000 m, where the mean temperature is less than 10°C and where frosts occur in at least 9 months of the year and often strike in January and February at the height of the growing season (Gade, 1970).

III. MORPHOLOGY AND ECOPHYSIOLOGY

A. QUINOA PLANT MORPHOLOGY

1. *General*

Quinoa is an annual gynomonoecious plant, varying in height from 0.7 to 3.0 m with an erect stem that may be either branched or unbranched, and alternate leaves (Fig. 3). Its growth cycle varies from 150 to 220 days.

2. *Root*

Quinoa seeds start to germinate a few hours after receiving moisture. The radicle grows to form a tap root from which secondary and tertiary roots develop, forming a highly ramified system (Gandarillas, 1979a; Lescano, 1981). Root depth is related to plant height, varying

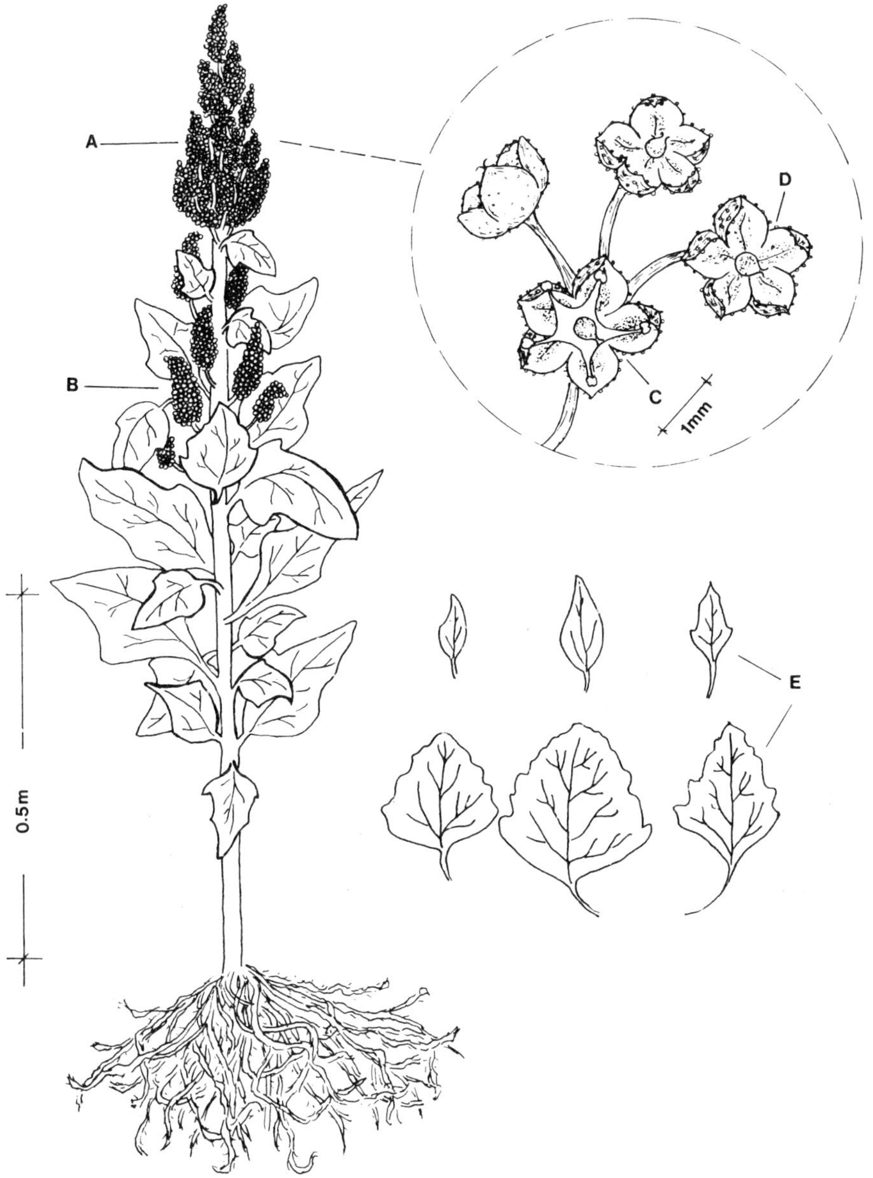

FIG. 3. The quinoa plant. A, Terminal inflorescence; B, axillary inflorescence; C, hermaphrodite flower; D, female flower; E, variation in leaf shape: top, apical leaves; bottom, basal leaves [for varieties Sajama, Amarilla de Marangani, and Baer (from left to right)].

from 0.80 m in plants 0.90 m tall to 1.50 m in plants 1.70 m tall, according to Pacheco and Morlon (1978, reported by Gandarillas, 1979a). Other investigators have estimated root depth at 30 cm (Gandarillas, 1979a; Lescano, 1981) or as little as 12.6–15 cm (Durán, 1980). Quinoa plants grown in Cambridge reached an average height of 1.80 m and were subject to strong winds in September and October, but almost all plants remained upright, which suggests that the deeper estimates are more accurate. The large and highly ramified root makes the plant resistant to drought.

3. *Stem*

Near the soil, the stem is round in cross section, becoming more angular where leaves and branches emerge. Its length varies from 0.50 to 2.50 m, depending on variety and environment. The amount of branching depends on the variety and on the sowing density. The stem cortex is very tough, whereas the medulla is soft when the plants are young and is dry and spongy at maturity. Stem color may be uniformly green, yellow, red, purple, or orange, or it may be green with stripes of another color (Lescano, 1981). At maturity, the color changes to pale yellow, or to red in some varieties. As in all species of the order Centrospermae, the reddish colors are due to betacyanins, not anthocyanins (Mabry *et al.*, 1963).

4. *Leaves*

The petiole is long and narrow and is grooved on its upper surface. The petioles of leaves that originate from the stem are longer than those of leaves that originate from branches (Gandarillas, 1979a). The lamina has three main veins that originate from the petiole (Hunziker, 1943; Lescano, 1981) and is polymorphic within a single plant, the lower leaves tending to be rhomboidal and the upper leaves lanceolate (Hunziker, 1943; Nelson, 1968). The laminae of young leaves are covered with a grainy vesiculate pubescence on the lower surface and sometimes also on the upper surface. The color of this layer varies from white to purple. In a few varieties the pubescence is completely absent (Gandarillas, 1979a). The number of indentations on the border of the lamina varies from 3 to 20, the number being characteristic of the variety (Gandarillas, 1968). The leaves on younger plants are mainly green under their layer of pubescence, but as the plant matures, they turn yellow, red, or purple.

5. *Inflorescence*

The inflorescence of quinoa is a panicle, having a principal axis from which secondary axes originate, and varies considerably in form among varieties. In the amaranthiform type of inflorescence the groups of flowers are directly inserted into the secondary axes, whereas in the glomerulate type the groups of flowers are inserted into tertiary (glomerulate) axes that originate from the secondary axes. (Lescano, 1981). The glomerulate inflorescence is believed to be the ancestral type (Gandarillas, 1974). Both types of inflorescences may be compact or lax according to the angle of insertion of the secondary axes. The length of the inflorescence varies from about 15 to 70 cm depending on variety and environment.

6. *Flowers*

As in all the Chenopodiaceae, the flowers are incomplete, no petals being present. Quinoa has both female and hermaphrodite flowers (Hunziker, 1943; Simmonds, 1965). The proportion varies according to variety (Rea, 1969; Aguilar, 1980), and some or all of the hermaphrodite flowers may be male sterile, having nonfunctional anthers (Nelson, 1968; Simmonds, 1971; Aguilar, 1980). A hermaphrodite flower has five perianth lobes, five anthers, and a superior ovary from which two or rarely three stigmatic branches emerge (Hunziker, 1943). Generally, the hermaphrodite flowers are located at the distal end of a group and the female ones at the proximal end (Gandarillas, 1979a).

7. *Fruits*

The fruit is an achene, sometimes covered by the perigonium, which is easily removed by rubbing (Lescano, 1981). The outer layer of the fruit is the pericarp, which has regular surface markings in the form of alveolar cells (Aellen and Just, 1943) and which may be translucent, white, yellow, orange, pink, red, brown, gray, or black (Lescano, 1981). The next layer is the episperm, which may be white, translucent, brown, brown-ochre, black-brown, or black (Ignacio *et al.*, 1976). The embryo takes up about 60% of the volume within the episperm and the endosperm about 40%. This high proportion of embryo accounts for the high protein content of the grain compared with cereals (Cardozo and Tapia, 1979). The fruit may be conical, cylindrical, or ellipsoidal in shape, and the size varies from 2.6 to less than 1.8 mm in diameter (Ignacio *et al.*, 1976).

The grains contain variable amounts of saponins, which have a bitter taste. The bitterness is removed by washing and/or friction before further processing or consumption. Any bitterness remaining after processing was found to be correlated with the presence of remnants of the pericarp, indicating that the saponins are located in this layer (Villacorta and Talavera, 1976).

B. CAÑIHUA PLANT MORPHOLOGY

1. *General*

Cañihua is an annual plant, highly branched and varying in height from 20 to 60 cm (Fig. 4). Its growth cycle varies from 120 to 150 days (García, 1953).

2. *Root*

The plant has a tap root and secondary roots, but these are not as large or as extensive as in quinoa (Velasco, 1968, reported by López, 1980). They reach a depth of 10–25 cm (León, 1964) and plants can be easily uprooted (Vargas, 1938). The color of the roots varies from white-cream to pale pink (Velasco, 1968, reported by López, 1980).

3. *Stem*

The stem of cañihua is round in cross section and is covered by a vesiculate pubescence. There are two ecotypes of cañihua: "saihua,"

FIG. 4. The cañihua plant. A, Hermaphrodite flower; B, variation in leaf shape: left, basal; right, apical.

an erect plant type with three–five basal branches, and "lasta," a semierect type with more than six basal branches. The stem color at maturity may be purple, pink, orange, or yellow, depending on the variety (Calle, 1980).

4. *Leaves*

The leaves are alternate with short petioles. The lamina is thick and covered with vesicles. At the base of the plant the laminae are rhomboidal and have three principal veins originating from the petiole (Hunziker, 1943), while near the apex, the petiole is almost naked and the leaves are almost sessile and cover the inflorescence (León, 1964).

5. *Inflorescence*

The inflorescences, whether terminal or located in the axils, are inconspicuous in their covering of leaves (Hunziker, 1943). The flowers are grouped forming spikes (Vargas, 1938).

6. *Flowers*

The flowers tend to be smaller than those of quinoa, 1–2 mm in diameter. According to Hunziker (1943), they may be hermaphrodite or male, but Lazarte (1972, reported by Bravo, 1975) states that on average 3.6% of the flowers are female, 1.1% hermaphrodite but male sterile, and 95.3% functionally hermaphrodite, with no male flowers. The five perianth lobes of the hermaphrodite flowers differ in shape and size and are covered with vesicles. The ovary is superior and has a two-branched stigma. The number of anthers varies from one to three, flowers with three anthers being rare (Hunziker, 1943).

7. *Fruit*

The fruit, as in quinoa, in an achene, in most cases covered by the gray perigonium (Hunziker 1943). The pericarp is thin and colorless and the episperm is shiny and may be black, dark brown, or brown (Calle, 1980).

C. ECOPHYSIOLOGY

1. *Environment*

The upper limit of cultivation of quinoa is about 4000 m, and cañihua is grown at even higher altitudes. Quinoa is grown in the mountains from 5°N in southern Colombia to 30°S in northeastern Argentina. At sea level, it is grown between 36 and 40°S in central Chile. The range of cañihua is much more confined, lying between

10°S in the Peruvian central Andes and 20°S in the southern Bolivian altiplano. Of the area under cañihua cultivation, 90% is in the region northwest of Lake Titicaca (Gade, 1970). Both crops are frequently grown on marginal soils, with problems of stoniness, poor drainage or excessively free drainage, low natural fertility, or pH values as low as 4.8 in Ecuador and Peru (Narrea, 1976a) and as high as 8.5 in the Bolivian salares (Tapia, 1979a).

Quinoa and cañihua are grown during the Southern Hemisphere summer, from September or October to May or June. The rains are concentrated during these months, the mean temperature rises, and frosts become less frequent. The total annual rainfall is 600–800 mm in the Ecuadorean Andes, 400–500 mm in the Peruvian central Andes, 500–600 mm around Lake Titicaca, 200–400 mm in southern Bolivia, and 800–1000 mm in central Chile.

The mean temperature in the altiplano ranges from 7 to 10°C. However, the range between the mean maximum and mean minimum temperature tends to decrease in the areas close to Lake Titicaca, the mean maximum at Puno (near the lake) being 14.5°C and the mean minimum being 2.6°C, whereas at Patacamaya, Bolivia, the mean maximum and minimum are 19 and 1°C, respectively (Aquize, 1977).

2. *Day length sensitivity*

Most of the range of quinoa lies at low latitudes and is not subject to great day length variation; however, varieties of the Chilean sea level type grow in summer days of up to 14 hours. The Chilean varieties Baer, Faro, Pichamán, Valdivia, and Litú have matured regularly at sites from the Loire Valley in France (47°N) to Loughborough in England (53°N), between 1979 and 1982 (C. L. A. Leakey, personal communication). Seeds of these varieties derived from two generations of mass selection in Europe were grown at Cambridge during the summer and were harvested 150 days after sowing, whereas the Peruvian variety Blanca de Junín took 230 days to reach maturity—considerably longer than the 180 to 200 days that it requires in Peru. Cárdenas (1949) reports that Bolivian varieties grown in Cambridge during the summer developed tall, bushy plants that did not flower, but that a Chilean variety produced fruits.

Sívori (1947) found that when Ecuadorian quinoa plants were grown in greenhouse conditions under continuous light, no flowers were formed, whereas at a 10-hr day length the flowers opened on day 97. At least 15 short days were necessary to induce anthesis in quinoa, and a further period of short days was required to induce fruit maturation. However, Fuller (1949) found that Bolivian quinoa plants would flower under a broad range of photoperiods but not under continuous illumination. The shorter the photoperiods and the more short photoperiods the plants were subjected to, the faster they flowered. Quinoa is thus a quantitative short-day species. Quinoa varieties from near the equator tend to flower later than those from high latitudes and the same altitude, even under fairly short days (Nelson, 1968).

The length of the vegetative period may depend not only on day length and latitude of origin, but also on altitude of origin. Two quinoa varieties collected from altitudes of 2500 and 4000 m, but from about the same latitude in Bolivia, were grown at the John Innes Institute, Norwich, England. They both flowered and fruited at about the same time in the greenhouse, but in the field the high-altitude variety flowered and fruited when it was 1.50 m tall, whereas the low-altitude variety grew to 2.0 m and was killed by frost when it was beginning to flower (Simmonds, 1965).

Quinoa races or ecotypes are evidently adapted to the length of the growing season in their place of origin. This means that in adapting the crop to temperate regions, particular attention should be paid to the high-latitude and high-altitude varieties.

It seems that no detailed studies of day length sensitivity in cañihua have been done, but Simmonds (1966) reports that cañihua plants grown from a stock bought at La Paz, Bolivia, grew well in the summer in England, both in the glasshouse and in the field.

3. *Frost resistance*

Reports of resistance to frost in quinoa are somewhat contradictory. Rea (1977) reported that the quinoa varieties Sajama and Kanccolla were susceptible to temperatures of −1°C in Aziruni, Puno, Bolivia, and found that seedlings were more susceptible than larger plants. However, Canahua (1977) found that temperatures of −3°C did not affect these varieties. Romero *et al.* (1977) reported that at an altitude of 3850 m in Cátac, Ancash, Peru, two trials in successive seasons—of 5981 and 3597 accessions, respectively—showed no evidence of frost resistance in quinoa. However, Canahua and Rea (1980) found that quinoa could tolerate frosts when they occur before flowering, but that after flowering, significant damage occurred. Three accessions from a collection of 144 were resistant to frosts of −3°C.

When quinoa varieties were planted on 15 January (i.e., at midsummer) in Puno, various degrees of frost resistance were detected. The variety Sajama was damaged by the first frosts in March and was killed in April, but Kanccolla and Blanca de Julí were more resistant, whereas Chewecca was damaged by a frost of −15°C in July, but by this time was already maturing (Canahua and Rea, 1980). At Illpa, Puno, 134 quinoa accessions were found to have some frost resistance and, of these, 12 were resistant to temperatures of −4°C (Valdivia, 1979). Most of the resistant accessions had red stems.

The Chilean varieties Baer, Faro, Litú, Valdivia, and Pichamán and the Peruvian variety Blanca de Junín were sown at Cambridge on 25 March and withstood seven frosts, one of them severe (−5°C), during their early growth. The late-maturing Peruvian variety remained in the field until 22 November and was not damaged by the autumn frosts. It was eventually harvested after being sprayed with paraquat in order to dry the foliage. These results support the higher estimates of frost resistance.

Rea (1977) reported that cañihua was resistant to temperatures of −3°C, but this is probably an underestimate of its resistance: at altitudes above 4000 m frosts are common throughout the growing season.

4. *Drought resistance*

Droughts are common in the altiplano and are usually due not to a deficiency of total rainfall but to a bad distribution of rains during the season (Aquize, 1977). Quinoa is regarded as a crop for dry years, able to withstand high irradiation, high evapotranspiration, reduced soil moisture, and low dew temperatures at night. In the drought of the 1976–1977 season in the altiplano, characterized by higher than average rainfall in September followed by 60 days without rain, quinoa fared better than potato, *Brassica* vegetables, barley, wheat, and many weeds (Canahua, 1977).

The drought resistance of quinoa and cañihua is probably mainly due to their deep, highly ramified root systems, but also to the vesiculate pubescence on the leaves. The vesicles contain crystals of calcium oxalate that are hygroscopic and control excessive transpiration. On days of high irradiation, quinoa leaves were found to feel humid when rubbed, whereas the leaves of other herbaceous plants were dry, and water stress was conspicuous in these plants (Canahua, 1977).

There is considerable variation in the response of quinoa varieties to diverse environmental stresses, as shown in Table IV.

5. *Vegetative and reproductive growth*

Flores (1977) defined five subperiods in the growth of quinoa:

Subperiod 1: from sowing to germination.
Subperiod 2: from germination to the formation of the first two true leaves.

TABLE IV. Responses of quinoa varieties to adverse conditions[a]

Variety	Lodging	Hail[c]	Drought	Flooding
Sajama	VS[b]	R	R	VS
Blanca de Julí	S	S	MR	R
Kanccolla	R	S	R	R
Rosada de Puno	R	R	R	R
Ajara (wild quinoa)	VR	S	VR	VR

[a]Data from Canahua (1977).
[b]VS, Very susceptible; S, susceptible; MR, moderately resistant; R, resistant; VR, very resistant.
[c]Conferred by compact inflorescences.

Subperiod 3: from the two-true-leaf stage to the appearance of the inflorescence.
Subperiod 4: from the appearance of the inflorescence to anthesis.
Subperiod 5: from anthesis to maturity.

Flores measured the lengths of the subperiods in plants from a range of sowing dates and obtained the results shown in Table V. Subperiods 3 and 5 are the longest, and subperiods 1 and 2 do not appear to vary in length between varieties. The time required for germination is determined by the soil humidity, but light quality influences the percentage of germination; light with a wavelength between 400 and 450 nm (from violet to blue) produces a decrease in the viability of seeds, particularly in pink-seeded varieties. Light with a wavelength higher than 730 nm (red) produces a decrease in the viability of white seeds. For this reason, higher sowing densities are recommended for the al-

TABLE V. Duration of subperiods (days) in the growth of quinoa in Puno

	Variety		
Subperiod	Sajama	Kanccolla	Blanca de Julí
1	11–57	11–57	11–57
2	5–9	5–9	5–9
3	45–51	45–56	45–56
4	11–31	20–29	20–29
5	60–80	65–106	69–109
Total	139–192	153–197	157–200

tiplano, where the levels of violet and ultraviolet radiation are high, than for the valleys (Arze *et al.*, 1977).

The relative growth rate of the plants increased uniformly for all varieties of quinoa tested between the twenty-ninth and seventy-first day after germination. After this, the relative growth rate in late varieties diminished so that their total vegetative period reached 200 days or more in Ayacucho, Peru (Ochoa, 1972).

In cañihua, the saihua (erect) types grew faster than the lasta (semi-erect) types in the period from sowing to 70 days after sowing. At this stage dry-matter production ceased in the saihua types, whereas the lasta types continued to grow and finally produced more stems and more dry matter than did the saihua types (Arze *et al.*, 1977).

IV. Reproductive Biology

A. BREEDING SYSTEMS

1. *Diversity of systems*

Quinoa has developed more than one breeding system, ranging from virtual cleistogamy perhaps to complete self-incompatibility. However, of a total of 84 accessions studied by Nelson (1968), only a few were placed in these extreme categories. It appears that gynomonoeicy is the predominant breeding system in quinoa, though within this system the proportion of hermaphrodite flowers on a plant varies from 2 to 99% (Rea, 1969).

The flowers of cañihua are wholly concealed within the leaves, and male-sterile flowers are rare (Lazarte, 1972, reported by Bravo, 1975), so it is apparently an effectively cleistogamous species.

2. *Self-compatibility*

Nelson (1968) assessed self-compatibility in quinoa by measuring the seed set on inflorescences enclosed in bags. One of the accessions studied, Rosada de Junín, set no seed in 18 selfing attempts, but set seed when cross-pollinated with another accession. Its pollen stained readily with cotton blue, indicating that it was viable. This variety is therefore probably self-incompatible. Rea (1969) observed that the red-stemmed variety Rosada de Junín and the white-stemmed variety Blanca de Junín did not breed true in trials, but appeared to have hybridized extensively with each other. When a sample of Blanca de Junín was grown in Cambridge, 30% of the plants had red stems, suggesting that hybridization had occurred in the previous generations. Plants grown in the field set seed, but no seed was produced by isolated plants grown in the greenhouse, nor by plants that were bagged. Nelson (1968) pointed out that bagging inflorescences does not allow partial self-incompatibility to be assessed, since low seed set can be attributed to damage to the flowers from the bagging process, heat and humidity, or insects, or to reduced pollination in still air. These factors cannot readily be identified and quantified.

3. *Gynomonoeicy*

Within an inflorescence of quinoa, both female and hermaphrodite flowers can be found in variable proportions (Rea, 1969); in the most extreme case only the apical flower of a group is hermaphrodite (León, 1964). The hermaphrodite flowers may be male sterile (Gandarillas, 1969). The proportion of these three flower types within an inflorescence is influenced by both genotype and environment, as shown in Table VI. A similar effect of greenhouse conditions was reported by Aguilar (1980), who found that three lines that were male sterile when growing outdoors in Puno developed hermaphrodite flowers when grown in a greenhouse. He suggested that low temperatures may inhibit the expression of male fertility in these lines.

Like quinoa, cañihua has some female and male-sterile flowers, but 95% of the flowers are hermaphrodite (Cano, 1971).

4. *Male sterility*

Male sterility, due to the anthers being nonfunctional in all the hermaphrodite flowers, was observed in two quinoa lines selected in Cha-

TABLE VI. Proportion of hermaphrodite and female flowers in four varieties of quinoa grown in greenhouse[a] and field[b]

		Flowers (%)		
Variety	Environment	Hermaphrodite male fertile	Hermaphrodite male sterile	Female
Sajama	Greenhouse	28.7	0.4	70.9
	Field	8	1	91
Kanccolla	Greenhouse	30.3	1.7	68.0
	Field	12	3	85
Blanca de Julí	Greenhouse	21.5	0.7	77.8
	Field	12	2	83

[a]Universidad Nacional Técnica del Altiplano, Puno, Peru (Rodríguez, 1978).
[b]Tahuaco, Puno, Peru (Calderón, 1980).

llapata, Bolivia (Gandarillas, 1969). When they were crossed with male-fertile plants, the F_1 was male fertile and in the F_2 generation a ratio of three fertile plants to one sterile was observed. In a sample containing male-sterile plants collected at Batallas, Bolivia, the progeny of hermaphrodite plants also provided evidence of a recessive gene determining male sterility, designated *ms* (Simmonds, 1971). However, the frequency of hermaphrodites in the progeny of male-sterile *ms ms* plants was variable and inconsistent with Mendelian ratios, which was thought to indicate a cytoplasmic influence. Aguilar (1980) found that a male-sterile line grown outdoors and exposed to pollen from other lines produced only 40% of male-fertile progeny. This was interpreted as indicating that both *Ms* and *ms* pollen were present, derived from *Ms ms* plants in the other lines. However, the cytoplasmic influence postulated by Simmonds (1971) would explain this result better.

More consistent evidence of cytoplasmic male sterility was found in a third male-sterile line selected at Challapata, which produced only male-sterile progeny in the F_1. The progeny of a backcross to the male-fertile line were also male sterile (Gandarillas, 1969). Similarly, the male-sterile line UNTA 292 produced only male-sterile plants in the F_1 generation and two successive backcrosses to three male-fertile lines. However, when this line was crossed with the variety Sajama, its progeny were male fertile, and in the F_2 fertile and sterile plants occurred in the ratio 3:1. This could indicate that Sajama possesses a dominant gene that restores male fertility in the cytoplasm of UNTA 292 (Aguilar, 1980). Reliable cytoplasmic male sterility and restorer genes could be immensely useful for the production of F_1 hybrid varieties.

5. *Temporal pattern of anthesis*

Anthesis in quinoa starts at the apex of each glomerulus or group of flowers. Hermaphrodite and female flowers are generally open at the same time (Gandarillas, 1979c). Most flowers open in the morning, and the maximum number of flowers open at midday (Ignacio and Vera, 1976). The number of open flowers is reduced by rain (Sacaca, 1978). Anther dehiscence occurs from early morning until late afternoon and is also highest at midday (Valdivia, 1978); large quantities of pollen are produced. Flowers remain open for 5–13 days (Erquínigo, 1970). In eight land races and five commercial varieties of quinoa, the average duration of anthesis was 14.5 days, and of dehiscence, 18.2 days. There was an average of 2.5% floral aberrations (Lescano, 1980).

In three ecotypes of cañihua, Lazarte (1972, reported by Bravo, 1975) found that some flowers opened in the morning, their stigmas remaining receptive for an average of 24.2 hr, whereas others opened in the afternoon and remained receptive for an average of 37.5 hr. Flowers remained open for 4–7 days (Cano, 1971).

6. *Rates of outcrossing*

Gandarillas (1979c) calculated the rate of outcrossing in quinoa for the conditions of the Bolivian altiplano. Green-stemmed plants were selected at different distances from fields of purple-stemmed plants, and their progeny were grown out. The results are shown in Table VII. Lescano (1980) estimated in eight land races and five commercial varieties of quinoa that the average rate of outcrossing was 5.8%.

These results show that although quinoa is generally considered an autogamous species, outcrosses can occur over considerable distances. This must be taken into account when it is necessary to isolate lines or varieties during a breeding program. However, different results may be obtained under conditions other than those of the altiplano since the rate of outcrossing is influenced by wind speed, the proportion of female and male-sterile flowers, and the presence of self-incompatibility.

In cañihua, Simmonds (1966) reported 0.1% outcrossing, but Cano (1971) reported 20%, a value that is rather high for a plant that appears effectively cleistogamous. It was suggested that the tendency for some flowers to be protandrous or protogynous may encourage outcrossing.

TABLE VII. Percentage of outcrossing in quinoa at different sowing distances from the pollinator

Distance (m)	Color of pollinator	Progeny: Number of green plants	Progeny: Number of purple plants	Outcrossing (%)
1	Purple stem, red seed	614	68	9.9
5		648	19	2.8
10		656	18	2.6
20		743	4	0.5
1	Purple stem, yellow seed	330	15	4.3
5		459	6	1.3
10		287	6	2.0
20		393	6	1.5

B. GENETICS

1. *Chromosome number reduction and endopolyploidy*

Gandarillas and Luizaga (1967) found not only polyploid cells, but also cells with 18, 27, and 36 chromosomes, in the radicles of quinoa. The chromosome number per cell was constant within the radicle in the cases in which more than one cell was observed. There was no correlation between chromosome number in the radicle and seed size. In root tips, cells with 45, 63, and even higher numbers of chromosomes were found, the cells nearest the apex having the lowest number.

In view of the high level of fertility in quinoa, it is likely that the sexual cells always have 36 chromosomes at the start of meiosis and that endomitosis during vegetative growth accounts for the higher numbers in the root tips. The lower numbers are less easily explained.

2. *Inheritance of Mendelian characters*

a. *Plant color.* Three basic patterns of plant coloration have been identified in quinoa (Gandarillas, 1974), namely, red plants with pigment in all parts; purple plants with pigment only in the apical leaves and inflorescence, which may turn yellow at maturity; and green plants with no pigmentation. The intensity of the color can vary, and Simmonds (1971) reported that when grown under low light intensities, pigmented plants may be misclassified as green plants. The results of crosses indicate that plant color is determined by a series of alleles at one locus, designated R for red, r^p for purple, and r for green, with R being dominant to r^p and r and r^p dominant to r (Gandarillas, 1968, 1974; Simmonds, 1971).

A major gene controls plant color in cañihua, red being dominant to green (Simmonds, 1966).

b. *Axil color.* Axillary pigmentation, a character that cannot be observed on red plants, is controlled by a single gene designated *Ax,* with pigmented axil being dominant to nonpigmented axil (Simmonds, 1971).

c. *Inflorescence type and color.* Although several inflorescence characters have an important influence on yield, the only factors that have been studied genetically are the type (glomerulate or amaranthiform) and color of the inflorescence (Gandarillas, 1979b). Inflorescence type is controlled by a single gene, designated *G,* with glomerulate being dominant to amaranthiform (Gandarillas, 1974). Inflorescence color is influenced by the allelomorphic series controlling color in other parts of the plant, *R*, r^p, and *r* (Gandarillas, 1974). However, the color intensity is also influenced by environmental factors (Simmonds, 1971).

d. *Seed color.* Since the pericarp is the outer layer of the harvested grain of quinoa, the pericarp color is usually called the seed color for convenience. The ancestral seed color is black. When a light-seeded quinoa was crossed with a light-seeded huauzontle (*C. berlandieri* ssp. *nuttaliae*), black-seeded progeny were obtained, indicating that light seed color is controlled by recessive mutations at different loci in the two species (Heiser and Nelson, 1974), and that mutant varieties have probably arisen several times independently. Coffee-colored seed has been found in archaeological remains (Gandarillas, 1979b), and this may have been the first mutant color.

In quinoa, red and yellow seed are both dominant to white, and black is dominant to yellow (Paca, 1970; Gandarillas, 1974). The results of crosses involving genotypes with coffee-colored seed are harder to interpret, and the suggestion of Gandarillas (1974) that seed color is controlled by two loci, with five and three alleles, respectively, seems to go beyond the available evidence.

The seed color of cañihua is determined by the endosperm color. Two studies have indicated that the color is determined by a single gene, black being dominant to brown (Paca, 1970; Simmonds, 1971).

e. *Saponin content.* When sweet-seeded, low-saponin quinoa plants, isolated from samples collected near Patacamaya, Bolivia, were crossed with bitter varieties, a 3:1 ratio of bitter to sweet was observed in the F_2 generation, indicating that high saponin content was determined by a single dominant gene, designated *D* (Gandarillas, 1974). However, semisweet varieties (e.g., Kanccolla, Blanca de Julí) exist, and it is likely that the amount of saponin is polygenically controlled. The genetics of this important character should therefore be studied in more detail, including crosses that involve semisweet varieties.

f. *Other seed characters.* Most varieties of quinoa have an opaque endosperm, but in some, known as chullpi varieties, the endosperm is translucent. This character is controlled by a single gene designated *Su*, opaque endosperm being dominant (Gandarillas, 1974).

In some varieties of quinoa from the Titicaca basin, the pericarp can be easily separated from the endosperm; this character is called koytu (Gandarillas, 1974) or ccoito (Tapia, 1979a) and is commonly found in low-saponin varieties. It is determined by a recessive gene (Gandarillas, 1974).

g. *Male sterility and gene linkage.* Simmonds (1971) found that the recessive gene determining male sterility, *ms,* was linked with the loci controlling plant pigmentation (*R*) and axil pigmentation (*Ax*) with the following recombination frequencies:

Ax--8%--*R*-----------35%-----------*Ms*

The weak *Ax–Ms* linkage was not detected directly. In the F_2 progeny of two crosses between lines that differed at these loci, Aguilar (1980) found 38 and 39% of recombinant plants. These values correspond to recombination frequencies of 52 and 54% in the gametes—not significantly different from the 50% expected for unlinked genes—and agree reasonably well with Simmonds' findings.

V. Diseases and Pests

A. PRESENT AND FUTURE PROBLEMS

When a crop is introduced into a new country, it often enjoys a period of freedom from pests and diseases. In order to anticipate the problems that will arise at the end of this period, three lines of evidence can be considered: first, the pests and pathogens that attack the crop in its region of origin, which may be transported to the new country or may have close relatives already there; second, those that are observed at low levels on experimental plots; and third, those that attack related plant species in the new country.

B. FUNGAL DISEASES

1. *Downy mildew*

This disease, caused by *Peronospora farinosa,* was the first reported on quinoa (García, 1947). It is also the most important and widespread, having been reported from Colombia, Peru, and Bolivia. Oospores of the fungus can be transmitted on seeds (Alandia *et al.,* 1979), and this was probably the source of *P. farinosa* observed on quinoa in Cambridge. Although the ideal conditions for the disease are high relative humidity and moderately low temperatures, it has been observed in parts of the altiplano where the annual rainfall is as low as 200–500 mm and the average temperature is as low as 6–10°C (Alandia *et al.,* 1979).

Yerkes and Shaw (1959) distinguished the species *Peronospora parasitica,* Cruciferae mildew, and *P. farinosa,* Chenopodiaceae mildew.

The term *Peronospora effusa,* applied to quinoa mildew (Otazú *et al.*, 1976), thus became a synonym of *P. farinosa*. However, Byford (1967) found that isolates of *P. farinosa* from sugar beet (*B. vulgaris*), fat hen (*C. album*), and spinach (*S. oleracea*) would only infect the host species from which they were isolated. He therefore proposed the following classifications: *P. farinosa* f.sp. *betae* on *Beta* spp.; *P. farinosa* f.sp. *spinaceae* on *Spinacia spp.; P. farinosa* f.sp. *chenopodii* on *Chenopodium* spp. This classification is supported by Johanson's (1983) finding that sugar beet mildew did not infect quinoa under greenhouse conditions and is partly supported by the finding of Alandia *et al.* (1979) that quinoa mildew did not infect spinach, beetroot (*B. vulgaris*), or cañihua. However, this last result suggests that further subdivision of *P. farinosa* f.sp. *chenopodii* is necessary, a suggestion confirmed by the failure of spores from *C. album* to infect *Chenopodium amaranticolor* or *Chenopodium capitatum* (Byford, 1967).

The main symptom of the disease is chlorotic lesions on the upper surfaces of the leaves, with a white or purple mycelium on the lower surfaces. The lesion may cover a whole leaf (Salas *et al.*, 1977), and severe early infections can become systemic, causing the plants to become dwarfed, chlorotic, and deformed (Alandia *et al.*, 1979).

Otazú *et al.* (1976) and Vásquez (1977) screened 145 and 444 germplasm accessions, respectively, for resistance to downy mildew at Puno, and obtained the results shown in Table VIII.

Peronospora farinosa infection is the only disease that has been reported

TABLE VIII. Resistance of quinoa accessions to downy mildew

Foliar area affected (%)	Classification	Accessions in category[a]	Accessions in category (%)[b]
0–4	Resistant	UNTA 140, UNTA 116, UNTA 60, UNTA 63, Tupiza	36.9
5–19	Moderately resistant	Kanccolla, Illimani, Ccoyto-1, UNTA 98, UNTA 97	53.4
20–49	Susceptible	Sajama, Oxfam	6.5
50–100	Very susceptible	UNTA 39, UNTA 18	0.4

[a]Data from Otazú *et al.* (1976).
[b]Data from Vásquez (1977).

in cañihua. It appeared during flowering but did not cause significant damage to plants (Tapia, 1979b).

2. *Brown stalk rot*

This disease was first observed in Puno in the 1974–1975 season and at present is frequently observed on the Peruvian altiplano (Alandia *et al.*, 1979). The causal agent has been identified as *Phoma exigua* var. *foveata* (Otazú and Salas, 1977). The pathogen is favored by low temperatures and high humidity and by the presence of wounds on the host, such as those caused by hail (Otazú and Salas, 1977).

The main symptoms are dark brown lesions with a vitreous edge, from 5 to 15 cm long, on the stem and inflorescence. Pycnidia are formed on the lesions. The stem is often shrunken, the plant may become chlorotic, and progressive defoliation toward the apex may occur. Artificially inoculated leaves have shown a necrotic hypersensitive reaction (Otazú and Salas, 1977).

Phoma exigua var. *foveata* infects potato foliage (Turkensteen, 1975) and has been isolated from potato tubers (Otazú and Salas, 1977) in Peru, and it is the causal agent of potato gangrene, a storage disease in the United Kingdom. *Phoma exigua* var. *foveata* isolated in quinoa caused foliar spots on potatoes and tomatoes and gangrene symptoms on potato tubers (Otazú and Salas, 1977). On the other hand, *P. exigua* var. *foveata* isolated from potato did not cause infection on wounded or unwounded plants of the quinoa varieties Sajama and Kanccolla under greenhouse conditions (Johanson, 1983), but this may have been because the temperature was too high for the pathogen to develop. The evidence suggests that potato–quinoa rotations should be avoided, though such rotations are in fact common.

3. *Stem Gothic spot*

This disease was observed during the 1974–1975 growing season, and the causal agent has been identified as *Phoma cava* (Salas *et al.*, 1977). The fungus is apparently favored by high relative humidity, and unlike *P. exigua* var. *foveata,* it does not require a wound to cause infection (Alandia *et al.*, 1979). The lesions, which occur mainly on stems but also on inflorescence branches and floral peduncles, are light gray with brown edges and are surrounded by a vitreous halo. They are 2–3 cm long and are said to have the shape of a Gothic window. These lesions produce pycnidia. In severe attacks the lesions can coalesce to girdle the stem, causing leaves and inflorescence branches to collapse (Salas *et al.*, 1977).

Among 145 germplasm accessions evaluated for resistance at Puno,

UNTA 135 was susceptible, Kanccolla and Sajama were moderately resistant, and Oxfam and Tupiza were resistant (Alandia *et al.*, 1979).

4. *Leaf spot*

This disease was described by Vilca (1972) and the pathogen was identified by Boerema *et al.* (1977) as *Ascochyta hyalospora.* It is apparently favored by high temperatures. The fungus is seed borne and was found on between 7.8 and 26.3% of the seeds in samples from Bolivia (Boerema *et al.*, 1977). The first symptom is light spots of indefinite area on the leaves. These become well defined, cream colored with a light brown edge, and may coalesce till they cover the whole leaf. At later stages pycnidia can be observed, and the leaves become dry and fall off (Vilca, 1972).

Seed transmission occurs when pycnidia are produced in the inner tissues. The fungus causes mild to severe browning in the roots and hypocotyl of seedlings; severely infected seedlings die (Boerema *et al.*, 1977). Some degree of resistance has been observed in the varieties Tupiza, Blanca de Chucuito, and Kanccolla (Salas *et al.*, 1977).

5. *Seed rot and damping off*

This disease was observed in 1980 in California. In an autumn planting, stem girdling and seedling collapse occurred in patches of the field. *Sclerotium rolfsii,* not previously reported as a quinoa pathogen, was isolated from affected seedlings. The saponin content of the seeds did not influence the development of the disease (Beckman and Finch, 1980).

6. *Gray mold*

This disease was observed on the quinoa variety Baer in Cambridge, and the pathogen was identified as *Botrytis cinerea.* Gray lesions of irregular shape were observed on the stems and inflorescences of mature plants. Where the central axis of the inflorescence was affected, the secondary axes sometimes collapsed. *Botrytis cinerea* also affected some plants growing under greenhouse conditions, causing leaf senescence and reduced height (Johanson, 1983).

C. BACTERIAL DISEASES

Bacterial blight is widely distributed around Puno and causes significant damage, especially when it occurs during grain development. The pathogen has not been fully identified and is described as a *Pseudomonas* sp. (Alandia *et al.*, 1979). The disease is seed borne, and its dissemination within the field is favored by rain, damp soil (Salas *et al.*, 1977), and mechanical wounds caused by hail (Alandia *et al.*, 1979).

D. VIRUSES

Alandia *et al.* (1979) reported a chlorotic mosaic of quinoa, probably caused by a seed-transmissible virus. Because quinoa is used as an indicator plant for virus testing, its response to a large number of viruses is known. Of those tested, many produce symptoms, but probably few would cause significant damage in the field.

A virus isolated from soil leachates in Wellesbourne, Warwickshire, England, was mechanically transmitted to quinoa, and also produced local lesions and systemic necrosis in *C. album*, cowpea (*Vigna unguiculata*), and *Phaseolus* beans. It can be isolated from leachates of infected quinoa roots and has been provisionally named *Chenopodium* mosaic virus (CMV), but its natural hosts are unknown (Tomlinson *et al.*, 1981).

E. INSECT PESTS

1. *The scope of insect problems*

Different insect pests attack quinoa and cañihua during germination, vegetative growth, reproductive growth, and seed storage (Zanabria and Mujica, 1977). In the salares of Bolivia, insects constitute an important limitation on quinoa production, causing losses of up to 40% in the Ladislao Cabrera region (Quispe, 1976, reported by Ortiz and Zanabria, 1979). In the Peruvian altiplano, insects cause losses of about 8% (Ortiz and Zanabria, 1979).

Quinoa insect pests can be classified as cutworms, mining and grain-destroying insects, biting and defoliating insects, and piercing and sucking insects (Zanabria and Mujica, 1977).

2. *Cutworms*

This group comprises several polyphagous species of the family Noctuidae, order Lepidoptera, including *Feltia experta, Spodoptera frugiperda, Spodoptera eridania, Copitarsia turbata,* and *Agrotis ypsilon.* The adult moths have a wingspan of 35–40 mm and have gray or beige forewings with dark stripes characteristic of the species. The hind wings are generally white, cream, or transparent. The caterpillars reach a maximum length of 35 mm and vary in color from light to dark gray. Some species have lines, varying in color from yellow-brown to gray, along their dorsal surfaces (Zanabria and Mujica, 1977). The caterpillars do the damage, cutting through the stems of seedlings and sometimes making it necessary to resow patches. They also attack the leaves of older plants, leaving only the veins (Lescano, 1981).

3. *Mining and grain-destroying insects*

a. *Leaf sticker (panicle destroyer).* This is probably the most important insect pest of quinoa in the altiplano. It has not been completely identified and is described as *Scrobipalpula* sp., family Gelechiidae, order Lepidoptera. The adult moths have a wingspan of 15–16 mm and are brown-gray or yellow-gray. The caterpillars reach a maximum length of 12 mm and vary in color from yellow-green to dark brown, with diffuse brown or pink spots on their dorsal surface (Zanabria and Mujica, 1977).

This pest is favored by warm, dry weather. The larvae mine the inflorescences of young plants and stick young leaves together to shelter their cocoons. Mature inflorescences and seeds are also attacked, leaving a white dust on the plants (Lescano, 1981). This gives the insect its Quechua name of kcona kcona, meaning "grain grinder" (Ortiz and Zanabria, 1979). The pest can also attack stored grain.

A moth probably belonging to this genus, and certainly belonging to the family Gelechiidae, was observed on quinoa in Cambridge.

b. *Quinoa moth and leaf and inflorescence caterpillar.* These two similar pests have been identified as *Pachyzancla bipunctalis* and *Hymenia recurvalis,* respectively, both of the family Pyralidae, order Lepidoptera (Ortiz and Zanabria, 1979). The adult moths of *P. bipunctalis* have a wingspan of about 25 mm and are pale yellow, whereas those of *H. recurvalis* are slightly smaller and are dark brown with a yellow spot and a darker transverse band on the forewing. The caterpillars of *P. bipunctalis* reach 20 mm in length, those of *H. recurvalis,* 17 mm. The two are similar in form and color, ranging from light to dark green with a dark brown head (Zanabria and Mujica, 1977; Ortiz and Zanabria, 1979).

The caterpillars destroy leaves and inflorescences and stick them together at the apex of the plant (Ortiz and Zanabria, 1979).

c. *Leaf miner.* This pest has been identified as *Lyriomiza brasiliensis,* family Agromyzidae, order Diptera. The adult fly is about 2.5 mm long and is black with yellow markings. The larva is vermiform, reaching about 3 mm in length, and is pale cream in color (Ortiz and Zanabria, 1979).

The larvae produce serpentine mines on the leaves and occasionally on stems. These may coalesce into blotches. The pest is favored by warm, dry weather (Ortiz and Zanabria, 1979). A fly belonging to the same family was observed in quinoa in Cambridge.

d. *Looper.* The adults of this species, *Perisoma sordescens,* are dark gray moths with a wingspan of 30 mm. The caterpillars reach about 20 mm in length and vary in color from pale green to yellow-cream. They destroy leaves and immature and mature seeds, and during severe attacks empty inflorescences are found (Zanabria and Mujica, 1977).

3. *Biting and defoliating insects*

This group includes three species of Coleoptera, *Epicauta latitarsis, Epicauta willei,* and *Epitrix subcrinita,* which are also potato pests. The adult beetles of both *Epicauta* species are about 15 mm long and have cylindrical bodies, but whereas *E. latitarsis* is black and hairless, *E. willei* is dark gray and is covered with yellowish gray velvety hairs. *Epitrix subcrinita* is a flea beetle about 2 mm long and is dark brown or shiny black (Zanabria and Mujica, 1977).

In all three species the damage is caused by the adults. *Epicauta latitarsis* and *E. willei* attack leaves and inflorescences. They are favored by dry and warm weather, and a severe attack can destroy entire fields in a few days. *Epitrix subcrinita* makes small perforations in the leaves and its attack is most serious at early plant growth stages (Ortiz and Zanabria, 1979).

4. *Piercing and sucking insects*

This group comprises aphids including *Mysus persicae* and *Macrosiphum* spp., leafhoppers including *Bergallia* spp., and thrips including *Franklinella tuberosi.* Feeding by these polyphagous species weakens the plant, but the damage that they cause by transmitting viruses is probably more important. All three groups of pests are favored by warm, dry weather (Ortiz and Zanabria, 1979). Black bean aphids (*Aphis fabae*) have been observed on quinoa in Cambridge.

5. *Insects found in cañihua*

Many of the pests found in quinoa are also found in cañihua. Pastor (1970) mentioned the following species as the most important: (1) cutworms: *Feltia experta, Spodoptera frugiperda,* and *Spodoptera eridania;* (2) panicle destroyer: *Scrobipalpula* spp. (kcona kcona); (3) beetles: *Epicauta latitarsis* and *Epicauta willei;* and (4) aphids: *Myzus* spp. and *Macrosiphum* spp.

F. NEMATODES

The false nodule nematode (*Nacobbus* sp.) and the cyst nematode (*Heterodera* spp.) have been reported on quinoa. *Nacobbus* sp. is a common pest, the females forming nodules on the roots (Alandia *et al.*, 1979). *Heterodera* is an occasional pest, the adult females forming yellow, white, or brown cysts on the roots.

Solano (1976) and Muñoz (1979) evaluated the resistance of quinoa varieties to *Nacobbus* sp. by growing plants in pots containing infested soil and obtained the results shown in Table IX.

G. BIRDS

Birds attack quinoa seedlings and mature inflorescences. In Cambridge about 40% of seedlings were attacked by birds, which destroyed the cotyledons. If the apex of the seedling was not damaged, the plant recovered. The plots in Cambridge were netted before maturity, and the portions of inflorescences that protruded through the net were completely stripped of seed. In the altiplano, losses of up to 40% occur in sweet varieties, especially around Lake Titicaca where pigeons are abundant (Mujica, 1977). Losses to birds are lower in bitter varieties (Aguilar, 1980), and it is probably for this reason that saponins have been retained in cultivated quinoas.

H. PESTS AND DISEASES FOUND ON *Chenopodium album*

Chenopodium album is the closest European relative of quinoa and cañihua and has been carried as a weed in European crops to North America, Australasia, and Africa, as well as to South America (Williams, 1963). It is therefore likely to be a source of pests and diseases if quinoa is cultivated outside South America. The fungi found on

TABLE IX. Resistance of quinoa varieties to *Nacobbus* sp.

Mean number of nodules/root	Classification	Varieties in category
0–0.9	Highly resistant	Chewecca, Real
1–2	Resistant	Kanccolla, Oxfam, Blanca de Julí, Pasankalla
2.1–3.9	Susceptible	Sajama, Illimani
>4	Highly susceptible	—

C. album include *P. farinosa, Ligniera verrucosa, Olpidium brassicae, Cercospora dubia, Cercospora beticola, Cercospora chenopodii, Verticillium albo-atrum, Septoria chenopodii,* and *Phoma lavendulae* (Williams, 1963). The insects include various species of collembola, thrips, aphids, Lepidoptera, and Diptera, and the nematode species *Aphelenchoides ritzema-bosi, Heterodera schactii,* and *Ditylenchus dipsaci* have also been found (Williams, 1963; Basset and Crompton, 1978).

VI. AGRONOMY

A. FARMING SYSTEMS

The agronomic practices used for quinoa and cañihua are mostly those of a subsistence agriculture that has changed little since the Spanish conquest, though in fairly flat areas such as the altiplano and the wider valleys, mechanization is becoming more common. Quinoa usually follows potatoes in the crop rotations of the altiplano, relying on the residue of the fertilizer applied to the potatoes, sometimes supplemented by an application of nitrogen (Rea *et al.*, 1979).

Quinoa requires a level, well-drained seed bed in order to avoid waterlogging of the small seed, but lack of moisture is often a problem in the altiplano and a technique named dry-season cultivation has been developed in order to combat this. A fallow field is ploughed in December in order to allow the rains from December to March to accumulate. It is ploughed again during the first week of April to kill the weeds and to break the soil capillarity so that the moisture is conserved. It is ploughed a third time and the crop is sown in September (Mujica, 1977).

B. SOWING

1. *Methods*

The following sowing techniques are used in the Andes (Tapia *et al.*, 1980):

1. Broadcast sowing. This technique, though common, makes weed control and any subsequent mechanized practices difficult.
2. Sowing in rows. This method is used where agriculture is mechanized. The row width varies from 40 to 80 cm. The seed is deposited

at the bottom of the furrow in dry areas or at the top of the ridge where rain is more abundant.

3. Group sowing. This technique is used in the salares (Lipez and Ladislao Cabrera in Bolivia), where rainfall is low. Four or five seeds are planted in holes about 40 cm in diameter and deep enough to reach humid soil. The holes are 70–120 cm apart (Rea *et al.*, 1979).

4. Mixed sowing. The field is first cultivated with a ridger and then sown broadcast, so that seeds are deposited both on ridges and in furrows. This assures establishment under either deficiency or excess of moisture.

5. Transplanting. Small plots of quinoa are sown at high densities and seedlings are transplanted to blank patches in maize fields. This technique is used in the Urubamba Valley, Cuzco, Peru.

2. *Dates*

The sowing of quinoa coincides with the onset of the rains in the Southern Hemisphere summer, in September or October. In Puno, sowings are made as early as August if moisture is available. The late-maturing altiplano variety Kanccolla can be sown only until mid-September (Mujica, 1977), whereas early-maturing varieties can be sown as late as November (León, 1964). In Concepcion, Chile, yields of the local varieties Baer, Litú, Pichamán, and Faro were 12% higher from a September sowing than from an October sowing; they were sharply reduced by sowing in November, probably due to the high temperature (28°C) and low relative humdity (55%) during flowering in January, which may have affected pollen viability (Etchevers and Avila, 1979).

When a valley variety (Blanca de Junín) and a sea level variety (Baer) were sown at Cambridge at three dates, the yields shown in Table X were obtained. Evidently, the earliest sowing date is the best. Even when sown at this date, Blanca de Junín had to be sprayed with

TABLE X. Yields (kg/ha) and harvest dates of quinoa at Cambridge in 1983

	Baer variety		Blanca de Junín variety	
Sowing date	Yield	Harvest	Yield	Harvest
25 March	4594	24 Sept	3317	11 Nov
14 April	3534	10 Oct	—	—
8 May	—	—	—	—

paraquat to dry the foliage. At the latest sowing date, weed competition was excessive and the quinoa seedlings could not develop. The sowing of 25 March was not affected by the frosts of April and early May, and when the field was eventually ploughed on 14 November, the remaining plants of Blanca de Junín had not been killed by frost. The possibility that quinoa is hardy enough for autumn sowing in Britain therefore merits investigation.

3. *Density*

Estimates of the optimum sowing density for quinoa vary widely. Blanco (1970) reported an optimum density of 4–6 kg of seed per hectare (1 kg contains about 300,000 seeds) for the Bolivian altiplano, whereas Canahua (1977) mentioned an optimum sowing density of 15–23 kg/ha in Puno. A density of 12 kg/ha has been recommended in Puno for mechanical drilling (Rea *et al.*, 1979). Velásquez (1968) found no significant differences in yield between sowing densities of 15, 20, and 25 kg/ha. However, Ortiz (1974) noted that a combination of high sowing densities (20–30 kg/ha) with high humidity produced small, weak plants with low productivity. Herquinio and Román (1975) obtained higher yields at a sowing density of 8 kg/ha than at 48 or 88 kg/ha, and they reported that the proportion of lodged plants increased at the higher densities. On the other hand, if the density is too low, the vegetative period is prolonged, maturity becomes uneven, and mechanical harvesting is difficult (Montenegro, 1976). When the Chilean varieties Baer, Faro, Litú, and Pichamán were drilled at row widths of 40, 60, and 80 cm, the yield per plant was higher at the wider spacings but the yield per unit area was significantly lower (Etchevers and Avila, 1979).

When the varieties Blanca de Junín and Baer were sown in Cambridge at different row widths and sowing densities within the row, the results shown in Table XI were obtained. The closest row spacing and the highest within-row density, equivalent to a seed rate of 15 kg/ha, gave the highest yields in both varieties. The 40-cm row width also gave the best weed control, the plants covering the ground 45 days after sowing.

Excess quinoa plants are sometimes removed by hand (Mujica, 1977). However, a correct sowing density, good seedbed preparation, and the use of good quality seed should make this operation unnecessary.

TABLE XI. Yields of two quinoa varieties sown at different densities

Row width (cm)	Seed/m (g)	Sowing density (kg/ha)	Yield (kg/ha)		Average values			
						Row width (cm)		
			Baer	Blanca de Junín	Seed/m (g)	40	80	Mean
80	0.2	2.5	3033	2566	0.2	3891	2260	3517
80	0.4	5.0	3511	2771	0.4	4791	2868	3952
80	0.6	7.5	3621	3283	0.6	5036	3103	4396
40	0.2	5.0	5181	3289				
40	0.4	10.0	5685	3840	Mean	4779	3131	3955
40	0.6	15.0	6530	4150	CV = 19.8%			

4. *Depth*

The small size of quinoa seed makes it vulnerable to both waterlogging and dehydration, so that particular care must be taken concerning the depth at which it is sown. Bornás (1977) reports an optimum sowing depth of 1.0–1.5 cm, whereas Mujica (1977) recommends a depth between 2 and 3 cm. When quinoa seeds were sown in pots at depths of 1, 2, and 3 cm, a lower proportion of seedlings emerged from the deeper sowings (Etchevers and Avila, 1979).

5. *Sowing methods for cañihua*

Cañihua is generally sown between September and October, and as it is a very minor crop, the soil is not so well prepared as for quinoa. It is generally sown broadcast, using between 4 and 8 kg of seed per hectare. One kilogram contains abut 1,000,000 seeds (Tapia, 1979b).

Cañihua yielded better when sown in rows, but no differences were found between yields at 25-, 30-, and 35-cm row widths (Cahuana, 1975).

C. FERTILIZER APPLICATION

Fertilizer is not generally applied to quinoa and cañihua. Quinoa usually depends on the residue of fertilizer from a preceding potato crop, but when quinoa is sown after quinoa an organic fertilizer such as sheep manure, guano, or peat is incorporated into the soil, and these have been shown to increase the yield (Calzada, 1951). However, many investigations have shown that quinoa responds well to applications of inorganic fertilizer, and rates of 80 kg/ha of N, 40 kg/ha of P_2O_5, and 0 kg/ha of K_2O (80:40:0) have been recommended for Puno (Mujica, 1977; Rea *et al.*, 1979; Condorena, 1979). These proportions reflect the high potassium and medium phosphorus content of the soils in Puno (Mujica, 1977) rather than any peculiarities in the requirements of the plant, but Etchevers and Avila (1979) found that dry-matter production in a pot experiment responded to applications of P_2O_5 or K_2O up to the equivalent of 450 kg/ha. These are remarkably heavy applications, even taking into account the fairly low fertility of the soil, which contained 7 ppm of available phosphorus, 0.2 mEq/100 g of soil of interchangeable potassium, and 1.6% organic matter. However, it is questionable whether the increase in dry-matter production would have been reflected in increased grain yield.

It is advisable that nitrogen applications should be divided, half of the dose being applied at sowing and the other half about 50 days later (Mujica, 1977).

In cañihua, both foliage production (for forage) and seed production are increased by fertilization, and a rate of 120:60:0 $N:P_2O_5:K_2O$ is recommended for Puno (de la Torre, 1969).

D. WEED CONTROL

In South America, quinoa is weeded by hand, but if it is to be cultivated in areas with mechanized agriculture and high labor costs such as Britain, chemical herbicides will have to be used. Inadequate weed control will not only reduce quinoa yields but also add to the weed seed bank for subsequent years.

Chaquilla (1976) reported that linuron (Afalon) at a dose of 1 kg/ha gave some control of weeds in Puno as a postemergence herbicide, but also showed some toxicity to quinoa, causing necrotic spots, smaller inflorescences, and later maturity. No preemergence herbicide was reported to work. However, Velazco (1977) reports that linuron (Afalon) and diuron (Karmex) applied postemergence at doses of 1.5 kg/ha controlled weeds and did not affect the yield significantly in Puno.

In an experiment at Cambridge, the preemergence herbicides trifluralin (Treflan) and metamitron (Goltix) and the postemergence herbicide propyzamide (Kerb) were tested on the wild quinoa Ajara and the cultivated variety PLQ-2-51. Propyzamide caused no phytotoxicity in quinoa, but its long residual effect could limit its use as a herbicide. Metamitron caused considerable damage to the wild quinoa at both 5.0 and 2.5 kg/ha, but less damage to the cultivated quinoa at the lower dose. Its suitability at various doses on different varieties should be investigated further. Trifluralin killed both quinoa varieties.

E. EARTHING UP

When quinoa plants reach about 40 cm in height, they are often earthed up, partially to strengthen them and partially to control weeds (Lescano, 1981). However, the plants grown in Cambridge were not earthed up, and although they were subject to strong winds in September, very few plants lodged.

F. PEST AND DISEASE CONTROL

Pests and diseases are traditionally controlled in Peru and Bolivia by the elimination of diseased plants, by the elimination of caterpillars and adult insects by hand, and by the burning of sulfur or old tires to deter the insects. *Scrobipalpula* spp. are also repelled by putting branches of the aromatic plant muña (*Hedeoma mandosiana*) in the quinoa inflorescences (Ortiz and Zanabria, 1979).

The fungicides Polyram-Combi, Cupravit OB 21, Manzate D, and Lanacol at a dose of 1.5 kg/ha were found to inhibit the growth of *P. farinosa* (Laura, 1977). Chemical control of insects is more commonly practiced (Zanabria and Mujica, 1977), and the insecticides and doses used are presented in Table XII.

G. HARVEST

At physiological maturity, the grains of quinoa become dry and hard and difficult to break with a fingernail. Th rest of the plant dries and in most varieties becomes pale yellow, and the leaves are shed. However, the seed heads remain intact, like those of other grain crops and unlike those of wild *Chenopodium* species, which shatter. Traditionally, the plants are pulled or cut with a sickle, then are left in windrows to dry completely. The plants are then threshed either on a threshing floor with sticks, animals, or vehicles, followed by winnowing, or else using

TABLE XII. Chemical control of quinoa pests

Group of insects	Insecticide	Dose/hectare
Cutworms	Aldrin 2.5 D	20–30 kg
	Heptachlor 2.5 D	20–30 kg
	Dipterex 2.5 G	20 kg
	Sevin 5 G	20 kg
Mining and grain-destroying insects	Metacide 50 EC	1.0 liters
	Roxion S	0.5 liters
	Tannaron 50 EC	1.5 - 2.0 liters
	Nuvacron 40 EC	2.5 - 3.0 liters
Biting and defoliating insects	Aldrin 2.5 D	20–25 kg
	Aldrex	0.3% solution
Piercing and sucking insects	Metacide 50 EC	1.0 liters
	Parathion 50 EC	1.5 liters

a stationary thresher. A Triton thresher produced threshed grain at a rate of 600 kg/hr (Mujica, 1977; Lescano, 1981).

Combine harvesting has been tried only on a small scale. It is successful provided that the plants are completely dry, which calls for an unbranched variety with uniform maturity, and provided that the machine is correctly adjusted so that grain is not lost nor chaff retained with the seed (Narrea, 1976a).

VII. Nutrition

A. METHODS OF INVESTIGATION

Determinations of the nutritional value of a product based on chemical analysis of nutrients should be confirmed by feeding experiments with animals, which may reveal problems of low palatability or toxicity. Both types of study have been conducted on the grain of quinoa, and chemical analyses have also been conducted on the leaves, which are used as a vegetable and as fodder, on the haulm and chaff, and on the grain of cañihua.

B. CHEMICAL COMPOSITION OF GRAIN

1. *Nutrients*

The crude protein content of quinoa is affected by environment and genotype, ranging from 11.90% in the variety Blanca de Junín to 14.03% in Blanca de Huancayo (Velázquez, 1959). Montenegro (1976) studied the Colombian varieties Nariño and Dulce de Quitopamba and obtained values of 16.8 and 17%, respectively, and de Etchevers (1980) analyzed six Chilean ecotypes and found values ranging from 10.9% in Lontué to 16.2% in Baer. The protein content of quinoa is thus generally higher than the 10–12% typical of wheat, which is in turn higher than that of other cereal crops. However, it is considerably below the 20–30% typically found in grain legumes.

Many analyses of the overall nutritional composition of quinoa grain have been summarized by Cardozo and Tapia (1979), and these results are compared with those for cañihua in Table XIII.

The essential amino acid compositions of quinoa and cañihua protein are compared with those of other foodstuffs in Table XIV. The

TABLE XIII. Nutritional value of quinoa and cañihua grain

Component	Number of determinations	Quinoa[a] Range (%)	Quinoa[a] Average (%)	Cañihua (%)[b]
Moisture	58	6.8–20.7	12.65	10.90
Protein	77	7.47–22.08	13.81	15.23
Carbohydrate	50	38.72–71.30	59.74	58.58
Fat	60	1.80–9.30	5.01	8.04
Cellulose	22	1.50–12.20	4.38	—
Fiber	30	1.10–16.32	4.14	3.85
Ash	60	2.22–9.80	3.36	3.40

[a]Data from Cardozo and Tapia (1979).
[b]Data from García (1953).

protein of both *Chenopodium* grains contains a high proportion of lysine, which is scarce in most cereal proteins, but is deficient in cystine.

The vitamin content of quinoa has been analyzed by Alvístur *et al.* (1953), by the US Department of Agriculture (reported by Pulgar Vidal, 1954), and by De Bruin (1964). The results, presented in Table XV, are rather contradictory and further analyses are needed.

The mineral contents of quinoa and cañihua are compared with those of maize and barley in Table XVI. The *Chenopodium* species compare favorably with the cereal species.

2. *Saponins*

Saponins are water-soluble glucosides that occur in the pericarp of quinoa (Villacorta and Talavera, 1976), but are absent from cañihua. They are soaplike compounds that foam when dissolved in water, reduce palatability due to their bitterness, and are toxic if they reach the bloodstream since they disrupt the membranes of red blood cells (Ballón *et al.*, 1976). They are usually removed from the grain by vigorous washing. Quinoa varieties differ in saponin content, from the bitter varieties typical of Potosí and Oruro in Bolivia to low-saponin varieties like Kanccolla and Blanca de Junín (Cardozo and Tapia, 1979) and the sweet varieties Sajama and Chewecca, which are almost saponin-free.

Glucose forms about 80% by weight of the molecule of all quinoa saponins, but these compounds can be divided into two groups, namely, triterpenoid glucosides and steroid glucosides derived from them (Bonner and Varner, 1965). The triterpenoid saponins have been

TABLE XIV. Crude protein content (percentage of dry matter) and amino acid composition (percentage of protein) of *Chenopodium* grains and other foodstuffs

Amino acid	Source						
	Quinoa[a]	Cañihua[b]	Wheat[c]	Barley[c]	Maize[c]	Soybean[c]	Skimmed milk[c]
Isoleucine	6.4	6.8	3.8	3.8	3.8	4.9	5.6
Leucine	7.1	5.8	6.8	7.0	12.0	7.6	9.8
Lysine	6.6	6.0	2.9	3.6	3.0	6.4	8.2
Methionine	2.4	1.8	1.7	1.7	2.2	1.4	2.6
Cystine	—	—	2.3	2.3	2.4	1.5	0.9
Phenylalanine	3.5	3.6	4.5	5.2	4.8	4.9	4.8
Tyrosine	2.8	—	3.1	3.4	4.0	3.5	5.0
Threonine	4.8	4.8	3.1	3.5	3.7	4.2	4.6
Tryptophan	1.1	0.8	1.1	1.3	0.9	1.3	1.3
Valine	4.0	4.6	4.7	5.5	5.1	5.0	6.9
Arginine	7.4	7.9	4.8	5.2	4.9	7.2	3.6
Histidine	2.7	2.5	2.2	2.2	2.9	2.5	2.8
Alanine	4.7	—	3.8	4.2	7.3	4.3	3.4
Aspartic acid	7.3	—	5.3	6.1	6.9	12.0	8.0
Glutamic acid	11.9	—	27.5	23.7	18.8	18.8	22.0
Glycine	5.2	—	4.0	4.0	4.0	4.2	2.0
Proline	3.1	—	10.0	9.9	9.1	5.5	10.0
Serine	3.7	—	5.0	4.6	5.1	5.6	6.1
Crude protein	13.0	14.1	10.7	11.9	9.0	36.5	34.1

[a]Data from Van Etten *et al.* (1963).
[b]Data from White *et al.* (1955).
[c]Data from Janssen *et al.* (1979).

TABLE XV. Vitamin content of quinoa grain (ppm of dry matter)

Vitamin	Reference: Alvístur *et al.* (1953)	Reference: USDA	De Bruin (1964), Color: Red	De Bruin (1964), Color: Yellow	De Bruin (1964), Color: White
Carotene	—	—	5.3	5.3	5.3
Thiamin	5.97	5.38	1.85	2.05	1.91
Riboflavin	4.56	3.04	—	—	—
Niacin	14.04	7.02	5.90	6.80	5.10
Ascorbic acid (total)	63.0	—	0.0	0.0	0.0
Tocopherol	—	—	59	52	46

separated into as many as five fractions, and the steroid saponins into two fractions, by chromatography (Ballón *et al.*, 1976).

The content and/or composition of saponins in quinoa have been assessed by the following methods:

1. Foam production. Seeds were shaken with water, and the amount of foam produced was measured (Rea and León, 1966).
2. Chemical extraction. Seeds were boiled and filtered, and the saponins were extracted and crystallized from the filtrate using alcohol, water, and diethyl ether (Machicao, 1965).
3. Chromatography. An extract in water was run on silica gel using a solvent mixture of chloroform, methanol, acetic acid, and water in the proportions 50:25:7:3. The bands were revealed using sulfuric acid (Ballón *et al.*, 1976).
4. Hemolysis. An extract from quinoa seeds was added to rabbit red blood cells. After 2 hr the amount of hemolysis was determined by

TABLE XVI. Mineral content of quinoa, cañihua, and cereal grains (mg/100 g of dry matter)[a]

Mineral	Quinoa	Cañihua	Maize	Barley
Calcium	85	110	6	61
Phosphorus	155	375	267	394
Iron	4.2	13.0	1.7	5.1

[a]Data from Nutrition Institute, Ministry of Health, Peru (Anonymous, 1974).

counting intact cells with a hemocytometer. The quinoa variety Real caused more hemolysis than did Blanca Común and Amarilla Común (Rea, 1948).

5. Fungal growth inhibition. The fungus *Trichoderma viride* was grown on potato dextrose agar, and drops of quinoa seed extract were added. Subsequent fungal growth was compared with that of a control culture (López, 1973, reported by Cardozo and Tapia, 1979).

Foam production is the simplest method of assessing saponin content and can easily be tested in the field, but it is possible that one of the other methods will prove to be better correlated with the toxicity or reduction in palatability caused by the saponins. The specificity of the hemolytic and fungal toxicity methods needs to be confirmed.

C. CHEMICAL COMPOSITION OF VEGETATIVE PARTS

1. *Composition of leaves*

Quinoa leaves, which have been used like spinach since pre-Columbian times, are known as "llipcha" in Quechua and "chiwa" in Aymara (Cardozo and Tapia, 1979). The protein content of quinoa leaves ranges from 2.79% of fresh weight in the variety Sajama to 4.17% in Blanca Amarga, and the lipid content ranges from 1.9% in Blanca Real to 2.3% in Blanca Amarga (Cornejo de Z., 1976). These levels compare favorably with those of other vegetables. During a 70-day growth period in southern Sweden, quinoa produced nearly 1000 kg/ha of extractable leaf protein, which placed it among the 10 most productive species out of 200 members of the families Chenopodiaceae and Amaranthaceae that were tested (Lexander *et al.*, 1970).

2. *Haulm and chaff composition*

Apart from the grain, quinoa was reported to produce 4 metric tons/ha of dry matter, and the prospect of using this as a forage is attractive (Tapia and Castro, 1968). The composition of the haulm and chaff, presented in Table XVII, suggests that this may be possible.

D. ANIMAL AND HUMAN NUTRITION

1. *Grain digestibility*

The digestibility of quinoa grain in sheep was estimated by obtaining the weight and composition of the grain consumed and the feces produced over a 10-day period (Ugarte, 1956). The results are sum-

TABLE XVII. Composition of quinoa haulm and chaff (%)

Component	Haulm	Chaff
Dry matter	92.37	90.9
Protein	7.53	10.7
Fats	1.59	—
Fiber	42.90	—
Ash	11.41	9.9
Nitrogen-free extract	36.57	—

marized in Table XVIII. The digestibility of raw, germinated, and cooked grain of quinoa (variety Illimani) and cañihua (variety Lasta Cupi) was determined using the Tilley and Terry *in vitro* technique. Dry-matter digestibility values of 61.2 and 62.56% were obtained for quinoa and cañihua, respectively. The digestibility was slightly increased by germinating or cooking (Arze and Alencastre, 1976).

2. *Animal productivity*

a. *Chicks.* Chicks fed on raw quinoa as part of a balanced diet for 30 days gained weight slightly less fast than when washed and cooked quinoa or maize was used, though the differences were not significant (Gandarillas, 1948). When chicks were fed substantial quantities of unwashed quinoa, some pathological effects on their internal organs were noted, due to the hemolytic action of the saponins (L. Villacorta S., personal communication). However, Cardozo and Bateman (1961) found that quinoa had detrimental effects in chicks even when the grain was washed. These effects were subsequently related to a deficiency of vitamins A and D (Cardozo and Dávalos, 1967), emphasizing the need

TABLE XVIII. Digestibililty, and contribution to the total digested, of quinoa nutrients in sheep

Nutrient	Digestibility (%)	Contribution (%)
Protein	80.63	11.23
Fats	67.82	2.37
Fiber	66.88	3.37
Nitrogen-free extract	85.48	52.04
Total	71.96	

to assess quinoa, or any other foodstuff, as part of a balanced diet. Thus used over a 56-day period, quinoa and cañihua were found to be acceptable in terms of weight gain, nutrient conversion, and mortality rate (Negrón *et al.*, 1976). Briceño and Canales (1976) found that cañihua could replace maize up to a proportion of 50% in chick diets without causing differences in weight gain over a 4-week period.

b. *Pigs.* Unwashed quinoa depressed the growth of pigs, presumably because of the hemolytic effect of the saponins, but quinoa cooked in water and used in a balanced diet was found to be comparable to powdered milk as a source of protein (Cardozo and Bateman, 1961).

c. *Cattle.* Used as a supplement to the diet of calves, quinoa produced greater weight gains than did the same proportion of wheat or *Vicia* beans, and the animals reached a commercial weight faster (Martínez, 1946).

d. *Rats.* Used as the sole source of protein in an otherwise balanced diet, quinoa produced rates of growth similar to those of powdered milk. In a depletion–repletion trial in which the rats were fed a nitrogen-free diet for 14 or 28 days and then given a protein source for an equal period, rats fed with powdered milk recovered 123 ± 2.2% of their weight loss, whereas rats fed with quinoa recovered 137 ± 3.2% (Alvístur *et al.*, 1953). However, unlike chicks and pigs, rats are tolerant of saponins (L. Villacorta S., personal communication).

e. *Humans.* Quinoa has been used in two experiments with Peruvian children who were recovering from malnutrition. In the first experiment, with children aged from 4 to 29 months, five diets based on potato and wheat and one based on quinoa and oats were compared. The acceptability and tolerance of all the diets were satisfactory, but on the quinoa-oat diet the mean apparent absorption of nitrogen and fat was significantly lower, which was attributed to the digestibility of the quinoa being low (López de Romaña *et al.*, 1978).

In the second experiment, diets based on whole quinoa grain and quinoa flour were compared with a casein control diet for children aged from 10 to 18 months recovering from malnutrition. The low digestibility of the quinoa grain limited protein and fat utilization, but milling significantly improved the digestibility. The results also confirmed that quinoa is suitable as a source of protein for humans (López de Romaña *et al.*, 1981).

VIII. Processing

A. Development of Methods

Until recently, quinoa has been processed almost entirely by the traditional methods of washing, with or without grinding, for household use. With the resurgence of interest in the crop, however, these processes have been converted to an industrial scale, and quinoa products are now available, packaged for supermarkets in the cities of Peru.

B. Elimination of Saponins

The major problem in the processing of quinoa is the elimination of the saponins from the outermost layer of the episperm (Villacorta and Talavera, 1976). Although low-saponin varieties exist, in Puno almost 75% of quinoa production is from bitter varieties because of their greater resistance to bird attack and to pests and diseases (Torres and Minaya, 1980).

Eliminating the saponins is quite easy on a household scale in the Andes. The grains are washed and rubbed with cold water and then are either cooked immediately or left to dry in the bright sunshine typical of the months after harvest. The grain must dry in a matter of hours to prevent fermentation or germination. The grain is then ground to flour or used whole. The saponins can also be eliminated on a household scale by toasting the grains and then rubbing them on stone mortars to remove the outer layers (Torres and Minaya, 1980). Both of these methods are hard to convert to an industrial scale. Wet and dry methods (Torres and Minaya, 1980) and a combined method (Ferrari, 1976) have been tried.

A machine was designed by Molina (1972) for washing and drying quinoa. The best treatment was found to be soaking for 30 min followed by agitation for 20 min in water at 21°C. The quinoa was adequately dried by being spread on trays in layers 1.8 cm thick, at an air temperature of 70°C and air speed of 5.8 m/sec for 160 min. No protein was lost in this treatment. However, the large amount of heat required made the process expensive (Torres and Minaya, 1980), though it might be economically viable if surplus heat from other industries could be used. Other problems with the method are the disposal of bitter, foaming water and the fact that if the soaking period is excessive, the saponins enter the interior parts of the grain (Vargas *et al.*, 1977).

In the dry methods, the pericarp is removed by machines similar to those used to remove wheat bran. A machine designed at the Institute of Agroindustrial Investigations, Lima, Peru, has produced some encouraging results. With the machine retaining 94.6% of the grain in processing, and producing processed grain at a rate of 850 kg/hr, the results shown in Table XIX were obtained (Torres and Minaya, 1980). The saponins, though not eliminated completely, were reduced to a level lower than that of the sweet variety Sajama.

The mixed process was used by Ferrari (1976) at a commercial mill in Oruro, Bolivia. The grains were first scarified and then washed, then centrifuged and sun dried. Virtually all the saponins were eliminated.

C. SUBSEQUENT PROCESSING

1. *Quinoa flour*

The efficiency of white-flour extraction from quinoa was found by Luna (1957) to vary between 50% in Blanca de Junín and 68% in Blanca de Puno, whereas Llerena (1973) found values between 80 and 90% in both quinoa and cañihua. The former values are lower than the 70–80% that is typical for wheat. However, Llerena (1973) considered that after elimination of the saponins, the whole grain should be used for flour production, because its outer layers are softer than those of cereal grains.

TABLE XIX. Saponin content (mg/kg of seed) of quinoa varieties with and without scarification

	Variety			
Treatment	Sajama	Blanca de Julí	Kanccolla	Witulla (red)
Not scarified	0.08	0.13	0.17	0.39
Scarified	—	0.04	0.05	0.04

The composition of quinoa flour is compared with wheat flour in Table XX. Quinoa flour has been tested as a partial substitute for wheat flour in bread, biscuits, and noodles. When a mixture of 90% wheat flour and 10% quinoa flour was used in bread making, the weight and volume of the loaf were not affected, but at substitution rates of 20, 30, and 40% the weight and volume were reduced and at 30 and 40% the loaf became brown (Luna, 1957).

When wheat flour was substituted by quinoa flour at levels of 30, 40, 50, 60, and 70% in sweet and savory biscuits, the nutritional value was increased, but at the 70% substitution rate the quality of the biscuits was affected (Luna and Quérzola, 1958). In noodles, substitution rates of 30 and 40% were acceptable, but at a rate of 50% the cooking quality, appearance, and taste were affected (Luna and Marchetti, 1957).

2. *Other processes*

In addition to the washed grain sold loose in street markets, various products of saponin-free quinoa are sold in 400-g packets in Peru. These include pearl quinoa (quinua perlada), which is simply washed; quinoa flakes (hojuelas de quinua), which resemble rolled oats; and quinoa–oat porridge (quinua–avena). These packets are marketed under the brand names Inca-Sur and Tres Ositos. The Peruvian Ministry of Health published 23 recipes using pearl quinoa for soups, stews, puddings, cakes, and drinks (Anonymous, 1961).

A product of cañihua, called cañihuaco, was found for sale in the street markets of Puno. It consisted of toasted and ground grain, apparently used for direct consumption with milk and sugar and for preparing puddings.

TABLE XX. Composition (%) of quinoa and wheat flours[a]

Component	Quinoa (scarified)	Wheat (white)
Moisture	13.40	14.40
Ash	3.63	0.63
Protein	12.75	12.50
Fat	5.55	1.20
Fiber	4.64	3.20
Carbohydrate	60.03	68.17

[a]Data from Luna (1957).

IX. Breeding Methods and Achievements

A. Historical Development

Although quinoa land races such as Blanca de Junín are mentioned by Llanos (1954), Ráez (1956), and Gorbitz and Luna (1957), serious attempts at the scientific improvement of quinoa started in 1965 at Patacamaya, Bolivia, in a program organized by the Food and Agriculture Organization of the United Nations (FAO), financed by the Oxford Famine Relief Committee (OXFAM) and the Bolivian government (Gandarillas, 1979c). Since then, several other breeding programs have been established. Cañihua improvement, on the other hand, has been confined to a small amount of germplasm evaluation, cytological studies, and the production of tetraploid plants with a view to crossing with quinoa (Gandarillas and Gutiérrez, 1973; Lescano, 1976). The more limited interest in cañihua is partially because of its apparently lesser potential, and partially because its flowers are small and virtually cleistogamous. Cañihua could, however, contribute hardiness, small plant size, and the absence of saponins if it proved possible to cross it with quinoa.

B. Germplasm Collections

The first germplasm collection of quinoa was formed by Flores and Morales in Puno in 1964 and collection of 1200 accessions was formed by the Bolivian Institute of Andean Crops in 1967 (Gandarillas, 1979c). The Universidad Nacional Agraria, La Molina, Lima, also has a germplasm collection (Salhuana *et al.*, 1977). The most complete and best organized germplasm collection of quinoa is probably that of the Universidad Nacional Técnica del Altiplano (UNTA), Puno, Peru. The collection has 1800 entries ranging in origin from southern Colombia to central Chile (Lescano, 1981) and is still expanding. It is stored in a well-designed building financed by the International Board for Plant Genetic Resources (IBPGR), in which low temperature and humidity are maintained without the use of power, but because of lack of funds some accessions are stored in improvised containers such as condensed milk tins. A germplasm collection of cañihua, with 430 accessions, is also kept at the UNTA (Anonymous, 1978). A collection of Chilean quinoa germplasm is maintained at the University of Concepción. This collection includes accessions from the island of Chiloe, which is probably the southern limit of quinoa cultivation (C. L. A. Leakey, personal communication). In 1982 a collection was established at Cambridge, containing 310 accessions of quinoa and 16 of cañihua, some collected from Peruvian markets and farmers, others being duplicates of accessions in Peruvian collections.

C. BREEDING OBJECTIVES AND METHODS

1. *Choice of objectives and methods*

The objectives pursued by quinoa breeders have mostly been those required to adapt the crop to more modern agricultural and processing methods. Lescano and Tapia (1977) have pointed out the needs of producers for higher yields and resistance to pests, diseases, and other environmental factors; of processors for low-saponin varieties; and of consumers for high protein quality. Gandarillas (1979c) has also mentioned the need for an erect stem and well-defined (i.e., few and large) inflorescences in order to compete with crops such as barley which have been introduced to the Andes. It is questionable whether protein quality is a wise breeding objective in a crop that is not used as a sole source of protein, and some of the other objectives may be in conflict. For example, the elimination of saponins causes susceptibility to birds and perhaps other pests, and the emphasis on seed production at the expense of vegetative growth may reduce the plant's tolerance of weed competition and other stresses.

Quinoa breeders have pursued their objectives by mass selection and hybridization. Mass selection—the improvement of local land races by elimination of defective genotypes—was successfully used in many crops when variable land races were common (Allard, 1960). In quinoa this is still the case: the product brought to market in the altiplano shows great variability in seed color, and few farmers grow a genetically pure variety. However, hybridization offers further possibilities for improvement, for example, by combining the low saponin content of the valley types with the short, less branched architecture of the altiplano types (F. Herquinio S., personal communication).

2. *Mass selection*

Farmers use this technique to maintain the purity of a variety for the characteristics that they regard as important (Lescano, 1977). For example, the Chilean varieties are uniform in seed size and color but vary in the compactness of the inflorescences. Mass selection of compact types was effective at Cambridge, although the genetic base of the population used had already been reduced by selection for early flowering in northern Europe (C. L. A. Leakey, personal communication). Some of the varieties obtained by South American farmers and breeders using mass selection are described in Table XXI.

TABLE XXI. Quinoa varieties obtained by mass selection

Variety	Place of origin	Type	Seed color	Seed size (mm)	Saponin content	Resistances	Suscep-tibilities	Breeder	Date	Reference
Kanccolla	Cabanillas, Puno	Altiplano	White	1.5	Medium	Mildew, *Nacobbus*	*Scrobipalpula*	F. Flores	1960	Rea *et al.* (1979)
Real	Coipasa and Uyni	Salar	Cream	2.0	High	Frost, drought	Cutworms	Tradi-tional variety	—	Rea *et al.* (1979)
Chewecca	Orurillo-A-sillo, Puno	Altiplano	White	1.2	Very low	Waterlogging	—	J. L. Lescano	—	Rea *et al.* (1979)
Blanca de Julí	Julí, Puno	Altiplano	White	1.4	Low	Mildew	*Nacobbus*, drought	A. Mo-rales	1969	Rea *et al.* (1979)
Blanca de Junín	Huancayo	Valley	White	1.5	Low	Mildew	—	Tantaleán	—	Rea *et al.* (1979)
Amarilla de Maranganí	Sicuani, Cuzco	Valley	Yellow	1.8	High	Lodging, mildew, other fungi	—	—	—	Rea *et al.* (1979)
Dulce de Quitopamba	Nariño, Colombia	Valley	White	1.5	Very low	—	—	—	—	Montenegro (1976)
Pasankalla	Puno	Altiplano	Purple	1.5	Low	—	—	Tradi-tional variety	—	Rea *et al.* (1979)
Baer	Central Chile	Sea level	Pale Yellow	1.2	High	—	—	—	—	Etchevers and Avila (1979)

3. *Hybridization*

Since most varieties of quinoa are self-fertile, a method of emasculation is needed in order to hybridize genotypes. In a technique described by Rea (1948), a glomerulus or group of flowers was chosen and the five or six most apical flowers were emasculated by removing the anthers with a needle before they had shed pollen, without damaging the stigmata. The rest of the hermaphrodite flowers were eliminated with a needle. (Forceps could also be used.) Any female flowers could be left. Pollen from another genotype was immediately placed on the stigmata with a fine brush, and the glomerulus was then covered with a grease-proof paper bag. This prevented pollen from elsewhere on the same plant from reaching the glomerulus. Grease-proof paper is suitable because it is translucent but, unlike plastic, does not cause condensation. Pollen was collected by shaking an inflorescence of the pollinator genotype into a paper bag, as is done with maize. The glomerulus was examined 5 or 6 days after pollination and any pollen-producing flowers that remained were removed.

In another technique, described by Gandarillas (1967), all the glomeruli of an inflorescence except two or three at the base were removed. In these glomeruli, the newly opened hermaphrodite flowers were emasculated or removed every morning, using a magnifying lens and a fine needle. The female and emasculated flowers were pollinated, and each glomerulus was covered with a grease-proof paper bag that could be removed the following morning to repeat the procedure. The process took up to 7 days, but it would eliminate the danger of self-pollination in the days after cross-pollination more thoroughly than did Rea's technique and would use more of the flowers.

Lescano and Palomino (1976) described a technique for emasculating a whole inflorescence. Before anthesis had occurred in any flower, the small and poorly formed glomeruli were removed. The hermaphrodite flowers were removed or emasculated, and the whole inflorescence was covered with a grease-proof paper bag. Receptive stigmas were recognized by their shiny white appearance, and after pollination all the flowers with dull stigmas were removed. Pollen was collected at midday, and if the female parent was not ready at the time when the pollen parent was at full anthesis, the pollen was stored in medicine capsules at 15°C. Immediate pollination was considered preferable, however.

All of these techniques depend on recognizing and removing hermaphrodite flowers before their anthers have dehisced. This is not easy, and it is probably important that it should be done early in the morning. It is because of this problem that Gandarillas (1979c) recom-

TABLE XXII. Quinoa varieties obtained by selection from hybrids

Variety	Parents	Type	Seed color	Seed size (mm)	Saponin content	Breeder	Date	Reference
Sajama	Line 547 (selection from Real) × Line 559 (sweet)	Altiplano × salar	White	2.0	Very low	H. Gandarillas	—	Gandarillas and Tapia (1976)
UNC-20	Blanca de Junín × Real	Valley × salar	White	1.8	Low	F. Herquinio S.	—	F. Herquinio S. (personal communication)
UNC-76	UNC-20 × Sajama	(Valley × salar) × (altiplano × salar)	White	1.8	Very low	F. Herquinio S.	—	F. Herquinio S. (personal communication)

mended that marker genes be used to distinguish hybrid progeny from the products of self-fertilization. This advice will become increasingly difficult to follow if quinoa breeding advances and more closely related, agronomically well-adapted types are crossed.

Emasculation would be simplified if hot water could be used to male-sterilize the flowers, as is done with rice (Poehlman, 1968). Flowers showed only slight scalding when submerged for 20 min in water at 41–45°C, though higher temperatures caused excessive damage (Aguilar, 1980), and this possibility deserves further investigation.

Some of the varieties produced by selection from hybrids are described in Table XXII.

X. Future Prospects

A. Prospects for South America

Although subsistence crops always attract less attention than commodities such as barley or maize, quinoa and cañihua are now being seriously investigated by the agricultural researchers of Peru and Bolivia, with some interest in Ecuador and Colombia and to a lesser extent in Chile. The area of quinoa cultivation in Peru has increased to perhaps 25,000 ha (Tapia, 1981) from its lowest value of 15,000 ha in 1975. Several germplasm collections have been set up, though the recurrent funding required to maintain and evaluate them, and to distribute material to breeders, is hard to obtain. Thus although the future of quinoa and cañihua is not assured, they at least stand a reasonable chance of a fair trial.

As long as subsistence farming continues in the Andes, quinoa should have a place in it, though a good deal of genetic diversity has probably been lost and will continue to be lost as breeders succeed in producing improved varieties. If the acceptance of quinoa products in the cities continues to increase, this will give a further stimulus to production by more modern methods. The experiments on substitution of quinoa in wheat products and the little-observed law requiring this in Bolivia are encouraging signs, though it is probably better that quinoa products should be marketed as such. The elimination of saponins on an industrial scale remains a formidable problem, though probably not insoluble in areas with reliable sunshine for drying, and the feasibility of growing low-saponin varieties should be further investigated.

It should also be possible to use quinoa extensively as an animal feed. The experimental results obtained in this area are not as encouraging as the composition of the grain would suggest, and more research needs to be done on the use of quinoa in balanced diets and the acceptability of low levels of saponins.

Cañihua, confined to the altiplano and probably specifically adapted to that region, is likely to remain a very minor crop, but its value as a source of genes for quinoa is well worth investigating.

B. PROSPECTS FOR BRITAIN

There is a need for additional break crops in cereal rotations in Britain, to control the weed and disease problems that arise from the continuous cultivation of cereals. The acreages of the crops that traditionally fill this role—*Vicia* beans, sugar beet, potatoes, and fodder crops—are limited by demand and by storage and processing capacity, and the acreage of oilseed rape, which has increased from 5000 to 300,000 ha between about 1965 and 1981 (Labuda, 1981), cannot go on increasing indefinitely. In agronomic terms quinoa is more suitable than other potential break crops, such as maize, soybeans, navy beans (baked beans), and even "leafless" peas, since it is hardy and tall enough to combine harvest. Unlike vegetable crops it does not require special planting or harvesting equipment, and the grain can be stored for long periods. However, all of these other crops meet a well-defined demand, and the main barrier to the cultivation of quinoa in Britain will be finding a market for the grain. Its only immediately forseeable use is as an animal feed, particularly for poultry, though in the longer term, large white-grained varieties might be used as a starch extender in processed foods, and perhaps eventually in quinoa products.

In order to be worth growing in Britain, quinoa would therefore have to be produced at a price competitive with feed wheat and barley. To achieve this will require the selection of genotypes that produce yields comparable to those of the cereals, at least in some parts of the country, though some shortfall in yield may be compensated for by a reduction in inputs of herbicides, fungicides, insecticides, and fertilizers. The yields that can be achieved will depend partly on whether the frost resistance of quinoa proves adequate for autumn plantings. The production of quinoa at a competitive price would probably also require a government subsidy, direct or indirect, comparable to those given to cereals and oilseed rape.

Any add-on costs incurred in the removal of saponins would need to be compensated by an even lower price. The choice between high- and low-saponin varieties would thus depend on the relative costs of washing and drying and of losses to birds, and the latter cannot be assessed until quinoa is grown in large plots without nets. It is worth considering the possibility of feeding washed quinoa to animals immediately *without* drying: quinoa is often used like this in Peru, but to do so on a large scale a farmer would need to invest a considerable amount in equipment.

The aim of most plant breeding is to make small changes in agronomically and commercially well-adapted varieties, but when crops are introduced to new countries and agricultural systems, they often require substantial modification. Examples of this process include the adaptation of sorghum and the soybean to North American agriculture after their introduction from Africa and Asia, respectively (Poehlman, 1968). Models for such comprehensive modification of plants have been called ideotypes (Donald, 1968; Davies, 1977). In the light of the requirements outlined above, the following quinoa ideotype, depicted in Fig. 5, is proposed for British agriculture:

1. Structural characteristics: short, thick stem; little or no branching; compact inflorescence; even maturity; early maturity; high harvest index; white or light-colored seed; and large seed.
2. Response to environment: responsive to nitrogen fertilization in terms of yield; tolerant of nitrogen fertilization in terms of vegetative growth; insensitive to day length; frost resistant; and drought resistant.

The sea level types from Chile already meet the requirements for short stature, early maturity, day length insensitivity, and frost resistance sufficient at least for spring sowing, and they are proving amenable to selection for compact inflorescences and absence of branching. If a high-saponin variety is acceptable, and if the other problems mentioned above can be overcome, mass selections from them could be grown commercially within a few years. If a low-saponin variety is needed, hybridization and further selection will be necessary, in which case the large- and white-seeded characteristics can probably be introduced at the same time.

It is of course possible that the costs of eliminating saponins and the losses to birds will, between them, rule out the cultivation of quinoa for grain in Britain altogether. In this case its potential as a forage crop might still be worth investigating.

C. PROSPECTS WORLDWIDE

Since it has a high level of drought resistance, quinoa could also be grown in warm temperate regions with low rainfall such as some parts

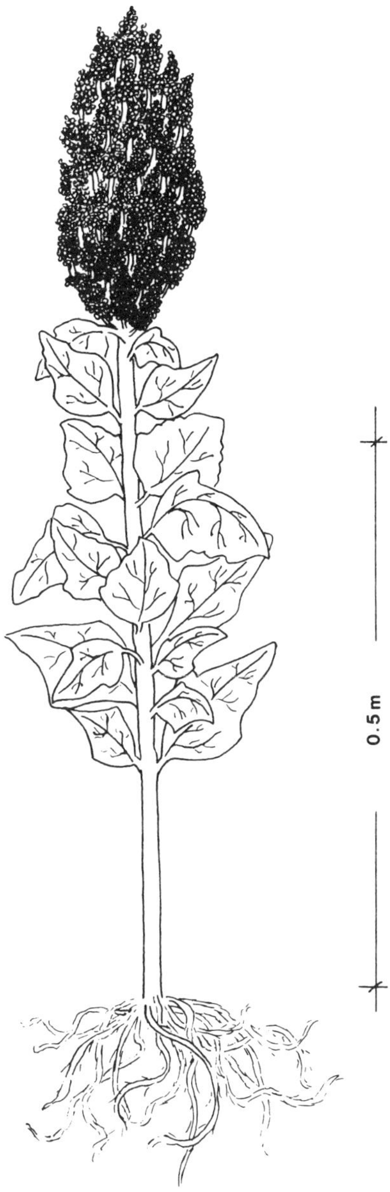

FIG. 5. A quinoa ideotype for British agriculture.

of Spain, Portugal, and the southwestern United States. The central Chilean varieties come from such latitudes. It could also be cultivated in highland-tropical regions similar to the central Andes, such as Ethiopia, the Himalayas, and perhaps parts of southeast Asia. It might be appropriate for the Consultative Group on International Agricultural Research to sponsor such development through its network of research institutes in the tropics. Such international interest would, we hope, raise the prestige of the crop and increase the resources available for its development in South America.

Acknowledgments

We are grateful to Ing. José Luis Lescano for giving us access to many of the publications cited here, to Mrs. Mónica Risi for drawing the text figures, and to Dr. Colin Leakey and Professor N. W. Simmonds for critical readings of the manuscript.

References

Aellen, P. (1929). Bietrag zur systematik der *Chenopodium.* Arten Amerikas. *Fedde, Rep. Spec. No. Regn. Veg.* **26,** 31–64.

Aellen, P., and Just, T. (1943). Key and synopsis of the American species of the genus *Chenopodium* L. *Am. Midl. Nat.* **30,** 47–76.

Aguilar A., P. C. (1980). Identificación de mecanismos de androesterilidad, componentes de rendimiento y contenido proteico en quinua (*Chenopodium quinoa* Willd.). M. S. Thesis, Universidad Nacional Agraria, La Molina, Lima, Peru.

Alandia, S., Otazú, V., and Salas, B. (1979). Enfermedades. *In* "Quinua y Kañiwa. Cultivos Andinos" (M. E. Tapia, ed.), Serie Libros y Materiales Educativos No. 49, pp. 137–148. Instituto Interamericano de Ciencias Agrícolas, Bogotá, Colombia.

Allard, R. W. (1960). "Principles of Plant Breeding." Wiley, New York.

Alvístur, J. E., White, P. L., and Collazos C., C. (1953). El valor biológico de la quinua. *In* "Anales del 4° Congreso Peruano de Química" pp. 1–10. Lima, Peru.

Anonymous (1961). "La Quinua. Gran Alimento Peruano." Instituto de Nutrición, Ministerio de Salud, Lima, Peru.

Anonymous (1974). "La Composición de los Alimentos Peruanos." Instituto de Nutrición, Ministerio de Salud, Lima, Peru.

Anonymous (1976). "Anuario Estadístico Agropecuario, 1976." Oficina Sectorial de Estadística e Informática, Ministerio de Alimentación, Lima, Peru.

Anonymous (1978). *In* "Plant Genetic Resources Newsletter," No. 37, p. 11. International Board for Plant Genetic Resources, Rome.

Aquize, J. E. (1977). Climatología del cultivo de la quinua. *In* "Curso de Quinua," pp. 119–126. Fondo Simón Bolívar, Ministerio de Alimentación, Instituto Interamericano de Ciencias Agrícolas, Universidad Nacional Técnica del Altiplano, Puno, Peru.

Arze B., J. A., and Alencastre M., S. J. (1976). Digestibilidad de los granos de la quinua (*Chenopodium quinoa* Willd) y cañihua (*Chenopodium pallidicaule* Aellen) en ovinos. *In* "Segunda Convención Internacional de Quenopodiáceas," pp. 166–171. Universidad Boliviana Tomás Frías, Comité Departamental de Obras Públicas de Potosí, Instituto Interamericano de Ciencias Agrícolas, Potosí, Bolivia.

Arze B., J., Reyes, P., Ramírez, D., Ramos, J. L., and Molina, F. (1977). Ecofisiología de la quinua. *In* "Curso de Quinua," pp. 75–80. Fondo Simón Bolívar, Ministerio de Alimentación, Instituto Interamericano de Ciencias Agrícolas, Universidad Nacional Técnica del Altiplano, Puno, Peru.

Ballón, E., Tellería, W., and Hutton, J. (1976). Aproximación a la determinación de saponinas por cromatografía de capa fina. *In* "Segunda Convención Internacional de Quenopodiáceas," pp. 89–94. Universidad Boliviana Tomás Frías, Comité Departamental de Obras Públicas de Potosí, Instituto Interamericano de Ciencias Agrícolas, Potosí, Bolivia.

Basset, I. J., and Crompton, C. W. (1978). The biology of Canadian weeds. 32 *Chenopodium album. Can. J. Plant Sci.* **58,** 1061–1072.

Beckman, P. M., and Finch, H. C. (1980). Seed rot and damping off of *Chenopodium quinoa* caused by *Sclerotium rolfsii. Plant Dis.* **64,** 497–498.

Blanco T., C. (1970). "La Quinua. Cómo se Debe Cultivar." Universidad Técnica de Oruro, Oruro, Bolivia.

Boerema, G. H., Mathur, S. B., and Neergaard, P. (1977). *Ascochyta hyalospora* (Cook & Ell.) comb. nov. in seeds of *Chenopodium quinoa. Neth. J. Plant Pathol.* **83,** 153–159.

Bonner, J., and Varner, J. E., eds. (1965). "Plant Biochemistry," 1st Ed. Academic Press, London.

Bornás C., E. A. (1977). Respuesta de la quinua (*Chenopodium quinoa* Willd) variedades Sajama y Kanccolla a la profundidad de siembra en cuatro clases texturales de suelo. Ingeniero Agrónomo Thesis, Universidad Nacional Técnica de Altiplano, Puno, Peru.

Bravo P., R. I. (1975). Análisis bibliográfico de quinua ((*Chenopodium quinoa* Willd) y cañihua (*Chenopodium pallidicaule* Aellen). Ingeniero Agrónomo Thesis, Universidad Nacional Técnica del Altiplano, Puno, Peru.

Briceño P., O., and Canales M., F. (1976). La cañihua (*Chenopodium pallidicaule* Aellen) como sucedáneo del maíz en raciones para pollos parrilleros. *An. Cient.* **14,** 151–163.

Byford, W. J. (1967). Host specialisation of *Peronospora farinosa* on *Beta, Spinacea* and *Chenopodium. Trans. Br. Mycol. Soc.* **50,** 603–607.

Cahuana F., L. (1975). Comparativo de rendimiento de cinco formas botánicas de cañihua por tres distanciamientos entre surcos. Ingerniero Agrónomo Thesis, Universidad Nacional Técnica del Altiplano, Puno, Peru.

Calderón P., G. (1980). Algunos resultados de la investigación de la quinua, obtenidos por la Estación Experimental Agropecuaria Puno (EEAP) centro Regional de Investigaciones Agropecuarias-Sur (CIAG-Sur) Instituto Nacional de Investigación Agraria (INIA). *In* "Segundo Congreso Internacional sobre Cultivos Andinos," pp. 13–30. Facultad de Ingenería Agronómica, Escuela Superior Politécnica de Chimborazo, Instituto Interamericano de Ciencias Agrícolas, Riobamba, Ecuador.

Calle C., E. (1980). Morfología y variedad de las cañihuas cultivadas (*Chenopodium pallidicaule* Aellen). *In* "Segundo Congreso Internacional sobre Cultivos Andinos," pp. 307–323. Facultad de Ingenería Agronómica, Escuela Superior Politécnica de Chimborazo, Instituto Interamericano de Ciencias Agrícolas, Riobamba, Ecuador.

Calzada B., J. (1951). "Variedades de quinua recomendadas para los sembríos de la sierra," Bol. Inf. No. 30. Dirección General de Agricultura, Ministerio de Agricultura, Lima, Peru.

Canahua M., A. (1977). Observaciones del comportamiento de quinua a la sequía. *In* "Primer Congreso Internacional sobre Cultivos Andinos," pp. 390–392. Universidad Nacional San Cristóbal de Huamanga, Instituto Interamericano de Ciencias Agrícolas, Ayacucho, Peru.

Canahua M., A., and Rea, J. (1980). Quinuas resistentes a heladas, avances a la investigación. *In* "Segundo Congreso Internacional sobre Cultivos Andinos," pp. 143–149. Facultad de Ingenería Agronómica, Escuela Superior Politécnica de Chimborazo, Instituto Interamericano de Ciencias Agrícolas, Riobamba, Ecuador.

Cano V., J. (1971). Biología floral de la cañihua (*Chenopodium pallidicaule* Aellen). Ingeniero Agrónomo Thesis, Universidad Nacional Técnica del Altiplano, Puno, Peru.

Cárdenas, M. (1949). Plantas alimenticias de los Andes de Bolivia. *Folia Univ.* **3,** 109–113.

Cárdenas, M., and Hawkes, J. G. (1948). Número de cromosomas de algunas plantas nativas cultivadas por los Indios en los Andes. *Rev. Agric.* **4,** 30–32.

Cardozo, A., and Bateman, J. V. (1961). La quinua en la alimentación animal. *Turrialba* **11,** 72–77.

Cardozo, A., and Dávalos, R. (1967). Las vitaminas A, D_3 y los efectos depresores en la quinua. *Jorn. Agron.* **2,** 1–6.

Cardozo, A., and Tapia, M. E. (1979). Valor nutritivo. *In* "Quinua y Kañiwa. Cultivos Andinos" (M. E. Tapia, ed.). Serie Libros y Materiales Educativos No. 49, pp. 149–192. Instituto Interamericano de Ciencias Agrícolas, Bogotá, Colombia.

Catácora G., A. G. (1977). Determinación del cariotipo en 5 lineas de quinua (*Chenopodium quinoa* Willd). Ingeriero Agrónomo Thesis, Universidad Nacional Técnica del Altiplano, Puno, Peru.

Chaquilla, O. (1976). Exploración de herbicidas en el cultivo de la quinua (*Chenopodium quinoa* Willd). *In* "Segunda Convención Internacional de Quenopodiáceas," pp. 127–129. Universidad Boliviana Tomás Frías, Comité Departamental de Obras Públicas de Potosí, Instituto Interamericano de Ciencias Agrícolas, Potosí, Bolivia.

Chimpén A., P. A. (1979). Determinación cariocinética y de aminoacidos en tres formas botánicas de cañihua (*Chenopodium pallidicaule* Aellen). Ingeniero Agrónomo Thesis, Universidad Nacional Técnica de Altiplano, Puno, Peru.

Cole, M. J. (1962). Interspecific relationships and intraspecific variation of *Chenopodium album* L. in Britain. II. The chromosome number of *C. album* and other species. *Watsonia* **5,** 117, 122.

Condorena P., J. B. (1979). Efecto de tres formulaciones N-P-K en ocho cultivares de quinua (*Chenopodium quinoa* Willd). Ingeniero Agrónomo Thesis, Universidad Nacional Técnica del Altiplano, Puno, Peru.

Cooper, G. C. (1935). Microsporogenesis in Chenopodiacae. *Bot. Gaz. (Chicago)* **97,** 169.

Cornejo de Z., G. (1976). Hojas de quinua (*Chenopodium quinoa* Willd) fuente de proteína. *In* "Segunda Convención Internacional de Quenopodiáceas," pp. 177–180. Universidad Boliviana Tomás Frías, Comité Departamental de Obras Públicas de Potosí, Instituto Interamericano de Ciencias Agrícolas, Potosí, Bolivia.

Davies, D. R. (1977). Creation of new models for crop plants and their use in plant breeding. *Appl. Biol.* **2,** 87–127.

De Bruin, A. (1964). Investigation of the food value of quinoa and Cañihua seed. *J. Food Sci.* **26,** 872–876.

de Etchevers, G. G. (1980). Composición química de algunas leguminosas y Chenopodiáceas de la provincia de Ñuble. *Cienc. Invest. Agrar.* **7,** 191–196.

de la Torre R., A. (1969). Efecto de cuatro niveles diferentes de N P K en fertilización de cañihua (*Chenopodium pallidicaule* Aellen). Ingeniero Agrónomo Thesis, Universidad Nacional Técnica del Altiplano, Puno, Peru.

Donald, C. M. (1968). The breeding of crop ideotypes. *Euphytica* **17,** 385–405.

Durán C., H. (1980). Estudio preliminar fenotípico y fenológico de siete cultivares nativos de quinua (*Chenopodium quinoa* Willd). Ingeniero Agrónomo Thesis, Universidad Nacional Técnica del Altiplano, Puno, Peru.

Erquínigo C., F. (1970). Biología floral de la quinua. Ingeniero Agrónomo Thesis, Universidad Nacional Técnica del Altiplano, Puno, Peru.

Etchevers B., J., and Avila T., P. (1979). Factores que afectan el crecimiento de quinua (*Chenopodium quinoa*) en el centro-sur de Chile. *Pap., 10th Lat. Am. Meet. Agric. Sci.*

Ferrari Q., C. (1976). Investigación para la utilización industrial de la quinua. *In* "Segunda Convención Internacional e Quenopodiáceas," pp. 186–188. Universidad Boliviana Tomás Frías, Comité Departamental de Obras Públicas de Potosí, Instituto Interamericano de Ciencias Agrícolas, Potosí, Bolivia.

Flores, A., F. G. (1977). Estudio preliminar de la fenología de la quinua (*Chenopodium quinoa* Willd). Ingeniero Agrónomo Thesis, Universidad Nacional Técnica del Altiplano, Puno, Peru.

Fuller, H. J. (1949). Photoperiodic response of *Chenopodium quinoa* Willd and *Amaranthus caudatus* L. *Am. J. Bot.* **36,** 175–180.

Gade, D. (1970). Ethnobotany of cañihua (*Chenopodium pallidicaule*) rustic crop of the Altiplano. *Econ. Bot.* **24,** 55–61.

Gandarillas, H. (1948). Efecto fisiológico de la saponina de la quinua en los animales. *Rev. Agric.* **4,** 52–56.

Gandarillas, H. (1967). Observaciones sobre la biología reproductiva de la quinua. *Sayaña* **5,** 26–29.

Gandarillas, H. (1968). "Razas de Quinua," Bol. No. 34. Instituto Boliviano de Cultivos Andinos, División de Investigaciones Agrícolas, Ministerio de Agricultura, La Paz, Bolivia.

Gandarillas, H. (1969). Esterilidad genética y citoplásmica de la quinua (*Chenopodium quinoa*). *Turrialba* **19,** 429–430.

Gandarillas, H. (1974). "Genética y Origen de la Quinua," Bol. No. 9. Instituto Nacional de Trigo, Ministerio de Asuntos Campesinos y Agropecuarios, La Paz, Bolivia.

Gandarillas, H. (1979a). Botánica. *In* "Quinua y Kañiwa. Cultivos Andinos" (M. E. Tapia, ed.). Serie Libros y Materiales Educativos No. 49, pp. 20–44. Instituto Interamericano de Ciencias Agrícolas, Bogotá, Colombia.

Gandarillas, H. (1979b). Genética y origen. *In* "Quinua y Kañiwa. Cultivos Andinos" (M. E. Tapia, ed.). Serie Libros y Materiales Educativos No. 49, pp. 45–64. Instituto Interamericano de Ciencias Agrícolas, Bogotá, Colombia.

Gandarillas, H. (1979c). Mejoramiento genético. *In* "Quinua y Kañiwa. Cultivos Andinos" (M. E. Tapia, ed.). Serie Libros y Materiales Educativos No. 49, pp. 65–82. Instituto Interamericano de Ciencias Agrícolas, Bogotá, Colombia.

Gandarillas, H., and Gutiérrez, J. (1973). Polyploidy induced in cañahua (*Chenopodium pallidicaule* A.) with colchicine. *Bol. Genet. (Engl. Ed.)* **8,** 13–16.

Gandarillas, H., and Luizaga, J. (1967). Número de cromosomas de *Chenopodium quinoa* Willd en radículas y raicillas. *Turrialba* **17,** 275–279.

Gandarillas, H., and Tapia, G. (1976). La variedad de quinua dulce Sajama. *In* "Segunda Convención Internacional de Quenopodiáceas," pp. 116–122. Universidad Boliviana Tomás Frías, Comité Departamental de Obras Públicas de Potosí, Instituto Interamericano de Ciencias Agrícolas, Potosí, Bolivia.

García G., J. (1953). "Estudio Químico de la Cañihua," Inf. No. 85. Estación Experimental Agrícola de La Molina, Ministerio de Agricultura, Lima, Peru.

García R., G. (1947). "Fitopatología Agrícola del Peru." Estación Agrícola de La Molina, Ministerio de Agricultura, Lima, Peru.

Giusti, L. (1970). El género *Chenopodium* en Argentina. I. Número de cromosomas. *Darwiniana* **16,** 98–105.

Gorbitz, A., and Luna de la F., R. (1957). "Estudios sobre la quinua on el Perú," Circ. No. 72. Estación Agrícola Experimental de La Molina, Ministerio de Agricultura, Lima, Peru.

Harlan, J. R. (1965). The possible role of weed races in the evolution of cultivated plants. *Euphytica* **14,** 177–188.

Heiser, C. B. (1963). Numeración cromosómica de plantas ecuatorianas. *Cienc. Nat.* **6,** 2–6.

Heiser, C. B., and Nelson, D. C. (1974). On the origin of the cultivated chenopods (*Chenopodium*). *Genetics* **78,** 503–505.

Herquinio S., F., and Román, F. (1975). "Estudio de la Densidad de Siembra en el Cultivo de la Quinua en Tres Campañas Agrícolas." Universidad Nacional del Centro, Huancayo, Peru.

Hunziker, A. T. (1943). Los especies alimenticias de *Amaranthus* y *Chenopodium* cultivadas por los Indios de América. *Rev. Argent. Agron.* **30,** 297–353.

Hunziker, A. T. (1952). "Los Pseudocereales de la Agricultura Indígena de América." ACME Agency, Buenos Aires, Argentina.

Ignacio Q., J., and Vera, R. (1976). Observación sobre la intensidad de floración durante diferentes horas del día efectuada en quinua (*Chenopodium quinoa* Willd). *In* "Segunda Convención Internacional de Quenopodiáceas," pp. 123–136. Universidad Boliviana Tomás Frías, Comité Departamental de Obras Públicas de Potosí, Instituto Interamericano de Ciencias Agrícolas, Potosí, Bolivia.

Ignacio Q., J., Fernández C., A., and Cortés G., J. (1976). Contribución al estudio morfológico del grano de quinua. *In* "Segunda Convención Internacional de Quenopodiáceas," pp. 58–60. Universidad Boliviana Tomás Frías, Comité Departamental de Obras Públicas de Potosí, Instituto Interamericano de Ciencias Agrícolas, Potosí, Bolivia.

Janssen, W. M. M., Terpstra, K., Beeking, F. F. E., and Bisalsky, A. J. N. (1979). "Feeding Values for Poultry," 2nd Ed. Spelderholt Institute for Poultry Research, Beekbergen, Netherlands.

Johanson, A. (1983). "The Resistance of Quinoa (*Chenopodium quinoa*) to Downy Mildew (*Peronospora farinosa*), Brown Stalk Rot (*Phoma exigua* var. *foveata*) and Grey Mould (*Botrytis cinerea*)." B.A. Research Project, Department of Applied Biology, University of Cambridge, Cambridge, England.

Kjellmark, S. (1934). Einige neue Chromosomenzhalen in der Familie Chenopodiaceae. *Bot. Not.* pp. 136–140.

Labuda, T. (1981). The oilseed rape crop in the U.K. *In* "Oilseed Rape Book. A Manual for Growers, Farmers and Advisers," pp. 13–20. Cambridge Agricultural Publishing, Cambridge, England.

Lanino, R. I. (1976). Informe preliminar sobre el cultivo de la quinua en el Altiplano chileno, zona de Isluga. *In* "Segunda Convención Internacional de Quenopodiáceas," pp. 21–22. Universidad Boliviana Tomás Frías, Comité Departamental de Obras Públicas de Potosí, Instituto Interamericano de Ciencias Agrícolas, Potosí, Bolivia.

Laura, R. (1977). Control químico del mildew (*Peronospora effusa* Grev.) en quinua. Ingeniero Agrónomo Thesis, Universidad Nacional Técnica del Altiplano, Puno, Peru.

León, J. (1964). "Plantas Alimenticias Andinas," Bol. Tec. No. 6. Instituto Interamericano de Ciencias Agrícolas-Zona Andina, Lima, Peru.

Lescano R., J. L. (1976). Cariotipo y ploidía en cañihua (*Chenopodium pallidicaule* Aellen). *In* "Segunda Convención Internacional de Quenopodiáceas," pp. 81–88. Universidad Boliviana Tomás Frías, Comité Departamental de Obras Públicas de Potosí, Instituto Interamericano de Ciencias Agrícolas, Potosí, Bolivia.

Lescano R., J. L. (1977). Métodos de mejoramiento. *In* "Curso de Quinua," pp. 63–65. Fondo Simón Bolívar, Ministerio de Alimentación, Instituto Interamericano de Ciencias Agrícolas, Universidad Nacional Técnica del Altiplano, Puno, Peru.

Lescano, R., J. L. (1980). Avances en la genética de la quinua. *In* "Primera Reunión de Genética y Fitomejoramiento de la Quinua," pp. B1–B9. Universidad Nacional Técnica del Altiplano, Instituto Boliviano de Tecnología Agropecuaria, Instituto Interamericano de Ciencias Agrícolas, Centro Internacional de Investigaciones para el Desarrollo, Puno, Peru.

Lescano, R., J. L. (1981). "Cultivo de la Quinua." Universidad Nacional Técnica del Altiplano, Centro de Investigaciones en Cultivos Andinos, Puno, Peru.

Lescano R., J. L., and Palomino L., C. (1976). Metodología del cruzamiento en quinua. *In* "Segunda Convención Internacional de Quenopodiáceas," pp. 78–80. Universidad Boliviana Tomás Frías, Comité Departamental de Obras Públicas de Potosí, Instituto Interamericano de Ciencias Agrícolas, Potosí, Bolivia.

Lescano R., J. L., and Tapia, M. E. (1977). Investigación en el mejoramiento de la quinua. *In* "Curso de Cultivos Andinos," pp. C1–C13. Instituto Interamericano de Ciencias Agrícolas - Zona Andina, Instituto Boliviano de Tecnología Agropecuaria, La Paz, Bolivia.

Lexander, K., Carlsson, R., Schalen, V., Simonsson, A., and Lundborg, T. (1970). Quantities and qualities of leaf protein concentrates from wild species and crop species grown under controlled conditions. *Ann. Appl. Biol.* **66,** 193–216.

Llanos M., G. (1954). "Quinua, Cañihua y Coyos," 2nd Ed., Publ. Inf. No. 2. Dirección General de Agricultura, Ministerio de Agricultura, Lima, Peru.

Llerena E., H. (1973). Ensayo de panificación con harina de dos variedades de quinua (*Chenopodium quinoa* Willd) y cañihua (*Chenopodium pallidicaule* Aellen). Ingeniero Argónomo Thesis, Universidad Nacional Técnica del Altiplano, Puno, Peru.

López, A., A. M. (1980). Evaluación biométrica de 340 líneas de cañihua (*Chenopodium pallidicaule* Aellen) del banco de germoplasma de la UNTA. Ingeniero Agrónomo Thesis, Universidad Nacional Técnica del Altiplano, Puno, Peru.

López de Romaña, G., Creed, H. M., and Graham, G. (1978). Alimentos comunes peruanos, tolerancia y digestibilidad en infantes desnutridos. *Arch. Latinoam. Nutr.* **28,** 419–433.

López de Romaña, G., Graham, G., Rojas, M., and McLean, W. C., Jr. (1981). Digestibilidad y calidad proteínica de la quinua: Estudio comparativo en niños entre semilla y harina de quinua. *Arch. Latinoam. Nutr.* **31,** 485–497.

Lorz, A. (1937). Cytological investigations on five Chenopodiaceous genera with special emphasis on chromosome morphology and somatic doubling in *Spinacia*. *Cytologia* **8,** 241–276.

Luna de la F., R. (1957). Ensayo de panificación con mezclas de harina de trigo y quinua. *Inf. Mens. Estac. Exp. Agric. "La Molina," Lima* **358,** 6–8.

Luna de la F., R., and Marchetti, I. (1957). Ensayo de elaboración de fideos con mezclas de harina de trigo y quinua. *Inf. Mens., Estac. Exp. Agric. "La Molina," Lima* **364,** 1–7.

Luna de la F., R., and Quérzola T., I. (1958). Ensayo de elaboración de galletas con mezclas de harinas de trigo y quinua. *Inf. Mns., Estac. Exp. Agric. "La Molina," Lima* **374,** 1–6.

Mabry, T. J., Taylor, A., and Turner, B. L. (1963). The betacyanins and their distribution. *Phytochemistry* **2,** 61–64.

Machicao, E. (1965). Las saponinas de la quinua. *Sayaña* **4,** 24–25.

Martínez C., C. F. (1946). "La Quinua. Divulgación Botánica, Agrícola y de Utilización Industrial y Culinaria." Dirección de Agricultura, Ministerio de Agricultura, Lima, Peru.

Molina A., V. (1972). Desarrollo de un metodo de lavado por agitación y turbulencia del grano de quinua. Ingeniero Agrónomo Thesis, Universidad Nacional Agraria, La Molina, Lima, Peru.

Montenegro, B. C. (1976). Investigación sobre la quinua Dulce de Quitopamba. *In* "Primera Reunión Binacional Sobre la Planificación de la Producción de la Quinua," pp. 47–56. Comité Interinstitucional Colombiano de la Quinua, Ministerio de Salud Pública, Instituto Colombiano de Bienestar Familiar, Pasto, Colombia.

Mujica S., A. (1977). "Tecnología de Cultivo de la Quinua," Bol. Tecn.—Ser. Quinua No. 2. Fondo Simón Bolívar, Ministerio de Alimentación Zona XII-Puno, Instituto Interamericano de Ciencias Agrícolas, Puno, Peru.

Muñoz S., D. H. (1979). Evaluación de 100 ecotipos de quinua (*Chenopodium quinoa* Willd) al ataque de *Nacobbus* sp. Ingeniero Agrónomo Thesis, Universidad Nacional Técnica del Altiplano, Puno, Peru.

Narrea R., A. (1976a). "Cultivo de la Quinua," Bol. No. 5. Dirección General de Producción, Ministerio de Alimentación, Lima, Peru.

Narrea R., A. (1976b). La producción de quinua en el Peru. *In* "Segunda Convención Internacional de Quenopodiáceas," pp. 51–63. Universidad Boliviana Tomás Frías, Comité Departamental de Obras Públicas de Potosí, Instituto Interamericano de Ciencias Agrícolas, Potosí, Bolivia.

Narrea R., A. (1977). El cultivo de la quinua y perspectivas de su incremento en el Perú. *In* "Primer Congreso Internacional sobre Cultivos Andinos," pp. 323–331. Universidad Nacional San Cristóbal de Huamanga, Instituto Interamericano de Ciencias Agrícolas, Ayacucho, Peru.

Negrón A., A., Alvarez G., E., and Calmet U., E. (1976). La quinua y la cañihua en raciones de pollos parrilleros en Puno, Perú. *In* "Segunda Convención Internacional de Quenopodiáceas," pp. 170–176. Universidad Boliviana Tomás Frías, Comité Departamental de Obras Públicas de Potosí, Instituto Interamericano de Ciencias Agrícolas, Potosí, Bolivia.

Nelson, D. C. (1968). Taxonomy and origins of *Chenopodium quinoa* and *Chenopodium nuttaliae*. Ph.D. Thesis, University of Indiana, Bloomington.

Ochoa B., V. (1972). Análisis de crecimiento de la quinua (*Chenopodium quinoa* Willd).

Ingeniero Agrónomo Thesis, Universidad Nacional San Cristóbal de Huamanga, Ayacucho, Peru.

Ortiz R., V. (1974). Densidades de siembra en quinua. *Av. Invest.* **3,** 3-4.

Ortiz R., V., and Zanabria, E. (1979). Plagas. *In* "Quinua y Kañiwa. Cultivos Andinos" (M. E. Tapia, ed.), Serie Libros y Materiales Educativos No. 49, pp. 121-136. Instituto Interamericano de Ciencias Agrícolas, Bogotá, Colombia.

Otazú, V., and Salas, B. (1977). La podredumbre marrón del tallo de la quinua (*Chenopodium quinoa*) causada por *Phoma exigua* var *foveata. Fitopatologia* **12,** 54-58.

Otazú, V., Aguilar A., P. C., and Canahua M., A. (1976). Resistencia en quinua (*Chenopodium quinoa*) al mildiú (*Peronospora effusa*). *Fitopatologia* **11,** 47-49.

Paca P., F. R. (1970). Herencia de colores de quinua (*Chenopodium quinoa* Willd) y cañihua (*Chenopodium pallidicaule* Aellen). Ingeniero Agrónomo Thesis, Universidad Nacional Técnica del Altiplano, Puno, Peru.

Paredes E., C. A. (1966). Estudio agro-botánico de la cañhiua. Ingeniero Agrónomo Thesis, Universidad Nacional San Antonio Abad, Cuzco, Peru.

Pastor B., L. R. (1970). Sistemática y morfología de los insectos que atacan al cultivo de la cañihua (*Chenopodium pallidicaule* Aellen). Ingeniero Agrónomo Thesis, Universidad Nacional Técnica del Altiplano, Puno, Peru.

Poehlman, J. M. (1968). "Breeding Field Crops." Holt, New York.

Pulgar Vidal, J. (1954). "La Quinua o Suba en Colombia," Publ. No. 3. Fichero Científico Agropecuario, Ministerio de Agricultura, Bogotá, Colombia.

Ráez, J. L. (1956). "Cultivo de la Quinua: Resultados Experimentales en el Cultivo de la Quinua," Inf. No. 52. División de Experimentación Agrícola, Dirección General de Agricultura, Ministerio de Agricultura, Lima, Peru.

Rea, J. (1948). "Observaciones Sobre Biología Floral y Estudio de Saponinas en *Chenopodium quinoa* Willd," Ser. Tec. No. 3. Ministerio de Agricultura, La Paz, Bolivia.

Rea, J. (1969). Biología floral de la quinua (*Chenopodium quinoa*). *Turrialba* **19,** 91-96.

Rea, J. (1977). Fomento de la producción agroindustrial de la quinua en Puno. *In* "Primer Congreso Internacional sobre Cultivos Andinos," pp. 141-147. Universidad Nacional San Cristóbal de Huamanga, Instituto Interamericano de Ciencias Agrícolas, Ayacucho, Peru.

Rea, J., and León, J. (1966). Determinación práctica del contenido de saponinas en quinua. *In* "Informe Técnico," No. 6, p. 190. Instituto Interamericano de Ciencias Agrícolas, San José, Costa Rica.

Rea, J., Tapia, M., and Mujica S., A. (1979). Practicas agronómicas. *In* "Quinua y Kañiwa. Cultivos Andinos" (M. E. Tapia, ed.), Serie Libros y Materiales Educativos No. 49, pp. 83-120. Instituto Interamericano de Ciencias Agrícolas, Bogotá, Colombia.

Renfrew, J. M. (1973). "Palaeoethnobotany." Methuen, London.

Rodríguez T., R. E. (1978). Determinación del porcentaje de autopolinización y cruzamientos naturales en tres variedades comerciales de quinua (*Chenopodium quinoa* Willd). Ingeniero Agronómo Thesis, Universidad Nacional Técnica del Altiplano, Puno, Peru.

Romero, A. (1976). Observaciones sobre el cultivo de la quinua en los Andes. *In* "Primer Reunión Binacional sobre la Planificación de la Producción de Quinua," pp. 85-90. Comité Interinstitutional Colombiano de la Quinua, Ministerio de Salud Pública, Instituto Colombiano de Bienestar Familiar, Pasto, Colombia.

Romero L., M., Gómez, P., L., and Mont K., R. (1977). Ampliación de la frontera agrícola en el Perú. *In* "Primer Congreso Internacional sobre Cultivos Andinos," pp. 111–118. Universidad Nacional San Cristóbal de Huamanga, Instituto Interamericano de Ciencias Agrícolas, Ayacucho, Peru.

Sacaca R., D. E. (1978). Biología floral de dos lineas Ccoito y Anaranjada (*Chenopodium quinoa* Willd). Ingeniero Agrónomo Thesis, Universidad Nacional Técnica del Altiplano, Puno, Peru.

Salas, B., Otazú, V., and Vilca, A. (1977). Enfermedades de la quinua. *In* "Curso de Quinua," pp. 143–149. Fondo Simón Bolívar, Ministerio de Alimentación, Instituto Interamericano de Ciencias Agrícolas, Universidad Nacional Técnica del Altiplano, Puno, Peru.

Salhuana M., W., Gómez P., L., and Romero L., M. (1977). Selección de colleciones similares en el banco de germoplasma de quinua de la UNA. *In* "Primer Congreso Internacional sobre Cultivos Andinos," pp. 382–389. Universidad Nacional de San Cristóbal de Huamanga, Instituto Interamericano de Ciencias Agrícolas, Ayacucho, Peru.

Simmonds, N. W. (1965). The grain chenopods of the tropical American highlands. *Econ. Bot.* **19**, 223–235.

Simmonds, N. W. (1966). Plant and seed colour in cañahua, *Chenopodium pallidicaule. Heredity* **21**, 316–317.

Simmonds, N. W. (1971). The breeding system of *Chenopodium quinoa*. I. Male sterility. *Heredity* **27**, 73–82.

Singh, H. (1961). "Grain Amaranths Buckwheat and Chenopods," Res. Cereal Crop Ser. No. 1. Indian Council of Agriculture, New Delhi, India.

Sívori, E. M. (1947). Fotoperiodismo en *Chenopodium quinoa*. Reacción de la cigota y gametofito femenino. *Darwiniana* **7**, 541–551. Argentina.

Solano L., M. A. (1976). Evaluación de 30 ecotipos de quinua (*Chenopodium quinoa* Willd) al ataque de *Naccobus* sp. Ingeniero Agrónomo Thesis, Universidad Nacional Técnica del Altiplano, Puno, Peru.

Suzuka, O. (1950). Chromosome numbers in pharmaceutical plants. *Rep. Kihara Inst. Biol. Res.* **4**, 57–58.

Tapia, M. E. (1979a). Historia y distribución geográfica. *In* "Quinua y Kañiwa. Cultivos Andinos" (M. E. Tapia, ed.), Serie Libros y Materiales Educativos No. 49, pp. 11–15. Instituto Interamericano de Ciencias Agrícolas, Bogotá, Colombia.

Tapia, M. E. (1979b). Kañiwa. *In* "Quinua y Kañiwa. Cultivos Andinos" (M. E. Tapia, ed.), Serie Libros y Materiales Educativos No. 49, pp. 205–216. Instituto Interamericano de Ciencias Agrícolas, Bogotá, Colombia.

Tapia, M. E. (1981). Informe sobre especies altoandinas de menor atención por las programas de investigación. *In* "Primera Reunión sobre Recursos Fitogenéticos de Interés Agrícola en la Región Andina," pp. 76–84. International Board for Plant Genetic Resources, Instituto Interamericano de Ciencias Agrícolas, Lima, Peru.

Tapia, M. E. (1982). "El Medio, los Cultivos y los Sistemas Agrícolas en los Andes del Sur del Perú." Proyecto de Investigación de los Sistemas Agrícolas Andinos, Instituto Interamericano de Ciencias Agrícolas, Centro de Investigación Internacional para el Desarrollo, Cuzco, Peru.

Tapia, M. E., and Castro, J. N. (1968). Digestibilidad de la broza de quinua y cañihua por ovinos mejorados y ovinos no mejorados (chuscos). *In* "Primera Convención de Quenopodiáceas," pp. 101–107. Universidad Nacional Técnica del Altiplano, Puno, Peru.

Tapia, M. E., Mujica S., A., and Canahua, A. (1980). Origen distribución geográfica y sistemas de producción en quinua. *In* "Primera Reunion sobre Genética y Fitomejoramiento de la Quinua," pp. A1-A8. Universidad Nacional Técnica del Altiplano, Instituto Boliviano de Tecnología Agropecuaria, Instituto Interamericano de Ciencias Agrícolas, Centro de Investigación Internacional para el Desarrollo, Puno, Peru.

Tomlinson, S. A., Faithfull, E. M., Webb, M. J. W., Fraser, R. S. S., and Primrose, S. B. (1981). Isolation and characterisation of a new soil-borne virus. *In* "31st Annual Report for 1980," pp. 87-88. National Vegetable Research Station, Wellesbourne, Warwickshire, U.K.

Torres, H. A., and Minaya, I. (1980). "Escarificadora de Quinua. Diseño y Construcción," Publ. Misc. No. 243. Instituto Interamericano de Ciencias Agrícolas, Lima, Peru.

Turkensteen, L. (1975). Hongos picnidioformantes asociados con el tizón foliar de la papa. *Fitopatologia* **10,** 83-84.

Ugarte C., J. L. (1956). Digestibilidad del grano de quinua en ovinos. Ingeniero Agrónomo Thesis, Escuela Nacional de Agricultura, La Molina, Lima, Peru.

Uotila, P. (1973). Chromosome counts on *Chenopodium* L. from S.E. Europe and S.W. Asia. *Ann. Bot. Fenn.* **10,** 337-340.

Valdivia, F. (1979). "Investigación en el Cultivo de la Quinua," Bol. Tec. No. 6. Estación Experimental de Puno, Instituto Nacional de Investigación Agraria, Puno, Peru.

Valdivia A., M. C. (1978). Biología floral de dos lineas de quinua (*Chenopodium quinoa* Willd). Ingeniero Agrónomo Thesis, Universidad Nacional Técnica del Altiplano, Puno, Peru.

Van Etten, C. H., Miller, R. W., Wolff, I. A., and Jones, Q. (1963). Amino acid composition of seeds from 200 angiosperm plants. *J. Agric. Food Chem.* **11,** 399-410.

Vargas, C. (1938). Nota etnobotánica sobre la cañihua. *Rev. Argent. Agron.* **5,** 224-230.

Vargas S., R., Begazo C., V., Moreyra L., P., Rojas P., H., Cochella V., T., Castro G., C., Soriano C., G., and Vega, C. (1977). "La Quinua como Sucedánea y Fortificante de la Harina de Trigo en Panificación Fideería y Galletería." Programa Nacional de Alimentación Popular. Instituto de Investigaciones Agro-Industriales, La Molina, Lima, Peru.

Vásquez D., C. G. (1977). Evaluación del mildiú (*Peronospora effusa* Grev) en 444 lineas del banco de germoplasma de quinua (*Chenopodium quinoa* Willd) de la Universidad Nacional Técnica del Altiplano. Ingeniero Agrónomo Thesis, Universidad Nacional Técnica del Altiplano, Puno, Peru.

Velásquez M., F. (1968). Efectos del sistema de siembra, densidad y estado de maduración sobre la produccion de quinua (*Chenopodium quinoa* var *Kcanccolla*). Ingeniero Agrónomo Thesis, Universidad Nacional Técnica del Altiplano, Puno, Peru.

Velazco C., M. S. (1977). Control químico de malezas en quinua (*Chenopodium quinoa* Willd) var Kankolla. Ingeniero Agrónomo Thesis, Universidad Nacional Técnica del Altiplano, Puno, Peru.

Velázquez G., D. (1959). Análisis cromatográfico de aminoacidos de variedades de quinua. *Agronomia (La Molina, Peru)* **26,** 257-265.

Vilca A., A. (1972). Estudio de la mancha foliar en quinua. Ingeniero Agrónomo Thesis, Universidad Nacional Técnica del Altiplano, Puno, Peru.

Villacorta S., L., and Talavera R., V. (1976). Anatomía del grano de quinua (*Chenopodium quinoa* Willd). *Ana. Cient.* **14,** 39-45.

Vorano, A., and García, R. C. A. (1976). La quinua (*Chenopodium quinoa* Willd) en la provincia de Jujuy. Informe preliminar de su situación actual y perspectivas futuras. *In* "Segunda Convención Internacional de Quenopodiáceas," pp. 19–20. Universidad Boliviana Tomás Frías, Comité Departamental de Obras Públicas de Potosí, Instituto Interamericano de Ciencias Agrícolas, Potosí, Bolivia.

White, P. L., Alvístur, J. E., Días, C., Viñas, E., White, H. S., and Collazos, C. (1955). Nutrient content and protein quality of quinoa and cañihua, edible seed products of the Andes mountains. *J. Agric. Food Chem.* **3**, 531–534.

Williams, J. T. (1963). Biological flora of the British Isles. *Chenopodium album* L. *J. Ecol.* **51**, 711–725.

Wilson, H. D. (1980). Artificial hybridisation among species of *Chenopodium* sect. *Chenopodium*. *Syst. Bot.* **5**, 253–263.

Wilson, H. D., and Heiser, C. B., Jr. (1979). The origin and evolutionary relationship of huauzontle (*Chenopodium nuttaliae*) domesticated chenopod of Mexico. *Am. J. Bot.* **66**, 198–206.

Winge, O. (1917). The Chromosomes. Their Number and General Importance. *C. R. Trav. Lab. Carlsberg* **13**, 131–275.

Witte, M. B. (1947). A comparative cytological study of three species of the Chenopodiacae. *Bull. Torrey Bot. Club* **74**, 443–452.

Woroschilov, W. N. (1942). Revision des especes de *Chenopodium* de la section *Ambrina* (Spach) Hook. Fil. *J. Bot. URSS* **27**, 33–47.

Yerkes, W. D., and Shaw, C. G. (1959). Taxonomy of the *Peronospora* species on Cruciferae and Chenopodiacae. *Phytopathology* **40**, 499–507.

Zanabria, E., and Mujica S., A. (1977). Plagas de la quinua. *In* "Curso de Quinua," pp. 129–142. Fondo Simón Bolívar, Ministerio de Alimentación, Instituto Interamericano de Ciencias Agrícolas, Universidad Nacional Técnica del Altiplano, Puno, Peru.

Seed Quality in Grain Legumes

ALISON A. POWELL, S. MATTHEWS, and M. DE A. OLIVEIRA

Department of Agriculture, University of Aberdeen, Aberdeen, Scotland

I. Introduction

Taken as a group of crops, the grain legumes (Table I), sometimes referred to as pulses, are ranked fifth in terms of annual world grain production, at around 150 million metric tons, after wheat (458 million metric tons), maize (452), rice (414), and barley (158) (Food and Agriculture Organization, 1982a). They have, in addition, a special place in the provision of human dietary needs because of the composition of their grains which contain more, and considerably more in the case of some species, protein (Table I) and oil than are ever found in cereal grains (Aykroyd and Doughty, 1964). The grain legumes contribute to

ISBN 0-12-040910-0

TABLE I. Grain legumes in world agriculture: Major and minor crops in terms of world production[a]

Species	Common name	Estimated world production (millions of metric tons in 1981)	Approximate protein in grain (%)
Major			
Glycine max	Soybean	88	40
Arachis hypogaea	Groundnut or peanut	19	27
Phaseolus vulgaris	Haricot, navy, or dwarf French bean[b]	16	22
Pisum sativum	Pea	16	22
Cicer arietinum	Chickpea	7	21
Minor			
Cajanus cajan	Pigeon pea or red gram		
Lens culinaris	Lentil		
Lupinus spp.	Lupins		
Phaseolus coccineus	Scarlet runner bean		
Phaseolus lunatus	Lima bean		
Psophocarpus tetragonolobus	Winged bean		
Vicia faba	Field bean or broad bean		
Vigna radiata	Mung bean or green gram		
Vigna mungo	Black gram		
Vigna unguicalata	Cowpea		

[a]Based on Food and Agriculture Organization (1982a).
[b]In this article this group is referred to as *Phaseolus* beans.

human diet both indirectly, in the form of protein supplements to animal feeds in the production of animal protein in developed countries, and directly. As a direct human food source grain legumes play an especially important role in developing countries, which is well exemplified by chickpea in Northern India where over 70% of the world's 7 million metric tons of this crop is grown (Ramanujam, 1976). Another attribute of grain legumes contributing to their importance in agriculture and common to all legumes in their symbiotic relationship with nitrogen-fixing *Rhizobium* bacteria found in root nodules. This allows the use of grain legumes in crop production systems that do not involve costly nitrogen fertilizers.

Two of the grain legumes, soybeans and to a lesser extent groundnuts, feature prominently in international trade. In 1980 around 22 million metric tons of soybeans valued at $6238 million were exported from the United States along with a further 3.6 million metric tons from Argentina and Brazil, most of which were imported by countries in Western Europe and by Japan (Food and Agriculture Organization, 1982b). The import of soybean grain and grain products by economically developed countries helps to fulfill the dietary expectations of these countries by providing plant protein to support the production of both high levels of animal protein and of vegetable oils for such products as margarine. Attempts to meet more of this demand for plant protein and oils from within the European Economic Community have led to rapid increases in the growing of oilseed rape (Ministry of Agriculture, Fisheries and Food, 1982), and more recently, dried, or so-called protein, peas in several European countries, including the United Kingdom. Two other seed legumes, peas and dwarf French or green beans, provide the most important convenience vegetables; canned or frozen forms of both are commonplace in many developed countries.

Most of the grain legumes are the subject of plant-breeding programs to serve the needs of both developed and developing countries (Simmonds, 1976), but the production of new, improved genotypes is only the first step. The ultimate objective is the production, distribution, introduction, and sustained use of seed of improved varieties. Thus, if the potential of new varieties is to be realized, seed production is especially important in order to ensure that the seeds sown are of a quality that leads to reliable crop establishment for growers. Both practical experience and documented reports, many of which are reviewed here, make clear that the quality of the seeds of grain legumes as received by the grower can be very variable.

Although the causes of poor seed quality in grain legumes appear diverse, from handling damage (Green *et al.*, 1966) to inappropriate storage conditions (Justice and Bass, 1978), research in recent years has revealed the importance of some basic physiological processes, such as deterioration (Roberts, 1973c) and imbibition (Powell and Matthews, 1978a), in determining seed quality in these crops. The purpose of this article is to examine the extensive literature on seed quality in grain legumes, with some of these basic processes in mind in order to construct a framework of understanding to guide practical work on seed production. Understandably, a great deal of attention has been given to the four crops (soybean, groundnut, peas, and *Phaseolus* beans) of particular importance to developed countries and this is reflected in the literature.

This article, which is an attempt to bring together research on physiological processes and practical considerations in seed production and evaluation, will cover the nature of seed quality, physiological and pathological aspects of quality, the influence of seed storage, the impact of mechanical damage on quality, and testing for seed quality.

II. Nature of Seed Quality

A. Aspects of Quality Recognized by Seed Testing

There are four aspects of seed quality recognized by seed testing, namely, analytical purity, germination percentage, seed vigor, and health. Many countries impose legal minimum standards for the analytical purity and germination required of a seed lot (the unit in which crop seeds are produced, tested, and sold) before the lot can be sold, indicating the importance of these aspects of quality to crop production.

The analytical, or physical, purity of a seed lot indicates how much of a seed sample is actually made up of the intact seed of that species and is expressed as the percentage of pure seed present. It therefore reflects the degree of contamination by broken seeds of the species, inert matter, and weed and other crop seeds. Some types of contamination, for example, empty florets in a grass seed sample, are innocuous, whereas, in contrast, weed seeds can be a very damaging component. The minimum analytical purity required of many grain legumes is 98% (by weight), with a maximum content of 0.1% (by weight) of other seeds (Anonymous, 1976b).

The germination percentage of a seed lot as referred to in seed testing is the percentage of seeds that produces normal seedlings, which gives an indication of the potential of the seed to establish in the field. Minimum standards require that commercial seed lots of soybean, broad bean, and pea should have germinations above 80%, *Phaseolus* beans over 75%, and field beans over 85%.

The third aspect of seed quality, seed vigor, is often considered alongside germination and gives a further indication of the ability of the seed to emerge under a wide range of field conditions.

Finally, two types of contamination by pathogens are recognized as influencing seed quality in general: first, pathogens that have little effect on seedling growth, but affect later stages of plant development, for example, smuts and bunts, and second, those that stunt or destroy seedlings, leading to poor establishment. Despite considerable interest in the nature and effect of seed-borne pathogens, there are few regulations controlling the level of infection in commercial seeds.

B. EFFECT OF QUALITY ON FIELD EMERGENCE AND STORAGE POTENTIAL

The influence of germination and vigor on field emergence and storage potential will be considered in this section. The effects of seed health are additional to these intrinsic properties of the seed and will be considered later (Sections IV and V).

Laboratory germination indicates the number of seeds that are viable, and therefore differences in field emergence arising from seed lots with vastly different laboratory germinations are not surprising. A number of workers have reported that laboratory germination predicts the field emergence of soybean (Athow and Caldwell, 1956; Agrawal and Singh, 1975; Tiwari *et al.*, 1978; Johnson and Wax, 1978), and in most cases the significant positive correlations obtained were attributable to large differences in the laboratory germinations of the seed lots tested. A similarly high correlation was found between the laboratory germination and field emergence of field bean (Hegarty, 1977), with germinations ranging from 73 to 99%. However, when seed lots with poor germinations were excluded, and only those above 85% germination (the legal minimum) considered, the correlation between laboratory germination and field emergence was no longer significant.

Problems of poor field emergence arising from low germinations should not occur in commercial seed lots due to the enforcement of minimum germination standards. However, despite the high germinations of commercial lots, large differences in field emergence can occur as a result of differences in what has been termed seed vigor. Delouche (1973) found that from 94 seed lots of soybean with germinations of more than 80%, 38 lots had field emergences below 70%, 9 below 50%, and 4 below 40%; more recently, the field emergences of 18 commercial lots from the United States were found to range from 17 to 90% (Oliveira *et al.*, 1984). In peas, the problem of poor field establishment of germinable seeds was recorded as early as 1903, when Hiltner drew attention to poor emergence, particularly in wet conditions. Many observations of the poor field emergence of peas have been made since and are reviewed by Matthews (1977). Field emergences of germinable seed have been reported as ranging from 62 to 85% in *Phaseolus* (Schoorel, 1957) and from 55 to 95% in field bean (Hegarty, 1977), with 20–75% of groundnut seed sown in the Sudan reported to be lost through emergence failure (Clinton, 1960). Poor establishment of lima bean has also been associated with vigor, particularly at low temperatures (Pollock and Toole, 1964, 1966). Thus, in many grain legumes differences in seed quality not reflected in seed lot germination, that is, seed vigor, have a major influence on field establishment.

Seed quality also influences the storage potential of seeds, that is, their ability to retain viability and vigor during a period of commercial storage. Poor initial seed quality reflected in the lower germination of aged seeds was found to reduce the storage potential of soybean (Byrd and Delouche, 1971), and Ellis *et al.* (1982) found that even small differences in germination among seed lots of chickpea, cowpea, and soybean resulted in differences in longevity; the viability of lots with initially lower germinations fell more rapidly. In contrast, Egli *et al.* (1978) found no relationship between initial germination and the storage potential of soybean, although the initial seed vigor was so correlated. Burris (1980) also found that the relative longevity of soybean seed batches with moisture contents ranging from 8 to 14% and stored at temperatures from −1 to 27°C for 3 years was predicted by initial vigor, as reflected in shoot weight. The rate of loss of viability of low-vigor lima beans was more rapid than high-vigor seeds in a range of storage conditions (Bass *et al.*, 1970). The decline in vigor of seed lots of peas during commercial storage has also been related to differences in seed lot vigor before storage (Powell and Matthews, 1978b).

II. Physiological Aspects of Quality

Many changes take place in the developing seed after fertilization. In the grain legumes, there are major changes in the size of the endosperm and the embryo, which is composed of two cotyledons and an embryo axis, as well as many biochemical changes, some of which lead to the laying down of food reserves (Pate and Flinn, 1977; Bils and Howell, 1963). At fertilization, the endosperm of grain legumes is initially large and expands rapidly, whereas there is little embryo growth despite rapid cell division. This is followed by the rapid enlargement of the cotyledon cells of the embryo, which absorb the endosperm and soon virtually fill the space originally filled by the liquid endosperm (Carlson, 1973; Bain and Mercer, 1963; Smith, 1973). As this takes place, the accumulation of food reserves occurs in the cotyledons, leading to an increase in dry weight (Pate and Flinn, 1977; Andrews, 1966) and resulting in the large living food reserves contained within the embryo that are characteristic of the grain legumes. These living food reserves are responsible not only for the importance of grain legumes as a food crop, but also for the particular significance of physiological aspects of seed quality exhibited in these crops.

The point at which seeds reach maximum dry weight has been described as physiological maturity (Harrington, 1972), and it is at this point that the vascular system connecting the plant and seed is severed, and the seed becomes an independent unit (Browne, 1978). In soybean, maximum seed quality is said to be reached at physiological maturity (Wahab and Burris, 1971; Delouche, 1974; Tekrony *et al.*, 1980), when maximum germination and vigor have been observed (Andrews, 1966). Harvesting seeds at different times during the physiological changes occurring before maturity appears to have little effect on seed germination and vigor. Indeed, immature pea seeds have been shown to withstand desiccation with no loss of viability (Matthews, 1973a) and little evidence of reduced vigor (Matthews, 1973b; Bedford and Matthews, 1975; Rogerson and Matthews, 1977; Nichols *et al.*, 1978). There are, however, a number of conflicting reports of the effects of differences in seed size, which may arise during seed development, on the quality of soybean seed. Higher germinations have been found from small seeds (Green *et al.*, 1965; Edwards and Hartwig, 1971; Tiwari *et al.*, 1978) and from large seeds (Ndunguru and Summerfield, 1975; Fontes and Ohlrogge, 1972; Burris *et al.*, 1971; Sivasubramanian and Ramakrishnan, 1974), whereas others report no (Johnson and Luedders, 1974) or little (Nangju *et al.*, 1980) effect of seed size.

The major physiological effects on seed quality, however, occur after physiological maturity. We shall consider the effects of two physiological processes on seed quality. The first process, seed aging, can occur at any time from maturity until the seed is sown; the second, imbibition damage, affects seed germination and vigor during the process of imbibition after sowing.

A. AGING

Aging involves the process of deterioration, the accumulation of irreversible degenerative changes in the physiological quality of the seed, until finally, the ability to germinate is lost. In a seed lot, the pattern of loss of viability over a period of time follows a sigmoid curve, which is typical of the survival curves of the many populations in which death of individuals is normally distributed (Roberts, 1972, 1973a). There is an initial period when few seeds die and germination remains high (Phase A, Fig. 1), followed by a rapid fall in germination as many seeds lose their viability (Phase B, Fig. 1) and a tail off to the curve as a few seeds retain viability for a longer time (Phase C, Fig. 1).

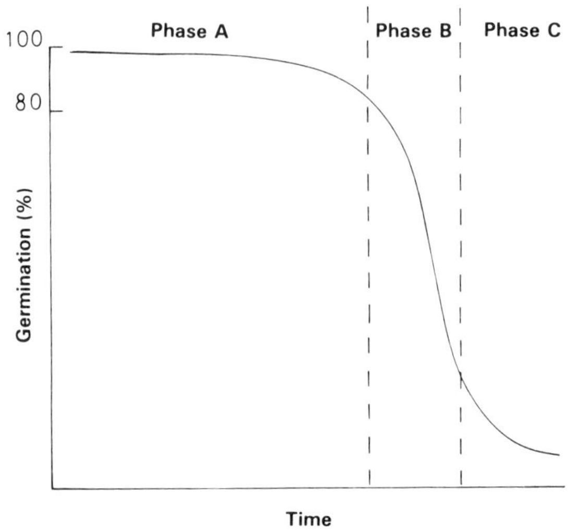

FIG. 1. Seed viability curve.

Studies of the aging process have often made comparisons between viable and nonviable seeds, or between seed populations with very different germinations. Any physiological changes observed in such comparisons may therefore be associated with death, or may be postmortem changes. The loss of viability is, however, the final stage of aging, and many deteriorative changes can occur before the ability to germinate is lost. Furthermore, it is the quality of commercial seed that concerns the farmer, and commercial seed lots have high germinations, lying on the initial slow decline of the viability curve (Phase A, Fig. 1). Thus, the physiological changes occurring during aging when there is little loss of germination are those most likely to cause differences in the quality of germinable seed, that is, differences in seed vigor.

The physiological changes that occur during aging in grain legumes are typical of the generalized sequence of changes proposed for all seeds (Delouche and Baskin, 1973; Roberts, 1973c). In our discussion of seed aging, we shall consider the evidence for these changes in grain legumes, drawing attention to those changes occurring before loss of viability that may influence seed vigor.

There are a number of physiological symptoms of reduced seed quality. Changes in seed color have been associated with low germination levels in lima bean (Pollock and Toole, 1966) and *Phaseolus* bean (Toole *et al.*, 1948) in both the laboratory and the field. A reduced rate of germination was found in soybean following artificial aging (Byrd and Delouche, 1971) and a reduced tolerance to suboptimal conditions for germination has also been observed in aged seeds (Burris *et al.*, 1969; Byrd and Delouche, 1971). Similarly, aged groundnut seeds sown in the field showed a slower rate of emergence, an increase in the proportion of abnormal seedlings, and reduced field emergence (Gavrielit-Gelmond, 1970). Even if successful establishment occurs, poorer growth of seedlings from aged seeds has been reported in *Phaseolus* bean (Toole and Toole, 1953; Toole *et al.*, 1957) and soybean (Burris *et al.*, 1969; Byrd and Delouche, 1971). There is some indication that the effect of impaired seed quality arising from aging can be carried through to the mature plants, with increased pollen abortion seen in peas and broad bean plants grown from aged seeds (Abdalla and Roberts, 1969).

Although the changes that take place at the cellular and metabolic level during seed aging have received considerable attention, they are still not well understood. This may be partly due to workers using different species, different methods of aging, and seeds from all three phases of aging (Fig. 1). These changes are often referred to as biochemical changes, reflecting a general tendency for workers to apply subcellular biochemical explanations to changes that are symptomatic of the more fundamental processes that might be occurring.

The leakage of solutes from seeds has often been associated with differences in seed quality reflected in both viability and vigor, and also with the degree of seed aging. Differences in the levels of solute leakage from seeds have been linked with viability since 1928 (Hibbard and Miller, 1928), when reduced resistance of pea seed soak water to electricity was observed as viability declined. The reduced retention of solutes associated with loss of viability has also been reflected in the increased electrical conductivity of leachates of soybean (Edje and Burris, 1970a; Abdul Baki and Anderson, 1973; Parrish and Leopold, 1978), groundnut (Pearce and Abdel Samad, 1980), lima bean (Pollock and Toole, 1966), black gram (Dharmalingam *et al.*, 1976), and pea (Powell and Matthews, 1977), in the leakage of [^{14}C]glucose and [^{14}C]leucine from soybean axes (Yaklich and Abdul Baki, 1975), and in the increase in total sugars in the leachate of aged soybean (Edje and Burris, 1970b).

Differences in solute leakage have also been observed in highly germinable seed lots taken from commercial sources, which did not clearly result from induced aging or prolonged storage. This has been seen for peas (Matthews and Bradnock, 1967, 1968), *Phaseolus* beans (Matthews and Bradnock, 1968), and soybean (Oliveira *et al.*, 1983). The electrical conductivities of the seed leachates were shown to be negatively correlated with the vigor of the seed lots and their ability to achieve good field establishment (Matthews and Bradnock, 1968; Oliveira *et al.*, 1983). Thus, seed lots that had high leakage giving high conductivity measurements exhibited poor field establishment and were low-vigor lots. Low levels of leakage and therefore low conductivities were indicative of high vigor. Similarly, in tests involving placing electrodes across a soaked seed, Levengood *et al.* (1975) demonstrated that in the early stages of imbibition, seeds giving smaller currents, that is, less electrolyte leakage, were associated with higher germination rates, more extensive growth, and fewer defective plants.

Such differences in leakage from viable seeds have been observed as a result of periods of aging in soybean (Edje and Burris, 1970a; Parrish and Leopold, 1978), groundnut (Pearce and Abdel Samad, 1980), black gram (Dharmalingam *et al.*, 1976), and pea (Powell and Matthews, 1977). These changes in leakage during induced aging at high temperatures and raised seed moisture contents are illustrated in Table II. In peas, the differences in leakage from both commercial seed lots (Matthews and Rogerson, 1977) and aged seeds (Powell and Matthews, 1977) have been related to the amount of dead tissue on the cotyledons. In view of the structure of grain legume seeds, with their large living cotyledons, it is perhaps not surprising that large differences in leakage can arise during aging due to the proportion of dead tissue present, giving rise to vigor differences before loss of viability. Powell and Matthews (1977) showed that even pea seeds whose cotyledons stain completely after a short period of aging have an impaired ability to retain solutes.

There have been many conflicting reports on the effects of aging on enzyme activity (Abdul Baki and Anderson, 1972). As early as 1920, McHargue proposed that seeds of nine species including cowpea and soybean could be divided into high- and low-viability classes on the basis of peroxidase activity. Much later, reduced activity of alkaline phosphatase and 3-phosphoglyceraldehyde dehydrogenase was observed in aged pea seeds (Harman *et al.*, 1976), and the reduced formation of formazan from tetrazolium chloride in aged soybean seed was interpreted as the result of reduced dehydrogenase activity (Edje and Burris, 1970b; Byrd and Delouche, 1971). In contrast, Edje and Burris (1970b) found no significant difference in the glutamic acid dehydrogenase activity (GADA) of soybean following different degrees of aging, and in *Phaseolus* bean, GADA was at a high level in some varieties even after loss of viability (James, 1968).

Measurements of oxygen uptake and carbon dioxide evolution have indicated changes in the rate of respiration and in respiratory quotient

TABLE II. Changes in solute leaching during aging[a]

Pea[b]			Soybean[c]			Groundnut[d]		
Days aging	Germination (%)	Conductivity (μS cm^{-1} g^{-1})	Days aging	Germination (%)	Conductivity (μS cm^{-1} g^{-1})	Days aging	Germination (%)	Conductivity (μS cm^{-1} g^{-1})
0	100	116	0	100	145	0	95	140
1	—	—	1	99	190	7	90	175
2	99	166	2	96	235	14	70	350
3	98	198	3	96	290	21	58	450
4	74	325	4	81	500	28	15	870

[a]As measured by the electrical conductivity of the seed soak water of pea, soybean, and groundnut following periods of accelerated aging.

[b]From Powell and Matthews (1977). Seeds aged in 94% rh at 45°C. Conductivity readings are the mean of 20 individual seeds soaked in water 24 hr.

[c]From Parrish and Leopold (1978). Seeds aged in 100% rh at 41°C. Conductivity readings taken from the leachate of six cotyledons after 30 min in water.

[d]From Pearce and Abdel Samad (1980). Seeds aged in 90% rh at 38°C. Conductivity measured for two replicates of 50 seeds after 24 hr in water.

(RQ) of both artifically aged seeds and seeds differing in vigor. Reduced oxygen uptake was observed in the axes of aged peas (Harman *et al.*, 1976), and Wahab and Burris (1971) reported that the respiration rate of axes from low-quality soybeans increased only 9 times during the first 72 hr germination, compared to 13 times increase in axes from high-quality seeds. Abdul Baki and Anderson (1973) found a positive correlation between soybean seed vigor and both oxygen uptake and carbon dioxide evolution. Although this work included axes from nonviable seeds, the data suggest that a similar correlation would be maintained in viable seed. In contrast, Abu-Shakra and Ching (1967) have shown a 10–40% greater uptake of oxygen by mitochondria from aged soybean than from unaged seeds. They suggested that the reduced vigor of aged but viable seeds resulted from the uncoupling of mitochondria, and therefore from a reduced phosphorylation efficiency. Byrd and Delouche (1971), however, observed little change in the oxygen uptake of soybean seeds during the early stages of deterioration, where increased carbon dioxide evolution resulted in an increased RQ. Reduced oxygen consumption occurred only after a decrease in germination and reduced seedling growth (Byrd and Delouche, 1971). Woodstock and Taylorson (1981a,b) suggested that aging results in a breakdown between the interlocking systems of glycolysis and the tricarboxylic acid cycle, leading to prolonged ethanol accumulation during the early stages of germination of low-vigor seed and to increased RQ.

Reduced synthesis of macromolecules may be a consequence of any changes in enzyme activity during aging (Delouche and Baskin, 1973; Roberts, 1973c). Harman *et al.* (1976) reported delayed protein synthesis and smaller amino acid pools in aged peas, although in soybeans the soluble amino acid fractions were found to be related more to variety than to age (Burris *et al.*, 1969). Reduced incorporation of ^{32}P into all nucleic acids and decreased protein synthesis were observed in aged soybean axes (Abdul Baki and Chandra, 1977), and good correlations have been obtained between vigor and both uptake and incorporation of [^{14}C]glucose and [^{14}C]leucine into carbohydrate and protein in viable and nonviable soybean seeds (Abdul Baki and Anderson, 1973) and axes (Yaklich and Abdul Baki, 1975). In nonviable field pea seeds (Bray and Chow, 1976) and soybean (Anderson, 1977), the failure to incorporate exogenously supplied radioactive amino acid into protein upon hydration was accompanied by loss of capacity to synthesize RNA. Evidence suggests that the reduced capacity for protein synthesis is, at least in part, due to an impaired translation mechanism (Bray and Chow, 1976; Abdul Baki and Chandra, 1977), although any damage to DNA would impair transcription.

Failure to synthesize DNA has been observed in nonviable pea axis tissue (Bray and Chow, 1976), and the observation of chromosome abnormalities in the root tips of aged peas and broad beans (Abdalla and Roberts, 1968; Roberts, 1973b) has provided evidence that some damage or changes to DNA occur during aging. In cases of extreme damage, this could result in impaired template activity of the DNA and in the reduced RNA and protein synthesis observed in aged seeds (Abdul Baki and Anderson, 1973; Yaklich and Abdul Baki, 1975; Bray and Chow, 1976; Anderson, 1977).

Much of the work examining the changes in aged seeds has been carried out with the aim of trying to identify the fundamental change(s) that occurs to initiate the process of aging. This might then provide the opportunity to halt aging and therefore improve seed quality. Many of the changes observed could occur as a result of membrane deterioration, and three lines of evidence support this hypothesis.

First, increased leakage, often the first symptom of aging, has been observed from viable pea seeds in which the cotyledons were made up of entirely living tissue (Powell and Matthews, 1979). In this case the reduced solute retention was not due to dead tissue on the cotyledons and was interpreted as indicative of impaired membrane integrity. Second, electron micrographs from aged but viable soybean axes have shown damage to mitochondrial membranes (Abu-Shakra and Ching, 1967), with dilated or inflated cristae and in some cases the absence of an intact outer membrane. Third, observations during the imbibition of soybean seeds have indicated membrane damage. Parrish and Leopold (1978) found that the increase in systemic (seed plus water) volume during imbibition was directly correlated with vigor and viability. The decrease in systemic volume in aged seeds (Parrish and Leopold, 1978) was interpreted as a reduced ability to develop turgor due to membrane deterioration. Subsequently, Parrish *et al.* (1982) demonstrated a reduction in turgor immediately on imbibition of aged seeds during the early stages of aging.

As a result of the implication of membranes in aging, a number of workers have examined the phospholipid components of membranes for evidence of deterioration in the early stages of aging. Two types of reaction have been recognized within membranes during aging: the formation of free radicals by peroxidation and the hydrolysis of phospholipids. The first of these, the formation of free radicals, can take place at both high and low seed moisture contents. Because of their high reactivity, free-radical production can result in the progressive inactivation of enzymes, denaturation of other proteins, and the disruption of DNA and RNA (Mead, 1976). Priestley *et al.* (1980) failed to detect free radicals in aged soybean, although because of their highly reactive nature, it is perhaps unlikely that they would accumulate sufficiently to be measured directly. Most work has therefore examined indirect evidence that free radicals are produced by looking at the consequences of peroxidation.

One approach to the search for evidence of peroxidation has been to examine any changes in the proportions of unsaturated fatty acids in phospholipids. Thus, the reductions in linoleic (18:2) and linolenic (18:3) acids observed in aged peas (Harman and Mattick, 1976) and soybeans (Stewart and Bewley, 1980) were said to result from their reaction with free radicals. However, these changes occurred either in the later stages of aging (Harman and Mattick, 1976) or after viability was lost (Stewart and Bewley, 1980). In contrast, Priestley and Leopold (1979) found no change in unsaturated fatty acids during soybean aging either before or after loss of viability.

An alternative approach in the search for evidence of peroxidation is to search for the products of the reaction. Thus the increase in the production of malondialdehyde by nonviable soybean (Stewart and Bewley, 1980) and in the release of carbonyl compounds during germination of aged but viable pea seeds (Harman *et al.*, 1978, 1982) have been interpreted as evidence for peroxidation. Other workers have, however, failed to detect hydroperoxides, other products of peroxidation, in either groundnuts (Pearce and Abdel Samad, 1980) or peas (Powell and Harman, 1984).

The second type of reaction that could occur in membranes during aging is hydrolysis of the phospholipids. The decline in the total phospholipid content reported in aged and nonviable groundnuts (Pearce and Abdel Samad, 1980), soybeans (Priestley and Leopold, 1979), and peas (Powell and Matthews, 1981a; Powell and Harman, 1984) was mainly attributable to loss of phosphatidylcholine. In peas, the association of this reduced phospholipid content with the high levels of solute leakage from living tissue (Powell and Matthews, 1981a) suggested that hydrolysis of phospholipids might be an early change in the aging process.

The overall evidence for either hydrolysis or peroxidation of membrane phospholipids as a primary cause of aging leading to reduced seed quality is clearly conflicting. Recent work (Powell and Harman, 1984) has indicated that this may arise as a result of the different conditions used by workers to induce rapid aging.

B. IMBIBITION DAMAGE

The second physiological factor that can give rise to differences in seed vigor in grain legumes occurs after the seed has been sown, during the process of imbibition. Such imbibition damage was first recognized in pea embryos (Powell and Matthews, 1978a) and was subsequently shown to occur in intact seed and to be a cause of vigor differences in commercial seed lots of that species (Powell and Matthews, 1979, 1980a). We shall describe the nature of imbibition damage, discuss evidence that indicates that it is a common phenomenon in grain legumes, and consider its role in determining seed vigor.

Imbibition damage was first observed when pea embryos (seeds with the testa removed) failed to stain with tetrazolium chloride following imbibition in water (Powell and Matthews, 1978a). This apparent cell death occurred as a result of rapid water uptake, since damage was reduced when embryos imbibed slowly in a polyethylene glycol solution (Table III, and Powell and Matthews, 1978a). Damage occurred only in the outer layers of cells of the cotyledons within the first 2 min of imbibition and was interpreted as the result of the physical disruption of cell membranes during the rapid inrush of water, causing cell death (Powell and Matthews, 1978a). More recent work (Powell and Matthews, 1981b) has illustrated that failure to stain actually resulted from the loss of the substrate for the dehydrogenase enzymes that reduce tetrazolium chloride to the red formazan, which indicates living tissue (Cottrell, 1948; Roberts, 1951). Although imbibition damage did not cause death of the surface cells, it was, however, clearly damaging, allowing loss of solutes which impaired cell function and re-

TABLE III. The percentage of cotyledons with abaxial surfaces showing complete tetrazolium chloride staining after three imbibition treatments[a]

Species	Imbibition treatment		
	Intact seed (water)	Embryo (water)	Embryo (PEG)[b]
Pea	95	20	75
Soybean	75	55	100
Vicia faba[c]	92	55	90
Phaseolus vulgaris[d]	75	45	100

[a]Complete staining indicates living tissue (A. A. Powell and S. Matthews, unpublished data).
[b]30% w/v solution polyethylene glycol.
[c]Field bean.
[d]Navy bean.

sulted in the failure to stain with tetrazolium chloride. This loss of solutes was reflected in the high conductivity of seed soak water (Powell and Matthews, 1978a). Embryos also showed reduced respiration and germination, a decline in the rate of food reserve transfer from the cotyledons to the growing axis, and a lower growth rate in the seedlings produced (Powell and Matthews, 1978a).

We have since observed imbibition damage, as reduced vital staining (Table III), and increased leakage in *Phaseolus* bean, field bean (Powell and Matthews, 1980b), and soybean (Semple, 1981; Oliveira *et al.*, 1983), which has led us to propose that it is common to all grain legumes. This proposal, and the hypothesis that imbibition damage results from the disruption of membranes (Powell and Matthews, 1978a), is supported by the work of Duke and Kakefuda (1981). They observed that when soybean, navy bean, pea, and groundnut were imbibed minus the testa, the outermost layers of cells of all species absorbed the normally nonpermeating pigment Evans blue after only 5–15 min imbibition. Embryos (minus the testa) showed poor retention of solutes. This was interpreted as being the result of cellular rupture during imbibition (Duke and Kakefuda, 1981). Larson (1968) also observed increased leakage and reduced growth of seedlings from pea embryos imbibed without the testa, compared to seeds imbibed intact. In addition, the observation that the immersion of embryo axes from lima beans in water for only 10 min results in reduced growth and ribonuclease development at a later period (Roos and Pollock, 1971) suggests that imbibition damage may also occur in this species. Thus, evidence is accumulating to suggest that imbibition damage occurs in many species of grain legumes, which gives emphasis to the importance of the testa in regulating the rate of water uptake into the seed.

The significance not only of the presence of the testa but also of an intact testa was illustrated by the more rapid water uptake and increased incidence of imbibition damage found in scarified seed (Powell and Matthews, 1979). Furthermore, the percentage of seeds with cracked testae in commercial seed lots of peas was positively correlated with their rate of water uptake and could be associated with the seed lots' vigor as expressed in both conductivity (Powell and Matthews, 1979) and field emergence (Powell and Matthews, 1979, 1980a). Low-vigor seed lots included a large proportion of seeds with cracks in the testa and seeds that imbibed rapidly and had high conductivities (Powell and Matthews, 1979), whereas high-vigor lots had little testa damage and imbibed slowly. In addition, the poor field emergence of low-vigor lots was associated with the greater incidence of imbibition damage when they imbibed in field conditions (Powell and Matthews, 1980a).

The reduced emergence associated with imbibition damage may occur as a result of physiological death, particularly in weak, possibly aged lots that are highly susceptible to imbibition damage, and/or because of increased predisposition to infection by soil-borne fungi (Powell and Matthews, 1980a). Infection of peas by the soil-borne fungus *Pythium* has previously been shown to be a major cause of emergence failure (Matthews, 1977). Increased predisposition may result from the dead tissue on the cotyledons acting as an initial site of fungal infection (Matthews, 1971) or from the leakage of solutes into the soil, causing an increase in inoculum potential (Matthews, 1971; Perry, 1973). That predisposition to infection is the more significant cause of emergence failure is indicated by the fact that fungicidal chemicals nearly always improve emergence (Jacks, 1963; Matthews and Bradnock, 1967).

Other investigations indicate that imbibition damage also affects germination and vigor in the intact seeds of several species. Among commercial seed lots of soybean (Oliveira *et al.*, 1983), lots that included many seeds with testa damage imbibed rapidly, showed high incidence of imbibition damage, and had low vigor as revealed by both high leachate conductivity and poor field emergence. In addition, Matheson (1983) found that soybean seeds with cracked testae showed greater predisposition to infection by *Pythium* when sown in soil. Reduced germination in soil was found for groundnut when the testa was removed or damaged (Carter, 1973), with little or no improvement following fungicide treatment. The poor germination of fungicide-treated seeds might have been due to the death of seeds as a result of imbibition damage. Soaking field bean in water also reduced germination and growth (Rowland and Gusta, 1977), and Adebona and Odu (1972) suggested that the decreased germination and increased leakage in cowpea observed after soaking might result from rapid water uptake causing membrane damage and solute loss.

Imbibition damage has therefore been shown to be closely associated with seed vigor in both peas and soybeans. Furthermore, the direct observation of imbibition damage in several species, and indirect evidence from other work, strongly imply that it is a major cause of low vigor in most grain legumes. Consequently, since the testa slows down water uptake (Powell and Matthews, 1978a), the incidence of cracks in the testa has a marked influence on seed quality. Although testa condition and the rate of water uptake largely determine the extent of imbibition damage, the condition of the embryo is also important. Similar rates of water uptake into different seed lots of peas, both in water (Powell and Matthews, 1979) and in soil (Powell and Matthews, 1980a), resulted in marked differences in the incidence of imbibition damage. This suggested that the embryos of the lots differed in their susceptibility to imbibition damage. Aged pea seeds have also been found to be more susceptible than unaged seeds to imbibition damage, again implying that the embryo condition determined susceptibility (Matthews *et al.,* 1980). Similarly, Woodstock and Tao (1981) found that aged soybean axes were less tolerant of rapid water uptake. Thus, although imbibition damage is important in determining vigor, the extent of damage appears to be influenced by the embryo's condition, especially the extent to which it has been subjected to the deteriorative processes of aging.

Imbibition damage may also provide an alternative explanation for the so-called imbibitional chilling injury reported in a number of species, including lima bean (Pollock and Toole, 1966; Pollock, 1969), *Phaseolus* bean (Pollock *et al.,* 1969), and soybean (Obendorf and Hobbs, 1970; Hobbs and Obendorf, 1972). This injury arises when seeds are subjected to low temperatures during early imbibition. Sensitivity to imbibition damage is greater at low temperatures in peas (Powell and Matthews, 1978a) and field and *Phaseolus* beans (Powell and Matthews, 1980b) and has several features in common with imbibitional chilling injury. In both situations, germination and growth are reduced, and chilling injury has been associated with rapid imbibition and is largely reduced if seed moisture content is raised before seeds are subjected to low temperatures (Eyster, 1940; Pollock, 1969; Obendorf and Hobbs, 1970). Moreover, the studies on lima bean (Pollock and Toole, 1966) were carried out on scarified seeds, so water would have had ready access to the dry embryo. Such observations lead us to suggest that the effects of low temperatures were in fact the result of imbibition damage, which was enhanced at these temperatures. An examination of embryo condition after imbibition at higher temperatures of the so-called chilling-sensitive species might well have also revealed damage that was not reflected in loss of viability. This view is supported by the observation that chilling injury can be avoided in soybean (Obendorf and Hobbs, 1970) and pea seed (Eyster, 1940) and in lima bean axes (Pollock, 1969) if dry tissues are allowed to take up water slowly at low temperatures from atmospheric conditions of high relative humidity.

IV. Pathological Aspects of Quality

Diseases of the seeds of grain legumes can be caused by what are termed biotic and abiotic factors. The biotic factors, in the form of microorganisms, have the more significant effect on seed quality, although abiotic factors such as nutrient deficiency can give rise to physiological disorders.

A. BIOTIC FACTORS

Diseases caused by biotic factors, namely, fungi, bacteria, and virsuses, and their effect on seed quality will be dealt with in turn.

1. *Fungi*

The fungi are the organisms most frequently associated with seeds, from the time that the seed is on the plant, through periods of storage, until the seed is sown. Over this period, two groups of fungi have been recognized, field fungi and storage fungi, the characteristics of which have been defined by Christensen (1972).

Field fungi are those that invade the seeds while they are on the developing plant in the field, during seed maturation, and after the crop is cut and swathed, but before it is threshed. When seeds have been harvested, dried, and taken into store, the activity of field fungi is usually arrested, as they require a high relative humidity (usually more than 95%) for growth. Field fungi may be saprophytes such as *Alternaria tenuis* and *Cladosporium herbarum*, or pathogens, whose spread into the next generation of the crop is seed borne. Of these, the most commonly occurring fungal pathogens (Table IV) are those that produce anthracnose or anthracnose-like diseases, with penetrating lesions in the stems and pods as well as degrees of leaf blight or foot rot (Neergaard, 1977). We shall, however, be concerned only with those fungi that affect seed quality in terms of the ability to germinate and establish a seedling in the field.

In contrast to field fungi, storage fungi are able to grow without free water, and do so on stored products. Most storage fungi are species of *Aspergillus* and *Penicillium*, which are active at 70–90% relative humidity and which do not usually invade seeds before harvest (Christensen, 1972). The activity of different storage fungi and their influence on seed quality are closely associated with both the storage conditions and the physiological changes occurring in the seed during storage. They will therefore be considered later (Section V) and only the role of field fungi in determining seed quality will be discussed here.

The fungi that have the greatest influence on soybean seed quality are *Diaporthe phaseolorum* var. *sojae,* the imperfect stage being *Phomopsis* sp., which causes pod and stem blight, and *Cercospora kikuchii,* the purple seed stain fungus.

TABLE IV. Seed-borne Coleomycetes of Leguminosae[a]

Host	Fungus: *Colletotrichum*	*Ascochyta*	*Phoma*	*Diaporthe (Phomopsis)*
Cajanus cajan	*gloeosporioides*	—	—	—
Cicer arietinum	—	*rabiei*	—	—
Glycine max	*dematium*	*sojiicola*	—	*phaseolorum* var. *caulivora* *phaseolorum* var. *sojae*
Phaseolus lunatus	*dematium* *lindemuthianum*	*boltshauseri*	*exigua*	*phaseolorum* var. *sojae*
Phaseolus vulgaris	*lindemuthianum* *dematium*	*boltshauseri*	*exigua*	*phaseolorum* var. *sojae*
Pisum arvense, *Pisum sativum*	*pisi*	*pinodes*, *pisi*	*medicaginis* var. *pinodella*	—
Vicia faba	*lindemuthianum*	*fabae*	—	—
Vicia spp.	*villosum*	*pisi*	—	—

[a]From Neergaard (1977).

Chamberlain and Gray (1974) found that *D. phaseolorum* was the predominant organism isolated from soybean seed, and it has been shown to be seed borne in a large proportion of seed lots produced in the United States (Ellis *et al.*, 1974a; Shortt *et al.*, 1981; Nicholson *et al.*, 1972), Canada (Wallen and Seaman, 1963), Puerto Rico (Ellis and Paschal, 1979), and Brazil (Bolkan *et al.*, 1976). The fungus first appears on the plant as pycnidia on the petioles of lower leaves, on broken lower branches, and on dry, poorly developed pods. The most important aspect of the disease, however, is its effect on the seeds. Infected seeds exhibit varying degrees of cracking of the seed coat, shriveling, and are frequently partially or completely covered with a white mold (Sinclair, 1976). The most significant effect on soybean seed quality is the association of reduced germination with increased incidence of infection by *D. phaseolorum* (Wallen and Seaman, 1963; Chamberlain and Gray, 1974; Tenne *et al.*, 1974; Wilcox *et al.*, 1974; Sinclair, 1977; Johnson and Wax, 1978; Grybauskas *et al.*, 1979). Ellis *et al.* (1974a) found that when 25% or more of the seeds within a lot were infected, both germination and field emergence were reduced, and significant correlations have been reported between the incidence of seed infection by *Diaporthe* and both field emergence (Wilcox *et al.*,

1974; Shortt *et al.*, 1981) and subsequent seedling vigor (Shortt *et al.*, 1981).

The purple seed stain fungus *C. kikuchii* has also been associated with a reduction in soybean seed quality (Sinclair, 1978b). This fungus colonizes the seed late in the season and characteristically appears as irregular blotches varying from light to dark purple, covering anything from a small spot to the entire seed coat. Discolorations are often accompanied by wide cracks in the seed coat. Infection has been reported to reduce the germination of purple-stained seed (Murakishi, 1951; Wilcox and Abney, 1973), and Wilcox and Abney (1973) also found that these seeds had consistently reduced field emergence. Other workers, however (Nangju *et al.*, 1980; Lehman, 1950; Sherwin and Kreitlow, 1952), did not observe these effects.

Other fungi that have been isolated from soybean and associated with reduced germination or field emergence are *Macrophomina phaseolina* (Chamberlain and Gray, 1974), *Colletotrichum dematicum* var. *truncata* (Sinclair, 1978a), *Aspergillus melleus* (Ellis *et al.*, 1975), *Alternaria* spp. (Sinclair, 1978b; Wilcox *et al.*, 1974; Tervet, 1945; Nittler *et al.*, 1974), *Sclerotinia sclerotiorum* (Nicolson *et al.*, 1972), and *Myrothecium roridium* (Schiller *et al.*, 1978).

The isolation of these fungi from soybean seed has revealed that they are most commonly associated with the seed coat. The mycelium of *D. phaseolorum* is abundant in the hourglass layer of the testa, whereas *C. kikuchii* is equally abundant in the hourglass and parenchyma cell layers (Ilyas *et al.*, 1975). Other fungi isolated from the seed coats of surface-sterilized seeds are species of *Alternaria, Aspergillus, Penicillium, Rhizopus, Fusarium,* and *Cladosporium* (Sinclair, 1978a). These observations clearly suggest that the seed coat is an important location of internally borne seed fungi that can reduce soybean seed quality.

The fungus *Diaporthe* also causes problems of seed quality in *Phaseolus vulgaris* (Ellis *et al.*, 1976; Bolkan *et al.*, 1976; Ellis and Paschal, 1979) and pigeon pea (*Cajanus cajan*) (Ellis and Paschal, 1979), causing reduced germination and field emergence (Ellis and Paschal, 1979). *Aspergillus* and *Penicillium* spp. have been isolated from *Phaseolus* seeds (Bolkan *et al.*, 1976), and Ellis *et al.* (1976) found that *Fusarium* spp., *Rhizoctonia solani, Diaporthe, Alternaria,* and *Macrophomina phaseoli* accounted for the majority of fungi recovered. Reduced germination and field emergence of *Phaseolus* bean was again associated with the incidence of internal seed-borne fungi.

The fungi most commonly found to be associated with groundnut fruits are soil-borne saprophytes (Garren and Higgins, 1947), such as *Rhizopus* sp., *Aspergillus* sp., *Sclerotium bataticola, Diplodia* sp., and species of *Fusarium*. Of these, *Diplodia* sp. and *S. bataticola* frequently invade the intercotyledonary space, producing a hyphal mat and causing internal discoloration and decomposition of seeds. Such fungal infection can reduce the germination of peanut seeds (Pettit *et al.*, 1971). Seed-borne inocula of *Aspergillus* and *Rhizopus* were found to be responsible for the establishment failure of groundnut in Israel due to pre- and postemergence damping off (Frank, 1969), and a 30% reduction in germination was observed in groundnuts infected with *Aspergillus niger* and *Rhizoctonia nigricans* (Lalithakumari *et al.*, 1972).

In peas, the seed-borne fungi *Ascochyta pisi, Ascochyta pinodella,* and *Mycosphaerella pinodes* have been found to cause poor germination and field establishment (Jones, 1927; Wallen and Stoko, 1950), particularly in conditions adverse to rapid germination such as low temperature and high soil moisture content (Jones, 1927). Shorter plants and more variable plant heights were produced from diseased seeds (Jones, 1927). Wallen and Stoko (1950) reported that from an examination of several hundred samples of Canadian-grown pea seed over a period of 10 years, *A. pisi* was by far the most common of the three fungi.

Macrophomina phaseolina and *Fusarium equiseti* have been isolated from both cowpea (Sinha and Khare, 1977) and mung bean (Nath *et al.*, 1970); in both species heavily infected seeds failed to germinate. In cowpea, partially infected seeds germinated but suffered from subsequent pre- and postemergence rot (Sinha and Khare, 1977). The germination of mung bean has also been found to be reduced in blotter tests when seeds were infected by *Botryodiplodia palmarum, D. phaseolorum* var. *sojae, Fusarium moniliforme,* and *Fusarium solani* (Nath *et al.*, 1970), with a similar effect in pot experiments where seeds were sown into inoculated soil. The viability and vigor of black gram seed have also been reported to be affected by the seed-borne pathogens *R. solani* and *Alternaria* sp. (Dharmalingam *et al.*, 1976).

2. *Bacteria*

Seed-borne bacterial diseases occur less frequently in grain legumes than do fungal diseases, and in both soybean and *Phaseolus* beans, only two species have been reported to influence seed quality. In soybean, Nicholson and Sinclair (1971) found that the incidence of *Pseudomonas glycinea* was significantly and negatively correlated with the inhibition of seed germination, and seed lots that had the highest incidence of bacteria had the lowest field emergence. A similar correlation has also been found for seeds infected by *Bacillus subtilis* (Ellis *et al.*, 1977; Tenne *et al.*, 1977). In *Phaseolus* beans, *Bacillus phaseoli* and *Bacillus medicaginis* var. *phaseolicola* cause seed-borne diseases. When seeds are only slightly infected, there is no effect on seed quality, but when infection is severe the seeds fail to germinate and disintegrate in soil (Zaumeyer, 1932).

3. *Viruses*

There are a number of examples of embryo-borne viruses reducing the viability of leguminous seeds. Pea seed infected by pea early browning virus becomes wrinkled and the seed coat becomes discolored (Bos and van der Want, 1962), and seed infected by pea seed-borne mosaic virus becomes small and cracked (Stevenson and Hagedorn, 1969, 1973). Soybean seed infected by mosaic virus has brown or blackish mottled seed coats and is smaller than healthy seeds (Phatak, 1974). Dunleavy (1976) reported a reduction in germination of 22% in such seed. Infection of cowpea by aphid-borne mosaic virus (Phatak and Summamwar, 1967), mung bean by mung bean mosaic virus (Phatak, 1974), and groundnut by groundnut mottle virus (Kuhn, 1965) all result in small, shriveled, and sometimes discolored seed.

B. ABIOTIC FACTORS

Although seed pathology refers primarily to the presence or absence of disease-causing organisms, seed health also includes physiological conditions that affect seed quality. Two such physiological conditions in grain legumes are hollow heart and marsh spot.

Hollow heart, or cavitation, was first described by Myers (1948) in New South Wales and is most common in wrinkle-seeded peas, although it has also been observed in field bean (Harrison, 1976). The seeds are outwardly normal, but following imbibition there is a sunken and sometimes cracked area in the center of the usually flat adaxial surface of the cotyledons. The cells lining the cavity are abnormal (Perry and Howell, 1965), containing little reserve material (Singh, 1974). High levels of hollow heart have been associated with pea seed lots that fail to emerge in the field (Perry, 1967; Gane and Biddle, 1973) and with seeds germinating more slowly and producing smaller seedlings (Noble and Howell, 1962; Harrison and Perry, 1973). Heydecker and Kohistani (1969) did not, however, observe such effects and concluded that hollow heart led to rotting of the cotyledons, predisposing seedlings to fungus infection.

Predisposition of pea seeds to hollow heart appears to be caused by the exposure of the mother plants to high temperatures during maturation or by drying immature seeds after harvest at high temperatures (Perry and Harrison, 1973). In peas the incidence of hollow heart then depends on the rate and quantity of water imbibed prior to germination (Heydecker and Feast, 1969; Perry and Harrison, 1973; Singh, 1974); rapid water uptake increases the incidence of the condition. Similarly, rapid imbibition of field beans in water resulted in higher incidence of hollow heart than when seeds were imbibed slowly on filter paper (Harrison, 1976).

Mineral deficiencies can also produce physiological disorders. Marsh spot, a disorder common in peas, particularly marrow fats, and to a lesser extent in *Phaseolus* beans and broad beans, results from a deficiency in manganese. Its name arises from its association with alkaline fen soils, which are rich in humus but deficient in manganese. The symptoms, like those of hollow heart, appear on the internal surfaces of the cotyledons as extended brown necroses, and cracks may appear when infection is severe (Neergaard, 1977). Internal symptoms are detectable 2–3 days after sowing, and the seedlings produced are weak and poorly developed.

V. Changes in Physiological and Pathological Aspects of Seed Quality during Storage

The aim of seed production is to maintain the maximum seed quality reached at physiological maturity (Section III) until the seed is sown. The whole of this period will be interpreted as seed storage. Deterioration of seed quality can occur both on the plant, that is, preharvest deterioration—which has been the subject of agronomic studies—and in seed storage, where research has considered the physiological changes that constitute aging.

A. Preharvest Deterioration

Preharvest or field deterioration of seeds can occur between physiological maturity and harvest and is often referred to as weathering, reflecting the considerable influence that the weather has on deterioration during this period. Most work has concentrated on the preharvest deterioration that occurs after the seed has dried down to a moisture content suitable for harvest, that is, harvest maturity, and has examined the effects of delayed harvest on seed quality (Fields and King, 1963; Green *et al.*, 1966; Wilcox *et al.*, 1974; Amable, 1976; Nangju, 1977, 1979). Field deterioration influences both the physiological aspects of seed quality and the incidence of seeds infected by fungi.

1. *Physiological aspects of seed quality*

Most attention has been given to the effects of preharvest deterioration on the ability of the seed to germinate. Delaying harvest after harvest maturity has been seen to reduce germination in both peas (Fields and King, 1963) and soybeans (Green *et al.*, 1966; Wilcox *et al.*, 1974; Amable, 1976; Nangju, 1977, 1979). Green *et al.* (1966) also reported an increase in the proportion of abnormal seedlings and poor field emergence in field-deteriorated soybeans. Tekrony *et al.* (1980b), on the other hand, observed little change in the germination of soybean produced in Kentucky when harvesting was delayed after harvest maturity, with only two instances of a decline, and these not until 50 days after harvest maturity. There was, though, a marked effect on seed vigor, which fell more rapidly (Tekrony *et al.*, 1980b), within 4 days of harvest maturity in one instance, and to an extremely low level within 30 days of harvest maturity.

The fall in germination seen after delayed harvest is often accompanied by a deterioration in the physical appearance of the seed. In soybean, poor germination was associated with a larger proportion of purple, wrinkled, and discolored seed (Nangju, 1977, 1979), and in peas, with cracked, split, and loose seed coats (Fields and King, 1963).

The environmental conditions occurring after seeds have reached the harvestable stage influence the degree of field deterioration. Deterioration of soybean after harvest maturity was particularly marked when seed was harvested after a period of heavy rain (Nangju, 1979; Green *et al.*, 1966), and in pea seeds when drying was delayed (Fields and King, 1963). Tekrony *et al.*, (1980b) reported a negative linear relationship between the minimum relative humidity and the time from harvest maturity to the first significant decline in the vigor of soybean; the corresponding relationship with temperature was negative and quadratic. The adverse effect of high relative humidities and temperatures is further illustrated by the common observation that early-maturing cultivars of soybean, which reach maturation before wet weather, show the greatest decline in vigor if harvest is delayed (Wilcox *et al.*, 1974; Tekrony *et al.*, 1980a). Work in the Missouri region of the United States has shown that if the sowing of early and midseason varieties is delayed, so that they mature after the wet conditions, improvements in both their laboratory germinations and field emergences have been seen, suggesting less field deterioration (Green *et al.*, 1965). Because of these observations, Tekrony *et al.* (1980a) suggested that by using late maturing cultivars and later sowing dates, soybean seed quality could be improved.

Although most work on preharvest deterioration concerns deterioration after the seed moisture content has decreased to harvest maturity levels, the influence of the environment during the period of seed desiccation cannot be overlooked as an influence on seed quality. Tekrony *et al.* (1980b) attributed a decrease in vigor and viability of one cultivar of soybean to the effect of high temperatures occurring during the desiccation period. This finding supported reports that temperature extremes such as hot, dry weather during soybean seed maturation resulted in lower quality seeds (Green *et al.*, 1965; Harris, *et al.*, 1965). Green *et al.* (1965) found that seed produced from later sowing dates, which underwent desiccation after hot weather had ended, generally exhibited higher laboratory germination and field emergence than did seeds in which desiccation took place during the hot weather. In lima beans, humid conditions during maturation or desiccation resulted in poor germination (Wester and Magruder, 1938).

Bleached seeds are a problem in several grain legumes and occur when periods of rain are followed by hot weather during seed maturation. These conditions can cause loss of chlorophyll and the production of bleached seeds most commonly in peas (Maguire *et al.*, 1973) and lima beans (Pollock and Toole, 1964). The stage of development defined by the term "maturation" is not, however, clear in these studies; it probably refers to the period between physiological and harvest maturity when rain is interrupting the normal process of desiccation. Bleached seeds show reduced vigor, which in peas is seen in increased leachate conductivity (Maguire *et al.*, 1973; Short *et al.*, 1977); decreased dehydrogenase activity, indicated by poor tetrazolium staining; a lowered respiration rate (Maguire *et al.*, 1973); and poor field emergence (Short *et al.*, 1977). Embryo axes from bleached lima bean seeds grew less (Pollock and Toole, 1966) and had a lower percentage emergence in the glasshouse (Abdul Baki, 1971) than did those from green seeds.

The preharvest deterioration of seeds under wet conditions has been associated with the rapid and uneven contact of seed tissues with water followed by drying (Moore, 1971). Moore proposed that uneven hydration and dehydration could produce fissures in the seed coat and cause the rupture of membranes in the embryo, leading to the early death of cells. He illustrated this field deterioration using vital staining in soybean, *Phaseolus* bean, lima bean, pea, and groundnut (Moore, 1965, 1971). In soybeans, the early-maturing cultivars commonly revealed more damage than later cultivars, and cultivars with light-colored seed coats were also more susceptible (Moore, 1965). Potts *et al.* (1978) suggested that this type of field deterioration resulting from fluctuations in moisture content might be avoided in soybean by using hard-seeded cultivars that are slow to imbibe. They found that an experimental hard-seeded cultivar retained viability longer than did a comparable cultivar from the same production environment. Embryo tissue of *P. vulgaris* was found to be more extensively damaged as a result of hydration than that of soybean (Moore, 1971).

2. *Fungal infection during preharvest deterioration*

Reduced seed quality following delayed harvest can also occur as a result of an increase in the percentage of seeds infected by fungal pathogens. In soybean, this mainly involves an increase in infection by field fungi (Kilpatrick, 1957; Athow and Laviolette, 1973; Nicholson and Sinclair, 1973; Wilcox *et al.*, 1974), whereas in peas increased infection by both field (Jones, 1927) and storage fungi (Fields and King, 1963) has been reported. Prior to maturity, the infection of soybeans by *Diaporthe* was found to be low (Kilpatrick, 1957), increasing gradually through and after maturity, until 100% of seeds were infected 6 weeks after maturity.

The incidence of fungal infection during field deterioration of seeds is influenced by environmental conditions. Most infection of soybean by *M. phaseoli* and *S. sclerotiorum* was found in seeds produced from early sowing dates, which were subjected to extended rainy periods, and early-maturing cultivars had a higher degree of infection than did later ones (Kilpatrick, 1957; Wilcox *et al.*, 1974). Similarly in peas, prolonged periods of rain before harvest resulted in greater incidence of *Ascochyta* infection (Jones, 1927), and greater infection by storage fungi was found after delayed harvesting or extended periods of field drying (Fields and King, 1962).

Some control of fungal infection during seed development has been achieved by applications of systemic fungicide sprays in soybeans (Ellis *et al.*, 1974b; Foor and Sinclair, 1977; Sinclair, 1981) and in *Phaseolus* beans (Ellis *et al.*, 1976). The subsequent seed produced had both improved seed germination and field emergence.

Thus, preharvest deterioration in the field is associated both with physiological deterioration or aging and with increased infection by fungi. The acceleration of both forms of deterioration by increased temperature and seed moisture content suggests that they are closely related. It is also possible that the damage and death of cells occurring as a result of repeated hydration (Moore, 1971) may predispose seeds to infection by both field and storage fungi.

B. POSTHARVEST STORAGE

Deterioration of seeds takes place during postharvest storage due to the inevitable process of aging. The conditions of storage, however, influence both the rate at which aging occurs and the activity of storage fungi and insects. The influence of seed storage on seed quality must therefore encompass the complex interactions between storage conditions, physiological changes during aging, and the activity of storage fungi and insects.

1. *Storage and physiological aspects of seed quality*

The two most important factors affecting the rate of aging and, therefore, the retention of seed viability in storage are seed moisture content and temperature. The moisture content of seed in storage is related to the relative humidity (rh) of the storage atmosphere (James, 1967; Roberts, 1972; Justice and Bass, 1978), since seeds are hygroscopic and take up or lose water until their moisture content is in equilibrium with the ambient relative humidity. There are many records of moisture equilibria values for seeds, including those of Harrington (1960), Roberts (1972), and Justice and Bass (1978). Grain legumes show the typical response of orthodox seed species (Roberts, 1972) to storage at high relative humidities and therefore high seed moisture content: seed longevity declines as relative humidity and moisture content (mc) increase. James *et al.* (1967) found that in conditions of high relative humidity (90% rh at 70°F) the viability of pea seeds declined to 4% in 12 months, but was maintained at 99% for 5 years in less humid conditions (50% rh at 50°C). Similarly, the viabilities of peas, *Phaseolus* bean, and broad bean all fell more rapidly when stored at high relative humidities (Sijbring, 1963).

In other work, the influence of moisture content on loss of viability has been examined by equilibrating seeds to different moisture contents before a period of hermetic storage. The loss of viability of soybean was greater when held at 17.5% mc than at 14.5% mc (Boakye-Boateng and Hume, 1975), and Burris (1980) found that the fall in germination of soybean was related linearly to increasing moisture content. Peas equilibrated to 18% mc lost viability rapidly, reaching 50% germination after only 15 weeks (Roberts and Abdalla, 1968), whereas at lower moisture contents (15.4 and 12.5%), a similar decline occurred after 35 and 100 weeks, respectively, and the viability of *Vicia faba* fell more rapidly at 19.4% mc than at 14.7% mc (Sholberg and Muir, 1979). Groundnuts also have limited longevity at higher moisture contents (de Tella *et al.*, 1976), although in this case, the moisture contents involved were much lower, with rapid loss of viability at 8.0 and 9.1% mc compared to 4.5 and 6% mc. Despite the general rule that longevity increases as seed moisture content declines, there is a suggestion that below certain moisture contents seeds deteriorate more rapidly (Bewley and Black, 1982). For example, pea seeds stored in 1% rh at 10°C revealed evidence of deterioration as determined by reduced vital staining and increased solute leakage (Powell and Matthews, 1977).

In most examples wherein reduced viability has been reported after storage at high relative humidity or moisture content, the temperature of storage was also high. Early work considered the effects of temperature alone on viability (Groves, 1917) and provided evidence that with increased temperature, viability declined. Groves (1917), however, noted that at any temperature, if the moisture content of the seeds was increased, viability decreased. In later investigations, the effects of the two factors of temperature and moisture content on viability were considered together for several grain legumes: soybean (Toole and Toole, 1953; Burris, 1980; Ellis *et al.*, 1982), pea (Roberts and Abdalla, 1968; James *et al.*, 1967), *P. vulgaris* (James *et al.*, 1967), *V. faba* (Roberts and Abdalla, 1968; Sholberg and Muir, 1979), groundnut (Ketring, 1971), and chickpea and cowpea (Ellis *et al.*, 1982). These investigations have shown that the effects of temperature and moisture content are constant and independent of each other. This appears to apply over a wide range of temperatures (−20–90°C) and between 5 and 25% seed moisture content (Ellis and Roberts, 1980). Harrington (1960) expressed the relationship of seed moisture content and temperature to loss of viability by his "rule of thumb" of seed storage, i.e., that a 10°F (5.6°C) reduction in temperature or a 1% reduction in seed moisture content doubles the storage life of the seed. This relationship has been more accurately described in viability equations for pea and broad bean (Roberts, 1972) and for chickpea, cowpea, and soybean (Ellis *et al.*, 1982). The information derived from the equations for pea and broad bean have also been presented as nomographs (Roberts and Roberts, 1972). These equations and nomographs make it possible to estimate the time taken for viability to decrease to a given level in various conditions of temperature and relative humidity, and also the combination of temperature and moisture content necessary to maintain viability above a given level for a certain period.

These studies on the influence of storage conditions on seed quality have concentrated on the loss of viability during storage, that is, the final stage of aging. There have been few investigations into the physiological changes occurring before loss of viability during more prolonged storage, compared to the many laboratory studies of changes during rapid aging (Section III,A).

In peas, increased leakage has revealed a decline in the vigor of germinable seeds of seed lots stored for up to 4 years in a commercial store (Powell and Matthews, 1977, 1978b; A. A. Powell and S. Matthews, unpublished data). Similar increases in leakage from stored soybeans (Srivastava, 1975; Verma and Gupta, 1975) have been associated with other indices of reduced vigor. Thus, reduced metabolic activity (Srivastava, 1975), reduced hypocotyl length, increased free fatty acids, and increased amounts of sugars and electrolytes in the leachate (Verma and Gupta, 1975) were found in soybean seeds showing increased leakage. Black gram seeds that leaked readily into soak water produced seedlings with reduced root and shoot lengths (Dharmalingam *et al.*, 1976), and a decline in the vigor of peas, broad beans (Abdalla and Roberts, 1969), and *Phaseolus* beans (Harrison, 1966) was reflected in a reduction in the initial growth rate of the seedlings. A high proportion of seeds producing abnormal seedlings has indicated a decline in quality of *Phaseolus* bean during storage (Toole and Toole, 1953; Vieira, 1966), as also did a slower rate of emergence (Vieira, 1966). Furthermore, Toole *et al.* (1957) found that following the storage of *Phaseolus* bean seeds in unfavorable conditions, the plants grown from them developed more slowly, reaching maximum flowering several days later than did plants from seeds stored in favorable conditions.

The evidence from prolonged storage experiments therefore indicates that physiological aging occurs, leading to loss of vigor. However, the paucity of this evidence and the recent proposal that the physiological changes during rapid aging may not be those of natural aging (Powell and Harman, 1984) suggest that there should be more extensive work done on noninduced physiological changes during seed aging.

The response of seeds to storage conditions is influenced by their initial condition as they enter store, which is largely determined by the degree of preharvest deterioration that has occurred. Amable (1976) found that the decline in the germination of soybeans in storage was most rapid after delayed harvest, and the shorter longevity of United States cultivars in India compared to local cultivars has been attributed to their maturation in the rainy season, which favors field deterioration (Gupta, 1976). The greater susceptibility of large-seeded cultivars of soybean to field deterioration was used to explain their poor storeability in comparison to small-seeded cultivars (Verma and Gupta, 1975). No indication was given in this work (Verma and Gupta, 1975) whether differences in stage of maturity could have contributed to the differences in seed size and extent of deterioration. Agrawal and Kaur (1975) also observed differences in the longevity of soybean, which were more likely to be related to seed condition than to their genetic origin. The high levels of leakage and increased fat acidity observed in seeds that rapidly lost viability also indicated that the seeds with short longevity were initially of low quality (Agrawal and Kaur, 1975). The influence of the year of production on the longevity of peas and *Phaseolus* beans (James *et al.*, 1967) suggested that preharvest weather conditions could have influenced the response of the seeds to storage.

Mechanical damage to seed during harvest can also affect seed storage potential. Reduced longevity was found in damaged soybean (Mamicpic and Caldwell, 1963; Grabe, 1965) and in seed batches of both groundnut (Gavrielit-Gelmond, 1970) and *Phaseolus* bean (Harty, 1977) showing signs of threshing damage. Toole and Toole (1953) also attributed differences in storage potential of *Phaseolus* to mechanical injury, and Harty (1977) emphasized that seed production should aim to produce the maximum normal germination at harvest to achieve good storage.

Comparison of the relative response of the grain legume species to storage is limited since few studies have included more than one species, and similar storage conditions were seldom used in different investigations. *Phaseolus* beans retained viability better than did lima beans and groundnut when stored at 10°C in 81% rh (Table V; Boswell *et al.*, 1940). However, following storage at 27°C in 78% rh, lima bean maintained germinability best and groundnut least well (Table V; Boswell *et al.*, 1940). Broad bean was found to have higher storage potential than *Phaseolus* bean when stored at a high relative humidity (62% rh; Table VI; Sijbring, 1963), whereas peas showed a large de-

TABLE V. Percentage germination of *Phaseolus* bean, lima bean, and groundnuts after storage[a]

	Storage conditions			
	10°C 81% rh[b]		27°C 78% rh	
Species	110 days	250 days	110 days	250 days
Phaseolus bean	83	91	60	0
Lima bean	60	61	54	26
Groundnut	71	68	0	0

[a]From Boswell *et al.* (1940).
[b]rh, Relative humidity.

TABLE VI. Percentage germination of pea, *Phaseolus* bean, and broad bean after storage for 16 months at 30°C in different relative humidities[a]

	Relative humidity		
Species	47%	55%	62%
Pea	89	73	5
Phaseolus bean	93	78	2
Broad bean	78	67	55

[a]From Sijbring (1963).

crease in viability. In other work, however, peas have been shown to retain viability well, with germinations of up to 78% recorded after 31 years storage (Haferkamp *et al.*, 1953) and with germinations greater than those of *Phaseolus* beans after storage for up to 36 (Toole *et al.*, 1948) or 60 months (James *et al.*, 1967) in a range of storage conditions.

Soybean seed has a reputation as an inherently bad storer (Delouche *et al.*, 1973). Its rapid decrease in germination is partially attributable to very small seed-to-seed variation, which results in a very steep slope in Phase B of the survival curve (Fig. 1) (Ellis *et al.*, 1982) and has been illustrated in both controlled environments (Ellis *et al.*, 1982) and in ambient conditions in the tropics (Boakye-Boateng and Hume, 1975). The viability equations have shown soybean to be particularly sensitive to storage temperature, with chickpea and cowpea being less sensitive (Ellis *et al.*, 1982). On the other hand, soybean was less sensitive to moisture content than were either of these species (Ellis *et al.*, 1982). The rapid deterioration of soybean is therefore largely attributable to the effects of temperature. In contrast, groundnut seed appears to be very sensitive to moisture content, with serious deterioration occurring within 2 years storage at a moisture content as low as 5% (Gavrielit-Gelmond, 1970). Similarly, de Tella *et al.* (1976) found that the reduction of seed moisture content from an initial 7 to 4.5% was necessary to maintain high germinations beyond 9 months of storage.

2. *Influence of storage fungi and insects on seed quality*

The viability and vigor of seeds held in postharvest storage is not only affected by intrinsic factors, but also by other organisms, namely, the storage fungi and insects. Seeds may become contaminated by storage fungi before harvest, but invasion does not usually occur until the seeds are in store. The major storage fungi reported in grain legumes

(Table VII) are *Aspergillus* spp., although *Penicillium,* the other major genus of seed storage fungi, has also been found.

The activity of these fungi during seed storage is influenced by the relative humidity of the store, and hence seed moisture content, and by storage temperature. Tervet (1945) reported increased isolation of storage fungi, particularly *Aspergillus* sp. from soybean as seed moisture content increased, which could be explained by the reduction in the latent period of spore germination that occurred as moisture content increased (Milner and Geddes, 1946). Increased storage temperature has also been associated with high levels of infection (Tervet, 1945; Milner and Geddes, 1945; Christensen, 1967), with maximum infection reported at either 40 (Milner and Geddes, 1945) or 45°C (Tervet, 1945). Increased incidence of infection of soybean by *Aspergillus glaucus* (Dorworth and Christensen, 1959) and cowpea by *A. glaucus* and *Penicillium* (Onesirosan, 1983) has been reported with increases in temperature, moisture content, and time in storage. High seed moisture

TABLE VII. Storage fungi isolated from grain legume species

Grain legume species	Fungal species	Reference
Soybean	*Aspergillus flavus*	Tervet (1945); Milner and Geddes (1945)
	Aspergillus glaucus	Tervet (1945); Milner and Geddes (1945); Christensen and Dorworth (1966); Christensen (1967)
	Aspergillus restrictus	Christensen and Dorworth (1966); Christensen (1967)
	Aspergillus ochraeus	Tervet (1945)
	Aspergillus niger, Aspergillus fumigatus	Tervet (1945)
	Aspergillus repens	Christensen and Dorworth (1966)
Phaseolus bean	*A. glaucus, A. restrictus, Penicillium*	Dorworth and Christensen (1959)
Cowpea	*A. niger*	Lalithakumari *et al.* (1972); Onesirosan (1983)
	Cladosporium herbarum, Rhizoctonia bataticola	Lalithakumari *et al.* (1972)
	A. flavus, Absidia sp., *Rhizopus* sp., *Penicillium*	Onesirosan (1983)
Pea	*Aspergillus* sp.	Carlson and King (1963)

contents resulted in greater infection of peas (Carlson and King, 1963) and *Phaseolus* beans (Lopez and Christensen, 1962) by species of *Aspergillus*. The importance of the interaction of seed moisture and temperature on the degree of infection was illustrated by the absence of infection up to 14.1% mc in soybean seeds stored at 5°C; at higher temperatures, lower moisture contents (12.5 and 13.3%) resulted in high levels of infection (60 and 87%; Christensen and Dorworth, 1966).

The most significant effect of infection by storage fungi on seed quality is to reduce seed viability. Soybean germination was found to decrease as seed moisture content increased to levels at which fungi grew readily (Tervet, 1945; Milner and Geddes, 1945), and in both soybean (Dorworth and Christensen, 1959) and cowpea (Onesirosan, 1983) the internal invasion of seeds by storage fungi preceded a decrease in germination. In addition, Saharan and Gupta (1973) have reported the total loss of emergence when soybeans were stored following inoculation with *Aspergillus niger, Aspergillus flavus,* or *Aspergillus tamarii.* The low germination of pea seeds following commercial storage has been attributed to *Aspergillus* infection (Fields and King, 1962), and the viability of pea seeds inoculated with *Aspergillus ruber* (Harman, 1972; Harman and Nash, 1972; Harman *et al.*, 1976), *Aspergillus chevalieri, Aspergillus amstelodami, Aspergillus repens,* and *Aspergillus restrictus* (Harman and Pfleger, 1974) declined more rapidly than did uninoculated seed when stored in 93% rh at 30°C. The infection of groundnut (Lalithakumari *et al.*, 1972) and *Phaseolus* beans (Lopez and Christensen, 1962) by storage fungi also caused reduced germination.

In addition to loss of viability, changes in seed physiology have been observed in seed infected by storage fungi. In early work on changes in the chemical composition of soybeans during storage (Milner and Geddes, 1946) a marked change was noted in the oil value and in both the total and the reducing sugars of seeds, which was proportional to the seed moisture content and extent of fungal growth. Increases in soybean fat acidity values have also been reported (Christensen and Dorworth, 1966; Christensen, 1967). Most information on physiological changes associated with infection is, however, available for peas, from the work of Harman and associates, who have compared the physiology of unaged seed both with aged, uninfected seed and with aged seeds inoculated with *A. ruber.* In aged, uninfected seeds they found reduced respiration, (Harman and Drury, 1973), enhanced solute leakage, and evidence of cell disorganization (Harman and Granett, 1972). There was also a delay in the onset of protein synthesis (Harman *et al.*, 1976), an increase in the release of volatile aldehydic compounds during germination (Harman *et al.*, 1978), and reduced

ATP and amino acid pools (Harman *et al.*, 1976). All these changes were enhanced in aged seeds that were inoculated with *A. ruber*. In addition, there was a further reduction in the unsaturated fatty acids of aged seeds associated with *A. ruber* infection (Harman and Mattick, 1976). Thus fungal invasion appeared to accelerate the normal processes of physiological aging. Harman and Nash (1972) proposed that the rapid deterioration of infected seed was induced by a fungal toxin, since the number of axes growing normally decreased more rapidly than the level of axis infection increased. Moreover, the fungus was present only in very small quantities or was even absent when the axis was killed, and extracts from infected seeds were toxic to healthy axes (Harman and Nash, 1972).

Insects also adversely affect seed quality during storage. The factors influencing insect development and the nature of the association of insects with different crop seeds, including grain legumes, have been extensively reviewed (Howe, 1972), and therefore only a few comments are made here.

Unlike the division described earlier for fungi, insects cannot be clearly divided into field and storage groups. A few species, e.g., *Bruchus pisorum,* are commonly found in stores, but are not storage species. They develop in the growing and ripening pea seed in the field, but emerge in store although they are unable to grow on the stored seed. Other species can pass to another generation in store, but fail to continue development, possibly because the seeds are too dry. Two groups of insect pests in seeds can, however, be distinguished: those that are more or less restricted to feeding in seeds and general scavengers able to deal with seeds along with organic debris. It is usually the scavengers that present the greatest hazard to germination since they selectively eat the embryo. Species adapted to live in seeds mostly feed on the cotyledon or endosperm and therefore cause little direct loss of germination, although it is possible that vigor may be reduced. They do, however, cause a loss of germination indirectly. Insect respiration can cause an increase in temperature and releases moisture that raises the relative humidity and subsequently the seed moisture content; thus, the seeds age more rapidly.

The bruchids are an important group of beetles that provide a good example of adaptability from life in growing seeds to life in stored seeds. Several species of major economic importance occur in grain legumes. *Bruchus pisorum* is a storage pest of garden and field pea, and cowpea is liable to severe damage by *Callosobruchus,* particularly *Callosobruchus chinensis, Callosobruchus rhodesianus, Callososbruchus maculatus,* and *Callosobruchus analis*. The bean weevil, *Bruchus rufimanus,* is found in cool temperate climates, whereas *Zabrotes subfasciatus* is found in tropical climates, and *Achanthoscelides obtectus* lives in warm temperate climates. The only bruchid genus of serious economic importance to crops other than peas and beans is *Carydon,* which is the principal pest of groundnuts stored in the shell and has become well established in Africa and India, and more recently in the West Indies and South America.

The rate of multiplication of storage insects, like that of storage fungi, is influenced by storage temperature and relative humidity, that is, seed moisture content, although the availability of food and light also affects development. In general, insect activity increases as temperature and relative humidity increase. This occurs over a temperature range of about 20°C for each species, from a poorly defined minimum temperature to a sharp maximum, with the optimum temperature differing for different processes. For example, the optimum temperature for the rate of oviposition is less than that for development. Insect activity also increases as seed moisture content is raised above 8–9%. The food availability for insect development depends on the amount of mechanical damage to seeds, the proportion of broken seeds, and, again, seed moisture content, since this affects the softness of the seed. Finally, insect development is influenced by light, since most insects exhibit a diurnal rhythm.

C. CONTROL OF SEED QUALITY DURING STORAGE

Seed temperature and moisture content emerge as the two factors that control preharvest deterioration and postharvest storage. Their influence lies both in their effect on the rate of aging and in the development of field and storage fungi and insects. Before harvest, there is little control possible of the conditions that determine the extent of deterioration. However, knowing the effects of delayed harvest, a valuable aim would be to harvest with a minimum of delay beyond harvest maturity. There is also the possibility of using systemic fungicide sprays to reduce fungal infection and to improve seed quality (Ellis *et al.,* 1974b, 1976; Sinclair, 1981).

It is, however, during the postharvest storage of seeds that the greatest opportunity to influence seed quality exists, through the control of the storage atmosphere. The degree of control needed for satisfactory storage will be influenced by the nature of the seed involved. The seed may be carryover seed on the farm, held in commercial stores, or intended for the maintenance of germplasm in long-term storage. Clearly, greater control is necessary to avoid even small degrees of genetic shift during germplasm storage than is necessary to prevent loss of viability in the carryover of seed from season to season. The methods used to control the storage atmosphere include ventilation, insulation, and refrigeration, with the use of sealed containers to maintain seed moisture content becoming increasingly common. These methods and their application in the different types of store were reviewed by Harrington (1972) and Justice and Bass (1978).

VI. Mechanical Damage and Seed Quality

A. The Nature and Effect of Mechanical Damage

Two types of mechanical damage can be distinguished in seeds: invisible or internal damage, which becomes evident only after the seed has germinated, and external visible damage.

There are two commonly recognized forms of internal damage. The first of these is most common in *P. vulgaris* and lima bean (Harter, 1930; Borthwick, 1932; Bainer and Borthwick, 1934; Anonymous, 1941) and produces abnormal seedlings in germination tests, in which parts of the seedling are absent or defective, usually as a result of damage to the epicotyl. Abnormal seedlings, in which the stem growing point and the first true leaves are missing, are referred to as baldheads; seedlings in which the two cotyledons are detached are termed snakeheads. Plants from both types of abnormal seedlings mature later and yield less than do those from normal seedlings (Harter, 1930; Anonymous, 1941).

Another common type of internal injury to grain legumes is transverse cracking (TVC), in which transverse breaks extend either partially or completely across the coytledons, severing the vascular elements (McCollum, 1953). The movement of reserve materials into the seedling is therefore impeded, the cotyledons remain swollen, and often the seedcoat is not shed. The susceptibility of *Phaseolus* beans (McCollum, 1953; Dickson *et al.*, 1973; Morris *et al.*, 1970; Pollock and Manalo, 1970), pea (Shull and Shull, 1932), and soybeans (Sorrells and Pappelis, 1976) to TVC has been associated with rapid water uptake. Thus the incidence of TVC in *Phaseolus* bean was increased under stress conditions of high sand moisture content (Pollock and Manalo, 1970) and when the rate of imbibition was increased following an ethanol treatment (Dickson *et al.*, 1973). Conversely, slow imbibition of soybean in mannitol resulted in a reduced number of transverse cracks. Transverse cracking has also been found to be more severe at low imbibition temperatures in soybean (Obendorf and Hobbs, 1970) and *Phaseolus* (Pollock *et al.*, 1969).

The cause of TVC is not clear, and several possible explanations have been suggested. Mechanical injury could occur as a result of handling during threshing and cleaning. However, McCollum (1953) and Pollock and Manalo (1970) reported TVC in hand-harvested *Phaseolus* bean, which suggests that harsh handling is not the cause of TVC. In both these reports, TVC was more apparent as germination conditions became progressively more stressful. Pollock and Manalo (1970) suggested that individual seeds took up water rapidly, causing uneven hydration and mechanical stresses leading to cracking. Possibly such stress causes cracking along any lines of weakness that may have formed as a result of repeated hydration and dehydration of the seed during preharvest deterioration (Moore, 1971).

External, visible damage to the seed varies considerably in its severity. At its worst, large proportions of the seed storage tissue may be lost, but seed-cleaning techniques usually eliminate this type of seed. In commercial seed, most mechanical damage is evident in the seed coat and can vary from slight damage to severe cracking and chipping or shattering of the seed coat (Hulbert and Whitney, 1934; Anonymous, 1941; Gibson and Clinton, 1953; Stanway, 1974, 1978). Where seed coat damage is most severe, seeds are often referred to as "splits" (Crosier, 1941; Stanway, 1974, 1978). In splits there is only one cotyledon in the seedcoat, or both cotyledons are outside the seedcoat. Schlub and Schmitthenner (1978) recognized that not all cell layers of the testa may be broken. They distinguished irregular breaks in the outer hypodermal layer of the seedcoat that expose the parenchyma layer, from mechanical damage in which all cell layers are broken. Moreover, slight damage to the seedcoat may not always be evident in the dry seed, being revealed only following imbibition (Powell and Matthews, 1979; Biddle, 1980).

Seedcoat damage has often been associated with poor germination in several species: *Phaseolus* beans (Atkin, 1958; Webster and Dexter, 1961; Barriga, 1961; Dickson, 1975; Dickson and Boettger, 1976; Duczmal, 1981), mung bean (Herath *et al.*, 1981), groundnut (Fowler, 1975), pea (Hulbert and Whitney, 1934), and in seed lots of soybean from commercial (Maeda *et al.*, 1977; Luedders and Burris, 1979) and experimental field harvests (Mamicpic and Caldwell, 1963; Green *et al.*, 1966). The selection of seeds without visible damage, and with varying degrees of seedcoat damage from lots of peas (Hulbert and Whitney, 1934) and soybean (Stanway, 1974, 1978), has shown that germination declines as the severity of damage increases. This explains the poor level of germination found in soybean seed lots including a large proportion of seeds with damaged seed coats (Luedders and Burris, 1979).

External mechanical damage may also influence the vigor of germinable seeds. In the laboratory, even when damaged *Phaseolus* beans germinated successfully, reduced seedling growth indicated that seed vigor was poor (Barriga, 1961; Dorrell and Adams, 1969; Dickson, 1975; Dickson and Boettger, 1976). The low vigor of damaged seeds is further reflected in their field emergence. Reduced field emergence was observed in soybeans with increased severity of laboratory-induced damage (Mason *et al.*, 1982), and selection of seeds showing differing degrees of damage from a seed lot of groundnuts showed a decline in field emergence with increasing seed coat damage (Gibson and Clinton, 1953). Furthermore, differences in the field emergence of seed lots of soybean (Green *et al.*, 1966; Luedders and Burris, 1979; Oliveira *et al.*, 1983) and pea (Powell and Matthews, 1980a) have been attributed to the extent of visible seed coat damage to seeds within the lot. In both species, the low vigor of lots with damaged seed coats was also reflected in high levels of solute leakage (Powell and Matthews, 1979; Oliveira *et al.*, 1983). This high leakage was attributed to a large proportion of dead tissue on the cotyledons that resulted from imbibition damage due to the cracks in the seed coat allowing rapid water uptake into the seed (Powell and Matthews, 1979; Oliveira *et al.*, 1983). The association of low vigor in pea seeds with seed coat damage was confirmed by Biddle (1980) in a survey of 122 commercial pea seed lots available in the United Kingdom.

In addition to these immediate effects on seed germination and vigor, mechanical damage has been found to reduce the longevity of *Phaseolus* beans (Toole and Toole, 1960), soybeans (Mamicpic and Caldwell, 1963), and groundnuts (Baskin and Delouche, 1971).

B. SOURCES OF MECHANICAL DAMAGE

There are three processes during which the handling of grain legumes has been shown to result in mechanical damage to the seed: the harvesting and processing stages of seed production and sowing. Although a large proportion of the world's grain legumes is not harvested mechanically, most attention to the effects of aspects of seed production on seed quality has been directed toward examining the effects of mechanical processes. This is clearly reflected in the literature.

During harvest, the main aim is to separate the seed from the parent plant or fruit, that is, the process of threshing, in which the basic equipment involved uses one or more cylinders rotating in relation to a fixed bar. The dried plants and fruits are disrupted to release the seeds, which fall through a screen and are collected. The threshing necessary to achieve efficient separation can cause mechanical damage. Harter (1930) noted that baldheads produced from machine-threshed *Phaseolus* beans did not occur in hand-threshed seeds and concluded that damage was caused by beans being violently struck by the teeth of the threshing cylinder or being thrown against the teeth of the concave during threshing. Reduced germination of *Phaseolus* beans has been reported following threshing (Toole *et al.*, 1951; Clark and Kline, 1965), with, in some years, the loss of germination being as high as 20% (Toole *et al.*, 1951). Internal injuries have also been reported in lima beans after machine threshing (Borthwick, 1932), which were absent or less frequent in hand-threshed seed. The observation that such injuries could be induced in hand-threshed seed by a mechanical shock prior to germination (Borthwick, 1932) supported the suggestion that threshing caused these injuries. Hand harvesting and threshing of soybean produced fewer splits (Green *et al.*, 1966) and higher germinations (Green *et al.*, 1966; Prakobboon, 1982) than did machine harvesting and threshing, and the reduced emergence of groundnut after machine decortication compared to hand shelling suggested that some mechanical injury had occurred (Fowler, 1975). In peas, higher leachate conductivities and poor vital staining were found in combined seed compared to hand-shelled seed (Biddle, 1981).

One of the aims of the seed-processing plant in seed production is to eliminate severely damaged seeds that are worthless for sowing. This process can, however, also produce damage, although less severe, when seeds fall into metal bins and come into contact either with metal surfaces or with other seeds. Bainer and Borthwick (1934) illustrated the occurrence of such damage in lima beans, in which impacts of low intensity produced internal damage and more severe impacts produced visible damage; in *Phaseolus* beans damage was shown to result from small falls, with the effect of a number of falls being cumulative (Anonymous, 1941). Mechanical damage arising from handling has been suggested as the cause of lower levels of germination than expected when seed lots of *Phaseolus* beans with high and low germinations were blended to produce a composite lot (Anonymous, 1941). Work simulating the falls that might occur during the processing of seed peas has shown an increase in the incidence of cracks in the seed coat during handling (Matthews *et al.*, 1980). Cracks in the seed coat were associated with increased leakage, that is, reduced vigor, which resulted from imbibition damage. The increased incidence of imbibition damage in field beans and *Phaseolus* beans after simulated processing treatments (Powell and Matthews, 1980b) also suggested that seed coat injury had occurred.

Although most attention has been given to the role of seed production in determining the extent of mechanical damage to seeds, damage can also occur during sowing. Hulbert and Whitney (1934) found up to 10% injury to peas during sowing, which could be minimized by mixing the seeds with graphite. Seed injury during sowing was also seen in *Phaseolus* beans (Dexter, 1966), and Wijandi and Copeland (1974) found a reduction in germination after *Phaseolus* seeds had passed through a planter.

C. FACTORS AFFECTING SUSCEPTIBILITY TO MECHANICAL DAMAGE

1. *Seed moisture content and severity of handling*

Seed moisture content and the severity of handling are the factors most commonly recognized as influencing susceptibility to mechanical damage. Two approaches have been followed in research on factors affecting mechanical damage: either examining the incidence of damage in field-harvested seeds or preconditioning seeds to different moisture contents in the laboratory before imposing handling treatments.

A limited amount of work has considered the effect of moisture content alone on the incidence of mechanical damage. *Phaseolus* bean seeds showed the greatest degree of laboratory-induced damage when handled at low moisture contents (Barriga, 1961; Duczmal, 1981), and when visible damage did not occur, the reduced vigor of normal seedlings indicated internal damage (Barriga, 1961). As the seed moisture content increased, damage due to handling decreased (Barriga, 1961; Duczmal, 1981). Biddle (1980) reported that the least seed coat damage occurred when peas were harvested at 30–40% mc, with an increase in damage at lower harvest moisture contents (18–19%). The importance of pea seed moisture content was illustrated further in a laboratory study (Matthews *et al.*, 1980) in which seeds were dropped from a height to cause damage. Seeds dropped 10 times at 6.1% mc included 27% with cracked testae, whereas no damage was visible after dropping at 24.0% mc. Fields and King (1963) found, however, that if the moisture content at harvest is too high, there is more damage, and they observed a reduction in the proportion of peas with damaged seed coats as harvest moisture fell from 43 to 24%.

Most work has, however, concentrated on the interaction between seed moisture content and severity of handling, which in field studies is mainly determined by the thresher cylinder speed. It is, however, more specifically the peripheral speed of the cylinder rather than the revolutions per minute that should be considered (Anonymous, 1941).

The incidence of mechanical damage in the form of either or both internal and external damage has been found to increase as seed moisture content is decreased and cylinder speed is increased in *Phaseolus* bean (Anonymous, 1941; Pickett, 1973; Singh and Linvill, 1977), soybean (Green *et al.*, 1966), and lima bean (Bainer and Borthwick, 1934). In soybean, increased damage was associated with the reduced moisture content arising from delayed harvest, and as cylinder speed increased, the percentage of seeds with cracked seed coats (averaged for all moisture contents) increased from only 2–8% in hand-harvested seed to 4–32% at 500 rpm and 17–49% at 900 rpm. An additional factor influencing the response of *Phaseolus* bean to threshing was the feed rate of the thresher (Pickett, 1973), with most damage occurring with a light feed rate of 91 lb of material other than grain (MOG) per minute compared to heavy (166 lb MOG min^{-1}) or ordinary threshing (100 lb MOG min^{-1}), particularly at high cylinder speeds. Operating the thresher at less than full capacity also increased the incidence of damage to soybean caused by the conveyor mechanism, where more damage again occurred at low moisture contents (13%; Hall, 1974).

The same interaction between moisture content and severity of handling has been shown using laboratory treatments to induce damage. Bainer and Borthwick (1934) dropped lima beans from different heights to produce velocities at impact equivalent to different thresher cylinder speeds and found that at any speed damage increased as seed moisture decreased, with a further increase in damage as cylinder speed increased. They also noted that while visible damage was greater at low moisture contents, internal invisible injury occurred at high moisture contents that could easily be overlooked.

Use of a centrifugal impactor to handle soybeans (Paulsen *et al.*, 1979) produced an increase in the percentage of splits as impactor speed increased and seed moisture content decreased. All seeds from the impactor showed less severe seed coat cracks (Paulsen *et al.*, 1979), but the cracks did not increase in number as impactor speed increased. In mung bean more damage was seen in seeds following several passes through a paddle thresher, especially at lower seed moisture contents (Herath *et al.*, 1981). *Phaseolus* beans at 8 and 10% moisture content were damaged after a number of drops of only 1 ft (Anonymous, 1941), whereas at a higher moisture content (12%) seeds could be dropped 17 times without injury.

Limited, and conflicting, reports suggest that seed moisture content can also influence planter injury during sowing of *Phaseolus* beans. Dexter (1966) reported that raising seed moisture content reduced injury, resulting in an improvement in emergence from 39 to 75% when seed moisture content was raised from 11 to 16%. In contrast, increased injury was found by Wijandi and Copeland (1974) when seeds were sown at 18% mc compared to lower moisture contents of 8.5 and 14%.

2. *Seed anatomical and morphological characteristics*

The susceptibility of grain legumes, and in particular *Phaseolus* beans, to mechanical damage sufficient to cause a decrease in germination and in vigor prompted investigations to try to explain susceptibility to damage. In this work, several anatomical and morphological characteristics were associated with susceptibility to mechanical damage.

In both lima bean (Kannenberg and Allard, 1964) and soybean (Agrawal and Menon, 1974), cultivars resistant to seed coat cracking were found to have thick seed coats, and in *Phaseolus* beans, Korban *et al.* (1982) emphasized that the uniformity of thickness of the testa was also important. Thus, seed lines with uniformly thick seed coats had the best resistance to cracking; cultivars with thick, but nonuniform, coats were susceptible. In contrast, despite their observation of significant cultivar differences in seed coat thickness in soybean, Caviness and Simpson (1974) found that these did not reflect differences in the extent of mechanical damage to the cultivars.

Seed lines of both lima beans (*Phaseolus lunatus*) (Kannenberg and Allard, 1964) and *P. vulgaris* (Dickson, 1975) with white seed coats have been found to be more susceptible to seed coat injury than are those with colored seed coats. As a result, comparisons of white and colored seed coats have been used to try to explain differences in susceptibility to damage. Kannenberg and Allard (1964) noted that not only were the seed coats of white-seeded lima beans thinner because the individual layers of cells were thinner, but also that the greater width of the cells meant that there were fewer cells per unit area of seed coat than in colored lines. In contrast, seeds of *P. vulgaris* with a significantly thinner parenchymatous layer of the seed coat were tolerant of seed coat cracking (Dorrell and Adams, 1969). The close adherence of this parenchymatous layer to the cotyledons of *P. vulgaris* seeds (Dorrell and Adams, 1969) has been associated with the resistance to mechanical damage of certain lines (Atkin, 1958; Dickson, 1975). In our own work on *P. vulgaris,* we have observed that the adhesion of the seed coat to the cotyledons makes it difficult to remove the seed coat from the tolerant colored cultivars, whereas it is easily chipped off in white-seeded lines.

In addition to these anatomical differences found between white and colored seed coats, the strength of the seed coat may be influenced by the lignin content, which is less in white than in colored lines of lima beans (Kannenberg and Allard, 1964) and in susceptible soybean cultivars (Agrawal and Menon, 1974). The lignin content of white seed coats of lima bean was only 1.1% of the total seed coat weight, compared to 15.1% in colored lines (Kannenberg and Allard, 1964).

Other seed characteristics that have been associated with susceptibility to mechanical damage are seed weight, density, size, and shape. Cracking of the seed coat and splitting of the cotyledons of *Phaseolus* beans decreased as seed weight increased, although cracking increased as seed density increased and the shape became more irregular (Dorrell and Adams, 1969). In contrast, regularly shaped, round-seeded peas were found to be more susceptible to drill injury than were irregularly shaped, wrinkle-seeded cultivars (Hulbert and Whitney, 1934). Furthermore, seed size was an important factor in round-seeded cultivars, with large seeds showing twice as much damage as small seeds (Hulbert and Whitney, 1934). Large seeds of soybean were also found to be more susceptible to damage induced by a centrifugal impactor (Paulsen *et al.*, 1979).

VII. Testing for Seed Quality

Methods for testing seed germination, purity, and health are well established and are included in the International Rules for Seed Testing (Anonymous, 1976a,b). Vigor tests are less well established in seed testing, although a handbook giving details of a number of standard methods has been published by the International Seed Testing Association (Perry, 1981).

A. Germination Tests

Germination tests (Anonymous, 1976a,b) aim to optimize the conditions for germination and growth so that the maximum number of seeds capable of germinating do so. The sample of seed, usually 400, is set to germinate either on absorbent paper or in moist sand under optimum conditions of temperature and light for the species. After a period of time, specified for each species (Anonymous, 1976b), the number of seeds producing normal seedlings is counted. Seeds producing abnormal seedlings that do not show the capacity for continued development into normal plants when sown in soil are excluded from the germination percentage. Three types of abnormal seedlings are recognized, namely, damaged, deformed, and decayed (Anonymous, 1976a,b).

B. ANALYTICAL PURITY

Tests of analytical purity (Anonymous, 1976a,b) involve separating impurities from pure seed. Impurities include weed and crop seeds of other species and inert matter such as broken seeds, chaff, pieces of leaf, and soil particles. When separation is complete, the pure seed is weighed and expressed as the percentage by weight of the whole sample. The susceptibility of grain legumes to mechanical injury, resulting in broken and cracked seed, adds to the problem of separating pure seed from inert matter. All pieces of grain legume seeds that are more than half their original size are considered as pure seed, although seeds with the seed coat entirely removed are classed as inert matter (Anonymous, 1976b).

The expression of analytical purity as a percentage by weight is sometimes not sufficiently precise. The percentage contamination by other seeds, expressed to the nearest 0.1%, can represent a wide range of seed numbers, from hundreds for small seeds to two or three for those of a size similar to the pure seed. Furthermore, the sample size is small in comparison to the quantity of seed used per hectare, and foreign seeds not present in the test sample may contaminate the field. To avoid contamination, a larger sample is examined, and the number of seeds of other species is counted and expressed as the number of seed per weight of seed examined.

C. HEALTH TESTS

Seed health tests may be carried out to fulfill one of a number of objectives: (1) to test for infection during a period of quarantine, (2) to determine the advisability of fungicide treatment, (3) to test for storage quality for seed or for subsequent use in feeds, (4) to eliminate the pathogens in seed certification schemes, or (5) to evaluate the planting value of seeds.

Health tests to evaluate seed planting value are partially comparable with the germination test: both aim to forecast potential field emergence and, to some extent, the health of the crop. Different test methods are needed to detect different diseases, but there are four simple, rapid tests that are widely used (Anonymous 1976b).

1. Direct examination of the seed, either unaided or at low magnification: fungi producing dark-colored sclerotia are detected this way, and discoloration caused by fungal and bacterial diseases is observed.
2. Microscopic examination of organisms removed by washing: the seed sample is immersed in water and shaken vigorously to remove spores, hyphae, etc. Excess liquid is removed by filtration, centrifugation, or evaporation, and the extracted material is examined microscopically.
3. Blotter test: seeds are set out on moist blotters as in the germination test and are maintained at high relative humidity at 20–30°C, which is a favorable condition for the pathogen. The pathogen is recognized by seedling symptoms or fungal growth.
4. Agar method: applicable to seed in which saprophytic species do not obstruct the identification of the pathogen. Seeds are surface sterilized using dilute hypochlorite and are plated out onto sterile nutrient agar jelly in a petri dish. The fungus grows out of the seed onto the agar and is identified by the color and form of growth.

For some diseases, however, there is no rapid test, and seeds have to be sown in unfavorable growth conditions in the glasshouse to await the development of symptoms. Bacterial diseases can also be identified by several bacteriological methods using phage or serological techniques. The types of test used for some pathogens of grain legumes are shown in Table VIII.

Seed health tests have not been adopted for legal and commercial purposes because the correlation between laboratory tests and field emergence depends on the testing procedure and the transmission and rate of increase of the pathogen (Neergaard, 1977).

D. VIGOR TESTS

In recent years the development of so-called seed vigor tests has been the aim of much work in which attempts have been made to relate laboratory measures of performance to the field emergence and storage potential of seeds. Seed vigor testing is not a legal requirement, but is often carried out by seed testing stations and seed companies to describe the quality of seed in a more discerning manner than is possible with the germination test alone. The additional information is then

TABLE VIII. Health test methods for seed-borne pathogens/diseases of grain legumes[a]

Category of seed-borne pathogen/disease	Health test procedure
Diaporthe phaseolorum	Agar
Mycosphaerella pinodes	Blotter, agar
Sclerotinia sclerotiorum	Blotter, agar
Alternaria tenuis	Blotter, agar
Ascochyta pisi	Blotter, agar
Ascochyta rabiei	Blotter, agar
Colletotrichum lindemuthianum	Blotter, agar
Fusarium spp.	Blotter, agar, seedling symptoms
Pseudomonas glycinea, Pseudomonas phaseolicola	Grow on beyond seedling to development of symptoms
Hollow heart	Blotter
Marsh spot	Blotter

[a]From Neergaard (1977).

used to aid decisions on the suitability of seeds for either early sowing or retention in stores for later seasons. There are two types of vigor test: direct and indirect. Direct tests aim to provide the adverse conditions that seeds may encounter in the field and to measure the seeds' response. Indirect tests measure aspects of physiological activity such as membrane permeability, enzyme activity, and respiration rate. Five of the vigor tests included in the International Seed Testing Association's Vigour Test Handbook (Perry, 1981) are applied to grain legumes. Two of these, the cold test and the Hiltner test, are direct tests, whereas the conductivity, accelerated aging, and tetrazolium tests are indirect.

The cold test (Fiala, 1981) subjects seeds to two adverse factors, a low temperature and soil-borne pathogens. Seeds are sown into a layer of soil adjusted to 40% water-holding capacity, which is laid on two water-soaked strips of filter paper. The papers are then rolled up loosely and held upright in a plastic container at 10°C and 95% rh for 7 days in the dark followed by 25°C with moderate lighting for 6 days. The seedlings are then evaluated. The original cold test carried out in trays or boxes filled with soil is still used frequently in the United States, particularly for soybean, and was described in detail by Woodstock (1976).

In the Hiltner test (Fuchs, 1981), seeds are sown into tightly packed, moistened "brick grit" and held in the dark at around 20°C for 10–14 days. Seedlings are then evaluated as normal and abnormal

(Anonymous, 1976a,b), and all normal seedlings are reported as the percentage vigor or percentage brick grit value. The test has been applied to large-grain legumes (Heydecker, 1969; Sivasubramanian and Ramakrishnan, 1974) and is described in the technical literature of the American Association of Official Seed Analysts (Woodstock, 1976).

The conductivity test was originally developed for vining pea seeds and is based on the association between the levels of solutes leached from different seed lots and their emergence in the field (Matthews and Whitbread, 1968). This was later developed into a routine test for the prediction of field emergence by Matthews and Bradnock (1967). The standardized method (Matthews and Powell, 1981) involves soaking 50 weighed seeds in 250 ml deionized water at 20°C for 24 hr, when the electrolyte leaching into soak water is measured with an electrical conductivity meter. Seed lots with high leachate conductivities have poor field emergence, that is, they are low-vigor lots, whereas high-vigor lots have low conductivities and emerge well (Fig. 2; Matthews and Whitbread, 1968). This relationship has been confirmed a number of times (Bradnock and Matthews, 1970; Perry, 1970; Perry and Harrison, 1970; Carver and Matthews, 1975; Scott and Close, 1976) and has led to a series of advisory recommendations regarding suitability of seed lots for sowing (Bedford, 1974).

The conductivity test has also been used as an indicator of field emergence in field beans (*V. faba*) (Fig. 2; Hegarty, 1977) and *Phaseolus* beans (Matthews and Bradnock, 1968, and Fig. 2). More recently, in soybeans, correlations of 0.67 (Yaklich *et al.,* 1979) and 0.89 and 0.92 (Fig. 2; Oliveira *et al.,* 1984) have been reported between the leachate conductivity of seed lots and field emergence. Yaklich *et al.* (1979) excluded all seeds with damaged seed coats from the conductivity test, which Tao (1978) had recommended in order to improve the repeatability of the test. In our own work (Oliveira *et al.,* 1984) a particular point was made of including all seeds whatever the condition of the seed coat. The use of all seeds probably explained the improved correlations obtained, since damaged seeds were shown to have high levels of leaching (Oliveira *et al.,* 1984). This difference in method was significant, not only because all seeds likely to be sown were used, but also because exclusion of seeds with damaged seed coats could eliminate from the test a major cause of low vigor, namely, imbibition damage (Oliveira *et al.,* 1984; see Section III,B).

The accelerated aging test was initially developed to predict the relative storage potential of seed lots of a number of crop species including soybean and *Phaseolus* bean (Delouche and Baskin, 1973), but has also been shown to predict the field emergence of soybean (Delouche, 1973)

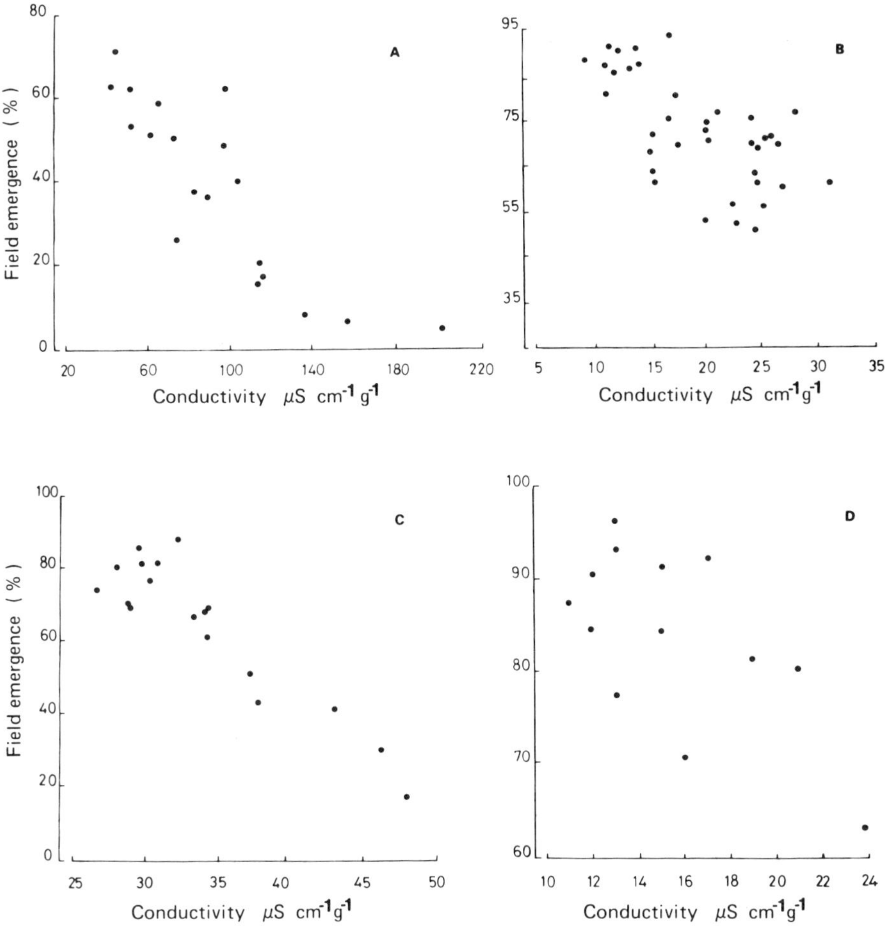

FIG. 2. The relationship between seed leachate conductivity and the field emergence of (A) peas ($r = -0.85$, $p \leq 0.001$), (B) *Phaseolus* beans (dwarf French beans; $r = -0.66$, $p \leq 0.001$), (C) soybeans ($r = -0.92$, $p \leq 0.001$), and (D) *Vicia faba* (field beans; $r = -0.67$, $p \leq 0.01$). [(A) From Matthews and Bradnock, 1968; (B) A. A. Powell and S. Matthews, unpublished data; (C) from Oliveira *et al.*, 1983; (D) redrawn from Hegarty, 1977, to include only lots with laboratory germinations >85%.]

and groundnut (Baskin, 1970). In the standardized method (Baskin, 1981), seed samples are held in individual accelerated aging chambers at high relative humidity and temperature. Under these storage conditions the rate of seed aging is accelerated (Section V). The germination of aged seeds is evaluated, and those seeds that produce normal seedlings (Anonymous, 1976a,b) are considered to be vigorous. Seed lots with a low germination count after aging are said to be low in vigor, emerge poorly in the field (Delouche, 1973), and lose viability rapidly in store (Delouche and Baskin, 1973). Seed lots that maintain a high germination after aging, that is, high-vigor lots, emerge well (Delouche, 1973) and retain viability longer in store (Delouche and Baskin, 1973). In effect, the test measures the relative position of the seed lots in Phase A of the survival curve (Fig. 1).

Different temperatures and times of aging have been suggested for different species. Baskin (1981) uses 100% rh at 40°C to age soybean for 72 hr, whereas McDonald and Phaneendranath (1978) recommended 48 hr at 41°C, and the combination of 72 hr at 42°C gave the best prediction of the storage potential of *Phaseolus* beans (Delouche and Baskin, 1973).

Accelerated aging has also been used to predict the relative vigor levels of seed lots of peas during prolonged storage in a commercial warehouse (Powell and Matthews, 1978b). In this case leachate conductivity of seeds after accelerated aging for 24 hr in 94% rh at 45°C was positively correlated with conductivity, and therefore vigor, after 1 year of storage.

Vital staining with 2,3,5-triphenyltetrazolium chloride is widely used in seed testing to predict seed viability by assessing the extent of staining on the embryo axes (Anonymous, 1976a,b). Moore (1973) has, however, described the use of tetrazolium staining of both the cotyledons and the embryo axis to evaluate vigor as well as viability. Both the color intensity and the staining pattern are considered, but according to Moore (1973) correct evaluation includes an appraisal of the presence, location, and nature of normal, weak, dead, and fractured tissues. Experienced seed testers can recognize from tetrazolium staining evidence of mechanical injury, damage from alternate hydration and dehydration during preharvest deterioration (Moore, 1965), preharvest freezing injury (Moore, 1967), heat damage and evidence of microorganism activity (Moore, 1973), and aging (Moore, 1968). The routine application of this test to grain legumes has been described for soybeans (Woodstock, 1976) and peas (Heydecker, 1969).

There has been some interest in both peas and soybeans in producing multiple indices of seed vigor. These consist of a composite evaluation of vigor drawn from the results of several different tests. Scott and Close (1976) reported a predictive equation including the laboratory germination percentage, hollow heart, and conductivity measurements to indicate pea seed vigor. This equation gave a better indication of field emergence than did laboratory germination alone.

Abdul Baki and Anderson (1973) suggested a multiple criterion measure of vigor in soybean. They calculated the correlation coefficient between a vigor index (the product of percentage normal germination and hypocotyl length in millimeters after 5 days at 25°C) and various biochemical tests on embryonic axes. They found good negative correlations between the vigor index and leaching of radioactive metabolite after feeding with [^{14}C]glucose or [^{14}C]leucine and a positive correlation with uptake of [^{14}C]leucine (Abdul Baki and Anderson, 1973). They did not, however, relate their results to field emergence. Three possible multiple criterion indices were proposed for soybean by Tekrony and Egli (1977). These were made up of combinations of the 4- and 7-day counts of germination from the laboratory germination test and germination after accelerated aging. The best index of field emergence taken over 3 years was one that combined the result of all three tests. However, even this index did not predict field emergence accurately and was very unsatisfactory in 1 year. Overall, the multiple criterion approach offered little improvement over the standard germination test (Tekrony and Egli, 1977).

VIII. Concluding Remarks

There are problems of seed quality leading to unreliable crop establishment in most grain legumes, as has been discussed. The causes of poor seed quality are both numerous and diverse, but even so there are several that are common to a number of species (Table IX). The many reports on variability of seed quality in grain legumes in different countries encompass events that reduce seed quality at several points on the way to emergence, including seed production, storage, and even after sowing (Fig. 3). There are, however, two basic physiological processes, aging and imbibition, that can often explain how particular instances of poor seed quality can occur, resulting in poor establishment through either reduced germination or vigor.

In countries with an established seed distribution organization, seed lots with less than the statutory minimum germination, which in grain legumes is around 80% (Section II,A), should never reach the grower. Even so, there are many reports of variable field establishment among highly germinable seed lots (Section II,B) due to differences in what has come to be termed seed vigor.

An important determinant of the vigor of a seed lot is its position on the initial slow decline of the viability curve (Phase A, Fig. 1), that is, the extent to which aging processes have already taken place. The

TABLE IX. Causes of reduced seed quality observed in different species of grain legumes

Cause of reduced quality	Soybean	Groundnut	*Phaseolus* bean	Pea	Pigeon Pea	Lima bean	*Vicia faba*	Mung bean	Black gram	Cowpea
Preharvest deterioration	+	+	+	+		+				
Infection by field fungi	+	+	+	+	+			+	+	+
Mechanical damage	+	+	+	+		+		+		
Deterioration in store	+	+	+	+			+		+	
Storage fungi	+	+	+	+						+
Storage insects		+	+	+						+
Imbibition damage	+		+	+			+			
Transverse cracking	+		+	+						

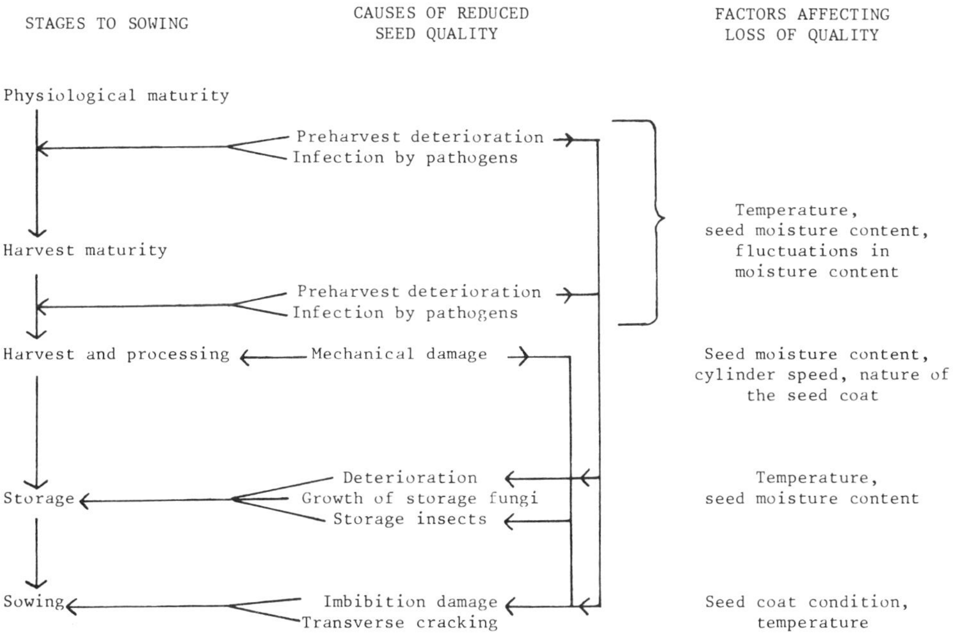

FIG. 3. Causes of reduced seed quality and their interaction.

position of the seed lot in the aging process (as expressed in Fig. 1) influences the establishment of many crop species (Matthews, 1980). This is, however, a particular problem in grain legumes because, we would suggest, of the combination of the physiological changes taking place during aging in Phase A (Fig. 1) and the structure of the grain legume seed, which consists of two large, living cotyledons and an embryo axis surrounded by a seed coat. The physiological changes during Phase A can be divided into three stages. First, increased leakage occurs from living cells of the cotyledons, possibly due to membrane damage (Section III,A), and is indicative of reduced vigor (Section VII). This is followed by the death of cells of the cotyledons, leading to the production of dead tissue, which further increases leakage. Third, death of parts of the embryo leads to the production of abnormal seedlings. At this point seeds have reached the end of Phase A, and further aging results in the loss of the ability to germinate and the seed lot enters the rapid decline in viability of Phase B (Fig. 1). Thus, the sequence of changes in the cotyledons during Phase A leads to a gradual decline in vigor before loss of viability. This contrasts with other species in which death of even a small proportion of normally living tissue within the seed would push the seed a long way through Phase A. The structure of grain legume seeds is such that Phase A is attenuated in comparison with other species, there being a relatively large amount of normally living tissue that can deteriorate and die before the ability to germinate is lost. Thus, the problem of vigor differences among seed lots of high and acceptable germination levels is especially common among grain legumes.

The decline in seed quality resulting from pathological causes (Section IV) is closely related to aging during storage (Section V). The rate of aging is determined by temperature and seed moisture content (Section V), both at preharvest (Section V,A) and during postharvest storage (Section V,B). These conditions are also associated with the increased incidence of infection by field fungi before harvest (Section V,A). It is possible that damage resulting from the alternate hydration and dehydration in these conditions increases the predisposition of the seeds to infection by field fungi. During postharvest storage, fungi become active at relative humidities above 70%, at which (Section III,A) seed moistures rise above 12–14%. Their adverse effect is thought to result from the enhancement of the aging process (Section V,B).

Clearly, a better understanding of the physiological and biochemical changes during aging, particularly those affecting the integrity of membranes, may point toward ways in which seed quality could be improved by controlling the aging process. Inconsistencies in the information presently available on aging (Section III,A) have led to the recognition of the limitations of the work so far, and in particular to the problems of relating the changes taking place during induced aging to those that may occur in natural aging. In the future, work giving more attention to natural aging might yield information having direct application to the control of aging and to the improvement of seed quality.

Events during the physiological process of imbibition, even in the first few minutes of the process, can have a crucial effect on vigor and, consequently, emergence. There are two ways in which imbibition influences vigor: through imbibition damage (Section III,B) and transverse cracking (Section VI,A). Imbibition damage results from the rapid uptake of water into cotyledons, causing cell death, possibly due to the disorganization or disruption of cell membranes. Imbibition damage is a major cause of low vigor where mechanical damage to the seed coat has occurred during harvest and/or processing (Section VI,B). Seed lots with a high proportion of seeds with damaged seed coats imbibe rapidly and have the high leakage and poor field emergence associated with low-vigor seeds. Thus, avoidance of mechanical damage to the seed coat has an impact on seed quality and not just on the appearance of the seed.

Rapid imbibition has also been associated with the incidence of transverse cracking (Section VI,A), which results in the production of abnormal seedlings. These cracks may occur along lines of stress produced during preharvest deterioration.

Both aging and imbibition damage have been associated with damage to cell membranes. Impaired membrane integrity may therefore explain the increased leakage of solutes from the seeds in both cases. Thus, the conductivity test (Section VII), in measuring the levels of solute leakage, is indicative of seed lot vigor whatever its cause. As a result, measurement of the leakage of electrolytes has emerged as a most useful test of vigor for several grain legumes (Section VII; Fig. 2) and may well be extended to other crops within the group. The incidence of imbibition damage is greater in aged seeds, in which the membranes are thought to be weakened and therefore more sensitive to physical disruption by rapid water uptake. Thus the ultimate determinant of seed quality may lie in the condition and resilience of cellular membranes.

REFERENCES

Abdalla, F. H., and Roberts, E. H. (1968). Effects of temperature, moisture and oxygen on the induction of chromosome damage in seeds of barley, broad beans and peas during storage. *Ann. Bot. (London)* [N. S.] **32,** 119–136.

Abdalla, F. H., and Roberts, E. H. (1969). The effects of temperature and moisture on the induction of genetic changes in seeds of barley, broad beans and peas during storage. Ann. Bot. (London) [N. S.] **33,** 153–167.

Abdul Baki, A. A. (1971). Biochemical differences between embryonic axes from green and sun-bleached lima bean seeds: Synthesis of carbohydrates, proteins and lipids. *J. Am. Soc. Hortic. Sci.* **96,** 266–270.

Abdul Baki, A. A., and Anderson, J. D. (1972). Physiological and biochemical deterioration. *In* "Seed Biology" (T. T. Kozlowski, ed.), Vol. 2, pp. 283–315. Academic Press, New York.

Abdul Baki, A. A., and Anderson, J. D. (1973). Vigor determination in soybean seed by multiple criteria. *Agron. J.* **71,** 755–759.

Abdul Baki, A. A., and Chandra, G. R. (1977). Effect of rapid ageing on nucleic acid and protein synthesis by soybean embryonic axes during germination. *Seed Sci. Technol.* **5,** 689–698.

Abu-Shakra, S. S., and Ching, T. M. (1967). Mitochondrial activity in germinating new and old soybean seeds. *Crop Sci.* **7,** 115–118.

Adebona, A. C., and Odu, A. (1972). On some effects of prolonged seed soaking on the germination of cowpea seeds. *Phyton (Buenos Aires)* **30,** 59–62.

Agrawal, P. K., and Kaur, S. (1975). Maintenance of germinability of soybean seeds from harvest to next planting under ambient conditions in Delhi. *Seed Res.* **3,** 81-85.

Agrawal, P. K., and Menon, S. K. (1974). Lignin content and seedcoat thickness in relation to seedcoat cracking in soybean. *Seed Res.* **2,** 64-66.

Agrawal, P. K., and Singh, J. N. (1975) Laboratory germination and field emergence in soybean *Glycine max. Seed Res.* **3,** 111-112.

Amable, R. (1976). The effects of harvest date and storage conditions on soybean seed quality. *In* "Grain Legumes" (E. V. Doku, ed.), pp. 109-118. Counc. Sci. Ind. Res., University of Ghana.

Anderson, J. D. (1977). Adenylate metabolism of embryonic axes from deteriorated soybean seeds. *Plant Physiol.* **59,** 610-614.

Andrews, C. H. (1966). Some aspects of pod and seed development in Lee soybeans. Ph.D. Thesis, Mississippi State University, State College (as cited by Tekrony *et al.,* 1980a).

Anonymous (1941). "A Study of Mechanical Injury to Seed Beans," Asgrow Monogr. No. 1., Assoc. Seed Growers Inc.

Anonymous (1976a). International Rules for Seed Testing. Rules 1976. *Seed Sci. Technol.* **4,** 3-49.

Anonymous (1976b). International Rules for Seed Testing. Annexes 1976. *Seed Sci. Technol.* **4,** 51-177.

Athow, K. L., and Caldwell, R. M. (1956). The influence of seed treatment and planting rate on the emergence and yield of soybeans. *Phytopathology* **46,** 91-95.

Athow, K. L., and Laviolette, F. A. (1973). Pod protection effects on soybean seed germination and infection with *Diaporthe phaseolorum* var. *sojae* and other microorganisms. *Phytopathology* **63,** 1021-1023.

Atkin, J. D. (1958). Relative susceptibility of snap bean varieties to mechanical injury of seed. *Am. Soc. Hortic. Sci.* **72,** 370-373.

Aykroyd, W. R., and Doughty, J. C. (1964). "Legumes in Human Nutrition." Food and Agriculture Organization, Rome.

Bain, J. M., and Mercer, F. V. (1963). Subcellular organisation of the developing cotyledons of *Pisum sativum* L. *Aust. J. Biol. Sci.* **19,** 49-67.

Bainer, R., and Borthwick, H. A. (1934). Thresher and other mechanical injury to seed beans of the lima type. *Bull.—Calif. Agric. Exp. Stn.* **580,** 3-30.

Barriga, C. (1961). Effects of mechanical abuse of navy bean seed at various moisture levels. *Agron. J.* **53,** 250.

Baskin, C. C. (1970). Relation of certain physiological properties of peanut seed to field performance and storability. Ph.D. Dissertation, Mississippi State University, State College.

Baskin, C. C. (1981). Accelerated ageing test. *In* "Handbook of Vigour Test Methods" (D. A. Perry, ed.), pp. 43-48. International Seed Testing Association, Zurich.

Baskin, C. C., and Delouche, J. C. (1971). Effects of mechanical shelling on storability of peanut (*Arachis hypogaea*) seed. *Proc. Assoc. Off. Seed Anal.* **61,** 78-84.

Bass, L. N., James, E., and Clark, D. C. (1970). Storage response of green and bleached lima beans (*Phaseolus lunatus*). *Hort. Science* **5,** 170-171.

Bedford, L. V. (1974). Conductivity tests in commercial and hand harvested seed of pea cultivars and their relation to field establihsment. *Seed Sci. Technol.* **2,** 323-335.

Bedford, L. V., and Matthews, S. (1975). The effect of seed age at harvest on the germinability and quality of heat dried seed peas. *Seed Sci. Technol.* **4,** 275-286.

Bewley, J. D., and Black, M. (1982). "Physiology and Biochemistry of Seeds," Vol. 2. Springer-Verlag, Berlin and New York.

Biddle, A. J. (1980). Production factors affecting vining pea seed quality. *In* "Seed Production" (P. Hebblethwaite, ed.), pp. 527–534. Butterworth, London.
Biddle, A. J. (1981). Harvesting damage in pea and its influence on vigour. *Acta Hortic.* **111,** 243–247.
Bils, R. F., and Howell, R. W. (1963). Biochemical and cytological changes in developing soybean cotyledons. *Crop Sci.* **3,** 304–308.
Boakye-Boateng, K. B., and Hume, D. J. (1975). Effects of storage conditions on germination of soybean (*Glycine max.* L. Merr.) seed. *Ghana J. Agric. Sci.* **8,** 109–114.
Bolkan, H. A., de Silva, A. R., and Cupertino, F. P. (1976). Fungi associated with soybean and bean seeds and their control in central Brazil. *Plant Dis. Rep.* **60,** 545–548.
Borthwick, H. A. (1932). Thresher injury in baby lima beans. *J. Agric. Res.* **44,** 503–510.
Bos, L., and van der Want, J. P. H. (1962). Early browning of pea, a disease caused by a soil and seed-borne virus. *Tijdschr, Plantenziekten* **68,** 368–390.
Boswell, V. R., Toole, E. H., Toole, V. K., and Fisher, D. F. (1940). A study of rapid deterioration of vegetable seeds and methods for its prevention. *U.S. Dep. Agric., Tech. Bull.* **708.**
Bradnock, W. T., and Matthews, S. (1970). Assessing field emergence potential of wrinkle seeded peas. *Hortic. Res.* **10,** 50–58.
Bray, C. M., and Chow, T.-Y. (1976). Lesions in post-ribosomal supernatant fraction is associated with loss of viability in pea (*Pisum arvense*) seed. *Biochim. Biophys. Acta* **442,** 1–13.
Browne, C. L. (1978). Identification of physiological maturity in sunflowers (*Helianthus annuus*). *Aust. J. Exp. Agric. Anim. Husb.* **18,** 282–286.
Burris, J. (1980). Maintenance of soybean seed quality in storage as influenced by moisture, temperature and genotype. *Iowa State J. Res.* **54,** 377–389.
Burris, J. S., Edje, O. T., and Wahab, A. H. (1969). Evaluation of various indices of seed and seedling vigour in soybean. *Proc. Assoc. Off. Seed Anal.* **59,** 73–81.
Burris, J. S., Wahab, A. H., and Edje, O. T. (1971). Effects of seed age on seedling performance in soybeans. I. Seedling growth and respiration in the dark. *Crop Sci.* **11,** 492–496.
Byrd, H. W., and Delouche, J. C. (1971). Deterioration of soybean seed in storage. *Proc. Assoc. Off. Seed Anal.* **61,** 41–57.
Carlson, J. B. (1973). Morphology. *In* "Soybeans: Improvement, Production and Uses" (B. E. Caldwell, ed.), pp. 17–66. Am. Soc. Agron., Madison, Wisconsin.
Carlson, L. E., and King, T. H. (1963). The effect of environmental factors on the quality of stored pea seed. *Proc. Minn. Acad. Sci.* **30,** 132–135.
Carter, J. B. H. (1973). The influence of the testa, damage and seed dressing on the emergence of groundnut (*Arachis hypogaea*). *Ann. Appl. Biol.* **74,** 315–323.
Carver, M. F. F., and Matthews, S. (1975). Respiratory measurements as indicators of field emergence ability in peas. *Seed Sci. Technol.* **3,** 871–879.
Caviness, C. E., and Simpson, A. M. (1974). Influence of variety and location on seed coat thickness of mature soybean seed. *Proc. Assoc. Off. Seed Anal.* **64,** 102–108.
Chamberlain, D. W., and Gray, L. E. (1974). Germination, seed treatment and micro-organisms in soybean produced in Illinois. *Plant Dis. Rep.* **58,** 50–54.
Christensen, C. M. (1967). Increase in invasion by storage fungi and in fat acidity values of commercial lots of soybeans stored at moisture contents of 13.0–14.0%. *Phytopathology* **57,** 622–624.

Christensen, C. M. (1972). Microflora and seed deterioration. *In* "Viability of Seeds" (E. H. Roberts, ed.), pp. 59-93. Chapman & Hall, London.

Christensen, C. M., and Dorworth, C. E. (1966). Influence of moisture content, temperature and time on invasion of soybeans by storage fungi. *Phytopathology* **56,** 412-418.

Clark, B. E., and Kline, D. B. (1965). Effects of water temperature, seed moisture content, mechanical injury and calcium nitrate solution on the germination of snap bean seeds in laboratory germination tests. *Proc. Assoc. Off. Seed Anal.* **55,** 110-121.

Clinton, P. K. S. (1960). Seed bed pathogens of groundnuts in the Sudan, and an attempt to control with an artificial testa. *Emp. J. Exp. Agric.* **28,** 211-222.

Cottrell, H. J. (1948). Tetrazolium salt as a seed germination indicator. *Ann. Appl. Biol.* **35,** 123-131.

Crosier, W. F. (1941). Split seeds in peas and beans. *Proc. Assoc. Off. Seed Anal.* **33,** 66-69.

Delouche, J. C. (1973). Seed vigour in soybeans. *Proc. Soybean Seed Res. Conf., 3rd, 1973,* pp. 56-72.

Delouche, J. C. (1974). Maintaining soybean seed quality. *In* "Soybean Production, Marketing and Use," Bull. Y-19, pp. 46-61. TVA, Muscle Shoals, Alabama.

Delouche, J. C., and Baskin, C. C. (1973). Accelerated ageing techniques for predicting the relative storability of seed lots. *Seed Sci. Technol.* **1,** 427-452.

Delouche, J. C., Matthes, R. K., Dougherty, G. M., and Boyd, A. A. (1973). Storage of seed in sub-tropical and tropical regions. *Seed Sci. Technol.* **1,** 671-700.

de Tella, R., Lago, A. A., and Zink, E. (1976). Effects of various moisture contents and fungicide treatments on the longevity of groundnut seeds. *Bragantia* **35,** 335-342.

Dexter, S. T. (1966). Conditioning dry bean seed (*Phaseolus vulgaris* L.) for better processing quality and seed germination. *Agron. J.* **58,** 629-631.

Dharmalingam, C., Ramakrishnan, V., and Ramaswamy, K. R. (1976). Viability and vigour of blackgram in India. *Seed Res.* **4,** 40-50.

Dickson, M. H. (1975). Improving bean seed quality. *N. Y. Food Life Sci. Q.* **8,** 9-10.

Dickson, M. H., and Boettger, M. A. (1976). Factors associated with resistance to mechanical damage in snap beans (*Phaseolus bulgaris* L.). *J. Am. Soc. Hortic. Sci.* **101,** 541-544.

Dickson, M. H., Duczmal, K., and Shannon, S. (1973). Imbibition rate and seed composition as factors affecting transverse cotyledon cracking in bean (*Phaseolus vulgaris* L.) seed. *J. Am. Soc. Hortic. Sci.* **98,** 509-513.

Dorrell, D. G., and Adams, M. W. (1969). Effect of some seed characteristics on mechanically induced seed coat damage in navy beans (*Phaseolus vulgaris* L.). *Agron. J.* **61,** 672-673.

Dorworth, C. E., and Christensen, C. M. (1959). Influence of moisture content, temperature and storage time upon changes in fungus flora, germinability and fat acidity values of soybean. *Phytopathology* **58,** 1457-1459.

Duczmal, K. W. (1981). Mechanical injury in seeds. *Acta Hortic.* **111,** 235-242.

Duke, S. H., and Kakefuda, G. (1981). Role of the testa in preventing cellular rupture during imbibition of legume seeds. *Plant Physiol.* **67,** 449-456.

Dunleavy, J. M. (1976). Pathological factors affecting seed germination. *World Soybean Res., Proc. World Soybean Res. Conf., 1975,* pp. 462-469.

Edje, O. T., and Burris, J. S. (1970a). Seed vigour in soybeans. *Proc. Assoc. Off. Seed Anal.* **60,** 149-157.

Edje, O. T., and Burris, J. S. (1970b). Physiological and biochemical changes in deteriorating soybean seeds. *Proc. Assoc. Off. Seed Anal.* **60,** 158–166.

Edwards, C. J., and Hartwig, E. E. (1971). Effect of seed size upon rate of germination in soybeans. *Agron. J.* **63,** 429–430.

Egli, D. B., White, G. M., and Tekrony, D. M. (1978). Relationship between seed vigour and the storability of soybean seed. *J. Seed Technol.* **3,** 1–11.

Ellis, M. A., and Paschal, E. H. (1979). Transfer of technology in seed pathology of tropical legumes. *In* "Seed Pathology—Problems and Progress" (J. T. Yorinori, J. B. Sinclair, Y. R. Menta, and S. K. Mohan, eds.), pp. 190–195. Fundacao Instituto Agronomico do Parana, Londrina, Brazil.

Ellis, M. A., Machado, C. C., Prasartsee, C., and Sinclair, J. B. (1974a). Occurrence of *Diaporthe phaseolorum* var. *sojae (Phomopsis* sp.) in various soybean cultivars. *Plant Dis. Rep.* **58,** 173–176.

Ellis, M. A., Ilyas, M. B., Tenne, F. D., Sinclair, J. B., and Palm, H. L. (1974b). Effect of foliar applications of benomyl on internally seed-borne fungi, and pod and stem blight in soybean. *Plant Dis. Rep.* **58,** 760–763.

Ellis, M. A., Ilyas, M. B. and Sinclair, J. B. (1975). Effect of three fungicides on internally seed-borne fungi and germination of soybean seeds. *Phytopathology* **65,** 553–556.

Ellis, M. A., Galvez, G. E., and Sinclair, J. B. (1976). Effect of foliar applications of systemic fungicides and late harvest on seed quality of dry bean (*Phaseolus vulgaris*). *Plant Dis. Rep.* **60,** 1073–1076.

Ellis, M. A., Tenne, F. D., and Sinclair, J. B. (1977). Effect of antibiotics and high temperature storage on decay of soybean seeds by *Bacillus subtilis. Seed Sci. Technol.* **5,** 753–761.

Ellis, R. H., and Roberts, E. H. (1980). Improved equations for the prediction of seed longevity. *Ann. Bot. (London)* [N. S.] **45,** 13–30.

Ellis, R. H., Osei-Bonsu, K., and Roberts, E. H. (1982). The influence of genotype, temperature and moisture on seed longevity in chickpea, cowpea and soyabean. *Ann. Bot. (London)* [N. S.] **50,** 69–82.

Essenberg, J. F. W., and Schoorel, A. F. (1962). The relation between the results of germination tests in the laboratory and the emergence in the field. *Lit. Overz Cont. Landb. Publ. Landls. Doc., Wageningen* **26.**

Eyster, H. C. (1940). The cause of decreased germination of bean seeds soaked in water. *Am. J. Bot.* **27,** 652–659.

Fiala, F. (1981). Cold test. *In* "Handbook of Vigour Test Methods" (D. A. Perry, ed.), pp. 28–31. International Seed Testing Association, Zurich.

Fields, R. W., and King, T. H. (1962). Influence of storage fungi on deterioration of stored pea seed. *Phytopathology* **52,** 336–339.

Fields, R. W., and King, T. H. (1963). The effects of early harvest and artificial drying on mold deterioration and quality of canning pea seed. *Proc. Minn. Acad. Sci.* **30,** 128–130.

Fontes, L. A. W., and Ohlrogge, A. J. (1972). Influence of seed size and population on yield and other characteristics of soybean (*Glycine max.* L. Merr.). *Agron. J.* **64,** 833–836.

Food and Agriculture Organization. (1982a). "1981 FAO Production Yearbook," Vol. 35. FAO, Rome.

Food and Agriculture Organization. (1982b). "1981 FAO Trade Yearbook," Vol. 35. FAO, Rome.

Foor, S. R., and Sinclair, J. B. (1977). Effects of fungicide sprays on soybean maturity, yield and seed maturity. *Fungic. Nematicide Tests* **32,** 122–123.

Fowler, A. M. (1975). Seed quality and seedling emergence of groundnuts. *Samaru Agric. Newsl.* **17,** 106-110.
Frank, Z. R. (1969). Localisation of seed-borne inocula and combined control of *Aspergillus* and *Rhizopus* rots of groundnut seedlings by seed treatment. *Isr. J. Agric. Res.* **19,** 109-114.
Fuchs, H. (1981). Hiltner test. *In* "Handbook of Vigour Test Methods" (D. A. Perry, ed.), pp. 21-27. International Seed Testing Association, Zurich.
Gane, A. J., and Biddle, A. J. (1973). Hollow heart of pea (*Pisum sativum*). *Ann. Appl. Biol.* **74,** 239-247.
Garren, K. H., and Higgins, B. B. (1947). Fungi associated with runner peanut seeds and their relation to concealed damage. *Phytopathology* **37,** 512-522.
Gavrielit-Gelmond, H. (1970). Moisture content and storage of peanut seed. *Proc. Int. Seed Test. Assoc.* **36,** 159-171.
Gibson, I. A. S., and Clinton, P. K. S. (1953). Pre-emergence seed-bed losses in groundnuts at Urambo Tanganyika territory. *Emp. J. Exp. Agric.* **21,** 226-235.
Grabe, D. F. (1965). Storage of soybean for seed. *Soybean Dig.* **26,** 14-16.
Green, D. E., Pinnell, E. L., Cavannah, L. E., and Williams, L. F. (1965). Effect of planting date and maturity date on soybean seed quality. *Agron. J.* **57,** 165-168.
Green, D. E., Cavannah, L. E., and Pinnell, E. L. (1966). Effect of seed moisture content, field weathering, and combine cylinder speed on soybean seed quality. *Crop Sci.* **6,** 7-10.
Groves, J. F. (1917). Temperature and life duration of seeds. *Bot. Gaz. (Chicago)* **63,** 169-189.
Grybauskas, A. P., Sinclair, J. B., and Foor, S. R. (1979). Surface disinfestation of soybean seeds for selective recovery of seedborne micro-organisms. *Plant Dis. Rep.* **63,** 887-891.
Gupta, P. C. (1976). Viability of stored soybean seeds in India. *Seed Res.* **4,** 32-39.
Haferkamp, M. E., Smith, L. S., and Nilan, R. A. (1953). Studies on aged seeds. I. Relation of age of seed to germination and longevity. *Agron. J.* **43,** 434-437.
Hall, G. E. (1974). Damage during handling of shelled corn and soybeans. *Trans. ASAE* **17,** 335-338.
Harman, G. E. (1972). Deterioration of stored pea seed by *Aspergillus ruber:* Extraction and properties of a toxin. *Phytopathology* **62,** 206-208.
Harman, G. E., and Drury, R. E. (1973). Respiration of pea seeds (*Pisum sativum*) infected with *Aspergillus ruber. Phytopathology* **63,** 1040-1044.
Harman, G. E., and Granett, A. L. (1972). Deterioration of stored pea seed: Changes in germination, membrane permeability and ultrastructure resulting from infection by *Aspergillus ruber* and from ageing. *Physiol. Plant Pathol.* **2,** 271-278.
Harman, G. E., and Mattick, L. R. (1976). Association of lipid oxidation with seed ageing and death. *Nature (London)* **260,** 323-324.
Harman, G. E., and Nash, G. (1972). Deterioration of stored pea seed by *Aspergillus ruber:* Evidence for involvement of a toxin. *Phytopathology* **62,** 209-212.
Harman, G. E., and Pfleger, F. L. (1974). Pathogenicity and infection sites of *Aspergillus* species in stored seeds. *Phytopathology* **64,** 1339-1344.
Harman, G. E., Khan, A. A., and Tao, K.-L. J. (1976). Physiological changes in the early stages of germination induced by ageing and by infection by a storage fungus *Aspergillus ruber. Can. J. Bot.* **54,** 39-44.
Harman, G. E., Nedrow, B. L., and Nash, G. (1978). Stimulation of fungal spore germination by volatiles from aged seeds. *Can. J. Bot.* **56,** 2124-2127.

Harman, G. E., Nedrow, B. L., Clark, B. E., and Mattick, L. R. (1982). Association of volatile aldehyde production during germination with poor soybean and pea seed quality. *Crop Sci.* **22,** 712–716.

Harrington, J. F. (1960). Seed storage and seed packages. *Seed World* **87,** 4–6.

Harrington, J. F. (1972). Seed storage and longevity. *In* "Seed Biology" (T. T. Kozlowski, ed.), Vol. 3, pp. 145–246. Academic Press, New York.

Harris, H. M., Parker, M. B., and Johnson, B. J. (1965). Influence of molybdenum content of soybean seed and other factors associated with seed source on progeny response to applied molybdenum. *Agron. J.* **57,** 397–399.

Harrison, B. J. (1966). Seed deterioration in relation to storage conditions and its influence upon germination, chromosomal damage and plant performance. *J. Natl. Inst. Agric. Bot. (G. B.)* **10,** 644–663.

Harrison, J. G. (1976). Hollow heart of field bean (*Vicia faba* L.) seeds. *Plant Pathol.* **25,** 87–88.

Harrison, J. G., and Perry, D. A. (1973). Effects of hollow heart on growth of peas. *Ann. Appl. Biol.* **73,** 103–109.

Harter, L. L. (1930). Thresher injury, a cause of baldhead in beans. *J. Agric. Res. (Washington, D.C.)* **40,** 371–384.

Harty, R. L. (1977). The influence of storage conditions on bean seed quality. *Queensl. Agric. J.* **103,** 534–535.

Hegarty, T. W. (1977). Seed vigour in field beans (*Vicia faba* L.) and its influence on plant stand. *J. Agric. Sci.* **88,** 169–173.

Herath, H. B., Don, R., and Jack, D. A. (1981). Investigation into the effect of damage caused by mechanical treatment of mungbean seeds at various moisture levels: increased moisture contents being obtained using a new quick method. *Seed Sci. Technol.* **9,** 853–860.

Heydecker, W. (1969). Report of the Vigour Test Committee 1965–1968. *Proc. Int. Seed Test. Assoc.* **34,** 751–774.

Heydecker, W., and Feast, P. M. (1969). Studies of the hollow heart condition of pea. *Proc. Int. Seed Test. Assoc.* **34,** 319–328.

Heydecker, W., and Kohistani, M. R. (1969). Hollow heart and poor stands of peas (*Pisum sativum* L.). *Ann. Appl. Biol.* **64,** 153–160.

Hibbard, R. P., and Miller, E. V. (1928). Biochemical studies on seed viability. I. Measurements of conductance and reduction. *Plant Physiol.* **3,** 335–352.

Hiltner, L. (1903). Die Keimungsvierhaltnisse der Leguminosenamen und ihre Beinflussung durch Organismenwirkung. *Arb. Biol. Abt. (Anst. Reichsanst.) Land-Forstwirtsch. Kaiserl. Gesundheitsamte* **3,** 1–102 (cited by Essenberg and Schoorel, 1962).

Hobbs, P. R., and Obendorf, R. L. (1972). Interaction of initial seed moisture and imbibitional temperature on germination and productivity of soybean. *Crop Sci.* **12,** 664–667.

Howe, R. W. (1972). Insects attacking seeds during storage. *In* "Seed Biology" (T. T. Kozlowski, ed.), Vol. 3, pp. 247–301. Academic Press, New York.

Hulbert, H. W., and Whitney, G. M. (1934). Effect of seed injury upon the germination of *Pisum sativum*. *J. Am. Soc. Agron.* **26,** 876–884.

Ilyas, M. B., Dhingra, O. D., Ellis, M. A., and Sinclair, J. B. (1975). Location of mycelium of *Diaporthe phaseolorum* var. *sojae* and *Cercospora kikuchii* in infected soybean seeds. *Plant Dis. Rep.* **59,** 17–19.

Jacks, H. (1963). Seed disinfection XVII. Field tests for control of damping off in pea seeds. *N. Z. J. Agric. Res.* **6,** 115–117.

James, E. (1967). Preservation of seed stocks. *Adv. Agron.* **19,** 87–106.

James, E. (1968). Limitations of glutamic acid decarboxylase activity for estimating viability in beans (*Phaseolus vulgaris* L.). *Crop Sci.* **8,** 403–404.

James, E., Bass, L. N., and Clark, D. C. (1967). Varietal differences in longevity of vegetable seeds and their response to various storage conditions. *Proc. Am. Soc. Hortic. Sci.* **91,** 521–528.

Johnson, D. R., and Luedders, V. D. (1974). Effect of planted seed size on emergence and yield of soybeans (*Glycine max.* (L.) Merr). *Agron. J.* **66,** 117–118.

Johnson, R. R., and Wax, L. M. (1978). Relationship of soybean germination and vigour tests to field performance. *Agron. J.* **70,** 273–278.

Jones, C. K. (1927). Studies of the nature and control of blight, leaf and pod spot, and foot rot of peas caused by species of *Ascochyta. Bull.—N. Y., Agric. Exp. Stn. (Ithaca)* **547.**

Justice, O. L., and Bass, L. N. (1978). "Principles and Practices of Seed Storage." Science and Education Administration, U.S. Dept. of Agriculture, Washington, D.C.

Kannenberg, L. W., and Allard, R. W. (1964). An association between pigments and lignin formation in the seed coat of the lima bean. *Crop Sci.* **4,** 621–622.

Ketring, D. L. (1971). Physiology of oil seeds. IV. Response of initially high and low germinating Spanish-type peanut seed to 3 storage environments. *Agron. J.* **63,** 435–438.

Kilpatrick, R. A. (1957). Fungi associated with flowers, pods and seeds of soybeans. *Phytopathology* **47,** 131–135.

Korban, S. S., Coyne, D. P., Weihing, J. L., and Hanna, M. A. (1982). Testing methods, variation, morphological and genetic studies of seed-coat cracking in dry beans (*Phaseolus vulgaris* L.). *J. Am. Soc. Hortic. Sci.* **106,** 821–828.

Kuhn, C. W. (1965). Symptomatology, host range and effect on yield of a seed transmitted peanut virus. *Phytopathology* **55,** 880–884.

Lalithakumari, D., Govidaswamy, G. V., and Vidhyasekaran, P. (1972). Isolation of seed borne fungi from stored groundnut seeds and their role in seed spoilage. *Madras Agric. J.* **59,** 1–6.

Larson, L. A. (1968). The effect soaking pea seeds with or without seedcoats has on seedling growth. *Plant Physiol.* **43,** 255–259.

Lehman, S. G. (1950). Purple stain of soybean seeds. *N. C. Agric. Exp. Stn., Bull.* **369** (as cited by Nangju *et al.,* 1980).

Levengood, W. C., Bondie, J., and Chen, C.-L. (1975). Seed selection for potential viability. *J. Exp. Bot.* **26,** 911–919.

Lopez, L. C., and Christensen, C. M. (1962). Invasion of and damage to bean seed by storage fungi. *Plant Dis. Rep.* **46,** 785–789.

Luedders, V. D., and Burris, J. S. (1979). Effect of broken seed coats on field emergence of soybeans. *Agron. J.* **71,** 877–879.

McCollum, J. P. (1953). Factors affecting cotyledonal cracking during the germination of beans (*Phaseolus vulgaris*). *Plant Physiol.* **28,** 267–274.

McDonald, M. B., and Phaneendranath, B. R. (1978). A modified accelerated ageing seed vigour test for soybean. *J. Seed Technol.* **3,** 27–37.

McHargue, J. S. (1920). The significance of the peroxidase, reaction with reference to the viability of seeds. *J. Am. Chem. Soc.* **42,** 612–614.

Maeda, J. A., Miranda, M. A. C., Arkcoll, D., and Zink, E. (1977). Influence of several external factors on the quality of soybean seed. *Bragantia* **36,** 179–186.

Maguire, J. D., Kropf, J. P., and Steen, K. M. (1973). Pea seed viability in relation to bleaching. *Proc. Assoc. Off. Seed Anal.* **63,** 51–58.

Mamicpic, N. G., and Caldwell, W. P. (1963). Effects of mechanical damage and moisture content upon viability of soybeans in sealed storage. *Proc. Assoc. Off. Seed Anal.* **5,** 215–220.

Mason, S. C., Vorst, J. J., Hankins, B. J., and Holt, D. A. (1982). Standard, cold, and tetrazolium germination tests as estimators of field emergence of mechanically damaged soybean seed. *Agron. J.* **74,** 546–550.

Matheson, S. (1983). Investigation of the susceptibility of soybean seed to *Pythium* infection and its fungicidal control. B.Sc. Agric. Honours Dissertation, University of Aberdeen.

Matthews, S. (1971). A study of seed lots of peas (*Pisum sativum* L.) differing in predisposition to pre-emergence mortality in soil. *Ann. Appl. Biol.* **68,** 177–183.

Matthews, S. (1973a). Changes in developing peas in relation to their ability to withstand desiccation. *Ann. Appl. Biol.* **73,** 93–105.

Matthews, S. (1973b). The effect of time of harvest on pre-emergence mortality in peas. *Ann. Appl. Biol.* **73,** 211–219.

Matthews, S. (1977). Field emergence and seedling establishment. *In* "The Physiology of the Garden Pea" (J. F. Sutcliffe and J. S. Pate, eds.), pp. 83–118. Academic Press, New York.

Matthews, S. (1980). Controlled deterioration: A new vigour test for crop seeds. *In* "Seed Production" (P. Hebblethwaite, ed.), pp. 647–660. Butterworth, London.

Matthews, S., and Bradnock, W. T. (1967). The detection of seed samples of wrinkle seeded peas (*Pisum sativum* L.) of potentially low planting value. *Proc. Int. Seed Test. Assoc.* **32,** 553–563.

Matthews, S., and Bradnock, W. T. (1968). Relationship between seed exudation and field emergence in peas and French beans. *Hortic. Res.* **8,** 89–93.

Matthews, S., and Powell, A. A. (1981). Electrical conductivity test. *In* "Handbook of Vigour Test Methods" (D. A. Perry, ed.), pp. 37–42. International Seed Testing Association, Zurich.

Matthews, S., and Rogerson, N. E. (1977). The influence of embryo condition on the leaching of solutes from pea seeds. *J. Exp. Bot.* **27,** 961–986.

Matthews, S., and Whitbread, R. (1968). An association between seed exudates and the incidence of pre-emergence mortality in wrinkle-seeded peas. *Plant Pathol.* **17,** 11–17.

Matthews, S., Powell, A. A., and Rogerson, N. E. (1980). Physiological aspects of the development and storage of pea seeds and their significance to seed production. *In* "Seed Production" (P. Hebblethwaite, ed.), pp. 513–526. Butterworth, London.

Mead, J. F. (1976). Free radical mechanisms of lipid damage and consequences for cellular membranes. *In* "Free Radicals in Biology" (W. A. Pryor, ed.), Vol. 1, pp. 51–68. Academic Press, New York.

Milner, M., and Geddes, W. F. (1945). Grain storage studies. II. The effect of aeration, temperature and time on the respiration of soybeans containing excessive moisture. *Cereal Chem.* **22,** 484–501.

Milner, M., and Geddes, W. F. (1946). Grain storage studies. III. The relation between moisture content, mould growth, and respiration of soybeans. *Cereal Chem.* **23,** 225–247.

Ministry of Agriculture, Fisheries and Food (1982). "Agricultural Statistics United Kingdom, 1980 and 1981." H. M. Stationery Office, London.

Moore, R. P. (1965). Natural destruction of seed quality under field conditions as revealed by tetrazolium tests. *Proc. Int. Seed Test. Assoc.* **30,** 995–1004.

Moore, R. P. (1967). Freeze injury to seed corn as evaluated in tetrazolium, and growth tests. *Proc. Assoc. Off. Seed Anal.* **57,** 138–140.
Moore, R. P. (1968). Seed deterioration symptoms as revealed by tetrazolium and growth tests. *Proc. Assoc. Off. Seed Anal.* **58,** 107–110.
Moore, R. P. (1971). Mechanism of water damage in mature soybean seed. *Proc. Assoc. Off. Seed Anal.* **61,** 112–118.
Moore, R. P. (1973). Tetrazolium staining for assessing seed quality. *In* "Seed Ecology" (W. Heydecker, ed.), pp. 347–366. Butterworth, London.
Morris, J. L., Campbell, W. F., and Pollard, L. H. (1970). Relation of imbibition and drying on cotyledon cracking in snap beans, *Phaseolus vulgaris* L. *J. Am. Soc. Hortic. Sci.* **95,** 541–543.
Murakishi, H. H. (1951). Purple seed stain of soybean. *Phytopathology* **41,** 305–318.
Myers, A. (1948). An abnormal condition of the cotyledons of *Pisum sativum* L. *Proc. Int. Seed Test. Assoc.* **14,** 35–37.
Nangju, D. (1977). Effect of date of harvest on seed quality and viability of soybeans. *J. Agric. Sci.* **89,** 107–112.
Nangju, D. (1979). Seed characters and germination in soybean. *Exp. Agric.* **15,** 385–392.
Nangju, D., Wien, H. C., and Ndimande, B. (1980). Improved practices for soyabean seed production in the tropics. *In* "Seed Production" (P. Hebblethwaite, ed.), pp. 427–448. Butterworth, London.
Nath, R., Mathur, S. B., and Neergaard, P. (1970). Seed-borne fungi of mung bean (*Phaseolus aureus* from India and their significance. *Proc. Int. Seed Test. Assoc.* **35,** 225–242.
Ndunguru, B. J., and Summerfield, R. F. (1975). Comparative laboratory studies of cowpea (*Vigna unguiculata*) and soybean (*Glycine max* under tropical temperature conditions. I. Germination and hypocotyl elongation. *East Afr. Agric. For. J.* (as cited by Nangju *et al.*, 1980).
Neergaard, P. (1977). "Seed Pathology," 2 vols. Macmillan, London.
Nichols, M. A., Warrington, T. J., and Scott, D. J. (1978). Pre-harvest treatment effects on some quality criteria of pea seeds. *Acta Hortic.* **83,** 113–124.
Nicholson, J. F., and Sinclair, J. B. (1971). Amsoy soybean seed germination inhibited by *Pseudomonas glycinea. Phytopathology* **61,** 1390–1393.
Nicholson, J. F., and Sinclair, J. B. (1973). Effect of planting date, storage conditions and seed-borne fungi on soybean seed quality. *Plant Dis. Rep.* **57,** 770–774.
Nicholson, J. F., Dhingra, O. D., and Sinclair, J. B. (1972). Internal seed-borne nature of *Sclerotinia sclerotiorum* and *Phomopsis* sp. and their effects on soybean seed quality. *Phytopathology* **62,** 1261–1263.
Nittler, L. W., Harman, G. E., and Nelson, B. (1974). Hila discolouration of Traverse soybean seeds; a problem of cultivar purity analysis and a possible indication of low quality seeds. *Proc. Assoc. Off. Seed Anal.* **64,** 115–119.
Noble, N., and Howell, P. (1962). Hollow heart, cavitation, depression in seed peas. *Seed Trade Rev.* **14,** 171.
Obendorf, R. L., and Hobbs, P. R. (1970). Effect of seed moisture on temperature sensitivity during imbibition of soyabean. *Crop Sci.* **10,** 563–566.
Oliveira, M. de A., Matthews, S., and Powell, A. A. (1984). The role of split seed coats in determining seed vigour in commercial seed lots of soybean, as measured by the electrical conductivity test. *Seed Sci. Technol.* **12,** in press.
Onesirosan, P. T. (1983). Effect of moisture content and temperature on the invasion of cowpeas by storage fungi. *Seed Sci. Technol.* **10,** 619–629.

Parrish, D. J., and Leopold, A. C. (1978). On the mechanism of ageing in soybean seeds. *Plant Physiol.* **61,** 365–368.
Parrish, D. J., Leopold, A. C., and Hanna, M. A. (1982). Turgor changes with accelerated ageing of soybeans. *Crop Sci.* **22,** 666–669.
Pate, J. S., and Flinn, A. M. (1977). Fruit and seed development. *In* "The Physiology of the Garden Pea" (J. F. Sutcliffe and J. S. Pate, eds.), pp. 431–468. Academic Press, New York.
Paulsen, M. R., Nave, W. R., and Gray, L. E. (1979). Soybean seed quality as affected by impact damage. *ASAE Pap.* **79-5057.**
Pearce, R. S., and Abdel Samad, M. (1980). Change in fatty acid content of polar lipids during ageing of seeds of peanut (*Arachis hypogaea* L.). *J. Exp. Bot.* **31,** 1283–1290.
Perry, D. A. (1967). Seed vigour and field establishment of peas. *Proc. Int. Seed Test Assoc.* **32,** 3–12.
Perry, D. A. (1970). The relation of seed vigour to field establishment of garden pea cultivars. *J. Agric. Sci.* **74,** 343–348.
Perry, D. A. (1973). Infection of seeds of *Pisum sativum* by *Pythium ultimum. Trans. Br. Mycol. Soc.* **61,** 135–144.
Perry, D. A., ed. (1981). "Handbook of Vigour Test Methods." International Seed Testing Association, Zurich.
Perry, D. A., and Harrison, J. G. (1970). The deleterious effect of water and temperature on germination of pea seed. *J. Exp. Bot.* **21,** 504–512.
Perry, D. A., and Harrison, J. G. (1973). Causes and development of hollow heart in pea seed. *Ann. Appl. Biol.* **73,** 95–101.
Perry, D. A., and Howell, P. J. (1965). Symptoms and nature of hollow heart in pea seed. *Plant Pathol.* **14,** 111–116.
Pettit, R. E., Taber, R. A., and Person, N. K. (1971). Microbial infestation of peanuts as related to windrow airing conditions. *J. Am. Peanut Res. Educ. Assoc.* **3,** 127–136.
Phatak, H. C. (1974). Seed-borne plant viruses—identification and diagnosis in seed health testing. *Seed Sci. Technol.* **2,** 3–155.
Phatak, H. C., and Summanwar, A. S. (1967). Detection of plant viruses in seeds and seedstocks. *Proc. Int. Seed Test. Assoc.* **32,** 625–631.
Pickett, C. K. (1973). Mechanical damage and processing loss during navy bean harvesting. *Trans. ASAE* **16,** 1047–1050.
Pollock, B. M. (1969). Imbibition temperature sensitivity of lima bean seeds controlled by initial seed moisture. *Plant Physiol.* **44,** 970–911.
Pollock, B. M., and Manalo, J. R. (1970). Simulated mechanical damage to garden beans during germination. *J. Am. Soc. Hortic. Sci.* **95,** 415–417.
Pollock, B. M., and Toole, V. K. (1964). Lima bean seed bleaching—a study in vigor. *Proc. Assoc. Off. Seed Anal.* **54,** 26–31.
Pollock, B. M., and Toole, V. K. (1966). Imbibition period as the critical temperature sensitive stage in the germination of lima bean seeds. *Plant Physiol.* **41,** 221–229.
Pollock, B. M., Roos, E. E., and Manalo, J. R. (1969). Vigor of garden bean seeds and seedlings influenced by initial seed moisture, substrate oxygen and imbibition temperature. *J. Am. Soc. Hortic. Sci.* **94,** 577–584.
Potts, H. C., Duangpatra, J., Hourston, W. G., and Delouche, J. C. (1978). Some influences of hardseededness on soybean seed quality. *Crop Sci.* **18,** 221–224.
Powell, A. A., and Harman, G. E. (1984). Absence of a consistent association of changes in membranal lipids with the ageing of pea seeds. *Seed Sci. Technol.*, in press.

Powell, A. A., and Matthews, S. (1977). The deterioration of pea seeds in humid or dry storage. *J. Exp. Bot.* **28,** 227–236.

Powell, A. A., and Matthews, S. (1978a). The damaging effect of water on dry pea embryos during imbibition. *J. Exp. Bot.* **29,** 1215–1229.

Powell, A. A., and Matthews, S. (1978b). Rapid evaluation of the storage potential of seed peas. *Acta Hortic.* **83,** 133–140.

Powell, A. A., and Matthews, S. (1979). The influence of testa condition on the imbibition and vigour of pea seeds. *J. Exp. Bot.* **30,** 193–197.

Powell, A. A., and Matthews, S. (1980a). The significance of damage during imbibition to the field emergence of pea (*Pisum sativum* L.) seeds. *J. Agric. Sci.* **95,** 35–38.

Powell, A. A., and Matthews, S. (1980b). The significance of seed coat damage in the production of high quality legume seeds. *Acta Hortic.* **111,** 227–233.

Powell, A. A., and Matthews, S. (1981a). Association of phospholipid changes with early stages of seed ageing. *Ann. Bot. (London)* [N. S.] **47,** 709–712.

Powell, A. A., and Matthews, S. (1981b). A physical explanation for solute leakage from dry pea embryos during imbibition. *J. Exp. Bot.* **32,** 1045–1050.

Prakabboon, N. (1982). A study of abnormal seedling development in soybean as affected by threshing injury. *Seed Sci. Technol.* **10,** 495–500.

Priestley, D. A., and Leopold, A. C. (1979). Absence of lipid oxidation during accelerated ageing of soyabean seeds. *Plant Physiol.* **63,** 726–729.

Priestley, D. A., McBride, M. B., and Leopold, A. C. (1980). Tocopherol and organic free radical levels in soybean seeds during natural and accelerated ageing. *Plant Physiol.* **66,** 715–719.

Ramanujam, S. (1976). Chickpea. *In* "Evolution of Crop Plants" (N. W. Simmonds, ed.), pp. 157–159. Longmans, Green, New York.

Roberts, E. H. (1972). Storage environment and the control of viability. *In* "Viability of Seeds" (E. H. Roberts, ed.), pp. 14–58. Chapman & Hall, London.

Roberts, E. H. (1973a). Predicting the storage life of seeds. *Seed Sci. Technol.* **1,** 499–514.

Roberts, E. H. (1973b). Loss of seed viability: Chromosomal and genetical aspects. *Seed Sci. Technol.* **1,** 515–527.

Roberts, E. H. (1973c). Loss of seed viability: Ultrastructural and physiological aspects. *Seed Sci. Technol.* **1,** 529–545.

Roberts, E. H., and Abdalla, F. H. (1968). The influence of temperature, moisture and oxygen on period of seed viability in barley, broad beans and peas. *Ann. Bot. (London)* [N. S.] **32,** 92–117.

Roberts, E. H., and Roberts, D. L. (1972). Viability monographs. *In* "Viability of Seeds" (E. H. Roberts, ed.), pp. 417–423. Chapman & Hall, London.

Roberts, L. W. (1951). Survey of factors responsible for reduction of 2,3,5-triphenyl tetrazolium chloride in plant meristems. *Science* **113,** 692–693.

Rogerson, N. E., and Matthews, S. (1977). Respiratory and carbohydrate changes in developing pea seeds in relation to their ability to withstand desiccation. *J. Exp. Bot.* **38,** 304–313.

Roos, E. E., and Pollock, B. M. (1971). Soaking injury in lima bean. *Crop Sci.* **11,** 78–81.

Rowland, G. G., and Gusta, L. V. (1977). Effects of soaking, seed moisture content, temperature and seed leakage on germination of faba beans (*Vicia faba*) and peas (*Pisum sativum*). *Can. J. Plant Sci.* **57,** 401–406.

Saharan, G. S., and Gupta, V. K. (1973). Influence of *Aspergilli* on soybean seeds in storage. *Phytopathol. Z.* **78,** 141–146.
Schiller, C. T., Hepperly, P. R., and Sinclair, J. B. (1978). Pathogenicity of *Myrothecium roridium* from Illinois soybeans. *Plant Dis. Rep.* **62,** 882–885.
Schlub, R. L., and Schmitthenner, A. F. (1978). Effects of soybean seed coat cracks on seed exudation and seedling quality in soil infested with *Pythium. Phytopathology* **68,** 1186–1191.
Schoorel, A. F. (1957). The use of soil tests in seed testing. *Proc. Int. Seed Test. Assoc.* **22,** 287–301.
Scott, D. J., and Close, R. C. (1976). An assessment of seed factors affecting field emergence of garden pea seed lots. *Seed Sci. Technol.* **4,** 287–300.
Semple, F. (1981). Investigation of imbibition as a cause of vigour differences in soybeans. (*Glycine max.*). B.Sc. Agric. Honours Dissertation, University of Aberdeen.
Sherwin, H. S., and Kreitlow, K. K. (1952). Discolouration of soybean seeds by the frogeye fungus *Cercospora sojina. Phytopathology* **42,** 568–572.
Sholberg, P. L., and Muir, W. E. (1979). Effect of heat treatment on the viability of faba beans. *Can. Agric. Eng.* **21,** 123–124.
Short, G. E., Loria, R., and Lacy, M. C. (1977). Effect of seed quality and seed treatment on yield of pea. *J. Am. Soc. Hortic. Sci.* **102,** 258–260.
Shortt, B. J., Grybauskas, A. P., Tenne, F. D., and Sinclair, J. B. (1981). Epidemiology of *Phomopsis* seed decay of soybean in Illinois. *Plant Dis.* **65,** 62–64.
Shull, C. H., and Shull, S. P. (1932). Irregularities in the rate of absorption by dry plant tissues. *Bot. Gaz. (Chicago)* **93,** 376–399.
Sijbring, P. H. (1963). Results of some storage experiments under controlled conditions (agricultural seeds). *Proc. Int. Seed Test. Assoc.* **28,** 845–851.
Simmonds, N. W., ed. (1976). "Evolution of Crop Plants." Longmans, Green, New York.
Sinclair, J. B. (1976). Seed-borne bacteria and fungi in soybeans and their control. *World Soybean Res., Proc. World Soybean Res. Conf., 1975* pp. 470–474.
Sinclair, J. B. (1977). The microcosm of the soybean seed. *Ill. Res.,* Winter, pp. 12–13.
Sinclair, J. B. (1978a). The seed-borne nature of some soybean pathogens, the effect of *Phomopsis* spp. and *Bacillus subtilis* on, and their occurrence in soybeans produced in Illinois. *Seed Sci. Technol.* **6,** 957–964.
Sinclair, J. B. (1978b). Micro-organisms affecting soybean seed quality. *Soybean Seed Res. Conf., 8th, 1978* pp. 6–10.
Sinclair, J. B. (1981). Fungicide sprays for the control of seed-borne pathogens of rice, soybeans and wheat. *Seed Sci. Technol.* **9,** 697–705.
Singh, B., and Linvill, D. E. (1977). Determining the effect of pod and grain moisture content on threshing loss and damage of navy beans. *Trans ASAE* **20,** 226–227.
Singh, D. (1974). Occurrence and histology of hollow heart and marsh spot in peas. *Seed Sci. Technol.* **2,** 443–456.
Sinha, O. K., and Khare, M. N. (1977). Site of infection and further development of *Macrophomina phaseolina* and *Fusarium equiseti* in naturally infected cowpea seeds. *Seed Sci. Technol.* **5,** 721–725.
Sivasubramanian, S., and Ramakrishnan, V. (1974). Effect of seed size on seedling vigour in groundnut. *Seed Sci. Technol.* **2,** 435–441.
Smith, D. L. (1973). Nucleic acid, protein and starch synthesis in developing cotyledons of *Pisum arvense* L. *Ann. Bot. (London)* [N. S.] **37,** 795–804.

Sorrells, M. E., and Pappelis, A. J. (1976). Effect of temperature and osmotic concentration on cotyledon cracking during imbibition of soybean. *Crop Sci.* **16,** 413-415.

Srivastava, A. K. (1975). Physiological studies on soybean seed viability during storage and its practical applicability. *Seed Res.* **4,** 56-61.

Stanway, V. (1974). Germination response of soybean seeds with damaged seed coats. *Proc. Assoc. Off. Seed Anal.* **64,** 97-101.

Stanway, V. (1978). Evaluation of "Forrest" soybeans with damaged seed coats and cotyledons. *J. Seed Technol.* **3,** 19-26.

Stevenson, W. R., and Hagedorn, D. J. (1969). A new seed-borne virus of peas. *Phytopathology* **59,** 105.

Stevenson, W. R., and Hagedorn, D. J. (1973). Further studies on seed transmission of pea seed-borne mosaic virus in *Pisum sativum. Plant Dis. Rep.* **57,** 248-252.

Stewart, R. R. C., and Bewley, J. D. (1980). Lipid peroxidation associated with accelerated ageing of soybean axes. *Plant Physiol.* **65,** 245-248.

Tao, K.-L. J. (1978). Factors causing variations in the conductivity test for soybean seeds. *J. Seed Technol.* **3,** 10-18.

Tekrony, D. M., and Egli, D. B. (1977). Relationship between laboratory indices of soybean seed vigor and field emergence. *Crop Sci.* **17,** 573-577.

Tekrony, D. M., Egli, D. B., and Balles, J. (1980a). The effect of seed production environment on soyabean seed quality. *In* "Seed Production" (P. Hebblethwaite, ed.), pp. 403-426. Butterworth, London.

Tekrony, D. M., Egli, D. B., and Phillips, A. D. (1980b). Effect of field weathering on the viability and vigour of soybean seed. *Agron. J.* **72,** 749-753.

Tenne, F. D., Prasartsee, C., Machado, C. C., and Sinclair, J. B. (1974). Variation in germination and seed-borne pathogens among soybean seed lots from three regions of Illinois. *Plant Dis. Rep.* **58,** 411-413.

Tenne, F. D., Foor, S. R., and Sinclair, J. B. (1977). Association of *Bacillus subtilis* with soybean seeds. *Seed Sci. Technol.* **5,** 763-769.

Tervet, I. W. (1945). The influence of fungi on storage, on seed viability, and seedling vigour of soybeans. *Phytopathology* **35,** 3-15.

Tiwari, D. K., Tiwari, J. P., and Agrawal, U. K. (1978). Evaluation of soybeans for high germinability and field emergence. *Seed Res.* **6,** 125-128.

Toole, E. H., and Toole, V. K. (1953). Relation of storage conditions to germination and to abnormal seedlings of bean. *Proc. Int. Seed Test. Assoc.* **18,** 123-129.

Toole, E. H., and Toole, V. K. (1960). Viability of stored snap bean seed as affected by threshing and processing injury. *U.S. Dep. Agric., Tech. Bull.* **1213.**

Toole, E. H., Toole, V. K., and Gorman, E. A. (1948). Vegetable seed storage as affected by temperature and relative humidity. *U.S. Dep. Agric., Tech. Bull.* **972.**

Toole, E. H., Toole, V. K., Lay, B. J., and Crowder, J. T. (1951). Injury to seed beans during threshing and processing. *U.S. Dep. Agric., Circ.* **874.**

Toole, E. H., Toole, V. K., and Borthwick, H. A. (1957). Growth and production of snap beans stored under favourable and unfavourable conditions. *Proc. Int. Seed Test. Assoc.* **22,** 418-423.

Verma, R. S., and Gupta, P. C. (1975). Storage behaviour of soybean varieties vastly differing in seed size. *Seed Res.* **3,** 39-44.

Vieira, C. (1966). Effect of seed age on germination and yield of field bean (*Phaseolus vulgaris* L.). *Turrialba* **16,** 396-398.

Wahab, A. H., and Burris, J. S. (1971). Physiological and chemical differences in low and high quality soybean seeds. *Proc. Assoc. Off. Seed Anal.* **61,** 58-67.

Wallen, V. R., and Seaman, W. L. (1963). Seed infection by *Diaporthe phaseolorum* and its influence on host development. *Can. J. Bot.* **41,** 13–21.
Wallen, V. R., and Stoko, A. J. (1950). Antibiotic XG as a seed treatment for the control of leaf and pod spot of peas caused by *Ascochyta pisi. Can. J. Res., Sect. C* **28,** 623–636.
Webster, L. V., and Dexter, S. T. (1961). Effects of physiological quality of seeds on total germination, rapidity of germination and seedling vigour. *Agron. J.* **53,** 297–299.
Wester, R. E., and Magruder, R. (1938). Effect of size, condition and production locality on germination and seedling vigour of baby Fordhook bush lima bean seed. *Proc. Am. Soc. Hortic. Sci.* **36,** 614–622.
Wijandi, S., and Copeland, L. O. (1974). Effect of origin, moisture content, maturity and mechanical damage on seed and seedling vigour of beans. *Agron. J.* **66,** 546–548.
Wilcox, J. R., and Abney, T. S. (1973). Effects of *Cercospora kikuchii* on soybeans. *Phytopathology* **63,** 796–797.
Wilcox, J. R., Laviolette, F. A., and Athow, K. L. (1974). Deterioration of soybean quality associated with delayed harvest. *Plant Dis. Rep.* **58,** 130–133.
Woodstock, L. W. (1976). Progress report on the seed vigour testing handbook. *Newsl. Assoc. Off. Seed Anal.* **50,** 1–78.
Woodstock, L. W., and Tao, K.-L. J. (1981). Prevention of imbibitional injury in low vigour soybean embryonic axes by osmotic control of water uptake. *Physiol. Plant.* **51,** 133–139.
Woodstock, L. W., and Taylorson, R. B. (1981a). Soaking injury and its reversal with polyethylene glycol to respiratory metabolism in high and low vigour soybean seeds. *Physiol. Plant.* **53,** 263–268.
Woodstock, L. W., and Taylorson, R. B. (1981b). Ethanol and acetaldehyde in imbibing soybean seeds in relation to deterioration. *Plant Physiol.* **67,** 424–428.
Yaklich, R. W., and Abdul Baki, A. A. (1975). Variability in metabolism of individual axes of soybean seeds and its relationship to vigor. *Crop Sci.* **15,** 424–426.
Yaklich, R. W., Kulik, M. M., and Anderson, J. D. (1979). Evaluation of vigor tests in soybean seeds: Relationship of ATP, conductivity, and radioactive tracer multiple criteria tests to field performance. *Crop Sci.* **19,** 806–810.
Zaumeyer, W. J. (1932). Comparative pathological histology of three bacterial diseases of bean. *J. Agric. Res. (Washington, D.C.)* **44,** 605–632.

Subject Index

Cumulative List of Authors

Numbers in **bold** face indicate the volume number of the series.

Cumulative List of Chapter Titles

Numbers in **bold** face indicate the volume number of the series.